Sacred Matters

Religion and Spirituality in Families

Sacred Matters

Religion and Spirituality in Families

Wesley R. Burr
Brigham Young University, USA

Loren D. Marks
Louisiana State University, USA

Randal D. Day
Brigham Young University, USA

Routledge
Taylor & Francis Group
New York London

Routledge
Taylor & Francis Group
711 Third Avenue
New York, NY 10017

Routledge
Taylor & Francis Group
27 Church Road
Hove, East Sussex BN3 2FA

Printed in the United States of America on acid-free paper
Version Date: 20110610

International Standard Book Number: 978-0-415-88744-1 (Hardback) 978-0-415-88745-8 (Paperback)

Library of Congress Cataloging-in-Publication Data

Burr, Wesley R., 1936-
Sacred matters : religion and spirituality in families / Wesley R. Burr, Loren D. Marks, Randal D. Day.
p. cm.
Summary: "Sacred Matters builds on earlier literature, adds new qualitative and quantitative data, and creates a conceptual framework and general theory (or model) about when, how, and why sacred matters are helpful and harmful in families"--Provided by publisher.
Includes bibliographical references and index.
ISBN 978-0-415-88744-1 (hbk.) -- ISBN 978-0-415-88745-8 (pbk.)
1. Families--Religious life. 2. Spiritual life. 3. Families--Research. I. Marks, Loren Dean. II. Day, Randal D., 1948- III. Title.

BV4526.3.B875 2011
249--dc23 2011020598

Visit the Taylor & Francis Web site at
http://www.taylorandfrancis.com

and the Psychology Press Web site at
http://www.psypress.com

Contents

Preface vii

1 Overview and Main Ideas in Sacred Theory 1

2 Forgiving 35

3 Asking and Seeking 53

4 Sacrificing 69

5 Loving Others 87

6 Aspects of Loving 101

7 Coping With Disagreements 123

8 Coping With Undesirable Behavior 147

9 Loving God 161

10 Generations 175

11 Morality 185

12 Psychosocial Aspects 195

13 Relationships With Other Perspectives 213

14 Researching Sacred Matters 243

15 Methods 263

References 289

Author Index 313

Subject Index 321

Preface

This book provides new research and a theory about ways the sacred parts of the human experience help and harm families. The research used multiple methods to gather qualitative and quantitative data from samples that included different religions, different stages of the life cycle, and different geographical areas. The findings led to an innovative conceptual framework and a theory that provides new, useful, and testable insights about *how*, *when*, and *why* sacred matters make a difference in families.

The book provides considerable evidence that when family members use sacred-based principles wisely it makes a difference in the quality of their lives, and it makes more difference than most theories in family studies suggest. All of the previous theories have truth and value, but they also are limited by the dominant assumptions in academia that emphasize the secular. The theory constructed in this volume complements the earlier theories, and when it is integrated with them it enriches and expands them.

The primary audiences for this book are scholars and students who are interested in better understanding why some families succeed and others fail. Researchers and practitioners in fields such as family studies, psychology, religion, philosophy, social work, and sociology will find that the ideas in this volume expand and enrich the ideas in their previous bodies of literature and describe new areas for research. Most family and religion texts pay little attention to the role of the sacred in families. Therefore this volume expands and improves graduate and undergraduate courses in religion and family, family studies, and programs that focus on family relationships, family processes, family development, and family therapy. It also enriches courses on religion and family, philosophy of religion, psychology of the family, sociology of the family, social work, and counseling.

The theory in this volume is called *sacred theory*, and it has four general ideas and a group of less general principles. Several of the less general propositions have been included in family studies in the last several decades. They deal with forgiveness, sacrifice, prayer, and sanctification, but these ideas have not been integrated into a more general framework. We review what has been learned about them, integrate the findings into a broader framework and theory, and describe a number of other principles about sacred matters that have not been included before in family studies.

Sacred theory is like the tip of an iceberg. It describes a group of sacred-based principles that can be easily identified, easily translated into the language of scholarly inquiry, and added to the field. There also are many other ideas about the sacred that are like the part of an iceberg below the surface. They are not as easily seen and described, and many of them are so complex they are not easily translated from the language of faith into the language of academia. We hope many of them will eventually be included in family studies.

Sacred matters generate strong emotions, and each person's background and approach influences how he or she responds to the sacred parts of life. Therefore it seems wise to share some of our experiences and beliefs because they have influenced this book. All three of us are husbands and fathers, and our families and the heritage and interaction in our extended families are important and precious parts of our lives. We are members of The Church of Jesus Christ of Latter-day Saints (The Mormon Church); and we have devoted considerable energy to learning about other religions by studying their bodies of literature, attending services, taking classes on world religions, and talking with many people in a variety of contexts about their views of the sacred. We are impressed with how much the many world religions have in common, and we believe each of them enriches humanity and has a great deal of value and truth. We also believe that no religion has a monopoly on truth and wisdom, and that all of them, including the church we belong to, have limitations and inadequacies. These views and our search for ideas that can help families led us to focus in this book on ideas that are widely shared by many religions rather than ideas that are provincial, controversial, fragmenting, or divisive.

Some readers may wonder what motivated us to write a book such as this, and our motives are easy to explain. We believe family life can be among the best and most wonderful and beautiful parts of the human experience; but it also can be among the worst and most painful and tragic parts. Family studies will become more relevant and helpful when the sacred becomes a more important part of the field, and this book is our attempt to help this happen.

The first chapter describes the four ideas that are the main assertions in sacred theory. The next 11 chapters describe less general propositions that are integrated with the four general ideas. Most of the less general principles are parts of an idea that is a central belief in most of the views of the sacred. It is the idea that people ought to *love* each other rather than relate in ways that emphasize such things as control, acquisition, manipulation, achieving, competing, independence, hedonism, exchange, fame, power, or fortune. However, the term love has many meanings, and we suggest that most of the ways this term is used have little to do with the sacred or the quality of marriages and families. Many of these differences deal with whether people view *love* as a noun or verb. These differences are analyzed in Chapter 5, and Chapters 6 through 8 then describe what our data suggest about what it means to be loving in families and how love *as a verb* makes a great deal of difference in families. There also are a number of principles in these chapters that deal with other aspects of family life, and we describe ways all of these principles can be applied by family members and professionals who work with families.

Chapters 13 and 14 are culminating chapters because they summarize, analyze, integrate, test, and look toward the future. Chapter 13 begins by describing how the ideas in sacred theory can be integrated with other theories such as symbolic interaction, transition theory, behaviorism, systems theories, and humanistic perspectives. We then describe seven competing ideologies that have emerged in nonsacred perspectives. These ideologies are compared with the ideas in sacred theory, and we describe how some of the competing ideas contribute to undesirable outcomes in families. We suggest that the competing ideas exact a high toll in families, but their role is not well understood by scholars, policy makers, or families because the study of the sacred has been so excluded from scholarly inquiry.

In Chapter 14 we describe new quantitative research that uses longitudinal data from the Flourishing Families Project at BYU. The findings corroborate several of the ideas in sacred theory, and suggest that commitment is more important than we previously thought. This chapter also describes a number of research projects that deserve attention in the future.

The usual pattern is to discuss the methods early in publications, but we describe our methods in the back of the book in Chapter 15. Our approach is like putting a tool shed in the backyard rather than the front yard. This way the tools are there for those who want them, and they don't interfere with the view in the front yard.

Additional information about the metaphysical, ontological, epistemological, paradigmatic, and definitional assumptions and agendas that underlie our theorizing and research can be found at http://familycenter.byu.edu/Assumptions.dhtml. Click on "Assumptions in Sacred Theory."

We appreciate the help and support of many people as we have worked on this project. Our wives, children, grandchildren, great-grandchildren, and extended families are the most precious and helpful parts of our lives and work, and we do not have words to adequately express how deeply we feel our appreciation for them. We also appreciate the support of the School of Family Life and the Family Study Center at BYU and School of Human Ecology at LSU.

We appreciate the scholars whose previous work laid the groundwork for this volume. This includes those who contributed to the *Contemporary Theories About the Family* volumes and the two *Sourcebooks* on family theory and methods. It also includes many years of creative and cumulative scholarship by a group of colleagues at Bowling Green University. This group has been led by Annette Mahoney and Kenneth Pargament. We also appreciate the work, friendship, support, and advice of David Dollahite and those who have assisted him in his research. We are also grateful for our collaboration with Kathleen Bahr in several projects over many years and for the volume she published with Howard Bahr titled *Toward More Family-Centered Family Sciences*. Their book was in many ways foundational to our work.

We appreciate Bert Adams, Terry Baker, Mae Blanch, Pauline Boss, Mark Butler, Tom Draper, Ralph Hancock, Sam Hardy, Alan Hawkins, Tom Holman, Stan Knapp, Brent Melling, Joe Ostenson, Emily Reynolds, Darwin Thomas, Richard Williams, and Brent Yorgason for the ways they assisted this project. They advised, encouraged, consulted, reacted, and suggested many useful ideas. Several groups of students at BYU and LSU were also thoughtful and creative in helping us find ways to improve the ideas in this book.

We are also thankful for the many ways Debra Riegert, Andrea Zekus, and Marsha Hecht at Routledge/Taylor & Francis have been helpful and for reviews of manuscript by Gina M. Brelsford, William Doherty, David Dollahite, W. Bradford Wilcox, and three other anonymous reviewers. These reviews were provided by the publisher and were unusually helpful. Our writing also benefited from editorial help by Jennifer Koski, Joy Stubbs, and Yaxin Lu. And, last but not least, none of this would have been possible without the contributions of the many people who shared their thoughts, feelings, and experiences in our interviews and discussions. They contributed immeasurably to the ideas in this volume, and we have a deep and lasting gratitude for them and what we have learned from our interaction with them.

Wes, Loren, and Randy

1

Overview and Main Ideas in Sacred Theory

Scholars have been studying religion in families for over a century, but this research is still "in its infancy" (Pargament & Mahoney, 2005, p. 193). It also has a number of serious limitations because it is "awash in data without adequate theoretical interpretive lenses," and "without a unifying coherent theory to interpret those complex empirical findings, the reader is left with the daunting task of unraveling conceptual spaghetti."[1]

This book improves this situation by adding new qualitative and quantitative data and creating a conceptual framework and general theory (or model) about *when*, *how*, and *why* sacred matters are helpful and harmful in families. We build on the earlier literature, and to do this we need to describe what has been accomplished and ways it can be broadened and enhanced.

PREVIOUS RESEARCH AND THEORIES

The Research

There have been three generations or stages in this research. The first generation began in the late 1800s and lasted till the end of the twentieth century. The studies during this stage focused on the correlation religious affiliation and participation have with family outcomes such as marital satisfaction and stability, and there were several hundred studies. There also have been several reviews of this research.[2] Therefore there is not a need for another detailed review, but there is a need to evaluate the methods, findings, and reviews and identify ways the theory and research can be enhanced and broadened.

The studies have large differences in quality, but the questions, methods, and findings remained the same for about a century. The review by Mahoney,

[1] Snarey and Dollahite (2001, pp. 647 and 649).

[2] The reviews were by Marciano (1987), Thomas and Cornwall (1990); Holden (2001); Mahoney et al. (2001); Snarey and Dollahite (2001); Dollahite, Marks, and Goodman (2004); and Mahoney (2010).

Pargament, Tarakeshwar, and Swank (2001) found that the strength of relationships with *distal* indicators is fairly low, but more *specific* and *proximal* aspects of religion were more strongly related. They also concluded that the relationships were "as impressive as the predictive power of other global risk factors of child or family problems that are highlighted in sociological and epidemiological research"[3] (p. 584).

Scholars gradually realized that this first generation of research did not appreciate the "complex nature of spirituality," and that much of it involved "simplistic, dichotomous thinking about the helpfulness versus harmfulness of religion" (Krumrei, Mahoney, & Pargament, 2009, pp. 380–381). This led Thomas and Cornwall (1990) to suggest that "it is time for the social scientists to ask more systematically what it is about religion that contributes," and further that "multivariate models will have to be developed where multiple dimensions of both family and religion are measured in an effort to assess how these variables may be related" (p. 989).

This plea by Thomas and Cornwall and two papers by Mahoney et al. (1999, 2001) started the second generation of research. The second stage focused on ways more specific aspects of religion are related to a variety of processes and outcomes.[4] It also began the study of these relationships in diverse families and unique conditions. For example, a study by Marks, Nesteruk, Swanson, Garrison, and Davis (2005) found that specific religious beliefs and practices were related to longevity, health, and well-being in African American individuals and families. The research in this stage also included studies about how specific aspects of religion help families cope with special needs, stressful situations such as disabilities and serious illnesses, and sexual abuse.[5] There also were studies about ways religion helps promote healthy development in adolescents and ways religious rituals influence activities in families.[6]

Ways the Research Can Be Improved and Expanded The first two generations of research were a valuable beginning, but the research in them also

---

[3] Mahoney et al. (2001) did a meta-analysis of 94 studies and found that when the research focused on distal factors such as affiliation with a religious denomination, the relationships were consistently positive but not strong. The correlation coefficients averaged around .05. However, when studies gathered data about the frequency of attendance at religious services, the correlations were a little higher, averaging .07. Relationships that dealt with more proximal aspects of religiosity such as the importance of religion, frequency of prayer, and Bible reading were still higher. They averaged around .15, and some of them accounted for as much as 46% of the variance.

[4] For example, Butler, Gardner, and Bird (1998); Butler, Stout, and Gardner (2002); and Beach, Fincham, Hurt, McNair, and Stanley (2008) focused on ways prayer is helpful in conflict resolution and therapy. Studies also began to examine ways forgiveness influences a variety of family processes such as marital satisfaction and conflict resolution (Fincham, 2003; Fincham, Beach, & Davila, 2004; Fincham et al., 2002; Worthington, 2005). Research also focused on ways religious practices are related to fidelity, commitment, conflict avoidance, and conflict resolution (Dollahite & Lambert, 2007; Lambert & Dollahite, 2006, 2008).

[5] Mahoney et al. (2001, pp. 583–584); Gall, Basque, Damasceno-Scott, and Vardy (2007); and Dollahite, Marks, and Olson. (1998).

[6] Smith (2003); Marks (2004); and Loser, Hill, Klein, and Dollahite (2009).

has a number of limitations, and there are ways it ought to be improved. Ten of these ways are relevant for the theory and research in this volume:

1. Only a few of the specific and proximal characteristics of the sacred have been studied, and there are many other aspects that deserve attention.
2. The research has focused only on the existence and strength of the covariation in the relationships. Therefore it provides little information about other characteristics of the relationships such as the shape of nonlinear relationships, thresholds, interactions, and the length of time for the effects of change to appear.
3. Little attention has been given to the role of contingencies or contextual factors, and Sullivan (2001) and Dollahite and Marks (2009) suggested that they are important.
4. "More in-depth and conceptually based measurement tools are needed to develop a richer, deeper understanding of the mechanisms that tie religion to family life" (Mahoney et al., 2001, p. 585).
5. There is a need for more integration. The previous studies are helpful, "but as a whole they present the contemporary researcher with a disjointed and fragmented account for religious influences" (Smith, 2003, p. 17).
6. Krumrei et al. (2009) argued that the majority of the research does not appreciate the complexity of spiritual phenomena, and they and Baucom (2001) suggested that more attention should be given to "specific religious beliefs and practices within the context of concrete life situations" (Krumrei et al., 2009, p. 380).
7. The research provides few insights about why some families with high religiosity are not successful and some families with low religiosity are successful. It is likely that some of the reasons for this are that some people are religious in some ways and not in other ways, that some of their behavior is consistent with their religious ideals and some is not, and that these patterns have been overlooked.
8. Most of the research has focused on ways religion is helpful, and more attention should be given to ways it can be harmful.
9. The research has focused almost exclusively on traditional families. Therefore little is known about the role of religion in nontraditional patterns such as same-sex coupling and parenting, nonmarital parenting, cohabitation, stepfamilies, polyamorous lifestyles, and single lifestyles.
10. The research in the first two generations focused on wholesome aspects of mainstream religions in the United States. These religions have experienced several reformations and counterreformations in the last several centuries, and many of them are more family-friendly than they were in the past. There have been many historical and cultural situations where religions have been neither noble nor helpful, and this means the existing research provides information about only a small part of the many different kinds and aspects of religion that have existed historically, that exist in the present, and that can exist. Therefore there are important limitations

to the conclusions and generalizations that can be made from the existing research, and there is a need for additional research about a broader range of religions and cultural conditions.

The Theories

During the first generation of research, there were no significant attempts to create theories about *why*, *how*, and *when* religion helps or harms families. Therefore the empirical research far outstripped the ideas about what the research means and how the ideas in the research can be applied by families and by professionals. This led to several unfortunate conditions. Scholars "found it difficult to integrate the findings from the various studies of families and religion because of the absence of a unifying theoretical perspective" (Snarey & Dollahite, 2001, p. 649), and the area was "correlation rich but explanation poor" (Marks & Dollahite, in press). Also, as Sullivan (2001) suggested, "the largest impediment to a more complete understanding of how religiosity affects marital functioning is that many studies have been exploratory in nature or empirically driven rather than theory driven" (p. 611).

Several groups began to create conceptual and theoretical models in the second generation. One group was led by Mahoney and Pargament.[7] They focused on "mechanisms through which religion may influence family relationships" (Mahoney et al., 2001, pp. 585–591), and suggested that psychosocial functions and the substantive elements are two different mechanisms. They also theorized that both of these mechanisms have the potential to facilitate and impede healthy family processes; and they developed a number of ideas about how substantive and psychosocial aspects of the sacred help and hinder marriage and parenting.

They also developed the relational spirituality framework that differentiates between processes in family formation, family management, and family transformation. This framework also has a number of ideas about ways relationships with the divine, perceptions of relationships as spiritual, and relationships with spiritual communities can be helpful and harmful (Mahoney, 2010). Many of the ideas this group developed are explained in more detail in later chapters and incorporated into the more general theory that is constructed in this volume.

A second group that began to create conceptual and theoretical models was Dollahite and Marks and their colleagues.[8] They conducted qualitative interviews with a sizeable sample of racially diverse, highly religious families and middle-aged couples living in different regions in the United States who were affiliated with the three major Abrahamic faiths of Christianity, Judaism, and Islam. The data from these interviews provided the basis for a model that describes how *contexts* influence *processes* and processes influence *outcomes*, and this model was one of the starting points for the theory building in this volume.

[7] Most of the theoretical contributions of this group are in Mahoney et al. (1999, 2001, 2003); Mahoney, Pargament et al. (2005); Pargament (1997, 2007); Pargament and Mahoney (2005); and Mahoney (2010).

[8] Most of the theoretical contributions of this group are in Dollahite and Marks (2005, 2009), Goodman and Dollahite (2006), Lambert and Dollahite (2006, 2008), and Marks (2005, 2006).

Smith (2003) also developed a model about the role of religion. His goal was to create "a more coherent, systematic account of how and why religion exerts significant positive effects on American youth" (p. 17). His model focused on three dimensions in the influence of religion: moral order, learned competencies, and social and organizational ties. His "moral order" and "social and organizational ties" are very similar to Mahoney's substantive and psychosocial dimensions. We have used Mahoney's terminology because the concepts are slightly more familial, whereas Smith's model deals with social processes generally rather than family processes.

The models that were created in the second generation dealt with all four of the key questions in theory building. The most elementary question is the *what* question raised by Thomas and Cornwall (1990): "What it is about religion that contributes" to family outcomes? (p. 989). Two of the other questions are the *why* and *how* questions. As Bengtson, Acock, Allen, Dilworth-Anderson, and Klein (2005) described: "This we believe is the purpose of theorizing—trying to understand and explain the *why* and *how* beyond the *what* of our data about families" (p. 4, italics in the original).

The fourth set of questions are the *when* questions. They deal with the conditions or circumstances that influence when aspects of the sacred are helpful and harmful, when relationships exist and don't exist, and when aspects of relationships such as shape and strength vary. They also deal with the "interactions" emphasized by Snarey and Dollahite (2001, p. 649).

Ways the Theories Can Be Improved and Expanded The theory building in the second generation was valuable because it provided more elaborate, useful, and insightful conceptualizations. It also moved the field well beyond the zero-order correlations between religiosity and valued outcomes; and provided new insights about the role of proximal and specific aspects of religion. However, the theories also have a number of limitations, and there are several ways they ought to be improved and expanded. Nine of these ways are relevant for this volume.

1. The previous models focused mostly on what and how questions, and little attention was given to the why questions. Ideas about why are elusive and speculative; and they are never complete or final in the study of phenomena such as religion and families, but they help provide understanding and insight. They also help with the application of the ideas, help in improving and revising theories, help stimulate new research, and help satisfy intellectual curiosity. Future scholarship should give more attention to the whys.
2. The previous theorizing also paid little attention to the when questions. The part of the Dollahite and Marks (2005, 2009) model that describes contexts began dealing with the when questions, but little has been done with how and why contextual variables make a difference in different social groups, in different situations, or at different points in the individual or familial life cycle; and scholars have not yet dealt with other issues such as the length of time for effects to appear when changes happen.

3. The conceptualization of the main terms remains problematic. Concepts such as religion, religiosity, spiritual, spirituality, and sacred have not been interdefined in an effective way, and they are used differently by different scholars. They continue to have overlapping, multiple, and sometimes ambiguous meanings. Therefore more work is needed to improve the way the basic terms are interdefined and operationalized.
4. The theory building also has remained close to the empirical data. This means the models are mini-theories or midrange theories, and there is little in this broad, general, and inclusive theorizing that is relevant in understanding the role of the sacred generally or in a wide variety of social conditions.
5. The theory building has focused primarily on the role of forgiveness, prayer, sacrifice, sanctification, and rituals; but there are many other aspects of the sacred that have been studied that ought to be included in the models, and there are many other aspects of the sacred that have not been studied that should be included.
6. The theorizing remains fairly fragmented because most of the work focuses on the role of specific phenomena individually rather than their role together, in interaction, as parts of an integrated whole, or as parts of a larger set of processes.
7. The theorizing deals with the existence, direction, and strength of relationships, but it does not deal with the more complicated aspects of relationships, such as their shape if they are nonlinear, interactions, and thresholds.
8. Like the research, the theorizing has been about wholesome aspects of mainstream religions in the United States. This means the theorizing is not very broad or general, and it should be viewed only as ideas about the role of positive aspects of a few religions in rather limited cultural and historical conditions. This also means the initial theorizing does not have ideas that are general and abstract enough to be relevant for and applicable to a wide range of historical, cultural, and religious conditions.
9. The theorizing has not been integrated with the conceptual frameworks or general theories that are widely used in the field (White & Klein, 2008). Another alternative would be to create a new conceptual framework or theory that is general and inclusive, but this also has not been done.

Thus the initial theory building in this area has been a valuable beginning, but it is only a beginning and has a number of limitations. There also are many ways and places where improvements can be made, and there is a need, in the cyclical relationship between theory and research described by Merton (1957) and Klein (2005, p.17), to *improve* and *expand* the theory and research. These are the goals in this book, and we try to move this area into a third generation. The first step is to improve the conceptualization.

CONCEPTS

One of the first challenges we encountered was the ambiguity and controversies in the way key terms such as *religion*, *spiritual*, *spirituality*, and *sacred* have been defined in the scholarly literature. This confusion in the conceptualization created a number of problems as we tried to integrate the previous research and theorizing. Therefore we focused first on these conceptual issues to try to find better ways to label, define, describe, illustrate, and operationalize the basic terminology.

Religion is the term that has been used most widely to describe the part of reality we are interested in. It is used the most in research and theory and in the names of journals; it is used to describe sections in the American Psychological Association and the National Council on Family Relations; and quite a number of scholars prefer this term.[9] Others prefer terms like spiritual or spirituality, and these also have been widely used.[10] However, all three of these terms have so much ambiguity and so many meanings and connotations that they have serious disadvantages.

A number of scholars have tried to improve the definitions of these terms,[11] but there is still little consensus, and they continue to be used in a variety of ways. We eventually concluded that *when dealing with general, broad, and inclusive theories*, the most useful term is sacred. Some of its advantages are that it is general and abstract and is relevant for a wide variety of cultural and denominational differences. Also, it is inclusive and broad while at the same time being fairly precise and focused. It is not as vague and all-inclusive as spiritual, and it shares useful elements with the term religion without including many aspects of religion that are of little interest to most scholars. It also avoids a number of the complicating connotations that come with the other terms. The result is that *sacred* has more advantages and fewer complications and disadvantages when thinking theoretically, and we and a number of others prefer it.[12] Another indicator of the value of this term is that some who prefer terms like religion and spirituality turn to the term sacred to define what they mean by the other terms (Mahoney, 2010). We particularly like the term *sacred matters*, which was introduced by Pargament and Mahoney (2005, p. 179).

It is difficult to create precise definitions of the primary terms in general theories, but it seems important to summarize our working definition of *sacred*. It refers to the parts of the human experience that are sufficiently awe inspiring that they transform the thinking and feeling of individuals from the ordinary, mundane, and routine into what is perceived as holy, hallowed, and sacrosanct. This transformation leads to high levels of reverence, adoration, deference, and respect.

[9] Young (1995) and Onedera (2008) are examples of scholars who prefer this term.

[10] Spiritual or spirituality are the primary concepts in Richards and Bergin (2005), Pargament (2007), Walsh (2009), and Mahoney (2010).

[11] Cashwell and Young (2005); Pargament and Mahoney (2005); Paloutzian and Park (2005); Pargament (2007); Zhai, Ellison, Stokes, and Glenn (2008); Walsh (2009); Swenson (2009); and Mahoney (2010) have all described the confusion in the terminology. Each of them has tried to improve it, but their proposed solutions have had little impact on later efforts.

[12] Berger (1967), Nottingham (1971), Bailey (1998), Bowker (2000), and Swenson (2009) are examples of others who prefer the term sacred.

These experiences include but are not limited to divine, heavenly, otherworldly, transcendental, numenal, and spiritual experiences and beliefs; and they frequently but not always provide the basis for religious experiences and religiously motivated behaviors.

One aspect of this definition is that a person cannot define a sacred experience for another person because the sacred is personal. Often those with similar experiences gather to share the results of their experiences; and they sometimes attempt to encourage or recruit others to have similar experiences. Multiple people in some groups may have such experiences, but the sacred is ultimately experienced, perceived, and defined by the individual. People can be coached to recognize certain feelings and experiences as "sacred," but in the end, it is the individual who ultimately experiences and judges the authenticity of the sacred.

One way of clarifying the way we conceptualize the sacred is to describe ways the term is similar to and different from related terms such as religion, spiritual, and spirituality. Some parts of religion are sacred and some are not; and some parts of spirituality are sacred and some are not. Therefore the term sacred includes some but not all aspects of religion and some but not all aspects of spirituality.

The term religion refers to organized, institutionalized, and denominational belief systems, practices, scripture, rules of worship, and institutionalized values—that is, the complex set of practices and ordinances by which humans derive order about the religious and how they fashion their actions. It generates doctrine, symbols, ethics, rituals, and performance expectations. It is often built on and around sacred experiences, but sacred experiences also can be disconnected from religion.

Religion is a less general concept than sacred because it is closely tied to organizations and behavior. Therefore religion is more easily operationalized by paying attention to which churches people join and their behavior as they respond to their beliefs and "search for significance in ways related to the sacred" (Pargament, 1997, p. 34). This means that focusing on measurable aspects of religions can be helpful in empirical research because such actions are close to what can be observed. However, the characteristics of religion that make aspects of it measurable also make it difficult to think more generally when using this term by being more abstract and general and rising above denominational, organizational, and behavioral aspects. Therefore the term religion is not very helpful in trying to create theories that are broad, inclusive, and relevant for a wide range of cultural and historical diversity.

The term sacred, on the other hand, has broader scope and does not connote or denote anything about behavior because it refers to relatively abstract experiences, perceptions, beliefs, or attributions. Conversely, the result of the broad and abstract nature of the term sacred is that it is not as helpful with empirical research because the logical connections between observations and the sacred are so distant—but it is easier to rise above cultural, denominational, historical, and situational differences and create understanding and insights into what, why, how, and when aspects of the sacred help and harm in society and in families, and why, how, and when it doesn't make a difference when people wish it did.

Our definition of the sacred is also quite different from spiritual and spirituality, which are broader, more inclusive, and variable. They also are more vague, subjective, personal, and difficult to define; and they refer to less institutionalized aspects of the human experience because they can include walking in the woods, football at LSU, listening to music, going to an art gallery, enjoying a sunset, or watching a butterfly emerge from a cocoon. Because so many aspects of the spiritual and spirituality lie outside the primary concerns in our research and theory building, we prefer to focus on the role of sacred matters.

Sacred experiences often involve emotion, but they also are different from many emotional experiences. People can have an emotive and special experience watching a sporting event, seeing a moving play about key social issues, or even attending a wonderful concert with stirring music. Those experiences become "sacred" only when a personal transformation occurs and the experience morphs from ordinary to holy.

Another issue about this conceptualization is whether the sacred is a part of reality. Some people believe the sacred is real in an absolute sense, and others believe it is imagined rather than real. We are among those who believe there are sacred realities that are important in an absolute or ultimate sense. But questions about whether these absolutes exist cannot be resolved with scholarly tools, and sacred processes make a difference in families whether they are real or imagined. Therefore sacred theory is primarily about the phenomenological aspects of the sacred, but they are an important part of reality. As James (1902) argued more than a century ago, "Name it the mystical region, or the supernatural region. . . . Yet the unseen region in question is not merely ideal, for it produces effects in this world" (p. 399). He also went on to explain that "*that which produces effects within another reality must be termed a reality itself*, so I feel as if we had no philosophic excuse for calling the unseen or mystical world unreal. . . . *God is real since he produces real effects*" (pp. 399, 400, emphasis added).

This principle was broadened and further developed by Thomas and Znaniecki (1918) and Thomas (1923), who argued that *a situation perceived as real is real in its consequences*. This leads to the conclusion that the phenomenological reality of the sacred leads to important consequences—whether they exist in a noumenological[13] sense or not.

Another aspect of these conceptual issues that deserves more elaboration has to do with the parts of the human experience that are given the most emphasis in the study of the sacred. The social sciences traditionally have focused primarily on cognitive, behavioral, affective, and relationship parts of the humane, and these are important in studying the sacred, but there is an aspect that in later chapters will be emphasized more than cognition, behavior, affect, and relationships. It is what happens in what is usually conceptualized as the human "heart." When there are beliefs, perceptions, or attributions about the sacred, they are experiential and

[13] The difference between noumenological and phenomenological is a conceptualization developed by Immanuel Kant. He used the term noumenological to refer to the absolute existence of reality that is independent of human observation, perception, or definitions. Therefore humans do not have direct access to the nature of noumenological reality. Phenomenological reality refers to the perceived and constructed human definitions about reality. Phenomenological perceptions of reality come from reason, empirical observations, and/or other sources of knowledge.

involve the heart in addition to these other phenomena. This part of the conceptualization of the sacred is difficult to describe clearly because it is so difficult to define phenomena such as the human heart, but because it is difficult doesn't mean it isn't important or real. Ideas such as having a hard heart or a soft heart, or something touching the heart are important when dealing with the sacred, and the term sacred is much better at identifying and describing these phenomena than terms like religion. Even though these parts of the human experience are elusive and difficult to define precisely, they are so important in our theorizing that this book is primarily a book about the heart and the experiential parts of being human. This is another reason we find the term sacred more helpful in our theory building than terms like religion and spiritual.

Even though the theory in this book is *about* and largely derived *from* the sacred, we do not turn scholarly inquiry into a religious activity or experience, or incorporate what philosophers call mystical epistemologies into scholarly inquiry. The theory in this volume merely uses ideas that are phenomenologically from and about the sacred.

As we shift the conceptualization and theorizing to a theory about sacred matters in families rather than focusing on religion, religions, spiritual, or spirituality, we recognize that different perspectives exist. We do not argue that any particular definition or version or approach is truer, better, more complete, more adequate, or more defensible than others. Most of the world religions have a great deal in common with regard to the sacred[14] regardless of their differences; and a central thesis in this book is that the quality of theory and research about families will improve and be more useful and cumulative when scholarship focuses on the nature and influence of the sacred.

We also note that all of the perspectives about the sacred, including our views, are limited and provide only a partial, incomplete, and sometimes inaccurate understanding of sacred phenomena. Further, each sacred perspective is influenced by its unique historical and cultural context, and each has disadvantages and inadequacies; but scholarship that focuses on the role of the sacred taps into aspects of reality that, when wisely used, are valuable in helping most people accomplish their family objectives.

A final aspect of the definition of sacred matters has to do with the sources or reasons for sacred experiences and perceptions. These sources can be theistic or nontheistic.[15] Theists have many reasons for believing in the sacred, and those who do not believe in god(s) also have experiences that are so awe-inspiring or transcendental that they create a sense of reverence, awe, respect, and holiness. For example, many who do not believe in god(s) are so committed to ideals such as liberty, equality, and freedom that they are sacred. Another example is the widespread view that Ground Zero in New York City is sacred for many people in ways that are independent of beliefs in god(s). These differences are important because the ideas in the theory that is constructed in

---

[14] Das (1947) and H. Smith (1992) assemble impressive evidence for these similarities.

[15] Pargament and Mahoney (2005, pp. 183–188) described a number of theistic and nontheistic sources of sacred beliefs and perceptions

this volume are valid, relevant, and important for both theistic and nontheistic views of sacred matters. Even if one argues that the sacred is not universally experienced or if some people have little experience with the sacred, it is universally important because everyone interacts with others who experience the sacred in important ways.

FOUR GENERAL IDEAS

After making these conceptual refinements, we began the process of trying to improve and expand the theorizing. Our goals were to use ideas in the previous research and theorizing, several strategies in the methodology of theory building,[16] and some new data and different kinds of data to build a conceptual framework and theory that (a) are more general, inclusive, and integrated than the previous theorizing, and (b) will provide better, more testable, and more useful explanations that are relevant for a wider range of religious approaches, specific situations, and cultural and historical conditions.

The main question we were concerned with was a slightly more general and complex version of the question asked two decades ago by Thomas and Cornwall (1990, p. 989): "*What is it about the sacred that helps and harms families?*" (emphasis added). The first thing we did as we tried to find answers to this question was to examine the previous literature and analyze and reanalyze the data in our observations and interviews to extract as many truth assertions or theoretical propositions as possible. This led to a list of about 50 generalizations that dealt with ways various dimensions of the sacred influence family processes and outcomes. These ideas dealt with the role of processes such as prayer, forgiveness, sacrifice, rituals, sanctification, turning the other cheek, patience, not being judgmental, being merciful, and so on. These propositions provided some understanding and explanation, but they had little generality, explanatory power, and integration. We then tried to integrate at least some of them by moving to a higher level of abstraction and grouping them under more general ideas. This led to the slightly more general idea that "loving others" in families includes 17 of the less general propositions.

This helped, but provided only a little bit of integration and additional explanation. We therefore tried to move to an even higher level of abstraction and seek more general ideas that would (a) be relevant for a wide variety of historical, cultural, and religious situations, (b) provide general propositions from which less general ideas could be deduced, (c) integrate the previous research and theory, (d) provide better explanation and understanding, (e) create ideas that are testable with empirical data, and (f) be an effective beginning point in theorizing about the sacred in families.

---

[16] The major contributors to this methodology have been Braithwaite (1953); Zetterberg (1965); Nagel (1961); Glaser and Strauss (1967); Stinchcombe (1968); Blalock (1969, 1971); Dubin (1969); Hage (1972); Gibbs (1972), Burr (1973); Glaser (1978); Burr, Hill, Nye, and Reiss (1979); Strauss and Corbin (1990); Denzin and Lincoln (1994); Gilgun (2001, 2005); Knapp (2009); Tudge, Mokrova, Hatfield, and Karnik (2009); and Jaccard and Jacoby (2010).

As we sought these more general ideas, we reexamined and reanalyzed our data and the 50 propositions in a variety of ways to see if they could be combined, integrated, or changed in ways that would provide clues about more general propositions or lead us in other ways to more general ideas. This led to a number of combinations and changes that did not prove fruitful. We also searched for ideas in other aspects of religion such as symbolism, traditions, religiosity, rituals, dogma and doctrine, and participating in joint activities; but they also did not help answer the key question.

Proposition 1

Eventually, as we were working with the less general propositions, the ideas about *sacred matters* and *sanctification* that were introduced by Mahoney et al. (1999, 2001; Mahoney, Pargament, Murray-Swank, & Murray-Swank, 2003) and expanded by Pargament and Mahoney (2005) started us on a line of analysis and reasoning that became more fruitful. They theorized that people can view many things as sacred, and that when phenomena are perceived as sacred this leads to individual and relational benefits, costs, and risks (Mahoney et al., 2003). Their ideas led to several studies about ways sanctification influences sexuality, parenthood, and health patterns and outcomes such as marital satisfaction and reactions to divorce,[17] and they argued that the process of defining aspects of life as sacred "has several implications for human functioning" and "should be of keen interest to the psychology of religion" (Pargament & Mahoney, 2005, p. 180).

We found some of these same patterns in our data. Some people we observed and interviewed believed aspects of their life were sacred, and these attributions or perceptions gave these phenomena substantial power in their lives. Others participated in religious activities for less sacred reasons, such as parental pressure or because it is the socially acceptable thing to do, and these less sacred religious parts of their lives had less power—less influence on other aspects of their lives.

As we analyzed these ideas about sanctification and our data, we found several ways to expand the previous theorizing, and several studies in other disciplines provided helpful insights. One of the helpful studies was Weber's (1904) analysis titled *The Protestant Ethic and the Spirit of Capitalism.* His data suggested there was a connection between an aspect of Calvinism and the rise of capitalism. According to Calvinism, one's work ethic and subsequent economic successes are tied directly to one's "election" by God. This notion places a high value on work and ties it to devotion and a desire to be chosen by God, and this contributed to the rise of capitalism because devoted people worked hard to achieve economic success and thereby prove their election. The empirical part of Weber's analysis dealt with religion and religious behavior, but his theoretical explanation was the more abstract idea that it was sacredness that made the difference because it was

[17] Mahoney et al. (1999); Mahoney, Carel et al. (2005); Mahoney, Pargament et al. (2005); Murray-Swank, Pargament, and Mahoney (2005); and Krumrei et al. (2009).

the attribution of sacredness to an aspect of life that is usually viewed as mundane that gave it power.

These ideas regarding the power of the sacred were also in the writings of Bīrunī in the eleventh century (Kamiar, 2009), in the work of other anthropologists (Murdock, 1934), and in the early psychological literature (James, 1902). In the empirical work by each of these scholars, they focused on aspects of religion and religious behavior, but when they sought explanations of their findings they turned to the more general and abstract idea that *sacredness increases the power of phenomena*. The results are not always beneficial, but they are powerful.

The same reasoning was used in Durkheim's volume on *The Elementary Forms of Religious Life* (1915). He analyzed the role of religions in a number of primitive cultures, and the idea that guided his work was also that the sacredness of aspects of religion gave them a powerful influence on other parts of reality. His summary of this idea is more individualistic than familial, but it is very insightful:

> The believer who has communicated with his god is not merely a man who sees new truths of which the unbeliever is ignorant; he is a man who is *stronger*. He feels within him more force, either to endure the trials of existence, or to conquer them. It is as though he were raised above the miseries of the world, because he is raised above his condition as a mere man" (Durkheim, 1915, p. 416; italics in the original).

Durkheim's summary of this idea is so close to poetry that Dave Dollahite arranged the flow of the ideas into this version:

> The believer who has communicated with his god
> Is not merely a man who sees new truths
> Of which the unbeliever is ignorant;
> He is a man who is stronger.
> He feels within him more force,
> Either to endure the trials of existence, or to conquer them.
> It is as though he were raised above the miseries of the world,
> Because he is raised above his condition as a mere man...
>
> Emile Durkheim

Our reasoning extended this theoretical idea beyond the initial proposition that sanctification leads to individual and relationship benefits, costs, and risks because it provides insight into *why* sanctification makes a difference. It also adds the idea that sacredness creates *salience and power* in the ways phenomena influence other processes and outcomes because when these same phenomena are not perceived as sacred they have less potency.

Different parts of the previous literature and the patterns in our data dealt with aspects of this general idea in slightly different ways. Figuratively speaking, this was like having a number of threads that were similar but slightly different. Separately, the threads did not form a pattern, and they provided little help in answering the key theoretical question we were asking. However, as we thought about the various ways these ideas have been used and can be used, this led us, with the help of some colleagues and students, to think about this cluster of ideas in a more general and abstract way; and we saw a pattern we hadn't seen before—a relationship we had not seen before.

To continue the analogy of threads, some of the threads are old and widely known, but they can be woven together in a new way that creates a new pattern—a new idea. The pattern provides an idea that is different from the individual studies, ideas, or threads. Also, it is greater than the sum of the parts because it provides a more general and abstract proposition that offers new insights, new explanations, and new understandings; and the central idea helps answer the key theoretical question we were asking. The resulting idea then became the most fundamental truth assertion in what we now call sacred theory, and it is:

Proposition 1: Experiencing parts of the human experience as sacred gives them a unique, unusually powerful, and salient influence.

A simpler way of summarizing this proposition is that *the sacred matters*, and, as one colleague put it, *it matters a lot*—irrespective of cultural differences, historical conditions, religious persuasion, and even participation. This idea is so powerful, relevant, and useful that it has the same keystone quality in our theorizing that *the invisible hand* had for Smith (1776), *survival of the fittest* had for Darwin (1859), *conditioning* had for Pavlov (1927), and *unconditional positive regard* had for Rogers (1951).

There are a number of characteristics of the sacred that help explain *why* Proposition 1 is true and helpful. The sacred inherently inspires awe and reverence. It deals with the parts of life that are unusually significant and sacrosanct, and that generate such deep respect that they lead to worship, commitment, devotion, dedication, and veneration. It deals with the extraordinary and hallowed rather than the ordinary. It inspires, amazes, and leads to wonder. It deals with the supernatural and numinous. Also, as Bahr and Bahr (2009) suggested, it deals with the transcendent, and as Pargament (2007) suggested, it deals with "boundlessness" and "ultimacy" (p. 39). It provides ideas and beliefs about the BIG questions in life that deal with the nature, meaning, and purposes of reality and human existence. Therefore by its very nature, the sacred occupies a unique, salient, and powerful place in the human experience.

We theorize that this idea is sufficiently powerful that experiences with the sacred make a great deal of difference, even in circumstances where people are not aware of the effects of their participation. Therefore Proposition 1 deals with more than just perceptions, beliefs, and discovery. It is an idea about experiencing and what the experiencing does to the heart. We also theorize that this idea is so general that it is relevant for many different perspectives about religion, religions, and the sacred. It also is sufficiently general that it is relevant for a wide range of cultural and historical conditions and a wide range of personal circumstances and perceptions; and this generality and profundity make this idea a strong beginning point in a theory about sacred matters in families.

Unfortunately, even though several versions of this idea were widely appreciated in the early years of the social sciences, the skepticism and ambivalence among scholars toward ideas about the sacred became so powerful by the middle decades of the twentieth century that the notion that the sacred matters was ignored in the conceptual frameworks and theories that became the dominant approaches in studying families (Hill & Hansen, 1960). And, unfortunately, this pattern continues up to the present time because this idea is not in any of the many summaries in the last half century of the widely used theories in family studies.[18] We think it is wise to resurrect this proposition, give it new life, and find new ways to use it to generate ideas that will help scholars and practitioners better understand what helps and harms families.

It is impossible to tell with the tools that are available in scholarly inquiry whether sacred phenomena are salient and powerful because phenomena such as God(s), heaven, hell, devils, life after death, and salvation exist noumenologically and phenomenologically, or just phenomenologically. For many of our purposes, however, this distinction is not central because the sacred is salient and powerful in families either way. Beliefs about whether sacred phenomena exist noumenologically are matters of faith, and scholarly inquiry does not have the tools to answer such questions. However, studying the ways families are influenced by experiences with the phenomenological aspects of the sacred can and ought to be a central concern in the study of families.

Many aspects of the sacred are salient and powerful for people of faith because they believe these aspects originate with God and are part of God's eternal, transcendental, and otherworldly plans for humans. But there are many who do not believe in the noumenological existence of God; yet many of them still have sacred phenomena in their lives, and many of the ideas in this book are relevant for them. Their beliefs are founded on secular rather than divine or theistic reasons. The basis for these ideas does not seem to us to be well articulated in the worldviews that undergird these philosophies, but these nontheistic experiences with the sacred have salience and power—whatever the source.

To summarize, the idea that experiences with sacredness create salience and power—irrespective of cultural differences, historical conditions, religious persuasion, and participation—is a truth assertion or proposition that became an assumption on which the rest of sacred theory is built. It is the most valuable and defensible intellectual bedrock we have seen for a theory about sacred matters in families.

There are several other analogies that illustrate the central and fundamental role of this idea in sacred theory. In a sense, it is an umbrella idea that covers all of the other ideas in the theory. In another sense it is a cornerstone idea. Or, as one colleague clumsily but insightfully put it, it is the kind of idea that provides the "overarching underpinning." If this idea is not true, sacred theory is irrelevant,

[18] The summaries after Hill and Hansen's (1960) were by Christensen (1964); Nye and Berardo (1966); Broderick (1971); Burr et al. (1979); Holman and Burr (1980); Thomas and Wilcox (1987); Winton (1995); Ingoldsby, Smith, and Miller (2004); Chibucos, Leite, and Weiss (2005); and White and Klein (2008).

inconsequential, and unimportant. However, to the extent it is true, sacred theory is built on a defensible and helpful foundation.

Proposition 2

Proposition 1 is so general that it is relevant for many aspects of the human experience, and it provides explanation and understanding about a wide range of phenomena. It can be applied to crosses, crucifixes, tombs, birthplaces, ideals, dreams, memories, hopes, experiences, emotions, books, poetry, revelations, legal systems, education, governments, and many other aspects of the human experience. However, in our theory building we are not interested in these other domains or phenomena, so they are residual. Rather, we are interested in ideas that can help *families* be effective. Therefore we applied this idea to family processes, and this led to a slightly less general truth assertion or proposition that is the second of four general ideas in sacred theory. It is:

Proposition 2: Experiencing parts of family life as sacred gives them a unique, unusually powerful, and salient influence in families.

This proposition provides valuable understanding and explanation about *why* the research has consistently found significant correlations between religious beliefs/activities and valued family outcomes. Also, based on the persuasive evidence about Proposition 1, from which this proposition is deduced, Proposition 2 also provides insight, explanation, and understanding about *why* scholars and practitioners who want to understand and explain what makes families effective and who want to develop programs to help families ought to give this idea a central role in their theories, research, and intervention programs.

Proposition 3

It would be easy to theorize that the parts of life that are perceived to be sacred are constructive and helpful in families because the vast majority of the previous research focused on the beneficial effects of wholesome aspects of widely respected religions; and the findings have demonstrated again and again that many aspects of the sacred are positively related to effectiveness in families. And, unfortunately, some of the earlier theorizing and much of the earlier research seems to be implicitly based on this generalization.

However, such a generalization ignores the reality that people can use aspects of the sacred in adaptive, good, and helpful ways, but they also can use them in maladaptive, bad, and harmful ways.[19] Propositions 1 and 2 do not help with these

[19] The idea that aspects of the sacred can be harmful was first described by Edmonds, Withers, and Dibatista (1972) and later expanded by Levinger (1976). It was further elaborated and illustrated by Scanzoni and Arnett (1987), Pargament (1997, 2007), Mahoney et al. (2001, 2003), Mahoney (2010), and Griffith (2010).

more value-laden differences because they deal only with the idea that aspects of the sacred are unique, salient, and powerful.

This reality led us to focus next on what it is about the sacred that is helpful in some circumstances and harmful in others. To help us find ideas about this question, we again turned to the data from our interviews and observations, and we eventually concluded that it is not the presence of the sacred, the presence of religion(s), or the presence of religiosity that is important in understanding when aspects of the sacred are helpful and harmful in families. It is variation in what people *do* as a result of their ideals and beliefs about the sacred that is important; and there can be (and is) considerable variation in what people do as a result of the sacred, even within the same family and same religious tradition. These insights led to the idea that became the third general proposition in the theory:

Proposition 3: It is variation in what people *do* as a result of their ideals and beliefs about the sacred that determines whether the sacred is helpful or harmful in families, and it is not the mere presence of religion in general or global religiosity that makes the difference.

In other words, it is how family members act as a result of their sacred beliefs that matters. It is not simply global religiosity per se or being a particular type of family such as highly religious, orthodox, or conventional. It is how family members *use* aspects of the sacred that is crucial because people can be religious generally and behave in some ways that are not helpful, and they can be low in religiosity and behave in ways that are helpful.

One of the earlier theoretical contributions that helped us arrive at this idea was Pargament's (1997) theory of religious coping. He focused on adaptive and maladaptive coping strategies people can use as they deal with stressful events and transitions. He and his colleagues developed an instrument called the Religious Coping Scale (RCOPE) to assess methods people use to cope (Pargament & Koenig, 2000), and this instrument has been used in subsequent research (Krumrei et al., 2009, p. 376).

Pargament's theorizing and research about how people "use" an aspect of the sacred parts of their life to help them understand and cope with stressors was useful to us because it helped us focus on one way of using aspects of the sacred. We then extended this reasoning to think about a broader array of ways people use what Mahoney et al. (2001) called the substantive and the psychosocial elements of religion, because we were interested in what happens in the routine and ordinary living in families, rather than just strategies that are used in coping with more profound and atypical stressors. As we found ourselves thinking about a broader array of ways of "using" the sacred, this was helpful because it included what family members do with the various aspects of the sacred in the ordinary, daily, everyday, and normal management of their lives and how variation in these ways of behaving changes the probability of other family processes and important family outcomes.

Proposition 4

As these ideas became clearer to us, they helped us focus on what seemed to be the next important question. That is, *what* is it that can help us understand *when* behaviors that result from the sacred are helpful and harmful?

As we examined and reexamined our interviews and observations, we eventually found an idea that is helpful in at least partially answering this question. It is the idea that ways of behaving that result from sacred matters can be consistent or inconsistent with a cluster of widely shared goals in families; and when behavior is consistent with these goals, it tends to be helpful. Conversely, the more behaviors are not consistent with these goals, the more they tend to be harmful. This insight then became the fourth general proposition in the theory:

Proposition 4: The more behavior is consistent with a cluster of widely shared goals in families the more it tends to be helpful, and the more it is inconsistent with these goals the more it tends to be harmful.

The value of this idea depends on what are viewed as the widely shared goals in families. There are many perspectives about the goals that are important in families, and there is more than a little controversy about them. Therefore it seems like a good idea to describe the cluster of goals we've used in our theory building and how and why we've used this particular group of goals.

This is another area where it is challenging to determine which parts of complex sets of ideas should be described first and which later. In some ways it would be better to describe the widely shared goals first and then the origins of and basis for the goals. On the other hand, there are several reasons why it would be better to describe first the origins and basis and then the goals themselves. This means we have another chicken-and-egg dilemma, and there are advantages and disadvantages to both of the strategies. Unfortunately, we had to choose one or the other of the strategies because both sets of ideas cannot be described first.

After evaluating the pros and cons of the two alternatives, we decided to describe the goals first and the basis for the goals second. Another complication is that the description of the origins of and basis for the goals is sufficiently complex that if we included them in this chapter, they would make this chapter way too long and complex. The goals are based on a number of metaphysical, ontological, and epistemological assumptions and on a model or definition of family. These philosophical assumptions and the model of family are too complex and involved to be included in this book, but they are published on the Internet, and we are submitting them to journals. The title of the publication containing these technical and philosophical parts of sacred theory is "Assumptions in Sacred Theory," and it is available at http://familycenter.byu.edu/Assumptions.dhtml.

Our observations and interviews suggest there are at least five areas where there are widely shared and important goals in families. How families strive to reach these goals plays out in infinitely variable ways in different cultures and subcultures, historical conditions, and technologies; and there is great variation in how effectively they are carried out. Our list is not exhaustive, but it is relevant for most people, and the ideas in it are sufficiently general that they are relevant for a wide range of cultural, religious, and historical conditions. We don't view these goals as an ultimate or comprehensive list that ought to be etched in stone. They are working tools that help provide a manageable model that we have found helpful in our theory building. The goals deal with (a) providing helping patterns, (b) meeting emotional needs, (c) providing a home, (d) balancing stability and change, and (e) avoiding and coping with "undesirables."

Providing Helping Patterns The irreducible core of family life is the cluster of experiences, connections, and emotions that derive from the birth process (Davis, 1984), and they create a need for complex patterns of *helping*. Infants and young children need vast amounts of help for many years if they are to survive, learn, grow, and thrive; and helping patterns continue to be important through the entire human life cycle if people are to successfully learn to understand, face, and manage the opportunities, challenges, and transitions that are encountered in the human life course. These helping patterns include the socialization of young and old, and they also include much more.

Families experience successes with regard to these helping patterns when they effectively help family members prepare intellectually, emotionally, spiritually, and socially to make the routine transitions in the life course that are expected in their community. This includes producing children who can be launched from their family of orientation and effectively assume adult responsibilities as they approach adulthood. It also includes preparing family members to let go of their children when they are ready to be launched, and for the changes that come with aging. Helping patterns also include helping family members acquire the ability to be creative, resourceful, humane, and resilient when they encounter unexpected and undesirable experiences. Failures result when families provide so little help that members are not able to effectively make these transitions and adjustments. These successes and failures can also be partial and involve many levels or degrees of effectiveness.

Meeting Emotional Needs Another area where there are widely shared goals for families, and where families encounter successes and failures, is in helping meet a group of the deep and meaningful emotional needs. Humans have deeply felt strivings for connection with others in intimate and caring relationships that involve support, love, and commitment. Public, occupational, and civic settings, and other secondary relationships tend to be transitory, variable, and optional, meaning that people tend to move in and out of these relationships, thus limiting individuals' ability to satisfy and meet their deeper human emotional needs in those settings. Therefore the deeper emotional needs of humans are only (at best) partially met in the transient, secondary, bureaucratic, public, less personal, and often market-oriented conditions that exist outside families and homes.

Many of the more important and deeply experienced emotions are best met in families that provide intimate, nurturing, stable, bonded, and humane relationships that involve "whole" persons across the entire life course. Family life is, for many, the part of the human experience that provides an optimal place for meeting many of these emotional needs.

Families vary a great deal in how well they meet emotional needs. Some families are so chaotic and dysfunctional that the people in them never learn how to create and maintain intimacy and closeness in supportive, tender, caring, enduring, bonded, and loving relationships. People who grow up in such families are often limited in their ability to experience affection, bonds, encouragement, predictability, celebration, and a sense of belonging and meaning. Success occurs when families are able to meet these emotional needs; failure occurs when these emotional needs are not met.

There are some human emotional needs that *are* met more effectively in the public realms than in familial parts of life. For example, family life is not very effective in meeting needs for novelty, excitement, adventure, unpredictability, and adrenaline-producing adventures. These needs or desires are usually met more effectively in nonfamily settings. The emotional needs that family life is especially suited for meeting are those for such things as connection, love, caring, nurturing, support, intimacy, stability, learning, coping, healing, and continuity.

Providing a Home A third area where there are widely shared goals in families is in creating, providing, and maintaining a *home*—in both a literal and ideal sense. The ideal condition in nearly all societies has been for the family to create and maintain homes. A home is where people can be "off-stage" (Goffman, 1959). It is the place "where they have to take you in." Other living arrangements such as dormitories, ships at sea, orphanages, rest homes, military housing, and foster homes are all temporary arrangements that are helpful when people do not have access to a family living in a home, but these are typically temporary or transitory substitutes that are less than ideal.

Families encounter successes with regard to this part of life when they consistently give and receive love and care, and manage what Maslow (1954) refers to as physiological needs—as well as coping with other needs relating to illnesses, accidents, exceptionalities, and bridging and bonding with other parts of life such as economic roles and resources, schools, medicine, law, entertainment, and the like. Thus success occurs when a family-in-a-home provides a sense of affectionate belonging and connection that helps people avoid feeling that they are alone, isolated, and lonely. Home is a success when it is a healthy base of operation—the center of people's lives and the place from which they move out to their more temporary, voluntary, and role-specific activities in work, sports, church, friendships, neighborhoods, and so forth. Metaphorically, the ideal family/home is the hub of the wheel of life, and spokes go out to other parts. Failures occur when people do not have a family-in-a-home that can accomplish these many parts of the ideal human condition, when they are not managed well, or when important parts of them are poorly accomplished.

Balancing Stability and Change A fourth area where there are widely shared family goals is in maintaining an effective balance between stability and change. Humans need enough stability to have predictability, safety, and a sense of order; but we also need the capacity to adjust to inevitable change, including ever-changing developmental shifts and an array of less predictable demands. A measure of stability, perhaps even considerable stability, is essential for the long-term, intimate, close, warm, nurturing, private, personal, and cherished parts of life that exist in families.

Families tend to be successful when the core relationships in them are permanent and predictable—and when they also have enough flexibility and adaptability that they can change when it is wise or needed. Failures are likely when there is chaos and unpredictability, and when people find it necessary to terminate marital and family relationships (particularly when these terminations recur; see Hetherington & Kelly, 2002). This aspect of family life can be operationalized with rates of divorce, disowning, running-away, desertion, and so on.

Avoiding and Coping With "Undesirables" Another area where there are widely shared goals for families has to do with undesirable experiences. There are a number of conditions in human life that are undesirable, and people try to avoid them. Some examples are accidents, illnesses, tragedies, loneliness, nihilism, and emptiness—rather than meaning, connection, intimacy, and purpose. The undesirables also include academic failures, addictions, gang involvement, violence, incest, delinquency, criminal behavior, unwanted pregnancies, rejection, and many forms of abuse such as sexual, physical, drug, and emotional abuse.

Successes tend to occur when families find ways to avoid these undesirables, and when families are resilient and effective in coping with undesirables when they cannot be avoided. Failures occur when families are not helpful in avoiding undesirable conditions, when they contribute to undesirables, and when they are not helpful in being resilient and effective in coping with them when they cannot be avoided.

Research shows that neighbors, coworkers, and friends can be (and often are) helpful to a degree in coping with these challenges, but the limits of these more transitory, voluntary, and superficial relationships typically tend to be reached quickly (Lee, 1987). There are important limits to how much people can turn to secondary relationships such as roommates, friends, and coworkers when they encounter serious challenges; and effective family life is well suited to providing the more involved and long-term caring, nurturing, support, and helpfulness that are needed when serious challenges are faced.

WAYS OF BEING HELPFUL AND HARMFUL

The ideas in the four general propositions provide insights about *why* sacred matters are salient and powerful in families and *what* it is about the sacred that determines whether it is helpful or harmful, but they provide little insight into *how* the behaviors that result from the sacred are helpful and harmful. After the above ideas were clear enough to describe them, we found ourselves wanting to better understand this "how" question; and this led us to examine our data further to try to glean insights about how harmfulness and helpfulness play out in families.

Our data suggest there are at least four ways sacred matters can be harmful in families. One of these ways appeared in several earlier studies in which it was found that aspects of the sacred were a mixed blessing rather than a simple matter of making things better or worse. These studies revealed that the sacred was simultaneously related to desirable and undesirable outcomes in complex ways. An example of this simultaneous relationship appeared in one study that found that sanctification was helpful in some ways yet also exacerbated psychological distress when there were negative life events such as a loss, violation, and/or desecration that were viewed as divine punishment (Pargament, Magyar, Benore, & Mahoney, 2005). The same finding also appeared in a study that focused on the role of sanctification in coping with divorce (Krumrei et al., 2009). The sanctification of divorce was positively related to adaptive coping strategies, but also positively related to spiritual struggles and depression. Phrased differently, *perceiving an endeavor as sacred raises the stakes*. If the goal or endeavor is realized, the meaning of the success is magnified; if the endeavor (i.e., marriage, parenting) fails, the pain and sense of failure are more acute.

A *second* way the sacred can be harmful is that family members sometimes misunderstand religious teachings or get carried away with them in ways that lead to excesses or extreme ways of behaving that are harmful. For example, parents sometimes "sanctify" excessively strict, punishing, or controlling behavior. Also, some become so committed to their own ideals that they reject and disown children who choose ways of believing and behaving that the parents do not think are right; and these patterns can be tragic and harmful.

A *third* way sacred matters can be harmful was identified by Mahoney et al. (2003). They pointed out that experiences such as unanticipated developmental transitions, uncontrollable crises, violations by family members, loss, conflict, and intrapsychic and institutional barriers can "challenge preset notions about how sacred family relationships operate" and that the resulting dissonance between the reality and expectations of sanctified family relationships may trigger feelings of spiritual failure, thereby exacerbating individual and relationship maladjustment (p. 229).

A *fourth* way the sacred can be harmful is that some ideals and beliefs about the sacred advocate ways of behaving that create harm. Our reading of history as well as our experiences and observations have led us to believe that there are many ways this occurs. One example is that some religious teachings have created and maintained gender discrimination and inequality in many cultures for millennia.[20] Another is religiously endorsed racial and ethnic discrimination. The idea of "manifest destiny" in nineteenth-century America was viewed by many as a sacred idea, yet the devastating impact it had on the families of Native Americans was a horrific tragedy. Also, two of the authors have lived in the southern part of the United States, Wes in the 1950s and Loren now, and we have seen examples of the

[20] Gallagher (2003) and Wilcox (2004) demonstrated that several religious traditions have been changing in recent years in the way they deal with gender issues to decrease discrimination and find ways to be more consistent with the needs and goals in families and with such ideals as equality, freedom, justice, and liberty.

religious sponsorship of racial hatred, disenfranchisement, and discrimination that creates harm in families and communities. It was more obvious in the 1950s and is now more subtle and implicit. Another example is that beliefs about the sacred have led to many wars and controversies that have caused harm in many families. Religions also have contributed to disfigurement, mutilations, and other forms of bodily abuse—even human sacrifice. A final example is that beliefs about the sacred are a primary source and vehicle of the current worldwide problems with terrorism that cause profound harm to nations and families, and there are many more situations where unhealthy patterns have been created and perpetuated by religions, at both societal and familial levels.

It is easier to identify ways the sacred is helpful. From the beginning of recorded history, humans have turned to many sources of ideas in their search for answers about life's most meaningful questions. They have turned to reason, and to many types of empirical observation. They have turned to art, literature, and philosophy. They have turned to the mystical and, more recently, many have turned to science to try to answer the profound and meaningful questions of life—a source not ideally suited for answering questions of meaning.

A large percentage of the human race also have turned to ideas about and from the sacred in this search. Sometimes they have turned to patterns in the earth and sky—especially to patterns with the sun, moon, planets, and stars—and viewed them as sacred. They also have turned to many different views about gods and the divine, and have provided some of the most subjectively satisfying and defensible ideas, ideologies, and answers, some of which are among the most enduring ideas and answers. The ideas from and about the sacred have been modified and refined over the centuries, and they will undoubtedly continue to evolve and change.

The traditions in the major world religions have been the most influential, powerful, and enduring, and it is not an accident or coincidence that these ideas also have become quite consistent with the needs of families. As people have turned to ideas about and from the sacred to provide answers, the answers that are less consistent with the needs of family life have gradually become less appreciated and tended to wane.

The result is that the major religious traditions provide ideas and answers that have a fundamental compatibility and helpfulness with the basic and enduring goals in family life, and it is likely that this compatibility has increased over the millennia. It also is likely that this compatibility will continue to increase in the future. The result of this symbiotic relationship between the sacred and familial is that people who are comfortable with the major religious traditions also tend to be more successful, as a group, than those who, for whatever reasons, tend to be less comfortable with the existing traditions about the sacred. A result is that when social scientists began gathering survey data in the 1930s about religiosity and family success, they found positive correlations.

This pattern is a form of a cultural survival of the fittest. The ideas that are not compatible with the goals in families tend to be rejected and fade, whereas the beliefs and approaches that are consistent with the goals in families are retained and emphasized. And over successive generations the more successful ways persist and flourish. In this winnowing process, sacred ideas help individuals and families find meaning, create order, and relate in ways that result in effective and successful homes and families. This relationship between the sacred and familial is extremely complex and multifaceted, and involves many different aspects of the sacred and the familial. It evolves and changes over time and in different social, economic, climatic, and governmental circumstances, but these are some of the reasons aspects of the sacred are helpful in families.

Thus we suggest that the most profound way the sacred can help families is that it can provide a set of ideas about the "big picture" in the human experience, and the ideas in the major world religions can provide clusters of time-tested ideas and answers about the most fundamental *whys* of life. These ideas in turn provide ideas that give meaning and purpose to existence. They provide ideas about the higher and most noble aspects of what it means to be human. They provide ideas that help create order, integration, and harmony in life generally and in family life in particular.

We are therefore suggesting that the sacred parts of the human experience provide individuals and families with a complex array of deeply meaningful ideologies, perspectives, values, ideals, prescriptions, hopes, strategies, limitations, constraints, proscriptions, and emotional experiences. These parts of the human experience are deeply ingrained into human minds, and, more importantly, into their hearts, and the insights provided by and about the sacred thereby help meet some of the most fundamental and basic needs of families.

These theoretical ideas seem helpful, but they are only a beginning in trying to better understand why the positive relationship between religiosity and valued family outcomes has so consistently recurred. It is likely that as future scholarly inquiry examines and tests these ideas, they will need to be refined and modified further because our first attempt to articulate them is undoubtedly limited and inadequate in many ways. There are still many questions about the why and the how that remain unanswered, so this is an area where there is a need for additional theorizing and research; but these ideas provide the beginnings of an explanation of the reasons sacred phenomena tend to help families.

THE BASIS

If we were to merely describe the above improvements and expansion in the theorizing and not describe the experiences and data that helped us arrive at them, there would be little evidence for their validity and they would have little credibility. Therefore it seems wise to also describe examples of our observations and some of the comments from our interviews because they provide data that undergird the validity of the ideas in the general propositions. A detailed description of the methods that were used in our interviews and observations is in Chapter 15, and some of them are described in other publications such as Dollahite and Marks (2009).

Interview Data

The majority of the people we interviewed indicated that the behavior in their families was fairly consistent with their religious ideals and led to fairly predictable results, but some interviews described situations where some who were generally religious did not behave in ways that were consistent with their ideals. For example, a recently married man in his middle 20s made the following observations about the home he grew up in:

> Our family was so religious when I was growing up that we went to church every week. My mother was clearly the leader in this, and she was intense in the ways she brought God and religion into our home. She did it in a very demanding way that was often critical and cynical; and when one of the kids did something they shouldn't, she'd talk about how God was displeased and we ought to feel guilty. She put more guilt on us than you can believe, and it was painful the way she treated us. Unfortunately, the words that best describe the way she treated us are brutal and abusive. I was the oldest and was an obedient child, so I didn't get yelled at as much as the others, and it was sad the way she treated my sister and brother who weren't as inclined to do what she wanted. Now that I'm away from the home and able to make my own choices, I don't want to have anything to do with her God and with her religion. There was little love and a lot of anger in our home, and my little sister hates my mother so much that whenever she can she stays with someone else on weekends when our mother is around the house. My brother is now away from home . . . and his resentment toward my mother and feelings of always being pressured and never loved has been getting in his way.

This description of a mother who was religious but also unkind and unloving shows the severe price the family paid for her inconsistencies. We elaborate more in Chapters 6 through 9 on ways being loving helps families and being unloving hurts families, but this situation illustrates that it is not global religiosity that matters. What matters is how people *act*—and whether these actions are consistent with the widely shared goals in families of behaving humanely, ethically, and morally consistent with their religious zeal and ideals.

A narrative from another individual illustrates the happier side of the ways family members use aspects of the sacred and their consequences:

> In my brother's family, they always put the gospel first in their lives. They go to church every week, and they make donations, and they make sure they serve others, and they do it as a family, and I think these things help them. They are also so kind and gentle with each other, and their happiness is exponential. I've never seen them unhappy. They have a common goal in their life that affects them in so many ways, and it brings them closer together and unifies them as a family. Whenever my family is around them, we feel happy too.

The following (and contrasting) description by a midwestern woman in her 70s illustrates how people who attend church regularly and view themselves as religious can behave in destructive ways, and how this leads to undesirable consequences:

> I love my father, but he also caused a lot of pain in our home. He always set very high standards for others, and when people didn't meet up to his view of what they ought to do he was very rejecting. My husband is a good man, but he also has his faults, and [my husband] was never good enough for my father. Dad criticized him all of the time to me and to everyone else, and he was never warm and accepting of him. My husband has grown and matured in many ways over the years and overcome many of his faults, but Dad went to his grave without ever accepting him as a son-in-law. As our children grew up, each one of them gradually turned away from their grandfather, and by the time Dad died none of our children wanted to have anything to do with him. Several of our children have also struggled in other ways, and I'm confident that the influence my father had in our home was an important source of their challenges. One of our sons struggled about so many things that he eventually took his own life as a 20 year old. I still love my father in ways, but there has been a lot of hurt, and it has been hard.

This father/grandfather who regularly attended his church was so rejecting, critical, and mean that he reportedly created a great deal of damage in his home, to his children, and even to his grandchildren. This further illustrates the pattern that what matters is not general religiosity but what people do with the more specific aspects of their religion.

A less extreme example of the negative side was described to us by a middle-aged father who, decades later, was still troubled by the hypocrisy he perceived:

> [My parents] were members of the synagogue and they went semi-regularly, all the holidays and some Friday nights, all the big events. They were key members of the synagogue. They might have fallen . . . into the trap of people who acted more spiritual in synagogue than they actually were. . . . They did it outwardly because . . . you need to be seen there . . . but I saw other sides of them and I thought, "This isn't very uplifting behavior." Maybe we [my wife and I] are sending mixed messages to our kids as well. We may be no different from my parents; we don't follow the letter of the law all the time either, not even close. That kind of hypocrisy bothers me.

Many of the theoretical concepts, ideas, and supporting narratives in this volume capture and illustrate ways the integrated use of the sacred benefits families. However, the positively integrated use of the sacred does not capture the whole spectrum of experience or truth. In these narratives we see how the inconsistent integration of sacred matters (e.g., through coercive or authoritarian means or misunderstandings) or a refusal of parents to *live* professed religious ideals can contribute to lasting harm—a common problem that has been referred to by one researcher as behavior-belief incongruence (Marks, 2002, 2004). Conversely, there are some people and families who would not be categorized as "highly religious" who model and integrate noble ideals in prosaic ways. A father of a son with severe developmental disabilities spoke of his own father in this way:

> My father was not a religious man but one of the things that I remember [from my childhood] is when we were working on the yard [at our] cabin in

> Minnesota. We children would get tired and leave and go play, but my father would always stay until the job was done. It would always impress me that I would be playing with my friends, and then I would still see my dad working on the same job, until the job was done. It always impressed me and has carried throughout my life that that's what men do. They accomplish the job. . . . I think the feeling that I have is, "Yeah, [having a child with severe disabilities] is tough, it is a disappointment. This is not fair." But I think that this is what you are dealt and this is what you play with. You don't just sit and whine and moan about it. You just get up and go to work and do the things that you need to do and deal with it. As far as spiritual things, I see from my father through his example that this is my job (to be a good father). I am to finish the job, so no matter what it takes or how long it is, you just stick to it and go to work, until the job is done. It is the father's responsibility—you are responsible, you are the support.

Observations

Our interviews provide useful data about many family processes, but *living* in a family provides insights about processes that are not revealed with interviews and questionnaires. Our observations in our own families and the families of the relatives, friends, students, and colleagues we have come to know well have revealed patterns that provide persuasive evidence about the propositions in this chapter.

One of these patterns is that when family members have put their love and devotion in the nonsacred parts of life, many of them have reaped more than a little bitter fruit. In several instances when we have seen family members turn to lifestyles away from the sacred, they have had a short-term sense of freedom and liberation that was greeted with enthusiasm, idealism, and optimism; but as the years passed, many of them encountered failures, including many different aspects of life, health, and death. We've seen it with drugs and depression, delinquency and rebellion, rejection and incarceration, loneliness and abuse, violence and betrayal, hate and poverty, disfigurement and premature deaths, suicides and deception, betrayal and sabotage, unhappiness and crime. Sometimes it has been with divorces and the abandonment of children, and sometimes with children being removed from homes by courts and other government agencies. It has been with the destruction of health and relationships, and tragic levels of physical, emotional, and mental pain. We are not trying to be melodramatic. We are talking about individuals we have known and loved and our close-at-hand observations.

Most of the time, people are fairly consistent over the years in terms of how they approach and integrate the sacred. However, we have observed a few situations where there have been dramatic changes in the way sacred matters were used, and we also have observed the consequences that tended to follow. Some have turned to the sacred, and the changes in their lives were not a panacea. They still encountered challenges and difficulties with illnesses and the life-changing transitions that are involved when people change the amount they value the sacred parts of life; but overall, we have seen increases in successes in some of the most meaningful parts of life and decreases in failures. The following two narrative accounts illustrate both a turning *from* and a turning *toward* the wise and harmonious use of the sacred:

One of my sisters decided as a teenager to live her life away from God and the church. A few years later her life fell apart. She had an affair, and her first marriage ended in divorce. She then had another affair with a different man and became pregnant for the second time while she was still in her teens. She married the second man, who also had two children from a former marriage. It was never a very enjoyable marriage, and she was the mother of three small children, and then they soon had another child. Shortly after the fifth and then a sixth child was born, and she couldn't cope with her situation. She tried to take her life, eventually lost her second marriage, spent time in a mental hospital, and eventually the state gave all of her children to other families. She wandered from one relationship to another for decades, a broken and unhappy woman searching for peace, love and happiness, but never finding them. Sometimes she married the man she was living with and sometimes she didn't. During these years, she lived a wild life and abused her health in a variety of ways.

When she was in her 60s, alone and with such poor health that she couldn't take care of herself, she found herself in a care center. She eventually was able to re-establish relationships with her children, but they have not become very deep, meaningful, or enjoyable relationships. Gradually, she realized she needed to make changes, and she tried to change her life and repent of the many wrongs in her life. As she returned to her spiritual roots, and tried to make peace with her God, her life gradually became more tolerable and eventually relatively enjoyable. She now lives several states away, and goes to church every week in the center, even though she is in such poor health I don't know how she does it or even stays alive. We talk on the phone often, and I try to show the love I feel for her and try to help her in any way I can, and we see each other as often as we can. She will probably carry a lot of pain to her grave, but her last years have had more peace and happiness than she knew for many years.

****

[My] brother got into trouble with the law when he was about 15. It started out with minor things, but eventually it became more serious, and he was placed in a correctional facility. When he got out, he didn't want anything to do with God or the church, and he stopped associating with the family. He moved to another state and lived quite the worldly life. Over the years, he had a number of affairs and had children with several different [women], but none of his families lasted very long or brought him or others much happiness. He never even knew about some of his children until they were adults. Alcohol, drugs, business problems, and run-ins with the law continued to be serious problems for him.

Members of the family would occasionally learn where he was living and try to visit him, but he didn't show much interest in them and didn't seem very receptive to their love. Later, when he was in his 60s, he came to a family reunion one year with the woman he was living with, and he seemed to enjoy being around the family more than he had. About two years later, he contacted the family and told them he was making some big changes in his life. He was married and was going to church. Even though his wife was a member of a different church, they went to church together and he was trying to put his life in order and do what was right. He was repenting and trying to be forgiven by

> Heavenly Father. He became active in his church and lived for about four years after this, and the last four years of his life were the happiest time of his life.

Our observations suggest that major changes such as these in the way people deal with the sacred are rare. The usual pattern is continuity in what people do with the sacred. Those who have lived in ways that were consistent with the ideals in sacred traditions have experienced relatively more successes and fewer failures. On the other hand, those who have not lived in these ways have had less stability in their family life, some finding complex patterns of successes and failures, and others finding few successes and many failures. The following two narratives illustrate ways different but stable lifestyles brought different results, one where the wise use of the sacred was helpful and one where a different lifestyle led to undesirable consequences. One father recalled:

> My wife and I both grew up in families that were effective in many ways, but there was also quite a bit of cruelty and pain in both families. As we were dating and starting our family, we talked about what we wanted and both of us wanted to pay more attention to God and his ways than was done in the families we grew up in. So, we read and studied in the scriptures to try to understand and draw close to God and do the kinds of things he taught. We have now been married over a half century and our grandchildren are starting their families; and we are so grateful we put God and his ways at the center of our family. We have had such a loving and close relationship with each other and with our children and grandchildren that they are a beautiful part of our life, and we try to be a beautiful part of theirs. Our children have tried to live the same way we try to live, and they are doing a better job of it than we did. Now, our grandchildren are all, so far, choosing the same patterns. We're counting our blessings . . . and are keeping our fingers crossed.

❖❖❖❖❖❖❖❖❖❖❖❖❖❖❖❖❖❖❖❖❖❖❖

> Our oldest daughter didn't choose to follow the lifestyle that we tried to teach her. She married a fellow that wasn't involved at all in religion, and she adopted his style. Unfortunately, their family life has not been very enjoyable. They fight a lot and have come close to divorce several times. Their children are now mostly grown, and two of them are into the drug culture and don't have anything to do with us or their parents. One of the sons in the family had a baby without being married and he seems to be more interested in his drugs and gambling than trying to be a good father or providing a good home. We worry about what kind of life the child [our great-grandchild] will have.

Another example of this was offered by another individual, who reported:

> One branch of our families was generally religious in that every member the family was active in their church and they went to church every week, but they also were good at holding grudges. It got so bad between two brothers that whenever one of them learned a certain brother was going to show up at a family gathering he would not attend, and both of them went to their graves with feelings of animosity and hatred.

The families of the children and grandchildren of these two brothers were dramatically different from the families of their more forgiving siblings. The children of the unforgiving brothers had resentments and animosities after they formed their own families, and the next two generations have had little contact, closeness, or love in their relationships with each other, as well as a number of other problems such as alcoholism, substance abuse, and crime. The brothers had five other siblings who were more inclined to forgive, and the families of their children and grandchildren were dramatically different. They were all closer and more loving. They remained close to each other throughout their lives, held reunions and other gatherings often, and were supportive and nurturing. It is likely that some of these differences are due to other things, but it also seems that the difference in the ways these two brothers used an aspect of the sacred (forgiveness) and the ways their siblings used this aspect was substantial, and this difference seems to have had an impact on the problems and successes in the two next generations.

Another related narrative from our sources reads:

> My father never learned how to forgive. All those who wronged him were SOB's and he let everyone know about it. His lack of forgiveness led to many hard feelings and resentments and interfered with feelings of love and kindness. And, in the same family, my mother was always loving, thoughtful and kind, and quickly and fully forgave all who wronged her. The contrast between my father's unremitting lack of forgiveness and the anger and hate this created [as opposed to mother's] healing balm was dramatic and powerful, and the ways these differences had an influence on those around them was a striking and potent influence in my life. I have tried to be like my mother and avoid being like my father, but it has been like swimming upstream.

We could add many other examples of these patterns from our interviews and observations, but these examples are enough to be persuasive, and they seem like enough for this chapter. To summarize, the data from our observations and interviews suggest that when family members deal with sacred matters in ways that are consistent with the widely shared goals in families it leads to desirable outcomes in families, and when they behave in ways that are not consistent with these goals it tends to lead to undesirable outcomes—not just for an individual but also for families, and often families across generations. Many of the specifics in how this plays out in specific parts of family life along with many more examples of these processes are described in Chapters 2 through 12.

OTHER IMPROVEMENTS

There are several other ways we think the theorizing in this volume improves and expands the earlier theorizing. Both the research and theory about religion in families have suffered from fragmentation, typically focusing on (at most) a few parts of the sacred and (at most) a few parts of the familial at a time. Neither the empirical nor theoretical work has been part of an integrated, general-level conceptual framework or theory. In the following chapters we integrate the previous research and theorizing about how sacred matters help and harm, and include all of it in a more comprehensive and coherent conceptual framework and theory. Also, we expand the theory by including a sizeable number of sacred phenomena that have not been parts of the previous theorizing and research.

An additional way we improve and expand the theorizing is with a rather extensive analysis of the philosophical assumptions and paradigmatic strategies we have used. They are described in *Assumptions in Sacred Theory*, a publication that is available at the http://familycenter.byu.edu/Assumptions.dhtml; and we have submitted them to a journal as well. This analysis will, hopefully, help us and others be better able to help assumptions be more consistent with theories and research. Thomas and Wilcox (1987) argued that much of the theory building about family unintentionally used more positivist views of the nature of family phenomena than the authors realized, and more than was wise. We hope that by being more explicit about the assumptions that are the intellectual underpinnings in our theorizing, we and others will avoid some of the incompatibilities and inconsistencies that have appeared in much of the earlier scholarship (Slife & Williams, 1995).

A VISUAL SUMMARY

We and many others find it helpful to have simple, summarizing, visual models of the ideas in general theories. Therefore we have devised the diagram shown in Figure 1.1. Proposition 1 is at the top because it is the most abstract and general idea. Propositions 2–4 are an interrelated cluster of ideas that are slightly less general, and they are in the box below Proposition 1. The rest of Figure 1.1 provides a glimpse into the ideas in sacred theory that are described in Chapters 2 through 12. The 5th proposition asserts that loving relationships are helpful in families, and Propositions 6–22 are less general ideas that are components or aspects of what it means to be loving. Propositions 23–30 are less general principles that deal with processes that are not subsets of what it means to be loving.

The figure also illustrates how hypotheses can be deduced from the theoretical ideas and tested in empirical research.

SUMMARY

This chapter began by summarizing and evaluating the previous empirical and theoretical literature, identifying a number of limitations in both as well as ways both empirical and theoretical scholarship on sacred matters in families can be improved and expanded. Next, there was an analysis of the conceptualization for the main ideas in this area of inquiry, and we suggested that the term sacred is more effective in building a general theory than terms such as religion, spiritual, and spirituality—even though these other terms have been used the most in the previous research and theory. We suggested that the complications and disadvantages with terms like religion and spirituality have caused problems and hampered the quality of the earlier scholarship.

This chapter then described a cluster of ideas that create a new conceptual framework and a general theory in family studies that uses ideas *from* and *about*

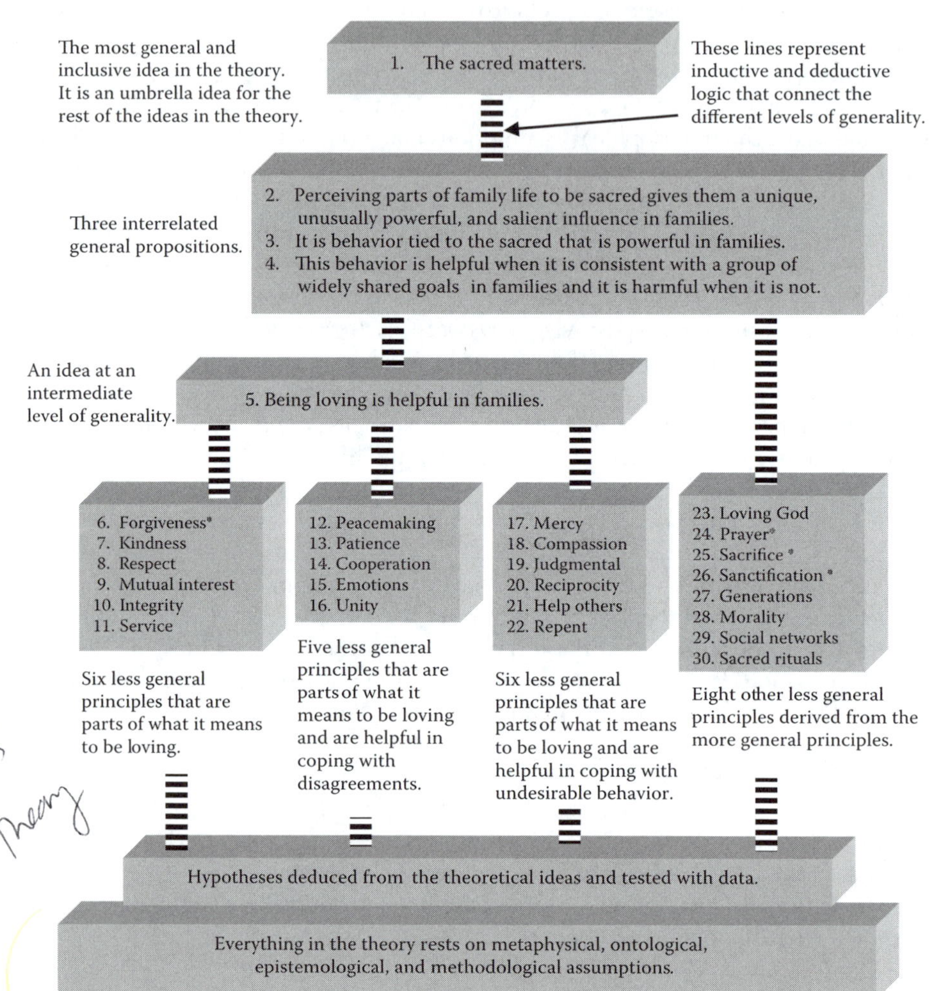

Figure 1.1 Summary of the main ideas in sacred theory.

the sacred. The theory has four general propositions about the role of sacred matters. These propositions assert that sacred matters are unusually salient and powerful in the human condition generally and in family life in particular; and they describe what it is about the sacred that makes a difference in families, as well as when behaviors that result from sacred beliefs and ideals are helpful and harmful. These general ideas set the stage for Chapters 2 through 12, which focus on ways specific aspects of the sacred make a difference in families. Chapter 2 begins this elaboration by discussing ways forgiving makes a difference in families.

There is a section in each of the next 11 chapters on ways to apply the ideas in each of the chapters. We do not have an "Applications" section in this chapter because the ideas in this chapter are so abstract and general that they are not directly applicable. The way the ideas in this chapter can be applied is to derive or deduce the less general ideas in Chapters 2 through 12 from these general and abstract ideas; and the less general ideas in these other chapters have considerable relevance for families, theorists, researchers, educators, and practitioners.

2

Forgiving

This chapter begins a series of chapters that discuss how "substantive elements" of the sacred help and harm families. The first idea we turn to is ways *forgiveness* is helpful in most circumstances but harmful in a few contexts and how the sacredness of forgiveness influences the effects it has on family processes and outcomes.

Forgiveness is discussed early in our theory building for several reasons. We want to begin with several concepts that have become parts of the scholarly study of family, and then move to concepts that have not been included in family studies. Also, forgiveness is the best example of what we would like to see done with ideas about and from the sacred. A few decades ago, forgiveness was viewed as a religious idea, not as a part of scholarly study; but it was "discovered" by scholars after Smedes (1984) published a volume titled *Forgive and Forget: Healing the Hurts We Don't Deserve.* Since then a large, impressive, and helpful body of literature has been created.

One reason the literature about forgiveness is an example of what we would like to see done with other ideas is that it is an area where religious literature and scholarly literature have been mutually helpful to each other. Both have benefited from the other, and we hope this pattern will be repeated many times in the future with other ideas that are still viewed as religious rather than scholarly. Before we describe the principle and related literature, we need to first define the key concepts.

DEFINING FORGIVENESS

There have been a number of debates in the last several decades about how forgiveness ought to be defined. Fortunately, there is considerable consensus emerging about some aspects of the definition, even though there are still debates and ambiguity about other parts of it. There is agreement that forgiveness is multifaceted rather than just being one simple dimension or process. One of the better definitions, by Denham, Neal, Wilson, Pickering, and Boyatzis (2005), begins, "Forgiveness is a transformation of one's affect, cognitive judgments, and motivations toward an offender" (p. 129). How is this done? The victimized individual assesses the harm done to him or her and then "makes an assessment of the harm done and acknowledges the perpetrator's responsibility but voluntarily chooses to cancel the debt, giving up the need for revenge, punishments, or restitution." Finally, and "importantly, one removes oneself from the negative emotions directly related to the transgression" (p. 129).

There are several parts of this definition that are helpful. It includes the idea of a transformation, and it includes the three components of changes in thinking, emotion, and motivation. As the negative emotion abates, forgivers continue to recognize that a wrong existed, but there are changes in their thinking so the offensiveness of the wrong does not continue to be a part of their present and future life. To illustrate these processes, we share the following true story from one of our sources:

> My wife's sister went through a phase of drug abuse and landed in trouble with the law. We were in grad school at the time and had no money, but upon promise of repayment we borrowed a couple thousand dollars for a bail bond. The payments did not come and, for years, we carried the twin burdens of resentment and financial debt. Every month during our [marital] budget meeting, the debt and resentment were both there with us. . . . I was reading in the Old Testament one day, where God commands Israel to forgive all debts during the seventh [Sabbatical] year. This sunk into my heart and I presented the idea to my wife, who told me she had been having similar thoughts. She was tired of being angry with her sister and having that point of tension [the unpaid debt] at the center of every conversation they had. We wrote a letter forgiving the debt in full, promising not to raise the issue again. The sense of healing was almost immediate. My only regret was that we didn't do it years earlier.

As scholars have tried to identify the processes that compose the rather complex process of forgiving, they have also suggested there are stages that can be identified and that each stage involves different cognitive, emotional, and behavioral aspects (Gordon & Baucom, 1998). Eventually, it is likely that scholars will discover further differences, such as how the process differs for the person who is doing the forgiving and the person who is forgiven. Also, it is likely that the process of getting ready to make a decision to forgive is itself complex, multidimensional, and involved, as illustrated in the experience above. The emotional aspects also probably have many components, and the behavioral aspects are probably also multidimensional.

We and others, such as Enright and Fitzgibbons (2000), prefer to add behavioral components to the affective, cognitive, and motivational aspects of the definition of forgiveness. Behavioral changes tend to, but don't always, follow changes in motivation, and we prefer to think that forgiveness includes the elimination of negative behaviors toward the offender.

One of the discoveries in the study of forgiveness is that it seems to have two dimensions that operate quite differently. A few scholars, such as Orden and Bradburn (1968) and Winch and Blumberg (1968), began arguing nearly a half century ago that positive and negative aspects of marriage are relatively independent of each other and operate in different ways. Some of us did not initially agree with this idea (Burr & Burgess, 1974), but as additional evidence was provided by Gray (1987) that positive (approach) and negative (avoidance) dimensions are independent in a wider array of psychological processes, we eventually agreed. This idea that there can be independent positive and negative aspects of an element that operate differently has now been included in studies of forgiveness (Fincham, 2000; Fincham & Beach, 2002; Fincham, Davila, & Beach, 2004, 2007; Gordon, Hughes, Tomcik, Dixon, & Litzinger, 2009), and enough evidence has accumulated that it seems fairly conclusive. This idea means that the absence of negative feelings may be fairly independent of the growth of positive feelings.

This insight about the relative independence of these two dimensions provides valuable insights into the nature of forgiveness. It suggests that the negative dimension includes such experiences as anger, anxiety, blaming, cognitive confusion, depression, discouragement, being punitive, grudges, emotional turmoil, psychological and physical aggression, avoidance, vengefulness, conflict, feeling one has a right to seek revenge or lash out at the offender, and being unforgiving. The positive dimension includes experiences such as positive affect, readiness to forgive, empathy, release from anger, bonds, closeness, motivation for approach and reconciliation, peace, trust, motivation for constructive communication, and compassionate and merciful views of the offender and events.

Apparently individuals can move from a neutral situation to a high level in both dimensions, and moving in one dimension tends to be independent of movement in the other. People can work through their negative emotions without creating positive emotions, and they can have positive emotions without working through their negative feelings. They can be low in both or high in both. These conceptual insights help clarify some rather complex aspects of forgiveness that are not dealt with in the religious literature, which merely suggests forgiveness is desirable and important.

Scholars are not in agreement about whether forgiveness should be defined as just eliminating the negative phenomena or as the elimination of the negative phenomena *and* a cultivation of positive attitudes, feelings, and behavior. Worthington (2005) suggested that it is different in noncontinuing and continuing relationships. In noncontinuing relationships, such as a random robbery or a medical error, "forgiveness is legitimately defined as giving up negative feelings, thoughts, motivations, and behaviors toward the offender" (p. 560). Comparatively, "when a betrayal or major disappointment occurs between romantic partners, family members, or close friends, forgiveness is defined as reducing of negative experiences coupled with replacing them with positive experiences" (p. 560). Like Worthington, Fincham and his colleagues (2004) argued that *both* the waning of negative *and* replacement with positive are helpful in family relationships.

Most scholars seem to agree with this distinction, but not all. There are some who think there are circumstances in continuing relationships where the cultivation of positive feelings may not be wise. For example, Legaree, Turner, and Lollis (2007) suggest it may not be wise when it is neither important nor safe to repair relationships, and Gordon, Baucom, and Snyder (2000) posit that "in some cases, these [positive] feelings may be impossible. Certainly the ability to experience compassion and warmth toward the offender may ideally be the best outcome, yet we do not believe this is necessary" (p. 220). Bass and Davis (1994) similarly stated, "Developing forgiveness and compassion for your abuser, or for members of your family who did not protect you, is not a required part of the healing process" (p. 160).

Ambiguity and debates continue about a number of other aspects of forgiveness. One ongoing debate is whether several other aspects, such as the communication of the forgiveness to the offender, should be included in the definition (Waldron & Kelley, 2008). Another is whether forgiveness involves an intentional decision to forgive or whether it is a process of discovery that cannot be willed. Legaree et al. (2007) suggest from their review that most scholars view the decision to forgive as possible and helpful (DiBlasio, 1998, 2000; Kaminer & Stein, 2000); but others, such as Mamalakis (2001), Patton (2000), and Hill (2001), argue that often when people try to deliberately decide to forgive, their efforts are fruitless. They suggest that most people seem to find it or discover it, almost as a by-product, when they move on to try to deal with issues other than forgiving. Debates such as these will undoubtedly continue well into the future, and future scholarship will probably provide new insights.

PRINCIPLES ABOUT FORGIVENESS

It is likely that forgiveness is relevant for all human relationships, but it is widely recognized that it is particularly important in family life. In fact, some have suggested it is the most important factor in whether families are successful (Fenell, 1993). One way of stating this generalization that is broader than just a part of the theory in this volume is *forgiveness is healing in human relationships, and the lack of forgiveness is damaging*. This principle is broader than the theory we are developing, but when it is applied to family life it yields the slightly less general principle that *forgiveness helps families find successes and avoid failures, and the lack of forgiveness is damaging in families*.

The scholarly literature is not the source of this principle because the idea existed long before modern scholars discovered its importance. The roots of the idea are embedded in the traditions of the world religions. The word *forgive* appears 43 times in the New Testament. Most of the time it is about God forgiving sins, but 11 of the 43 times the word *forgive* appears it is about humans forgiving. We see three themes in these verses: (a) God can and will forgive sins, (b) humans ought to forgive others as many times as they are offended, and (c) humans will be forgiven by God only if *they* are forgiving.

In the Lord's Prayer or "Our Father," which is held sacred by many Christians, Jesus's model of how to pray includes the phrase: "Forgive us our debts *as* we forgive our debtors" (Matthew 6:12, KJV, emphasis added). The pivotal and conditional phrase "as we forgive our debtors" seems to reference at least two aspects of forgiveness—the timing and the degree. Is one's offering of forgiveness immediate or painfully slow? Is it provisional, constrained, and insincere, or pure and full? Indeed, a rephrasing of the forgiveness phrase of the Lord's Prayer might well read: "Our Father which art in Heaven . . . Please do not forgive me in full, until I have forgiven in full." This emphasis on cleansing one's own heart first is illustrated in the following narrative from a father and husband we interviewed:

> We're people, we screw up . . . but as we invite God into our life and He forgives us of our sins and as we present ourselves to Him, He changes us and makes us more like Him and . . . the desires of our hearts change and we develop friendship with God. . . . The whole meaning of life is to get to know God and to become like Him and to do the same sorts of things that He is invested in. And I'm sure that I fall way short and still have a lot that I don't see and mess up on but . . . [because I'm] a Dad, you see your kids make efforts to please you and to do what you want and to imitate you, you don't get upset that they didn't do better. It's just amazing that they even want to try, you know. So rather than focus on the shortcomings, it's just about trying to relate to God and to get to know Him better.

Forgiveness is thus a central and important idea in Christianity, and the lack of forgiveness is a serious wrong. As Fernando (1985) argued, forgiveness is not exclusive to the Judeo-Christian tradition. It is found in Buddhism too. In fact, forgiveness is an important theme in many world religions.

One of the reasons we believe this principle is true and powerful in families is because of comments made by people we have interviewed about the role of forgiveness in their lives. For example, another individual we spoke with explained:

> The presence and absence of forgiveness has been a powerful part of my life and it has made an important difference in my own family and in my extended family. I watched resentments continue for decades among some of my uncles and watched it destroy their relationships and add to the hurt in the lives of many around them. Their inability to forgive began early in their lives with childish things and continued as adults with more substantial things, and it lasted until they were all in their graves. As their resentments toward each other festered and grew, it got so they would not attend family gatherings if they learned a certain brother would be there.

As illustrated earlier, another reason we believe forgiveness has an influence on family successes and failures is because we have observed forgiveness (and the lack of it) in our own families and families. We have also seen abundant examples and counterexamples in counseling and educational settings. In sum, we have observed over the decades that willingness to forgive has made an important difference in families. We have watched some who have been unwilling to forgive others for small indiscretions and some who have found it in their hearts to forgive major offenses. Some of these situations, for good or ill, have influenced more than one generation. As we have watched forgiveness for both small and major offenses, we have seen the healing balm dissipate negative affect and help families move on with kindness and compassion. The following example illustrates these observations:

> [Our neighbor's] husband [had an affair that] led to a pregnancy. When the wife learned of the affair, she was hurt and furious, and considered divorce. In the next several months they decided to try to re-create the kind of marriage

they had wanted. It was difficult, but she was forgiving and he was repentant, and they worked hard at their marriage. It is now about 15 years after this situation, and they have become a loving and effective family, and have found many successes they probably would not have found without forgiveness.

THE SCHOLARLY LITERATURE

The scholarly study of forgiveness has created a number of new and important insights about the principle of forgiveness. It provides information about the nature of forgiveness, how it ought to be defined, and how it can be observed and measured. It also provides new and persuasive evidence of the validity and importance of the principle, reveals how it helps in families, and outlines ideas and steps for helping people increase their ability and inclination to be forgiving.

When forgiveness became a topic in the social sciences, the strategy that was almost universally used was to administer nonstandardized questionnaires. Gradually instruments that paid more attention to reliability and validity were developed (e.g., Al-Mabuk, Enright, & Cardis, 1995; Barry, Worthington, Parrott, O'Connor, & Wade, 2001; Hargrave & Sells, 1997; Subkoviak et al., 1995; Wade, 1989.)

Process Rather Than Event

There is accumulating evidence that forgiveness is qualitatively different for the minor slights, forgetfulness, hurts, and misunderstandings that are a part of everyday interaction, than for serious breaches in relationships such as abuse, betrayal, and infidelity. Forgiveness can be accomplished quickly and easily in long-term and committed relationships when the offenses are about minor conflicts and everyday hurts (Fincham et al., 2004), but the process is more complex and involved as the seriousness of the wrongs increases.

Several scholars have argued there are stages in this sequencing. Apparently, when many people say "I forgive you," this declaration may be more of a decision to try to forgive rather than a culmination of the process. Indeed, incompletely resolved feelings of anger or resentment about the transgression often intrude later in the relationship and take longer to resolve (Fincham, Hall, & Beach, 2005, p. 217).

A three-stage model of forgiveness was developed by Gordon and Baucom (1998). They suggested there is an impact stage, a definition stage, and a "moving on" stage. One of the important findings from a series of studies using their model (Gordon & Baucom 1998, 2003; Gordon, Baucom, & Snyder, 2005) is that as people move through the stages, they deal with the negative dimension of forgiveness early in the process and the positive dimension later. Insights such as this move our understanding of forgiveness well beyond the rather simple and uncomplicated idea in the sacred literature that forgiveness is a good and important thing.

Consistent with Gordon and Baucom's work, Enright's (2001) model also emphasizes that forgiveness is more of a process than an event. He viewed forgiveness as a journey through the four phases: an uncovering phase, a decision phase, a work phase, and a deepening phase. This model has also received some empirical support (Enright & Fitzgibbons, 2000). Sometimes the stages in these models overlap and are dealt with in different orders, but the models that have suggested stages are helpful because they divide the rather complex processes in forgiving into more manageable parts.

Ways Forgiveness Is Helpful

There are a number of different research questions that have been addressed in the literature, and reviews by Enright and North (1998), Worthington (2005), and Fincham et al. (2004; Fincham, Hall, & Beach, 2006) chronicle the progress. One of the areas of research has examined the effects of forgiveness on the forgiver. More specifically, this area has focused on effects on physical, mental, relational, and spiritual health (Harris & Thoresen, 2005). In the early days of the research, claims about positive benefits outweighed supporting data. Thus far, however, no studies have found harmful effects, and a few have documented beneficial effects. For example, Toussaint, Williams, Musick, and Everson (2001) found from a national survey that forgiveness was associated with fewer negative health symptoms in a sample of elderly people. This is an area where additional research is needed because no "direct" evidence indicates that "either situational or dispositional unforgiveness is related to long-term health or disease. The lack of direct evidence is not surprising, given that the notion of unforgiveness and the means to measure it are fairly recent developments" (Harris & Thoresen, 2005, p. 322).

A number of studies have focused on the relationships between forgiveness and marital processes and variables. Fincham, Stanley, and Beach (2004, 2006, 2007) have reviewed this literature, and the cumulative findings are consistent and persuasive. The research focused mostly on the traditional outcomes in marital quality such as satisfaction, happiness, and adjustment, but the research also includes relationships with other aspects of marital relationships such as conflict, hostility, aggression, communication, retaliatory and conciliatory responses, emotional and intellectual intimacy, trust, and commitment. None of the studies found unexpected or negative relationships between forgiveness and desirable aspects of marriage, and many of them found relationships that were encouraging. For example, Fenell (1993) found that spouses report that the ability to ask for and offer forgiveness is viewed as one of the most important factors contributing to marital longevity and marital satisfaction. Gordon et al. (2005) noted that many marital therapists view forgiveness as a vital part of the healing process necessary to overcome profound marital threats such as infidelity; and Fincham et al. (2006) concluded that it is also important in healing relatively minor but damaging "everyday relational harms" (p. 415).

Gordon et al. (2009) undertook a review of the research a few years later, and they summarized that "the association between forgiveness and relationship functioning has been well documented" (p. 2). More specifically, greater forgiveness has been associated with higher levels of dyadic adjustment (e.g., Gordon & Baucom, 2003; Paleari, Regalia, & Fincham, 2005), greater empathy (McCullough et al., 1998), more positive communication patterns and less psychological aggression (Fincham & Beach, 2002), and greater intimacy and closeness in the relationship (Finkel, Rusbult, Kumashiro, & Hannon, 2002; Gordon & Baucom, 2003). The Gordon et al. (2009) review further noted, based on studies from three different research teams (Fincham & Beach, 2002; Finkel et al., 2002; Gordon & Baucom, 2003), that "lower levels of forgiveness are associated with poorer relational adjustment, intimacy, and closeness, and higher levels of psychological aggression" (p. 2).

Even though this research advances knowledge in important ways, research leaders in this area still observe that scholarly "work on forgiveness in marriage is in its infancy" (Fincham et al., 2006, p. 425). Both Fincham et al. (2006) and Worthington (2005, pp. 557–573) laid out impressive agendas for future research, arguing, for instance, that "the biggest challenge facing the field is the need to integrate theory, research, and practice" (Fincham et al., 2006, p. 425). This volume is an attempt to help cope with this challenge.

Most of the previous research has focused only on the existence and strength of the relationship between forgiveness and marital outcomes. But some recent research has begun to study more complex aspects of this relationship, and there are indications that the relationships may be more complicated than most of the studies have appreciated. For example, Bradbury and Fincham (1991) suggested that the context in which forgiveness occurs is likely to be important—a point to which we return later.

An issue that is slightly different is the effects of forgiveness on familial processes and variables. So far, there is much less literature about relationships between forgiveness and family variables than there is between forgiveness and marital variables. In the Battle and Miller (2005) review they found "few references . . . to the concept of forgiveness" in theories about family processes and "that forgiveness is also virtually absent…" (p. 229).

An exception to this omission is Böszörményi-Nagy's contextual approach (Böszörményi-Nagy, 1987; Böszörményi-Nagy & Krasner, 1986; Böszörményi-Nagy & Spark,1973;), and the later refinements by Boss (2002) and Walsh (2003). This model does not explicitly give forgiveness center stage, but it emphasizes processes that are close to it. The model focuses on the balance of fairness, or equitability, in family systems and the dynamics of loyalties, interpersonal trust, and relational ethics that contextual therapies help families confront. Böszörményi-Nagy (1987) argued that the balance of fairness is a "fundamental force in holding family and societal relationships together through reliability and trustworthiness" (p. 204). Further, his idea of what he called "rejunction; reworking the impasse" (Böszörményi-Nagy & Krasner, 1986, p. 215) is close to what is here conceptualized as forgiveness.

Coleman (1998) has identified several reasons for the lack of attention to forgiveness in systems theories. She suggested that the emphases on the transactional nature of relationships, circularity, and relational patterns diverted attention away from individuals' behaviors such as forgiveness. Systems theorists were so focused on such processes as patterns in communication, power relationships, and affective patterns that forgiveness fell outside their intellectual net.

Battle and Miller (2005) were able to draw a number of tentative conclusions from the research in this area: "Individuals with higher levels of dispositional forgiveness—that is, those who have a greater tendency to forgive those close to them after transgressions—are more likely to experience higher quality relationships . . . in their families" (p. 232).

Research after this 2005 review continued to provide new insights about the effects of forgiveness on family processes. Maio, Thomas, Fincham, and Carnelley (2008) found with longitudinal data that children modeled the forgiveness-related behavior of parents, and that forgiveness had a variety of positive effects, including greater expressiveness and cohesion, emotional stability, agreeableness, extraversion, and less conflict. They also found some different effects in different family relationships. The amount of forgiveness of children by parents had more influence on the propensity of children to forgive than the amount spouses forgive each other and the amount children forgive parents. Gordon et al. (2009) similarly found that forgiveness was related to marital satisfaction, parenting alliances, parental conflict, and children's perceptions of the quality of marital functioning. Future research on issues such as these will undoubtedly add many more insights about the results of forgiveness.

There is another body of literature that also seems relevant. It is about the role of what has been called the law or norm of reciprocity (Deutsch, 1973; Gouldner, 1960). This is the idea that patterns of behavior tend to be contagious. One simple example of this idea is "getting up on the wrong side of the bed." When one family member is grouchy in the morning, it tends to spread fairly fast to others. This idea suggests that forgiveness tends to produce more forgiveness, and the lack of forgiveness tends to produce less forgiving.

Not many ideas are accepted broadly in the social sciences and viewed as important in fields as diverse as anthropology, economics, sociology, psychology, and family studies, but one of these few is the law of reciprocity. Lévi-Straus (1967) argued that this idea lies at the heart of human culture and this is a central idea in the work of Jourard (1971) and Guerney (1977).

The literature about reciprocity tends to focus primarily on patterns of the same type of behavior escalating, but our observations and interviews suggest that this idea should be broadened to include "similar" kinds of behavior. This suggests that when people are forgiving it creates more forgiveness and also increases similar kinds of behavior such as mercy, lack of judging and condemning, cooperation, kindness, respect, consideration, and helpfulness. By comparison, the lack of forgiveness tends to produce similar kinds of behaviors such as unkindness, lack of mercy and cooperation, more arguing and fighting, striving to win, combativeness, resistance, and defensiveness. Figure 2.1 is a visual summary of the findings about the effects of forgiveness and the lack of it on family processes and outcomes.

Ways Forgiveness Is Harmful

The scholarly study of forgiveness has almost exclusively emphasized its beneficial effects, but there is a little research indicating there are circumstances where it can also be harmful. For example, Murphy (2002) suggested that

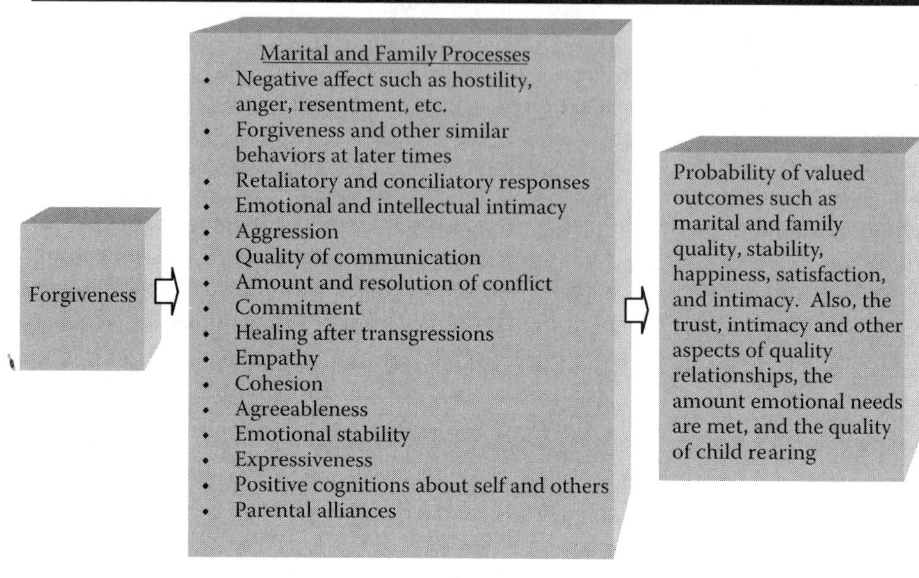

Figure 2.1 Processes and outcomes influenced by variation in forgiveness.

forgiveness may have some long-term costs that have not been detected with cross-sectional research. Also, McNulty (2008) has suggested that "there are a number of reasons to expect that the frequency of partners' transgressions should moderate the effects of forgiveness. For instance, forgiveness may remove the accountability necessary to motivate changes in the transgressing partner" (p. 171). McNulty also went on to explain that removing accountability "may allow more frequent problems to worsen over time. Further, forgivers faced with numerous transgressions may feel frustrated or betrayed in a manner that is qualitatively different than in those with relatively few partner transgressions to forgive" (pp. 171–172).

McNulty (2008) studied these issues with longitudinal data and found some replicated correlations between forgiveness and marital outcomes, but some more novel interactions also appeared. When spouses were rarely negative, forgiveness was positively related to satisfaction and to a (lower) severity of problems; but both of these relationships became inverse when spouses were frequently verbally negative. These findings suggest that there may be some circumstances where forgiveness may not be wise, or that at least the timing may be important.

This research also suggests that there is a need for more study of the ways forgiving may create problems or be harmful in other ways. We need studies that will provide information about the conditions that influence when and how forgiveness is helpful—and when it may be wise to delay forgiveness, not forgive, or forgive conditionally, so that forgiveness does not become harmful or destructively enabling.

REASONS FORGIVENESS IS HELPFUL

The religious body of literature encourages forgiveness, and the scholarly body of literature documents that relationships exist between forgiveness and a number of variables, but they are limited in the information they provide about *why* forgiveness helps. Our observations and interviews suggest that forgiveness is important because of what happens inside people (and then in their relationships) when there are wrongs or offenses that are forgiven or not forgiven. When we humans feel wronged, there apparently are a number of negative emotions and motivations that tend to build up and be retained, sometimes for long periods of time. Some of these emotions are resentment, frustration, and anger. Some of the motivations often include finding ways to retaliate or get even.

If we retain these feelings and motivations, and especially if they become intense, they have a number of predictable and undesirable effects. Our minds and hearts increasingly become cankered with negative affect, and this tends to color our perceptions, leading us to attribute more evil and aggressiveness to the intentions of others than may actually exist. Also, we tend to find ourselves motivated to act in retaliatory ways, even though we may usually be loving and kind. We then find ourselves being mean and vicious to the very people we love the most. The result is that the negative emotion that is created and retained because of unforgiving feelings leads us to be more unloving than we would otherwise be. But when we forgive we lose a host of phenomena that interfere with our desires to be loving, and we are able to be loving and kind rather than mean and unkind.

Chapters 5 through 8 discuss a number of ways loving helps in marriages and families, and we believe these chapters are the most powerful and useful parts of sacred theory. Therefore anything that helps families be loving helps them find successes and avoid failures, and this is one of the powerful reasons forgiveness is so important. Other scholars such as Cheong and DiBlasio (2007) have argued that it is important to view forgiveness as salient in families because it is such an important part of what it means to love others. It helps us be accepting, kind, understanding, and helpful rather than rejecting, condemning, and hurtful.

Our aim is that these beginning ideas (about how and why forgiveness helps) will contribute to future empirical and theoretical work examining these processes. However, these ideas also are only a beginning; there is a need for future scholarship that will provide more insights.

SACREDNESS

There is another aspect of the scholarly study of forgiveness that also deserves attention. It has to do with the sacredness of forgiveness. Worthington (2005) explained that "in the mid-1980s, when most people thought about forgiveness, they associated it with religion. Even if people were not religious, common culture had imported the term *forgiveness* from religious usage" (p. 2). He then noted that the concept changed over the next several decades: "As society became more postmodern and multicultural, though, forgiveness broke free of the confines of religious communities and even religious connotation" (p. 2).

The result is that a term that was once viewed as a part of the sacred has become secularized in the way it is used in the scholarly community. This secularization of forgiveness has been another repetition of the pattern that was so dominant in the middle decades of the twentieth century wherein sacred matters were ostracized by, or at least excluded by, social scientists as they examined aspects of life they viewed as important. We suspect this secularization was not an intentional distortion. It was just more of the modus operandi or standard operating procedure in the academic community—a pattern we are trying to change.

This unfortunate condition of secularizing forgiveness in the scholarly community is understandable because of the traditions in academia that became prevalent after the struggles between science and religion that began in the sixteenth century. However, the main thesis in this book is that *the sacred matters* and *it matters a great deal*. Therefore sacred theory suggests that the secularization of forgiveness is a loss that should be corrected because scholarship that ignores the sacred has less quality than scholarship that includes and pays attention to it.

The first step in correcting this problem is to recognize that the concept of forgiveness is much older than the scientific method and older than the modern version of academia, and its deepest roots are not in secularized science or the academy. The roots of forgiveness are in the sacred, and scholarship about it will be the most effective, defensible, and helpful when attention is paid to the role of the sacred aspects of forgiveness as well as the many other important aspects of it, such as defining it carefully, finding ways to measure it, and learning more about ways it is helpful and harmful in families. There is more to forgiveness than just the sacred aspects of it, and therefore it is good that forgiveness broke free of the "confines" of religious communities, but we need to deal with the sacred *and* secular in an inclusive rather than exclusive way.

> The roots of forgiveness are in the sacred, and scholarship about it will be the most effective, defensible, and helpful when attention is paid to the role of the sacred aspects of forgiveness.

After we became aware of the difference between the secular and sacred views of forgiveness, we included this difference in some of our interviews, and our data suggest several ideas. First, we learned that the secularization of forgiveness is a characteristic of the academic community. Many in the general public still appreciate the sacred aspects of forgiveness. Second, we learned that the sacredness of forgiveness is not a categorical situation where people view it as either sacred or secular. It is a continuous variable that has many subtle degrees because forgiveness is viewed as something that is relatively more and less sacred. Third, we learned that sacredness is an attitude or perception people bring to the forgiving process rather than a property of what is being forgiven or not forgiven.

One of the important aspects in this area of inquiry is how the sacredness of forgiveness makes a difference in families. Again, the second proposition in sacred theory is the idea that experiencing parts of family life as sacred gives them a unique, unusually powerful, and salient influence in families. When this idea is applied to forgiveness—that is, when forgiveness is viewed as sacred—this increases the power and salience it has in families. There is considerable evidence that Proposition 2 is true generally, but there is no research that tests whether it is true with regard to forgiveness.

As we discussed these notions with about 30 people, a number of ideas emerged about how people think sacredness makes a difference. More systematic research is needed that gathers data from larger samples, but this initial exploration of these differences provides a few ideas that are suggestive, and they can be studied more systematically in future research.

Some suggested that the way sacred forgiveness may be different is in the motivation for forgiving, the priority and importance of forgiving, and how easy it is to forgive. Some we discussed these ideas with indicated they believe sacred forgiveness is quicker and more complete. Some also said they think sacred forgiveness leads to a deeper sense of peace and harmony after the forgiveness.

Some suggested that secular forgiveness is more likely to be influenced by social pressures, societal views, and individualistic desires; and when forgiveness is viewed as sacred there is less likelihood of looking for ulterior motives. Others suggested that when forgiveness is viewed in secular ways, it is more likely to be given in an exchange way, to get something in the future; and when it is sacred, it is less likely to be conditional or exchange oriented. Others suggested that when forgiveness is viewed as sacred, this moves it away from a selfish process and becomes more selflessness because it is done for nonself reasons, at least for them.

Others suggested that when forgiveness is viewed as part of a divine and sacred process tied to the atonement of Christ, It helps people see their own imperfections and need for forgiveness, and can help them be more forgiving. Others suggested that when forgiveness is sacred, it is deeper and more meaningful because it involves a relationship with deity, and family members realize they are a part of something that is divine. Also, when forgiveness is sacred it may be more involved with the soul, not just the body; and there may be a "higher" level of motivation, more nobility, and forgiving for higher reasons rather than just instrumental reasons.

Some suggested that the problems associated with undesirable behavior are removed from the relationship more completely when forgiveness is sacred. Some also indicated they believe some offenders feel freer to change their heart and behavior when the forgiveness is ultimately a divine rather than human process. The problem of family members not allowing others to change their heart, motivation, and behavior is a serious problem in many families because there is such a tendency in many families to resist genuine morphogenesis, leading to many family members continuing to treat offenders in the "same old way" and viewing them as offenders even though they are genuinely trying to change.

Also, some view forgiveness as a "gift" from God that is part of the grace of God, and these characteristics provide a depth and power that can be very powerful, and deepen and strengthen the motivation and ability to forgive as well as the effects of the forgiveness in a relationship. Some also believe that the injunction to "pray for them that despitefully use you, and persecute you" (Matthew 5:44) helps people be receptive to use the gift of a forgiving heart.

Thus our data suggest that scholars would be wise to view the sacredness of forgiveness as a contingency or contextual factor as they study the role of forgiveness in families. Theorists, researchers, and practitioners ought to pay attention to how much family members view forgiveness as something that is sacred because it makes an important difference in the way forgiveness influences other family processes and outcomes.

These ideas about the ways sacredness may change the effects of forgiveness are based on very little data because we added this issue to our interviews after most of them were completed, and so we have data from only a few individuals. This means our data are meager and from a very small number of people. Therefore these ideas are still theoretical, speculative, suggestive, and tentative rather than conclusive, but they are a beginning. There is a need for more systematic research with larger and more diverse samples to see how widespread these differences are and if there are other differences.

GOOD AND BAD

There is another group of ideas that are important to understanding the ways forgiveness makes a difference in families. They have to do with differences in the way "good" things and "bad" things influence family processes and outcomes.

The core of these ideas is that bad things in families tend (a) to make a difference in a more dynamic and dramatic way than good things and (b) to create change in families more than most good things. The research about whether "bad is stronger than good" was reviewed by Baumeister, Finkenauer, and Vohs (2001), and their review focused on a wide range of topics. They found that the "greater power of bad events over good ones is found in everyday events [and] major life events. . . . Bad emotions, bad parents, and bad feedback have more impact than good ones, and bad information is processed more thoroughly than good" (p. 323). This is significant because "the self is more motivated to avoid bad self-definitions than to pursue good ones. Bad impressions and bad stereotypes are quicker to form and more resistant to disconfirmation than good ones" (p. 323). In the effort to discover *why* bad events, bad interactions, and bad contexts seem to be more influential than good ones, various explanations (including diagnosticity and salience) help explain some of the difference in outcomes, but the greater potency of bad events is still evidenced, even when these variables are controlled. Further, Baumeister and colleagues noted that "hardly any exceptions (indicating greater power of good) can be found" and concluded, "Taken together, these findings suggest that bad is stronger than good, as a general principle across a broad range of psychological phenomena" (p. 323).

We have detected this same pattern in our observations and interviews about forgiveness in families. When incidents of undesirable behavior occur in families, and forgiveness does not occur, it has several effects on other family processes. Negative affect increases, and a variety of other negative consequences either begin or are accelerated. Some of them are suspicion, defensiveness, aggression, disagreeableness, negative cognitions about self and others, and reluctance to communicate freely and openly. In situations where families already have a substantial amount of these negative processes, an additional incident where forgiveness does not occur tends to accelerate and exacerbate these negative processes. If these negative patterns and processes become long-term trends, they have powerful deleterious effects on outcomes.

When incidents occur and there is forgiveness, our data suggest that the effects are less dramatic. If the family has relatively few of the above negative processes, the forgiveness tends to merely maintain the status quo. The incidents of forgiveness don't usually make much of a difference in what is happening. Also, if a family already has a substantial amount of the negative processes, a few incidents of forgiveness also don't usually have much impact or create much change.

These different patterns are consistent with the idea that bad is generally stronger than good. In Chapter 6 (see p. 103), we describe some of our earlier research that found this same pattern with regard to kindness and unkindness in families. High unkindness was considerably more strongly related to family effectiveness than high kindness (Lee et al., 1997). Therefore our data add further credence to the suggestion by the Baumeister group (2001) that this idea should be viewed as "a general principle across a broad range of psychological phenomena" (p. 323). Our data also suggest that this idea ought to be generalized even further. In addition to having a role in psychological processes, it also is true for a broad range of family processes. Therefore the generalization that *bad things in family life generally have more influence than good things* should be another of the principles in sacred theory because "various studies reveal long-term harmful consequences of child abuse or sexual abuse, including depression, relationship problems, revictimization, and sexual dysfunction, even if the abuse occurred only once or twice" (Baumeister et al., 2001, p. 326).

This suggests that one or a few "bad" incidents can be very powerful in families, and one or a few "good" incidents generally have less of a dramatic and dynamic effect. Also, even one incident such as sexual infidelity or a major breach of trust can create a great deal of change in families, whereas years of good incidents merely maintain the status quo, have little discernible influence, and create little change.

There is an analogy that is helpful in understanding these differences. When raising a flower or vegetable garden, incidents of watering, fertilizing, having sunshine, and maintaining the appropriate temperature keep the garden growing; they maintain and enhance but the separate incidents of nurturing do not each make a big difference. However, even one undesirable event such as pulling plants up, having unusually high heat, freezing, having no water for a while, overfertilizing, or a misplaced foot can make a dramatic difference. These negative events all create significant change. Thus positive events do not usually produce significant change, but negative events often can and do.

This pattern of bad usually being stronger than good in a variety of ways is discussed in several later chapters, and it is another reason research and theorizing ought to focus on more specific aspects of the sacred rather than global religiosity. In our view, this will help the theorizing and research become more precise, profound, and (more important) helpful.

A concluding thought about the differences in the effects of "good" and "bad" is that some families who have high religiosity may behave for many years in ways that are consistent with their ideals with regard to most aspects of life; but just a few incidents when family members behave in ways that are not consistent with their ideals can be powerful. The few incidents of behaving badly may make much more difference in families than the more numerous good things. It is widely recognized that one area where this occurs is with trust. Family members can experience years of good experiences that build trust, but it can be destroyed by one bad situation where a family member acts in an untrustworthy way.

FORGETTING

Forgiving is frequently coupled with forgetting. We often hear the two words *forgive* and *forget* put in the same sentence as though they are inseparable or parts of the same process. For example, the title of the volume by Smedes (1984) that began the study of forgiveness is *Forgive and Forget: Healing the Hurts We Don't Deserve*, illustrating the tendency to link these two together. We suggest that these are actually two very different processes and should be studied and used separately.

The definition of forgiving on pages 35–38 states that forgiving is different from forgetting, and it includes a continuing acknowledgment of the existence of wrongs. We suggest that forgetting is not only a different process and a very complex process—maybe even more complex than forgiving.

If people forget about offenses, the memory of the offense is out of their awareness, which opens them up to the possibility of being hurt again. There is a saying that is common in our culture: "Hurt me once, shame on you. Hurt me twice, shame on me." This suggests that it is wise to remember, at least in some ways, former hurts and offenses. As Tutu (1998) has argued, "Forgiveness is an absolute necessity for continued human existence . . . but almost always we should not forget that there were atrocities, because if we do, we are then likely to repeat those atrocities. . . . [They] will return to haunt us" (p. xiii).

Yet on the other hand, part of the process of dealing wisely with hurts and offenses is to find ways to not have them continue to be a problem in the present and future. The goal is to find strategies to take painful parts of the past out of relationships but still have enough memory that one is not unwisely vulnerable. This idea is similar to forgetting, but it isn't truly forgetting. It is forgetting in some ways and not forgetting in other ways. It means that the wrongs cease to be parts of the current and future in relationships, but there is still a memory of past situations.

When family members are wise, these memories are not thought about and talked about as though they deal with the parts of the relationship that are the present and future. This means that wrongs are not brought up again and again when there are problems in the present or future, even if the offender offends again. Yet at the same time, there is an awareness of the wrongs that is tucked away in the mind that is retained and used when it is wise to use it. It is not wise to use this memory to destroy present and future possibilities, which can exist if the past wrongs are removed from the present and future of the relationship. This rather complicated process helps people genuinely repent and improve, because the old baggage isn't thrown out but is removed from the present and future so it doesn't keep people and relationships from growing and changing.

The following comment from one of our interviewees illustrates these differences between forgiving and forgetting in family relationships:

> I like to forgive, but I don't like to forget because if you forget something then it is like it never happened in your life, and it could happen again. Like with Saul in the Bible, he they tried to kill [David] a whole bunch of times and [David] ran away, and [Saul] decided to not kill him, and [David] forgave [Saul]. Then [Saul] said, "Why don't you come back with us" and [David] said, "I'm not going to come back with you." [David] didn't want it to happen again. He forgave [Saul] but he wasn't going to forget what happened.

Rituals can be helpful ways to put things out of a relationship. The past things a couple or family is trying to "put out" of their lives can be burned, buried, tied to a balloon and released, and the like. Another strategy for putting things out of relationships is to have "funerals" for them. Indeed, it is so difficult for many people to let go of former problems that these strategies can be very helpful for many families.

It may be that the sanctification of forgiveness is relevant in finding ways to remove past offenses from the present and future in relationships. It also might be that it is easier to remove past offenses with "sacred" forgiveness. Again, this is only a theoretical idea, but it has potential and is intriguing. It is also now an empirical question that we hope receives attention in future research.

Forgetting has not received the same attention in either the sacred literature or the scholarly literature as forgiveness, and it deserves more attention than it has had. We need to clarify the conceptualization and the processes that are involved in learning how to remove from a relationship some things that were previously painful and where forgiveness has occurred, because bringing up previous problems again and again interferes with the relationship being able to move on from those problematic situations.

APPLICATIONS

An increasing number of programs have been developed to help people learn how to be forgiving and to help them forgive. There have been family life education programs (Al-Mabuk et al., 1995; Burchard et al., 2003; Ripley & Worthington, 2002) and therapeutic programs (Al-Mabuk & Downs, 1996; Coyle & Enright, 1997; DiBlasio, 1998; Freedman & Enright, 1996; Gordon et al., 2000; Worthington, 1998). The effectiveness of many of these programs has been studied empirically, and the results in all of them have shown discernible improvements in forgiveness and marital and family outcomes. In the Fincham et al. (2006) review of this research, they argued that the research about these programs is limited because it deals, so far, only with modest and short-term parts of the forgiving process. Again, more is needed.

SUMMARY

In this chapter, forgiveness was identified as a leading example of a social science research domain where work from both sacred and academic sources can be integrated to enhance conceptual and practical understanding of a given family-related issue. The chapter discussed the idea that forgiveness helps families find successes and avoid failures, and that a lack of forgiveness is damaging to both individuals and families. We addressed the emergence of a growing scholarly literature about the nature and measurement of forgiveness that beneficially augment scriptural and sacred treatments of the concept, and noted that the scholarly work is beginning to examine ways forgiveness relates to marital and family phenomena. This research was reviewed, evaluated, and summarized, and some new ideas were introduced about how and why forgiving helps families.

The chapter also outlined some complexities and nuances relating to forgiveness. These included (a) whether forgiveness is the cessation of negative thoughts and emotions or whether the process must include the replacement of negative affect with positive affect; (b) the varying conditions under which forgiveness can be helpful or harmful; and (c) whether or not forgiving should include forgetting. The greater relative salience of “bad” actions (over “good”) in families was discussed—and forgiveness was posited as a vital coping resource in dealing with the failures, insensitivities, and harms that occur in all families. We presented the careful and multifaceted examination and consideration of forgiveness from diverse secular and sacred perspectives as a model for what we hope to see in the future. When other significant issues, including sacrificing (Chapter 4), loving others (Chapter 5), and coping with undesirable behavior (Chapter 8), receive the level of thoughtful attention from sacred and secular perspectives that forgiveness has, we believe that the results will be synergistic—and that they will benefit both academic and applied family professionals in ways that will matter to real families in the real world.

3

Asking and Seeking

This chapter adds a principle about ways *asking* for help from spiritual sources and seeking help in other ways help and harm families. When humans ask and seek help about and from the sacred, it is often through activities such as prayer, meditation, worshipping, fasting, listening, contemplation, blessings, reading sacred writings, consulting with spiritual leaders, spiritual imagery, support groups, and attending church services. When they receive spiritual information, comfort, or assistance, persons of faith sometimes report that it is through some form of inspiration, revelation, and/or spiritual enlightenment. In unusual situations, people have reported experiencing voices and/or personal visitations from Gods, angels, or deceased loved ones (e.g., Boss, 1999). More often, however, it is subtle experiences such as new insights, clarity, comfort, dreams, feelings, or promptings.

People indicate that these processes sometimes occur with their five senses, but many also say that there are other sensory processes involved in this communication. These other senses can be called a sixth sense or a group of additional senses. The five senses are experienced in specific locations in the body. Hearing is in the ear, and tasting is in the mouth, but the senses about the sacred are different. They tend to occur in more diffused places and in more subtle ways.

The diffused and delicate nature of sacred messages makes it difficult to describe them, the location where these messages occur in the body, and how they are received. Some people indicate that these messages are experienced or felt more than heard; and they are usually described as a delicate and peaceful experience, but sometimes as intense and involving warm or burning sensations. One way of describing them is "a still, small voice" or a "soft voice," and another is as a "burning in the bosom" or as the mind being "opened" or "enlightened." Still another way of describing them is that one might become aware of an idea or thought in one's mind that doesn't seem to come from one's own thoughts, reasoning, or sensory experiences. It just appears; or, as one of the people we interviewed described this process, it just drops into the mind.

This is another area where the concept of the *heart* is helpful. We describe in more detail in Chapter 9 (pp. 165–167) what we mean by the term heart, but the term is already well understood by most people. Many people describe their spiritual communication as feelings or experiences in their heart or their soul. These are elusive and intangible ways of conceptualizing, but the process of communication with the spiritual has intangible, transcendental, and unique qualities.

Those who do not use or are not aware of these spiritual senses have a difficult time understanding or appreciating this form of communication, but it is the same with the five senses. If individuals do not have the ability to see, hear, or smell, they have a difficult time understanding what these sensory experiences are like in those who have them. Also, those who have experiences with their five senses have a difficult time explaining to someone who doesn't have these experiences what they are like. However, those who are able to see, hear, or smell understand and appreciate these experiences. Experiencing spiritual messages seems to be similar in that, as with the five physical senses, they are real to those who have the capacity to experience them, and they at least partially understand and appreciate the processes involved.

Many who believe in the reality of communication and connection with the sacred view it as a valuable resource in their lives generally and in their family life specifically. For them, this communication provides information and ideas they wouldn't otherwise have. It opens possibilities and ways of doing things they believe are helpful and facilitating. Also, when members of families share their sacred experiences with others in their family, the sharing can help comfort and inspire, help resolve differences, sometimes help cope with undesirable behavior, and ultimately increase bonds and love.

THE PRINCIPLE

The thesis of this chapter is that there is a principle behind these processes that is helpful in understanding family dynamics and helping families find successes. It is the idea that *wisely asking and seeking help from spiritual sources helps families find successes and avoid failures*. This idea denotes that when individuals and families seek spiritual help it can bring a variety of resources, insights, capacities, calming influences, and ways of coping that help them succeed.

Sources of the Principle

The idea that prayer and other ways of seeking assistance are helpful has been widely shared for so long in the world's religious traditions that it is difficult to identify where it originated. The injunctions to "ask" and "seek" are repeated many ways and times in the Bible. One widely quoted reference is "Ask, and it shall be given you; seek, and ye shall find; knock, and it shall be opened unto you" (Matthew 7:7). The same injunction is in the Qur'an: "And your Lord says; 'Call on Me: I will answer your prayer'" (Qur'an, 40:60). And, as Beach et al. (2008) suggest, "A spiritual activity that appears to be omnipresent in religious life is prayer. Prayer is a spiritual activity common to all the 'Abrahamic' traditions (i.e., Judaism, Christianity, and Islam) and one that has strong parallels in other religious traditions" (p. 645).

Interestingly, most of the injunctions about asking and seeking in the sacred literature seem to deal with individualistic rather than familial prayer. However, it is a minor logical leap to generalize to the idea that asking and seeking can be helpful to families; and our data seem to support this extension.

Our reasoning behind positing that *asking and seeking* are useful is difficult to describe. We suspect we only partially understand it, but it seems to have truth and importance. A central reason we promote this idea is that there seems to be harmony between asking and seeking and the cluster of widely shared goals in families that are part of sacred theory.[1] When people participate in asking and seeking, they are inherently in a relationship where they are in a subjugated and dependent position, and in a position of openness and receptiveness rather than arrogance, domination, and control, or having a "hardened" or closed heart and mind. This humble harmony is illustrated in the following comments of a father as he reflected on the births of his children:

> I felt like I had a special calling when they were born. When they first come out, that is when I feel like my calling has begun. I don't think that calling ends when they turn thirty. I think a father's calling is always a father's calling. So, whether you're fathering a forty-five-year-old man or a two-year-old son it's a very special calling. It means God has entrusted me with these four spirits to help them grow and to teach them the things that He thinks I need to teach them. So, I think if I don't teach them I'll be accountable, and it means that God has entrusted me and called me, and He wants me to be a father.

As this father's thoughts and feelings illustrate, the birth process and the nurturing that accompanies it are sufficiently demanding and consuming that they create feelings in people that lead them to feel they need help and assistance—including, and perhaps especially, divine assistance. New parents become a part of something that is larger and more profound than themselves, and the generative pull and processes that emerge tend to engender a certain type of humility and openness that is consistent with turning to the sacred for help and in an attitude of appreciation and thankfulness (Hawkins & Dollahite, 1997). This means that the process of parenting and asking and seeking have a harmony that is mutually facilitative and helpful—even though we may not yet have a very adequate understanding of these processes.

These ideas suggest it is not defensible to argue that this principle was created with the scientific method or in scholarly literature because it predates the scholarly study of it. It clearly originates in sacred traditions and literature that predate the scientific method and modern academia.

The observations of the authors also provide one of the sources of this principle. We have watched prayer help change the attitudes and behavior of families

[1] These widely shared goals are described in Chapter 1, and they are built on a model of family that is described in a separate publication. The separate publication is available on the Internet at http://familycenter.byu.edu/Assumptions.dhtml and is also being submitted to a journal that publishes theories about family life.

we have tried to help. Also, we have experienced the ways prayer and meditation have opened our own hearts and minds, and how it has helped sustain us and add to our hope and resolve as we have faced serious challenges with the health and welfare of our children and loved ones. Thus we are among those who believe this principle is a powerful and important idea.

Research

There has been considerable research about several aspects of seeking help from the sacred. Most of the research has focused on individual rather than familial phenomena, including myriad studies that examine the connections between *prayer* and *coping* with aspects of physical and mental health such as depression, blood pressure, immune system functioning, mortality, traumas, and crises (Benson, 1996; Dossey, 1993; Elkins, Anchor, & Sandler, 1979; Harvey, Stein, Olsen, & Roberts, 1995; Larson & Larson, 2003; Lindgren & Coursey, 1995; McCullough, 1995; McIntosh, Silver, & Wortman, 1993; Ohaeri, Shokunbi, Akinklade, & Dare, 1995; Poloma & Pendleton, 1991; Shams & Jackson, 1993; Townsend, Kladder, & Mulligan, 2002; Williams, Larson, Buckler, Heckman, & Pyle, 1991).

Some research also has addressed the role of seeking spiritual help in psychotherapy (Richards & Bergin, 2005, Chapter 9). These bodies of research have consistently found that seeking help from and about the sacred generally has a positive influence in many areas, and the research is sufficiently consistent and impressive that prayer and other forms of seeking help from the sacred are widely viewed as beneficial (Koenig et al., 2001). This is even true among many professionals who are not personally religious, because prayer can "soften or eliminate negative processes. For example, a frustrated husband who turns to prayer may or may not 'regain perspective,' 'break negative thought cycles,' or 'relax,' . . . but at least he has *not* turned to alcohol, drugs, or violence" (Marks, 2008, p. 680).

This is significant given that an estimated 80% of domestic violence is alcohol related (Kroll & Taylor, 2003). Consistent with William James's argument that God is real because a belief in God produces real effects, we see that prayer can also have empirical effects. Scientists cannot prove or disprove that prayers are heard and answered, but specific participants who have reported turning to prayer during difficult times illustrate that prayer may wield force as a behavioral alternative to violence (Marks, Nesteruk, Hopkins-Williams, Swanson, & Davis, 2006) and problem drinking (Lambert, Fincham, Marks, & Stillman, 2010).

The earliest reference we know of that focuses on the relationship between prayer and family processes and outcomes is Crocker's (1984) essay that suggests communication in couples can be enhanced by prayer. The first empirical study we are aware of was Gruner's (1985) study of 208 religious couples from four different religious denominations in California. The findings were that prayer had a significant positive relationship with marital adjustment and that it also facilitated coping with marital and family problems. Gruner further found that prayer had a more positive influence on marital adjustment than Bible reading.

Another study, by Abbott, Berry, and Meredith (1990), gathered questionnaire data from 206 married adults from 20 different denominations in two midwestern metropolitan areas and found that 63% of the sample "almost always" sought help or assistance from God with family difficulties. An additional 18% frequently asked God for help. Over 29% reported almost always receiving some form of guidance or inspiration from God with family problems, and another 32% said they frequently received divine assistance (Abbott et al., 1990, p. 446). The majority of the sample reported that religion was helpful, and that the assistance was primarily in the form of enhancing the family's social network and encouraging family members to petition God for help with family problems. Those who reported more social support and divine help also reported higher levels of family satisfaction (Abbott et al., 1990, p. 443).

Greeley's (1991) analysis of survey data from several large samples in the United States in the 1970s and 1980s yielded clear and impressive results. The author concluded that when couples prayed *together* it was "a very powerful correlate of marital happiness, the most powerful we have yet discovered" (p. 189).

Robinson (1994) collected qualitative data from 30 individuals and focused on the relationship between religiosity and marriage. She included prayer as one aspect of religiosity, but did not separate prayer from other aspects of religiosity. Therefore this study provides only an indirect and fairly inconclusive type of evidence about the role of prayer in families.

Butler and Harper (1994), in a theoretical essay, used systems theory to develop a triangular model of husband–wife–God. They suggested that through a couple's shared belief system concerning their Deity, including God's interest and involvement in the marriage, their God can become a functional member of the marital system. They then hypothesized that couples who have this type of a triadic relationship allow God to operate more intimately and frequently within the couple relationship than many other relationships, including relationships with other members of their family—an idea that harmonizes with the concept of sanctification introduced later by Mahoney et al. (2003).

Butler and Harper (1994) then suggested that couples may use various methods to establish, maintain, and interpret their triadic relationships with their Deity, and the authors identified prayer as one such method. They posited that spouse or marital prayer "invokes God's participation and guidance in the day's forthcoming marital interactions, and provides opportunity for accountability . . . at its close" (p. 279). Prayer therefore helps invoke or activate the couple–God triangle, changing the interactional system, and potentially leading to meaningful shifts in couple interaction. This idea is illustrated in some recent qualitative research. Qin and Mei, a married couple who are Christian converts and immigrants from Taiwan, explain:

> *Qin (Husband):* We look up [to the Lord]. Just like a triangle, both of us look up to the Lord; the distance between us is more and more narrow [as we grow closer to Him], otherwise we would be more far away. This gives me great encouragement.
>
> *Mei (Wife):* The husband and the wife are different individuals, but now we have God. We were usually unpleasant with each other for some little things such as shopping or education. But now God is above, Qin said look up to the Lord, let God be the Lord of our family,

we [still] have distance [between us], but we are closer when we look upon the Lord.

Qin (Husband): The most important [issue] is the two commandments our Lord Jesus gave us: love your Lord and love one another. The same in a family, the Lord is the head of our family. He loves us, and there will be love in the family. I was very busy before on Mathematics research, not much time to consider my family. Now I value the family time following God's commandments. Since the Lord is the head, we should really let Him be the head of our family. We try our best to do [this].

The next study that focused on the role of prayer in marriage and family was by Butler et al. (1998). They used the Butler and Harper (1994) model as the theoretical orientation in a structured interview of 26 spouses who were characterized as "religious" by a close acquaintance. They used a qualitative, hermeneutic approach to investigate the effects of prayer on couple interaction during conflict, and the findings revealed that "overall, prayer appears to be a significant 'softening' event for religious couples, facilitating reconciliation and problem solving" (p. 451).

They identified six ways prayer was helpful. It invoked an experience of relationships with Deity. It deescalated hostile emotions and reduced emotional reactivity. It enhanced relationship and partner orientation and behavior. It facilitated empathy and unbiased perspectives. It increased self-change focus and encouraged couple responsibility for reconciliation and problem solving (Butler et al., 1998, p. 451).

The Butler et al. (2002) team followed up their 1998 study with questionnaire data from a geographically diverse sample of 217 spouses. They found prayer to be significantly related to an impressive number of couple processes. Prayer contributed to a perceived meaningful relationship with Deity, and this prayer-invoked relationship contributed to a sense of emotional validation from Deity in addition to mindfulness of and accountability to Deity. It also assisted with conflict resolution process through decreasing feelings of contempt, hostility, and enmity—and through lessening emotional reactivity. Couples also reported that prayer enhanced their productive focus on behaviors they perceived to be beneficial to their partner, and contributed to an increased understanding of their partner's perspective. Prayer also reportedly increased their "commitment to focus on self-change independent of their partner," which is significant because "self-change focus can be an expression of healthy personal responsibility and change initiative in relationships" (p. 31).

The study also confirmed the hypothesis that prayer engenders couple responsibility for reconciliation and problem solving, making Deity's role in helping "more characteristic of a 'therapist-coach' than a judge or problem solver for the couple. Couple responsibility is facilitated by the 'incremental coaching' that was reported to be an effect of prayer" (Butler et al., 2002, p. 31).

A series of recent studies also provide additional evidence about the ways prayer influences other family processes. Fincham, Beach, Lambert, Stillman, and Braithwaite (2008) found in correlational studies that prayer for a partner accounted for unique variance in satisfaction beyond that contributed by positive and negative behaviors and concluded that commitment was an intervening variable that mediated this relationship. They later conducted a series of experimental studies and found that prayer for a partner led to more gratitude, willingness to forgive, cooperation, satisfaction with sacrificing for the relationship, alcohol intake, and infidelity (Fincham, Lambert, & Beach, 2010; Lambert, Fincham, Braithwaite, Graham, & Beach, 2009; Lambert, Fincham, Marks, et al., 2010; Lambert, Fincham, Stillman, Graham, & Beach, 2010). Sanctification of the relationship was an intervening variable in the relationship with fidelity, and praying with a partner also contributed to unity and trust (Fincham et al., 2010). They also found that prayer was helpful in a skill-based family life education program, and that, in their sample, prayer for a partner made a difference whereas prayer that was not for a partner did not.

Ellison et al. (2010) used data from the National Survey of Religion and Family Life (NSRFL) to study the ways race, ethnicity, and religiosity shape relationship quality. They found that the amount family members participated in prayer or other religious activities with their partner or children at home was related to relationship quality even when other aspects of religiousness were controlled; and the greater religiousness of African American and Hispanic couples compared to non-Hispanic whites suggested that the in-home worship activities may make less difference in the non-Hispanic white families. No interaction effects were found with race and ethnicity.

Our interviews provide additional information and evidence that asking and seeking are helpful in families, as illustrated with the following comments. The first is from a Jewish mother:

> *Sarah:* When we take the time out, when we light the [Sabbath] candles Friday night, that's a time that I feel really close to [my children]. . . . We [ask a] blessing and after we say the blessing . . . I always say a prayer of thanks for my children. . . . When we sit across the table from each other, my husband and I, and the Sabbath candles are lit, and I see the kids, there is something I get from that that is *so deep*. It's just a feeling that [all is right in the world] . . . it doesn't matter what else is going on. Right in that circle . . . it's awe-inspiring (Marks, 2002, p. 70).

Many families, including Sarah's, found praying, asking, and seeking together to be rewarding and helpful. A college student recalled the following memories from her youth as her family conducted their evening family prayer, and some of the benefits it brought to their home

> Ever since I was little we've had a special way of doing our family prayer. When it is time for the prayer, we start singing "Let us gather in a circle," and all six of us gather in a circle in the living room and kneel down. Then, after the prayer, we have two little chants we always say. One is what we call our family motto and the other is our family theme. We change them every once in a while, and they help remind us what we are striving for as a family. Then, we all stand up and give each other a big group hug. It is just this little thing we do almost every night, and I think it has blessed our family a lot. It has helped

us be close to each other, and to feel the spirit together in our home, and be close to the Lord, and love each other.

The two following comments from people in different faiths further illustrate ways asking and seeking humbly and wisely are helpful:

(Congregational mother) Abby: [I pray] for the qualities that I need to make this marriage and this family here work. Often I need courage . . . patience . . . [the] ability to be more loving and understanding. And, I'm often . . . asking . . . because that's [what I need]. (Dollahite & Marks, 2009, p. 380)

****

(Latino Catholic father) Carlos: I pray . . . for guidance on how to resolve other problems. . . . I pray for patience. I pray for [God to] allow me to see how . . . to avoid problems, avoid losing my patience, [and] how to help my children be better persons. (Dollahite & Marks, 2009, p. 380)

THEORY BUILDING ABOUT WHY, HOW, AND WHEN ASKING AND SEEKING ARE HELPFUL

More research is needed about the role of asking and seeking in families, but there have been enough studies that have found impressive results to provide a basis for theorizing about why, how, and when asking and seeking help in families can be helpful. Several of the early studies, such as those by Abbott et al. (1990), Greeley (1991), and Robinson (1994), dealt with fairly general processes and began the theorizing. For example, Greeley observed: "It may be that the prayer interlude provides husbands and wives with time away from the other responsibilities of their common and individual lives in which they can share affection and common values and thus reinforce their relationship" (p. 190). He further reasoned that couples often begin to pray together because the relationship is already perceived as good, and their joint prayer tends to validate and improve the relationship even more.

Most of the later studies focused on fairly specific processes couples and families experience when they are dealing with conflict. The Butler et al. (2002) team examined their findings in a way that began the theorizing about how prayer helps in dealing with conflict. They grouped their findings into three interrelated processes: (a) creating and maintaining a meaningful relationship with their Deity that leads to (b) emotional softening in conflict and problematic situations, which helps move them away from negative affect and toward neutrality, which helps them (c) move toward reorganizing and reorienting toward a sense of personal responsibility for problem solving that helps with conflict resolution. More simply, prayer helps with relationships, neutrality, and responsibility (Butler et al., 2002, p. 33). These concepts are illustrated in qualitative work by Marks (2002) in which a Christian mother explains:

We have disagreements [in our marriage], we have things we don't see the same sometimes, and faith is a source of help. We can pray about things

> together and the Lord can help us work things out. Sometimes one person has to give in and accept the other person's point of view, [but] it helps to be able to pray about things. The Lord, He's the best counselor you could ever have. I don't know how marriages can work without God. I'm sure that there are people who are so compatible that they can still get along but (our faith) has been really helpful [for us]. (p. 105)

Several insights by Lambert and Dollahite (2006) are also important parts of the theorizing about the role of prayer. Their data indicated that when faith and prayer are integrated into the marital relationship, processes are different in three different phases of the conflict process: problem prevention, resolution, and reconciliation. They also found that prayer was one of the aspects of religiosity that helped people avoid, cope, and reconcile.

Beach and colleagues' (2008) recent conceptual framework included several theoretical ideas that are virtually identical to the three main ideas in the Butler et al. (1998, 2002) model. The Beach team apparently based their conceptual and theoretical model on their clinical and/or personal experience, but their insights are impressive because several of their ideas are similar to the ideas of the Butler team—and the ideas from the Butler team were not referred to in the text or cited in the references. In short, two highly experienced but independent teams in different regions of the nation working with different populations developed similar core conceptualizations regarding how prayer influences marriage.

One of the theoretical ideas that was independently constructed by both the Butler and Beach groups is that *prayer tends to help people maintain and regain relationships.* The Butler team focused on the relationship with Deity, and the Beach team similarly focused on ways prayer tends to help people retain and regain perspective about the long-term goals in their interpersonal relationships. The Beach group built on the Fincham and Beach (1999) idea that in conflicted situations it is typical for people to shift their attention to short-term goals that are emergent in the conflict situation and to divert their attention from more wholesome, shared, long-term goals such as love, compassion, and understanding. The short-term and emergent goals may include becoming concerned about such things as winning the current argument, getting even, showing up the other person, or getting one's own way. The Beach group argue that prayer tends to help individuals affirm and focus on the more long-term goals in their relationship.

The available scholarship and our own experience lead us to believe that a key question in most marital conflicts is: "Would I rather fight to be 'right' or be 'wrong' and get along?" Genuine prayer (whether personal or shared) provides an opportunity to consider and respond to this question in a way that returns focus to long-term relational goals and away from petty ego and pride and the desire to be "right."

The second theoretical idea that both the Butler and Beach teams describe is that prayer tends to help soften emotional negativity and break negative thought cycles. This notion relates to previous work by Gottman (1999), Fincham (2003), and Wile (1993) about states that have been conceptualized as emotional flooding, emotional-state dependence, and self-soothing.

The third idea shared by the Butler and Beach models has to do with conflict resolution and problem-solving skills. As prayer helps people focus on wholesome aspects of their divine and interpersonal relationships and move toward emotional neutrality, this contributes to their ability to use conflict resolution and problem-solving skills they already have. It may also promote a willingness to learn and use new skills.

The Beach group (2008) adds several other unique theoretical insights about ways prayer tends to be helpful in family processes, especially in dealing with conflict or other difficult situations. For example, they suggested that prayer tends to help tap into new sources of motivation. This can occur because prayer tends to "create a longer time perspective, a factor that has been shown to prompt cooperation and investment in the relationships" (p. 655).

The Beach group also theorized that prayer may be used to prime "implemental intentions" or plans for achieving a desired goal that guide future behavior (Bargh, Gollwitzer, Lee-Chai, Barndollar, & Trötschel, 2001; Gollwitzer & Moskowitz, 1996). For example, spouses could pray for help in "showing love," and they could include in their request pleas for "assistance in identifying opportunities for loving behavior and acting on them as they arise" (Beach et al. 2008, p. 655).

Beach et al. (2008) also drew on the work of Gottman (2002a, 2002b), Novak and Vallacher (1998), and Fincham, Stanley, and Beach (2007) to introduce another theoretical idea. They began by distinguishing between "influence processes" and "control processes." *Control processes* are intraindividual processes that influence behavior. *Influence processes* are when a person's behavior is influenced by what others do. They then theorized that prayer tends to alter both control and influence processes in ways that open possibilities that can be difficult to acquire in other ways. For example, especially in conflictual and other emotionally charged situations, prayer has the capacity to help people change such things as the way they view offenses, perspective taking, soothing, rumination, propensity toward forgiveness, willingness to sacrifice one's wishes for the sake of a relationship, negative reciprocity, and ability to accommodate aspects of a relationship that cannot be readily changed. These changes may also involve "not just one discrete outcome but a series of linked events unfolding over time in an iterative process" (p. 660).

This process is captured in the following juxtaposed quotes from a wife and husband who, though interviewed separately, both referenced the ways prayer was an important influence vis-à-vis each other:

> *Jessica:* In our family . . . [Joseph's] an excellent role model. The kids need to be able to look up to him and see the God in his life . . . [so] that they'll want to pattern their lives after him. It's always great for kids to be able to look up to their Dad and see someone that they respect. . . . I've seen him changing over the years. He loves the Lord and wants to do what pleases Him . . . modeling what he sees as being valuable for the kids to see. He has an important role in being like Jesus to the kids. A lot of our understanding of who God is comes through fathers, because God is presented as a father in

the Bible. If a kid grows up having a father who is loving and kind and supportive and strong, I think it is easier for them to understand God and who He is. . . . The kids see in their father aspects of God, a perfect God.

Joseph: I see her get up every morning and take time to read scripture and pray and I just see that it's not separate from the rest of her day and that it influences the way she does [everything]; the way she interacts with me and the kids and everybody in the community. It's central, it's pervasive [it makes me want to be better]. (Marks, 2002, pp. 79–80)

Beach et al. (2008) theorized that these ways prayer influences families can be transformative processes, and suggested that "the transformative potential of prayer may represent its most potent potential contribution" (pp. 656–657). We agree that these processes can be transformative in marital and family situations.

Similarly, even though we understand that the Beach team was primarily interested in transformational processes, we also believe that abruptly transformative processes are so rare that the "most potent potential contribution" of these ideas is not their value in transformative processes. It is in their help with the routine and everyday processes in marriage and family.

The Beach team (2008) made a small but qualitative shift from their preceding article (Fincham, Stanley, & Beach, 2007) involving their definition of transformation. In their 2007 paper, *transformation* was defined as "sudden and discontinuous" and "nonlinear" (pp. 286, 288). In the 2008 paper, the authors illustrated how transformation may, in many instances, be "cumulative" or "compound." This explanation of how small, positive movements may transform the marriage across time will be more palatable to many readers than the nonlinear definition of marital transformation. In a review of the Beach team's progressing work on marital transformation, we posited:

> The Second Law of Thermodynamics states, "All physical or chemical changes tend to proceed in such a direction that useful energy undergoes irreversible degradation into a randomized form called *entropy*" (Lehninger, 1982, p. 362). If we prefer the language of the poet over that of the basic sciences, we can turn to Yeats, "Things fall apart; the centre cannot hold; mere anarchy is loosed upon the world." If the principles of entropy and the trend toward disorganization and loss apply to marital relationships at some level—and if Doherty (2001) is correct in asserting that one of the greatest dangers to marriage is the steady current of daily living that pulls us downstream toward dis-integration—then Beach and colleagues are onto an issue of critical importance with "cumulative" transformation. Viewed in this light, marital transformation is not solely expressed as a one-time, anomalous phenomenon that happens to a few couples on the edge of the bell curve; it may also be a process that perennially produces revitalizing marital energy in many lasting marriages. (Marks, 2008, p. 684)

A concluding thought about this theorizing is that it also seems likely that the different ways of seeking spiritual help may influence different family processes in different ways. For example, praying probably has different effects than fasting, and fasting while praying probably has unique effects. Also, meditation, worship, and contemplation probably influence family processes in unique ways, and it is possible that the differences between individual and family prayers may provide related but differing influences. We do not know of any empirical or theoretical work that focuses on these differences, and this also suggests that more research and theory are needed about these differences.

WAYS ASKING AND SEEKING CAN BE HARMFUL

As with all aspects of the sacred, there also can be a dark side to this principle; and leading scholars in this area have also focused on the negative aspects of prayer (Beach et al., 2008; Butler & Harper, 1994). They have pointed out that individuals and families can use prayer in devious and destructive ways. We have previously argued that "certain forms of prayer that abdicate personal action may lead *away* from [healthy] objectives and toward a type of passive fatalism that seems incongruent with marital intervention and training" (Marks, 2008, p. 682). Phrased differently, there are praying couples that may expect God to do their marital work for them. Such an approach not only may be unhelpful, it can be negligent and destructive.

Another cautionary note offered by Butler and Harper (1994) and Beach et al. (2008) is that religious couples who are embroiled in conflict and are highly reactive to one another emotionally might exploit the couple–God system in unwholesome ways. They might define and interpret aspects of their relationship with the divine in ways that could perpetuate and fixate conflict through such strategies, invoking spouse–God alliances or other dysfunctional triangulation rather than helping to resolve and cope effectively. For example, praying "God, if you want my marriage to work, help my spouse to not be such an aggravating jerk" is far less active and facilitative than "God, please soften our hearts and help us to be more patient and understanding with each other" (Marks, 2008, p. 682). There is probably a contingency with regard to the principle of asking and seeking. It is that this process is helpful when family members use asking and seeking in wise, ethical, humane, and humble ways, and harmful when used in opposite conditions such as being selfish, exploiting, manipulating, and controlling (Beach et al., 2008; Fincham et al., 2008). These are the reasons we added the word *wisely* to the principle about asking and seeking.

VISUAL SUMMARIES

When the Butler group and the Beach group organized the ways asking and seeking help families, they both suggested that these processes help family members create, maintain, and enhance relationships. We also like the idea of separating these effects from the other effects, and Figure 3.1 is a visual summary of the ways asking and seeking influence relationships. The other ideas in the literature about the ways asking and seeking help families all deal with how they help families with regard to preventing and coping with challenges such as disagreements and undesirable

- Facilitates communication (Crocker,1984)
- Variables such as marital and family adjustment and satisfaction (Gruner, 1986; Abbott et al. 1990; Greeley, 1991, p.189)
- Promotes a sense of God's involvement intimately and frequently, and perceptions of divine help, inspiration, and guidance(Abbott et al. 1990; Butler & Harper, 1994; Butler et al., 1998)
- Provides emotional validation from Deity in addition to mindfulness of and accountability to Deity (Butler & Harper, 1994)
- Enhances other-orientation and behavior beneficial to others (Harper et al., 1998)
- Facilitates empathy and unbiased perspectives (Harper et a., 1998)
- Facilitates willingness to forgive, gratitude, satisfaction with sacrificing, cooperation, unity, trust, alcohol intake, and infidelity (Lambert et al., 2009, 2010, 2010a, Fincham et al., 2010).
- Shares affection and common values thereby reinforcing, validating, and improving relationships
- Increases ability to accommodate aspects of relationships that cannot be readily changed
- Helps people focus on wholesome aspects of divine relationships
- Provides a time away from other responsibilities when family members can share affection and common values and thus reinforce their relationship
- Enhances the quality of communication
- Enhances the quality of the social network
- Increases empathy and commitment
- Creates a sense of having someone to turn to for ideas, answers, and guidance
- Provides a perception of being able to get new ideas and possibilities

Figure 3.1 Family processes that are influenced by asking and seeking that help families create, maintain, regain, and enhance relationships.

behavior. We have grouped these ideas into two areas and summarized them in Figure 3.2. The way these ideas are organized in Figure 3.2 focuses on only one of the three phases that are described by Lambert and Dollahite (2006)—how asking and seeking can help with the coping part of conflict. We have organized the ideas this way because so little has been done so far with the avoidance and reconciliation aspects of dealing with problems such as conflict and undesirable behavior.

APPLICATIONS

The ideas in this chapter have a number of implications for families and practitioners in the family field, but scholarship about the ways professionals should and should not deal with asking and seeking is still nascent. Doherty (1995), Richards and Bergin (2005), Onedera (2008), and Walsh (2009) have begun to explore these complex issues, but much more still needs to be done.

The strategies that are helpful in enhancing spiritual communication undoubtedly depend on the orientations and perceptions family members have about the sacred, but there may be insights that can be contributed by the scholarly community. For example, our experiences suggest that there is a cyclical quality to the

Ways asking and seeking help keep negative affect from being disruptive

- Enhances emotional softening in conflict and problematic situations that helps move people away from negative affect and toward neutrality (Butler et al. 1998)
- De-escalates hostile emotions and emotional reactivity and breaks negative thought cycles (Butler et al., 1998)
- Lessens feelings of anger, contempt, and enmity
- Increases relaxation responses
- Helps prime implemental intentions
- Helps cope with emotional flooding and over dependence on emotions
- Promotes self-soothing

Ways asking and seeking help families prevent and cope with conflict and problems

- Facilitates effective coping strategies (Gruner, 1986)
- Helps people use conflict and problem solving skills they already have and use new skills
- Helps people move toward reorganizing and reorienting toward a sense of personal, couple, and family responsibility for problem solving (Butler et al., 1998)
- Increases focus on and emphasis on self-change independent of others (Butler et al., 1998)
- Facilitates empathy and unbiased perspectives
- Helps change control and influence processes in ways that open possibilities that can be difficult to acquire in other ways
- Helps focus on long-term perspectives and goals rather than getting caught up in short-term goals that are emergent in difficult situations and divert attention from more wholesome shared long-term goals such as love, compassion and understanding
- Helps people reorganize and reorient toward long-term goals
- Promotes an attitude of being humble, subjugated, open, receptive, and dependent
- Helps reconciliation after there are disagreements or problems (Butler et al., 1998)

Figure 3.2 Other family processes influenced by asking and seeking.

process of asking and seeking. When people try to participate in the process of asking and seeking and take the time to try to communicate spiritually, this seems to increase both their ability and inclination to do it more as well as their ability to be more effective in the future. And, conversely, as people avoid or ignore this type of communication, they seem to lose the abilities and the gifts they have.

Another way of applying the ideas in this chapter is to compare and contrast these ideas with the ideas in several philosophies or perspectives that are very different from the notion that asking and seeking help from spiritual sources is helpful. One approach would be to do this analysis in each chapter as we go, and another strategy is to describe all of the ideas in sacred theory first and then make these comparisons. We have decided to use the second alternative, and these important comparisons and issues are discussed in Chapter 13 (pp. 213–229).

SUMMARY

This chapter discussed the idea that asking and seeking help with regard to the sacred parts of the human experience helps families find successes and avoid failures. We noted a growing scholarly literature about the nature and measurement of different ways of asking and seeking help with and from the sacred, and this literature was reviewed, evaluated, and summarized. The most promising area of research and conceptualization regarding asking and seeking has examined prayer. Sacred literature has dealt extensively with prayer, but the treatment of prayer in this domain has been almost exclusively focused on personal or individual prayer (as illustrated by the Psalmists of the Old Testament offering their prayers to their God). Little of the sacred literature explicitly addresses marital or family prayer. Social science research in this area followed a similar pattern by initially focusing on individual prayer. Related scholarship has revealed several (mostly positive) correlations between prayer and various aspects of physical, emotional, and psychological well-being, but research addressing familial-level praying, asking, and seeking has been scant.

Important empirical and conceptual developments emerged from the Butler group and Beach group that have indicated that certain expressions of individual and marital prayer seem to beneficially influence marital processes and may even be transformative—although we reported some dangers as well. Although the sacred and scholarly literatures on asking and seeking are not as complementary or integrated as those addressing forgiveness (see Chapter 2), important foundational work has been done in connection with asking, seeking, and praying at the marital level. Asking and seeking remains a neglected topic at the family level, both conceptually and empirically. Given the typically positive and recurring correlations between prayer and individual-level wellness, and the early promise of conceptual and theoretical work addressing prayer at the marital level, we wait with anticipation for badly needed work at the family level.

4

Sacrificing

This chapter focuses on the role of sacrificing in families. Our goals are to describe a principle, review the previous literature about this principle, and expand and improve the related theory and research.

This chapter is similar to the last two chapters in that all three of these topics have become parts of scholarly inquiry in addition to having a long history in the major world religions. On the other hand, this chapter is a little different from the previous two because sacrifice received some attention by social scientists in the early years of the social sciences. For example, James (1902) argued that "the impulse to sacrifice is the main religious phenomenon. It is a prominent, a universal phenomenon certainly, and lies deeper than any special creed" (p. 303).

As secular perspectives came to dominate the social sciences during most of the twentieth century, the theorizing and research about sacrifice received less attention. However, this pattern has changed in the last several decades, and it is again a topic that is studied theoretically and empirically.

DEFINITIONS AND A PRINCIPLE

Our first goal is to describe how we are using this concept because sacrifice has several different meanings. Bahr and Bahr (2009) recently reviewed a number of different ways scholars have used the term *sacrifice* in contexts that vary from family life to concentration camps. Their analysis is very thorough so there is no need to review the many definitions again. We found their review useful because it helped sensitize us to the importance of the concept, the variety of ways it has been defined, and a number of issues that are associated with it, but we still need to describe the way we are using this term.

In addition to the word *sacrifice* having multiple meanings, the meanings also have changed over time. It first appeared as a combination of the two words *sacer* and the *facere*. *Sacer* refers to sacred, holy, consecrated, hallowed, or dedicated to a divinity; and *facere* refers to making, acting, taking action, being active, composing, or writing. Thus the combination of the two words into the Latin *sacrificium* and eventually into the English word *sacrifice* literally means to make something holy or sacred.

The usual pattern in modern dictionaries is to list the process of making something sacred as the first definition of this term. Then other meanings are listed, such as offering animals, plants, or a human life to a deity, and the calculated (but not necessarily sacred) process of giving up, destroying, surrendering, destroying, permitting injury to, or forgoing a valued thing or something that is prized for the sake of something of greater value or having a more pressing claim. Other definitions are a loss incurred in selling something below its value and a bunt in baseball designed to advance another player. We use the term *sacrifice* in all of these ways, except for the baseball definition.

Van Lange, Rusbult et al. (1997) suggested that it is helpful to make another distinction "between the concepts of sacrifice and costs" (p. 1374). Many events may be costly but not involve sacrifice (e.g., having a car accident or losing a bet). Costly experiences may originate in a partner's behavior or something that is external to the relationship, but sacrificing refers to forfeiting of self-interest. Also, sacrificing may or may not be experienced or psychologically framed as costly, and it may or may not be distasteful. Costs are inherently linked to the experience of dissatisfaction, but sacrificing can be, and often is, "intended to further positive goals—to promote the well-being of a partner or relationship" (p. 1374).

Sacrificing probably has many facets and dimensions, but the theorizing in this chapter deals only with variation in the amount or quantity of sacrificing and the ways several other factors influence the effects of this variation. Other aspects will probably be included in the future as sacred theory is refined and improved, but it is important at this stage of the theory construction to keep the conceptualization and theorizing simple enough to be manageable.

Sacrificing varies a great deal in families. Parents, for example, are inclined to or find themselves in situations where they sacrifice many things. Others, especially at certain developmental stages, such as the very young, do much less sacrificing. Also, some family members choose to sacrifice more than others. This means that, in addition to the many ways sacrifice can change and evolve qualitatively, the amount of sacrifice is a continuous variable that can vary quantitatively between low and high amounts.

There is some previous literature that illustrates that paying attention to the amount of sacrificing is relevant. Bellah, Madsen, Sullivan, Swidler, and Tipton (1985) argued that marital commitments and family obligations in America are threatened by a pervasive "therapeutic individualism" that devalues the concept of sacrifice. They then asserted that there is a trend among Americans to emphasize individualism and freedom over relationships based in commitment and obligation, and posited that the perceived value of sacrifice is fading. For example, they suggested:

> Even the most secure, happily married of our respondents had difficulty when they sought a language in which to articulate their reasons for commitments that went beyond the self. These confusions were particularly clear when they discussed problems of sacrifice and obligation. While they wanted to maintain

> enduring relationships, they resisted the notion that such relationships might involve obligations that went beyond the wishes of the partners . . . They were troubled by the ideal of self-denial the term "sacrifice" implied. (p. 109)

Even though they argued that there are social forces that are decreasing the amount of sacrificing in modern societies, studies by Stanley, Whitton, Sadberry, Clements, and Markman (2006) and Whitton, Stanley, and Markman (2007) document that sacrificing exists in modern family life; and in some situations there is an impressive amount of it—more than many scholars acknowledge (Dollahite & Thatcher, 2008).

With the concept of sacrifice defined in this way, it is possible to describe a principle about the role of sacrifice in families. The principle is the main thesis in this chapter and an important part of sacred theory. It is the idea that *variation in the amount of sacrificing in families influences the amount families flourish.* Sacrificing, however, doesn't always have the effects that are suggested by this principle because there are some circumstances and conditions that influence when and how this principle operates. Five of these qualifying aspects are discussed later in this chapter.

SOURCES OF THE PRINCIPLE

The idea that sacrificing is a good thing for humans generally with regard to their spiritual progress and growth is a central idea in all of the major world religions, especially the Abrahamic religions of Judaism, Islam, and Christianity. It is implicit in many of their traditions and explicit in situations such as the offerings by Cain and Abel (Genesis 4:3–5) and Abraham being asked to sacrifice his son Isaac (Genesis 22:1–19).

However, the religious bodies of literature about sacrifice tend to deal with the value of sacrifice for individuals. The idea that sacrifice helps families flourish is an extension of this notion that we have not found in the sacred literature. Myers (1983) was the first we know of to suggest that sacrificing is an important part of family processes, and there is a growing body of research that addresses this idea (Fincham, Stanley, & Beach, 2007). Our observations in our own families and the comments by people we have interviewed provide additional evidence that this principle is important, but before we describe the insights provided by our experiences and interviews, it seems wise to review the previous scholarly literature about this principle.

THE SCHOLARLY LITERATURE

The study of sacrifice was not a part of family studies in most of the twentieth century. Research about it was almost nonexistent (Bahr & Bahr, 2001, 2009), and the term doesn't even appear in the titles or indexes of most texts or summaries, such as Goode's propositional inventory (Goode, Hopkins, & McClure, 1971), or *Journal of Marriage and Family* decade reviews, or any of the handbooks or summaries of theories and methods in the field (Arcus, Schvaneveldt, & Moss, 1993; Burr et al., 1979; Christensen, 1964; Sussman & Steinmetz, 1987). However, a number of scholars have begun to suggest in recent years that sacrifice should have a more central role in the social sciences generally (Mizruchi, 1998; Myers, 1983) and family studies in particular (Bahr & Bahr, 2001, 2009; Fincham, Stanley, & Beach, 2007). For example, Bahr and Bahr (2001) stated: "Self-sacrifice is a powerful and essential part of social life generally, and family life in particular. It merits a more substantial place in contemporary theory" (p. 1231).

A little research about the role of sacrifice in organizational behavior began to appear in the 1970s (Baefsky & Berger, 1974; MacCrimmon & Messick, 1976; Schwartz, 1975). These studies are helpful because of their innovations in conceptualization and measurement, but they are of little value in understanding the role of sacrifice in family processes. A few studies have also focused on the role of sacrifice in close relationships, but most of this research deals with temporary relationships rather than permanent or family relationships (Berscheid, 1985; Clark & Mills, 1979; Holmes & Boon, 1990). The result is that these studies are helpful in some general ways but very limited in facilitating greater understanding of sacrifice in *family* systems.

A few studies have focused on aspects of sacrifice that are not related to the principle in this chapter. For example, Stanley and Markman (1992) measured satisfaction with sacrifice, but viewed it as a component of commitment, and this did not provide information about the effects of sacrificing in families. Others, such as Stanley (1998) and Turillo, Folger, Lavelle, Umphress, and Gee (2002), studied factors that influence propensity to sacrifice, as well as antecedents of sacrifice, and this research also provides no information about the effects of sacrifice in families.

Ways Sacrifice Is Helpful

The studies by Van Lange, Rusbult et al. (1997) were among the first that focused on the effects of sacrifice in dating and marital relationships. They carried out a series of six studies that examined ideas about sacrifice that were based on interdependence theory (Kelley & Thibaut, 1978; Thibaut & Kelley, 1959), and they found those who reported more willingness to sacrifice also reported greater satisfaction, commitment, and relationship persistence. In fact, "willingness to sacrifice accounted for an average of 40% of the variance in dyadic adjustment" (p. 1388). When they controlled for the amount of commitment in relationships, "sacrifice accounted for a significant unique variance in adjustment" (pp. 1388–1399).

Van Lange, Rusbult et al. (1997) also developed four theoretical reasons sacrifice enhances functioning in relationships (pp. 1375–1376). The first is the law of reciprocity. Namely, sacrifice enhances the probability that others will reciprocate with additional acts of sacrifice. Van Lange and colleagues argued that unless there are other factors that come into play, family members generally will not "take a free ride" and respond to sacrifices with exploitation. Further, the tendency for reciprocity leads to patterns of beneficially reciprocal sacrifice and effectiveness in families. This theoretical reason is an application of the law of reciprocity that was developed by Gouldner (1960) and Deutsch (1973) and was described on page 43.

The second theoretical point suggested by Van Lange, Rusbult et al. (1997) is that sacrifice tends to solve problems for family members, and this tends to create congenial options for others. Sacrifice also seems to exert more global beneficial effects, and this leads to a variety of prosocial behaviors such as helpfulness and loving gratitude, which also help families flourish.

The following narrative from a father captures this tendency of facilitating helpfulness and gratitude. Tom, whose daughter Megan died of leukemia, explained what she had taught him:

> We went to give blood at a church blood drive. I was just happy because I'd just gotten a penicillin shot and they wouldn't take my blood. Sandra, my wife, had given her blood and our friend Clyde was there giving blood. Megan went over and held his hand while he had that blood drawn, because she knew what it was like to have needles poked in your skin and she felt for him. She couldn't do much but she could hold his hand, and she did that. The impact that has on me just tells me that a little bit of loving concern for others goes a long way, not just in the life of either person in the interaction, but in the people who see that. It makes you want to go forth and do likewise.

It is noteworthy that in this case Tom was influenced by his daughter Megan's example, even though her act did not even involve him directly.

The third reason mentioned by Van Lange, Rusbult et al. (1997) for emphasizing sacrifice in families is that sacrificing tends to create a general "climate" of trust and cooperation in which other relationship-building behaviors become increasingly probable. They explained: "When partners develop generalized habits of pro-relationship transformation, they are more likely to seek out and identify patterns of interaction for which little or no sacrifice is called [for]" (p. 1376) and where congenial solutions are sought.

The fourth benefit of sacrifice identified by Van Lange, Rusbult et al. (1997) is that "sacrifice serves a communicative function, providing relatively unambiguous evidence of the individual's pro-relationship orientation" (p. 1376). Sacrificing has "surplus value," yielding positive consequences above and beyond the direct impact on the behavior of others. For example, acts of sacrifice tend to enhance the conviction that others can be relied on to behave in prorelationship ways (cf. Holmes, 1989; Holmes & Rempel, 1989); and there is evidence that these ways of behaving lead to other benefits such as willingness to accommodate rather than retaliate when others behave poorly (Gottman, 1979; Jacobson & Margolin, 1979; Rusbult, Bissonnette, Arriaga, & Cox, 2008).

Wieselquist, Rusbult, Foster, and Agnew (1999) also focused on the role of sacrifice in a series of studies. They theorized that sacrifice is an important part of a positive cyclical growth process in relationships. However, they viewed sacrifice as one of several types of prorelationship behaviors, and their model highlights the role of trust and commitment so much that their findings provide little information about the role of variation or differences in sacrifice as a unique process. This means their research provides only a little evidence for the validity of the principle that is the main concern in this chapter.

Van Lange, Rusbult et al. (1997) also found that sacrifice and commitment were related, and several other scholars have focused on the role of commitment (Fincham, Stanley, & Beach, 2007; Stanley & Markman, 1992). We find the way they dealt with commitment a little puzzling because variation in commitment seems to have little value to professionals such as therapists and educators who are trying to help families or family members who are trying to be as *effective* as possible. It doesn't seem very meaningful to think of intervention or educational programs designed to increase commitment per se (there is little joy in being committed to a miserable relationship). Family life education students frequently ask a variation of the question, "Should unhappily married parents stay together for the sake of their children or should they get divorced?" Such a question references level of commitment, but there are other vital factors in play as well. We believe that this question implies a false binary choice that one may *either* (a) stay married and stay miserable, *or* (b) divorce and escape unhappiness. There are several other choices and potentialities—one of which is to stay married and committed and to create (or re-create) a happy and effective marital and family life (Doherty, 2001). Variation in the inclination and willingness to sacrifice and the amount of sacrificing are potentially potent factors in helping people change their beliefs and behaviors to try to improve their family effectiveness. Therefore sacrificing seems like a relevant and important variable that deserves more attention. And, to the extent the positive relationship between commitment and sacrificing is relevant, the most theoretically meaningful way to think about this relationship is to think of the amount of sacrificing as both influencing and reflecting the amount of commitment.

This reasoning extends the cyclical model proposed by Wieselquist et al. (1999) and implies that greater attention should be directed to the way the amount of sacrifice influences other processes. For example, the Wieselquist team's model emphasizes that variation in trust influences dependence, which influences commitment, which influences prorelationship behaviors such as sacrifice. To us, it is more meaningful and potentially helpful to professionals and families to think of how prorelationship factors such as sacrifice influence trust, dependence, and commitment; how variations in all of these processes probably have a reciprocal and cyclic effect on each other; and how all of the various versions of these positive cycles probably help the flourishing of families. We recall an older and wiser Abraham Maslow revising his "hierarchy of needs" near the end of his life to posit that *inter*dependence, not "self-actualization," reigns as the crowning achievement in life (Covey, 2004). Viktor Frankl (1984), in clear criticism of the younger and individual-focused Maslow, stated: "What is called self-actualization is not an attainable aim at all, for the simple reason that the more one would strive for it, the more he would miss it. In other words, *self-actualization is possible only as a side-effect of self-transcendence*" (p. 133, emphasis added). In this idea, both Maslow and Frankl were preceded by the Christian teaching that "he that findeth his life shall lose it: and he that loseth his life for my sake shall find it" (Matthew 10:39).

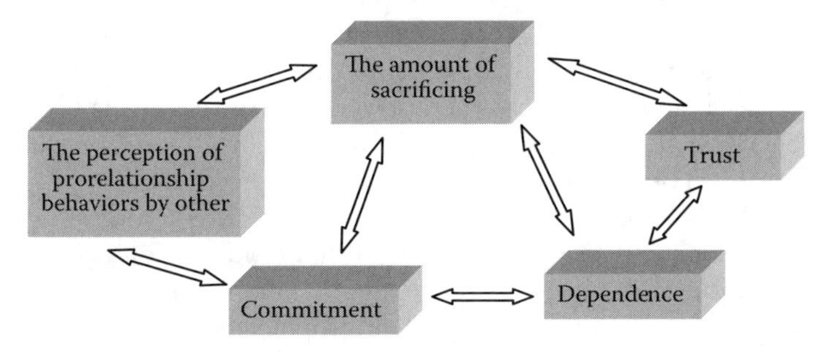

Figure 4.1 Revision of the Wieselquist model to highlight the effects of sacrifice.

Figure 4.1 is an attempt to visually illustrate this way of rearranging the issues that we think are more relevant theoretically, empirically, and practically. There are probably many more arrows that could be put in this diagram because so many things influence other things, but this version of the model highlights the role of the amount of sacrifice, and the ways it probably influences other family processes. Figure 4.1 does not include the various valued outcomes such as marital and family stability, satisfaction, and effectiveness, but the theoretical idea is that all of the various versions of these positive cycles have a positive influence on family functioning.

There is additional evidence about the principle in this chapter that came from a study where it was not expected. When Pargament et al. (1998) were developing scales of negative aspects of the spiritual, they gathered data about a concept they conceptualized as self-neglect, and they expected it to be negatively related to the ability to cope with stress. When they analyzed their data, they found that the relationship was positive rather than negative. Their analysis of this unanticipated finding suggested that the usual way social scientists think about sacrifice is to view it negatively, but their data confirmed that decreasing the emphasis on self while focusing on sacrificing and serving tends to be helpful (Pargament et al., 1998, pp. 86–87). A narrative from a Hurricane Katrina survivor in a study by one of the authors captures this idea:

> [A]fter the storms . . . the main thing that I can see that actually has come out of it for me is . . . it has been a humbling experience and it has changed my life in a way that I really can't even explain. [H]elping [other] people, that [is what] helped me to cope. . . . I took on so much other stuff helping other people [that] it kind of drowned out what I was going through and God fixed it. So while I was trying to fix somebody else['s situation], God was fixing *mine*. I . . . just continued to stay in prayer and helped those that needed help [and in the process, God helped me]. (Silva, Marks, & Cherry, 2009, p. 236)

In a review of the relatively limited research on sacrifice, Impett, Gable, and Peplau (2005) observed that several studies found that sacrifice was positively related to "a variety of relational benefits, including increased satisfaction and a greater likelihood of persistence over time" (p. 327). A later study by Stanley et al.

(2006) provided additional evidence about the relationship between a peripheral aspect of sacrificing and marital adjustment and distress. The Stanley team gathered data from 38 married couples about their satisfaction with sacrifice, and these data discriminated between couples who became distressed versus nondistressed over time. Sacrifice attitudes predicted the maintenance of relationship adjustment over time even better than earlier relationship adjustment.

In addition to the empirical research, several essays argue for the significance of sacrifice. For example, Boulding (1973) suggested from an economic perspective that "grants," a form of sacrifice, influence identity and commitment (pp. 28–30). Additionally, Myers (1983) argued from an anthropological point of view that sacrifice promotes solidarity and morality—and that it changes the nature and quality of relationships.

The contextual theory developed by Böszörményi-Nagy and Spark (1973) and expanded later (Böszörményi-Nagy, 1987) argues that the sacrifices parents and others in earlier generations make for people create "invisible loyalties," and when people behave in ways that are consistent with these loyalties by sacrificing to create good families for their children (and otherwise helping the next generations) they have harmony and effectiveness in their lives. Böszörményi-Nagy further argued that considerable human pain and pathology result when people fight or ignore the reality of these loyalties. More recently, Bahr and Bahr (2009) have similarly argued that sacrifice is "a powerful source of human bonding and community solidarity" (p. 10).

To summarize, there is a modest amount of research about the relationship between sacrificing and family functioning, and the research supports the validity of the principle; but few of the studies have measured the actual amount of sacrificing. Most have focused on some type of sentiment about sacrificing. For example, studies have focused on participants' (a) perceptions regarding sacrifice, (b) satisfaction with sacrifice, (c) willingness to sacrifice, and (d) perceptions that sacrifice is not harmful. These phenomena seem to be close enough to the amount of sacrifice that they are relevant, and they provide some evidence for the principle. But, as Stanley et al. (2006) suggested, "the links between sacrifice-related *sentiments* and [actual] sacrificial *behaviors* is a matter to be teased apart in future research" (p. 291, emphasis added).

Figure 4.2 provides a visual picture of the ways the existing literature suggests sacrificing helps in families. This figure does not show the cyclic patterns in the way many of these processes probably influence each other because it highlights just the aspects of family dynamics that seem to be influenced by sacrifice. These ideas do not have a large amount of data that support them because we are still in the early stages of trying to understand these complicated relationships, but we hope this theorizing will stimulate new research and theories about these ideas, and that it will lead to additional refinements, improvements, and expansion of these tentative beginnings.

New Research After we became aware of the idea that sacrifice is helpful in families, we found ourselves gathering data in a variety of ways to see if we could acquire additional evidence that argued for or against the validity

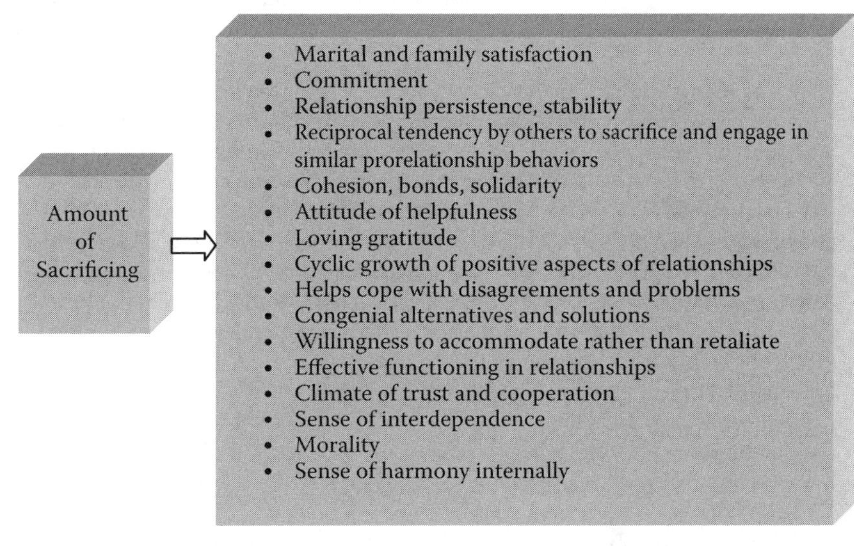

Figure 4.2 Ways research suggests that sacrifice helps families.

of this idea. This led us to reflect on experiences we have observed in our own families, and we have found many situations that argue for it and illustrate its validity. The following example illustrates some of the beneficial effects sacrifice can have:

> Our second son had muscular dystrophy. We watched his muscles become weaker and weaker until he passed away at the age of 23. It was challenging in a lot of ways to see his body gradually become weaker, and it demanded more than a few sacrifices from us as parents and also from his brothers and sister. I remember one day when he was in the third grade and his older brother was in the fifth grade. Their elementary school was about four blocks from our home. Steve wore braces at the time, and could still walk, but as I looked out the window, I saw Ken carrying Steve on his shoulders. I was so touched as I watched. And, after they were home I told Ken how I appreciate how he helped Steve. His comment was, "Well . . . he's my brother." Steve's illness helped all of us learn patience, service, caring, consideration, and love . . . and also appreciation and gratitude in ways we wouldn't have without it. At the time we were highly involved with coping with his illness, we were more aware of the sadness of his situation and the challenges it brought than the blessings; but as the years have passed, we have come to better understand the many blessings his illness brought to our family. Even though there were many difficult sacrifices during those years, the blessings he and his situation brought were so much more important that we cherish the opportunity we had to have him in our home.

A different situation in one of our families further illustrates the ways sacrificing can bring blessings. After one of our fathers turned 90, he wasn't able to do as much for himself and needed more and more care. In the words of his daughter:

> He was living in a retirement center, but as he got weaker they didn't have the resources to provide the help he needed. We thought about having him move to a facility that could provide more care, but eventually decided that as a family that we would take turns to always have someone be at the home at mealtime to help dad eat. One brother volunteered to coordinate having someone there, and he was the one who came most of the time. This lasted for about 4 years, until Dad passed away, and as I look back on that time, it was a wonderful blessing for all of us. It was an opportunity for us to show our love for him. He had always been such a loving and caring person all his life, and we then had a situation where we could help care for him. And, he was so appreciative of what we did. It took some time out of our schedules, and sometimes it was a challenge to find someone who could be there for every meal, but these previous experiences during that stage of his life and our lives helped our love and his love grow.

As these stories illustrate, the meaningful and influential aspects of sacrifice are often not the task itself, but the beauty in the care and motive behind it. If the driving motivation is unfettered love, then even experiences such as spoon-feeding an aged father can be "wonderful blessing[s]" and cherished and precious memories.

Continuing on the path of motives and purity of intentions, we briefly turn to an additional example from the family of one of the authors:

> My grandpa was among the most generous and considerate persons I have ever met. After he passed away, I was looking at a thought book that contained several detailed, handwritten notes. It contained a discussion of the story of the Good Samaritan (Luke 10:30–37). Two "religious" men passed by a wounded victim who had fallen among thieves—but the last, a "lowly" Samaritan, bound the man's wounds, provided all the care he could, and then paid for additional care as well. Grandpa had identified three attitudes in this story: 1) The thief: "What is yours is mine, if I can take it" (Grandpa called this mindset *Offense*); 2) The priest: "What is mine is mine, if I can keep it" (Grandpa called this mindset *Defense*); and 3) The Samaritan: "What is mine is yours, if you need it" (Grandpa called this mindset *No Fence*). Twenty years later, the depth of Grandpa's words still strikes me. He had "no fence" around his property when it came to helping those in need.

Our interviews have also provided additional evidence for the validity and importance of this principle. One of the fathers we interviewed described how sacrifices he was asked to make for his family helped him as a father:

> When I was in high school, my brother was handicapped and was in a wheelchair. During the day he sometimes needed to go to the bathroom, so we agreed I would meet him at a certain time at the restroom and I would help him because he needed to be lifted out of his chair and held while he was on

> the toilet. We did this each noon, so I was always late getting to the lunch room to be with my friends, but I didn't really mind.
>
> Now as a father, I realize that the service to my brother helped me learn a lot of patience. I am not a slow person. I'm a very hyper and fast personality, and these experiences helped me learn how to slow down and help others; and now several members of my family need help in several ways, and I think that the way I now interact with my family is totally different because of the sacrifices I had to make in our family as I was growing up. I am a much better father and I am closer to my children because of those experiences.

The choice to commit time and energy to a child is often a sacred choice that involves the giving of self. For a few of the parents we interviewed, whose children's lives had hung in the balance for a period of time, this commitment seemed particularly vital. Ethan, whose son Bryce eventually received a heart transplant that saved his life, recalled this challenging incident:

> When Bryce had his fifth open heart surgery, he really had a hard time keeping his heart beating. Bryce just wouldn't settle down to keep his neck still and so they were essentially going to have to put him back on the ventilator, which is an awful experience. Bryce hates it. Well, they called me. It was about midnight. We had been at the hospital all day and they said, "Bryce's gonna have to settle down or we're going to have to put him out." And I said, "You can't do that. It would just destroy him emotionally." He was really kind of at his limit. So I jumped in the car and rushed up there and said, "What do I have to do to prevent you from putting him under again?" They said, "He has got to hold his head still." So, I held his head, I held his head all night. It was one of the hardest things because he was just groaning. He would go in and out of sleep. It was a long night, but it was a great experience. (Dollahite & Marks, unpublished raw data)

Megan, the daughter of Tom, died of leukemia at age 5 after unsuccessful treatment and lengthy hospitalization. Tom recounted, with considerable emotion, his thoughts about being there for her:

> I was always there for her. Megan got my time. She had leukemia and I was going to make sure that I spent time with her when I wasn't at work. Maybe the hospital is the part we like to forget but can't. When her pain got to the point that she couldn't go to the bathroom, I was the one that did her bedpans for her. She would only let me do it; I was the one that did that. It wasn't a thing for Mom, and she didn't want anybody else in the room. She kicked everybody out of the room; nurses, Mom (Mom had to be outside the door), and I would get the bedpan as best as I could under her bottom without hurting her. Moving the sheets hurt her. It was not a good thing. But she let me do that for her, and I was able to take care of her needs, and it helped me that I was the only one she'd let do it. You wouldn't expect bedpan shuffling to be a wonderful memory, but it was. She trusted me to do my best job not to hurt her, and that was special to me that she let me do that, (Marks & Palkovitz, 2007, pp. 217–218)

Ways Sacrifice Can Be Harmful

The research about the role of sacrifice does not uniformly suggest it is helpful. As Impett et al. (2005) suggested in their review, "Successful relationships require some willingness to set aside personal interests and desires. But, sacrifice cannot always be a useful strategy" (p. 327). They then addressed the question of when it is harmful to place the interests of others ahead of one's own, and they concluded: "Empirical research has shown that subverting one's true wishes and desires in a relationship is associated with increased psychological distress and decreased relationship satisfaction" (p. 327; see also, e.g., Cramer, 2002; Fritz & Helgeson, 1998; Gottman & Krokoff, 1989).

They also pointed out that considerable feminist literature argues that sacrificing is frequently stifling and destructive. Lerner (1985, 1988), Jack (1991), and Jordan (1991) have argued that many women have schemata of how females should behave that include silencing many of their thoughts and feelings, self-negation, paying attention to the needs of others but not themselves, and sacrificing their individual interests—and that these problems are so severe that they can lead to depression. We do not interpret this as a blanket argument against sacrifice in general but against *excessiveness* in sacrifice, and this is a commencement point for us to begin identifying circumstances that help us understand when sacrificing is helpful and harmful. Jack and Dill (1992) found data that provided some support for the idea that excessiveness is harmful. They found a positive relationship between depressive symptoms and the belief that women should act in gender-prescribed ways to maintain romantic relationships, and that doing so is detrimental to their own self and interests. Page, Stevens, and Galving (1996) found the same pattern with males, suggesting that this is not a pattern for just females and that excessive sacrificing, when it does occur, tends to have negative consequences for both males and females. Boulding (1973) also argued that excessive sacrifice is destructive, stating, "sacredness, like every other virtue . . . becomes a vice if there is too much of it . . . up to a point, both sacrifice and sacredness give meaning and significance to human life and are positive values [but they are not helpful in excess]" (pp. 98–99).

This reasoning and data suggest sacrifice is one of the many aspects of family systems where Aristotle's golden mean is also relevant. Sacrifice in moderation tends to have beneficial effects, but when it is excessive it tends to have harmful consequences. Therefore excessiveness is an important contingency that should be included in theory and research about the role of sacrifice.

Whitton et al. (2007; Whitton, Stanley, & Markman, 2002) added the idea that perceptions about sacrifice influence the effects of sacrificing. They theorized that perceptions about the frequency and reciprocity of sacrifice make a difference, as do perceptions about the harmfulness of sacrifice, independent of excessiveness. In some situations, sacrifices are perceived as harmful, and in others they are not. They theorized that the more sacrifices are perceived as harmful, the greater the probability of undesirable consequences such as depression and the lower the probability of relationship effectiveness. The Whitton et al. (2007) study provided more persuasive evidence than the Jack and Dill (1992) study because the Whitton team gathered data from 145 couples about sacrificing *behavior* rather than just beliefs about what people ought to do.

We suspect that these insights about the role of self-neglect and harmfulness should be combined with the ideas discussed earlier about the role of excessiveness with regard to sacrifice. As we try to put these three ideas together, we theorize that moderate levels of self-neglect are helpful, but when the neglect becomes excessive or when the sacrificing is genuinely harmful to family members (for example, with destructive enabling behaviors), the direction of the relationship changes. Sacrificing when there are moderate levels of self-neglect is positively related to family flourishing and negatively related to undesirable consequences, such as stress and depression. However, when the self-neglect is excessive and/or harmful, the sacrificing will at some point correlate negatively with individual mental and physical health, as well as to less flourishing and positive outcomes on a familial level. To extend this concept, "If Mama ain't *healthy*, ain't nobody happy." Strong, healthy parents who are willing to make necessary sacrifices are needed, but silent martyrdom helps no one in the long run.

A series of studies by Neff and Harter (2002) and Impett et al. (2005) suggest another contingency that should be included in theorizing about sacrifice. These authors examined sacrifice from an approach–avoidance motivational perspective (Carver & White, 1994; Gray, 1987). Approach motives "focus on obtaining positive outcomes, such as a partner's happiness or enhanced intimacy," but avoidance motives focus on avoiding "negative outcomes such as conflict, disapproval, or loss of interest in the relationship" (Impett et al., 2005, pp. 328–329; see also Gable & Reiss, 2001). Impett and colleagues suggested that "people may feel differently toward their partners and their relationships, depending on whether they sacrifice for approach or avoidance motives" (pp. 328–329). When they sacrifice to please their partner (an approach motive) this contributes to greater satisfaction from knowing they have cared for and responded to their partner in a loving manner. In contrast, when they sacrifice to avoid disappointing others (an avoidance motive) they tend to feel resentment or other negative emotions that distract from their satisfaction (Impett et al., 2005).

The data in these studies revealed that approach motives for sacrifice were positively associated with personal well-being and relationship quality, but avoidance motives were negatively associated. Sacrificing for avoidance motives was particularly detrimental to the maintenance of relationships over time.

The data from our observations and interviews suggest that there is another contingency that also influences the effects of sacrifice. It is whether the sacrificing is voluntary. When it is voluntary, there are many benefits, but when it is forced, compulsory, or involuntary, we suspect that the positive effects decrease and it brings undesirable things into families such as resentment, resistance, and less cooperative behaviors.

SACREDNESS

Our theory, observations, and interviews suggest another contingency that influences the effects of sacrificing in families. It has to do with the amount the sacrificing is perceived to involve the sacred. When family members give in and go along with another family member's wishes when there are differences of opinion, or when people go out of their way to purchase something for another family member, many people do not view these relatively mundane and routine sacrifices as sacred. However, when family members devote their time and energy to care for a child, spouse, or elderly parent, they may view it as dedication, charity, and love that are parts of a larger view of what is sacred. It can even be viewed as a form of consecration of their life or efforts, and in these circumstances the sacrifices are sanctified.

> The greater the sacredness of sacrificing the more unique, powerful, and salient the effects of the sacrificing on other family processes and valued family outcomes.

Our data suggest that much of the sacrificing that occurs in families does not have a sacred or sacred quality to it, but some of it is sanctified; and when it does involve sanctification Proposition 2 on page 16 is relevant. This proposition asserts that *perceiving parts of family life to be sacred gives them a unique, unusually powerful, and salient influence in families.* This leads to the conclusion that the greater the sacredness of sacrificing, the more unique, powerful, and salient the effects of the sacrificing are on other family processes and valued family outcomes. One example of this difference is in the writings of the concentration camp survivor Viktor Frankl (1984), who recounted:

> [You] may ask me why I did not try to escape what was in store for me after Hitler had occupied Austria. Let me answer by recounting the following story. Shortly before the United States entered World War II, I received an invitation to come to the American Consulate in Vienna to pick up my immigration visa. My old parents were overjoyed because they expected that I would soon be allowed to leave Austria. I suddenly hesitated, however. The question beset me: could I really afford to leave my parents alone to face their fate, to be sent, sooner or later, to a concentration camp, or even to a so-called extermination camp? Where did my responsibility lie? Should I foster my brain child, logotherapy, by emigrating to fertile soil where I could write my books? Or should I concentrate on my duties as a real child, the child of my parents who had to do whatever he could to protect them? I pondered the problem this way and that but could not arrive at a solution; this was the type of dilemma that made one wish for "a hint from heaven" (p. xv).

It was at this point, Frankl explains, that the decision became sacred:

> It was then that I noticed a piece of marble lying on a table at home. When I asked my father about it, he explained that he had found it on the site where the [Nazis] had burned down the largest Viennese synagogue. He had taken the piece home because it was a part of the tablets on which the Ten Commandments were inscribed. One gilded Hebrew letter was engraved on that piece; my father explained that this letter stood for one of the [Ten]

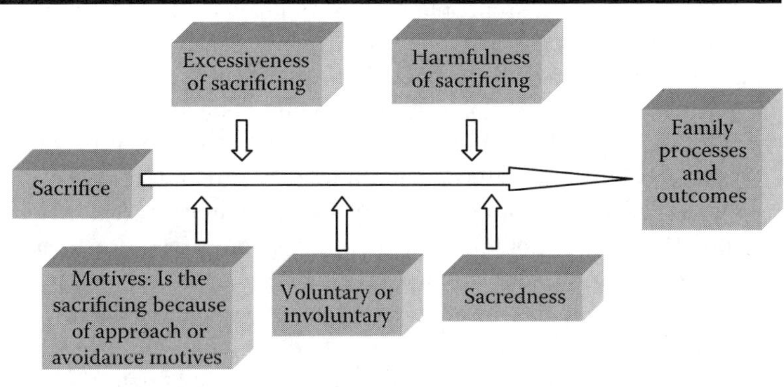

Figure 4.3 Contextual factors that influence the effects of sacrifice.

> Commandments. Eagerly I asked, "Which one is it?" He answered, "Honor thy father and they mother that thy days may be long upon the land." At that moment I decided to stay with my father and my mother upon the land, and to let the American visa lapse. (pp. xv–xvi)

Like Frankl, several people in our interviews suggested that when sacrificing has sacred components, it increased the power of the sacrificing. They indicated that sacrifices that do not involve the sacred tend to have less profound effects, and those that include the sacred tend to have more meaningful, deeper, and more significant effects. It also may be that this occurs for both the beneficial effects of wise sacrificing and the harmful effects of excessive, harmful, and/or involuntary sacrifices.

We do not know of previous research that has studied the differences in the role of sacrificing that is sanctified compared to sacrificing that has little sanctification, so this is another unknown that can be resolved only with future research. We suspect future research will show that it is a helpful distinction, and we describe later in this chapter several reasons why we think this distinction is important and how it makes a difference when we try to understand the effects of sacrificing on family processes and outcomes.

Another aspect of the sacredness of sacrificing is that the scholarly literature about sacrifice is similar to the literature about forgiveness. It tends to ignore the sacred aspects of sacrificing, and thereby has virtually secularized this concept. Part of the irony of this is that the roots of the word *sacrifice* mean to "make sacred," but that meaning has been excised in the scholarly literature. We hope that sacred theory will help the scholarly study of sacrifice refocus on the nature and effects of sacrifice's sacred core (Figure 4.3).

APPLICATIONS

Stanley et al. (2006) suggest that even though we are in the "early phases" of theory and research about the role of sacrifice in family life, there are a number of practical implications in what is known. For example, the research provides a basis for clinicians and educators to help people understand how accommodation, compromise, helping, and assisting, even when it is difficult, can be helpful in marriages and families. Individuals usually, especially in distressed relationships, focus on how their partner can change, and clinicians can encourage a shift in focus to aspects of life that people have more control over than their partner's behavior—such as ways they can give to their partner in meaningful and salient ways.

Also, people can be taught the value of being willing to give unselfishly to their partners; that commitment is not merely "hanging in there through thick and thin," but that commitment coupled with sacrifice can foster not just survival but qualitative improvements. In some ways, the research about sacrifice provides a basis for clinicians who may otherwise feel reticent about emphasizing altruism to teach clients that it can help lead to satisfying and loving relationships that last (Stanley et al., 2005).

The ideas in this chapter have many implications for families and professionals who try to help families. It is likely, however, that these implications are more complex than just encouraging sacrifice in families or teaching people how to value and participate in sacrificing, because they are tied to larger issues in our culture that put a great deal of pressure on people to emphasize individualistic, materialistic, hedonistic, and selfish goals rather than altruistic devotion in families.

Another way of applying the ideas in this chapter has to do with the idea that when sacrificing is perceived to be a part of the sacred, it acquires a unique salience and power. Family life educators can include this idea in courses and encourage students to think about whether this idea has relevance in their personal lives or the lives of others they know. Because it is possible to have theistic and nontheistic reasons to view phenomena as sacred, educators can also have students discuss ways this can be done among those who have theistic reasons and those who do not. Also, when religion is important to clients in therapy, therapists can find ways to help clients understand these ideas and help them explore the possibility that they might find these ideas to be helpful in coping with their challenges. These strategies would need to be carefully and sensitively used, but they may be especially helpful when working with clients who are so caught up in individualism, egoism, and hedonism that they have little appreciation for the value of sacrificing and helping others.

We are not aware of any programs that have been developed by therapists or family life educators to specifically help family members increase their inclination to sacrifice or better understand the contextual factors that influence when sacrificing is helpful or harmful. Based on the ideas in this chapter, however, we hope this will be an area where programs will be developed and tested in the future.

SUMMARY

This chapter discussed the idea that sacrifice in families can be helpful and harmful in families. There is a growing scholarly literature about the nature of sacrifice and the ways it influences family processes and outcomes, and this literature was reviewed and integrated. Additional evidence from our experiences and interviews about the validity and importance of sacrificing was also described.

To summarize, sacred theory suggests there are five contingencies or contextual factors that influence the effects of sacrificing. They are excessiveness, harmfulness, whether the sacrificing is motivated by positive or negative reasons, whether the sacrificing is voluntary or not, and the amount of sanctification. All of these ideas about the role of contingencies rest on very little research and theorizing. Therefore it is important to include them because making them explicit will help us understand where the field is with regard to these ideas at the present time, but it is also important to remain tentative and skeptical about these ideas until additional theorizing and empirical research provide more evidence about them.

5

Loving Others

There are many ways family members can relate to each other. They can be loving or mean. They can treat others as objects to be controlled or conquered. They can be cooperative or competitive. They can be close or distant, empathetic or sympathetic, authoritarian or equalitarian, affectionate or unaffectionate. They can be open to innovations and changes or rigid and closed. They can be critical and demeaning or inspiring and uplifting. They can be gentle and tender or forceful and harsh, consistent and predictable or inconsistent and contradictory, friendly and soft or demanding and cruel, and so forth.

Of all of the many possibilities in the ways family members can relate to each other, there is one way that is a central theme in all of the major world religions; and our observations and interviews suggest that it is very helpful in families. It is the idea that *loving relationships in families increase the probability of successes, and unloving relationships increase the probability of failures.*

According to our data this idea is one of the most important and useful ideas in sacred theory, and it may be the most powerful and important one. It also is so complex and multifaceted that four chapters are devoted to it. We deal with some of the more general aspects of this idea in this chapter, and in Chapters 6 through 8, we discuss some of the less general aspects or facets of what it means to be loving in families.

SOURCES OF THE PRINCIPLE

We encountered this idea first in the Judeo-Christian tradition. When Christ was asked which of his teachings was the most important, he said:

> Thou shalt love the Lord thy God with all thy heart, and with all thy soul, and with all thy mind. This is the first and great commandment. And the second is like unto it, Thou shalt love thy neighbor as thyself. On these two commandments hang all the law and the prophets. (Matthew 22:27–40)

The Golden Rule is one of the ways of encouraging people to be loving, and it is a central idea in most religious traditions. When Confucius was asked by his disciple Tzu Kung "Is there any one maxim which ought to be acted upon throughout one's life?," he replied: "Surely the maxim of charity is such: 'Do not unto others what you would not they should do unto you'" (Giles, 1976, p. 37).

There also are many examples of this idea in the Hindu literature: "Do not to others what ye do not wish done to yourself; and wish for others too what ye desire and long for, for yourself—This is the whole Dharma, heed it well" (Das, 1947, p. 262). In Islam, one of the *hadith* quotes Muhammad as saying: "None of you truly believes until he wishes for his brother what he wishes for himself" (Ibrahim & Johnson-Davies, 1976, p. 56).

This ideal in the religious traditions is a fairly individualistic idea because it deals with people being loving in general. But our data suggest that this notion ought to be generalized to family processes, and it is a simple logical step to make this generalization. Our observations and data suggest that this idea undergirds and provides the basis for a philosophy of life that is profound, helpful, and humane; and it is one of the most important ideas that exists about what helps families flourish.

The teachings in the major world religions are the most original or the basic source as the idea has existed there for centuries, long before modern scholarship and our experiences. But there is another source we also have found meaningful—that is, the idea is also an important theme in literature, poetry, and the arts. It is a central idea in literature as old as Homer's *Odyssey* and in many of Shakespeare's plays. It is in literary traditions throughout the world in works such as Tolstoy's *Anna Karenina*, Browning's "How Do I Love Thee?," and Tyler's *Searching for Caleb*.

As we add this idea to sacred theory in a way that will give it a central role, our first task is the same as with most of the other ideas. We need to define how we are using the main terms.

DEFINING LOVING

There are at least three different strategies in defining and studying love and loving. Two of these approaches have been widely used in the literature, and one of them is rarely used. One of the widely used approaches is a *typological* approach, and it is the strategy used by Bahr and Bahr (2009, Chapter 3) in their attempt to help the study of family become more consistent with what goes on in families. In this strategy, the goals are to improve the understanding of love by describing different types of love. Bahr and Bahr (2009) reviewed a number of earlier typologies such as those by Fromm (1956), Sorokin (1967), May (1969), Berscheid and Hatfield (1978), Sternberg (1988), and Sternberg and Barnes (1997). They then created a three-page table of typologies that is quite complex (pp. 82–84), and is illustrative rather than exhaustive. For example, the table does not include typologies created by Rubin (1973), Powell (1974), Laswell and Lobsenz (1980), or Noller (2005). The number of publications that take this typological approach to conceptualizing love demonstrates that many scholars prefer this strategy.

The Bahr and Bahr (2009) review and analysis is recent, more complex, nuanced, insightful, profound, and more useful than any of the work they review and use. After their review and analysis, they expanded on the earlier work by describing a different type of love, which they called *family love*, and as they described this type or conceptualization of love, they combined "concepts and propositions in questions that may guide research" (p. 116). Their synthesis provides:

> a paradigm of family love, involving three propositions about attributes of love necessary to healthy individual and family life. First, love is accepting, or generous. Second, it is enduring. Finally, it is other-oriented, familial, or altruistic in the sense that it aims to foster the well-being of others . . . The core of this model is the altruism of kinship. The emphasis is not on love as emotion, but rather as a set of moral responsibilities. In this approach, love is action, not mere feeling. (p. 117)

The typological strategy of describing and differentiating between various kinds or types of love is useful because it refines the conceptualization, is intellectually broadening, and provides insights about the complexity and multifaceted nature of love. However, this strategy is also limited because it does not move beyond conceptual issues or aspects of love. It develops concepts, but does not use the conceptualizations to create theoretical ideas and research that have practical value to families who are trying to learn what they can *do* to be effective. The focus on types is also not very helpful to professionals such as therapists and educators who try to help families. The limitations of this strategy are illustrated by how much the various typologies are ignored by later scholars, who just keep adding more and more types—as though more types will be helpful. These limitations of the typological approach have prompted us to prefer a different strategy.

A second strategy that is used extensively in the earlier literature can be called a *descriptive* strategy. The goals in this approach are to do such things as describe what is done in families with regard to the various types or aspects of love, and do comparative research to learn more about social, cultural, or racial differences, about historical changes in love, and/or about differences in the ways people behave in different developmental stages or parts of their life cycle. There is a very large body of literature that uses this approach to conceptualizing and studying love, illustrated by the work of Shorter (1975), Ruddick (1989), and Lakritz and Knoblauch (1999).

The descriptive research approach also has value. It expands insights and increases appreciation for diversity. It also increases understanding of the changes in love, but, like the conceptual approach, it stops short of the value and utility that are added when there are theories that provide testable and useful explanations that can be applied by family members and practitioners who try to help family members improve the quality of their families.

Our goals are to expand and improve the ideas in the previous work by trying to discover and/or create theoretical ideas that provide insights about what family members can *do* or *change* to maximize the probability that their family life will flourish rather than encounter the many different kinds of failure that can occur in families. This means we are seeking ideas that have utility, ideas that family members and professionals can use. Concepts, typologies, descriptive data, and analyses are a helpful foundation in the search for these theoretical insights, but our goals are to add to what they do and to try strategies different from the typological or descriptive approaches because these strategies don't take us very far in dealing with our agenda.

Our agenda therefore leads us to try a third strategy, which is a little different. It can be called a *theorizing* strategy. It relies heavily on clarifying the conceptualization of love or loving, but takes a different approach to creating typologies and doing descriptive research. It focuses on aspects of loving that can vary or change and that make a difference in the probability of families finding successes and failures.

One of the differences in the ways we prefer to conceptualize love and loving is that most of the previous literature has defined and studied love by viewing it as a noun. Most unabridged dictionaries, such as the *Random House Dictionary of the English Language: The Unabridged Edition*, have 20 to 25 different definitions of *love*, and almost all of these definitions denote forms or aspects of love that are nouns that deal with cogitative or emotional aspects of affection, desire, attachment, endearment, or strong liking. These definitions of *love* as a noun focus on what people experience or possess rather than on what they do or can do.

When love is a noun it is something that is possessed. It may lead to action, but the action is a response to what is possessed rather than a form of love that is action. Therefore when love is viewed as a noun, the nature of what is denoted is not inherently a behavior. On the other hand, when love is conceptualized as a verb, it is defined as action or behavior in what is denoted. It is conduct, deeds, and performance. It is things family members do. It deals with behaviors that involve attentiveness, caring with concern, and consideration. It involves a degree of thoughtful striving and watchfulness that includes interest that is active rather than passive. It is engaging and takes effort. It includes a degree of benevolence, unselfishness, solicitude, and kindness in what people do rather than in what they possess or experience; and it has a degree of anxious but not overly anxious involvement.

We suspect that love as a verb (actions or behaviors) is usually intertwined with love as a noun (feelings, experiences, and emotions). We also believe feelings can lead to behaviors and behaviors can lead to the feelings. But even though they can be intertwined—and they frequently are related—it is helpful for several reasons to conceptually separate love as a noun and love as a verb.

One reason this is useful is because many people think of love only as a noun, not as a verb. One way we have seen this is when marriages are in trouble and one of the spouses says something like "I don't love her anymore." This person is seeing the lack of love as a noun and one of the sources of his marital difficulties. In these situations, we have found it useful to help these individuals think about how they "don't love her anymore" by reframing the idea and saying such things as "you don't have love (noun) for him (or her) anymore because you don't love (verb) him (or her) anymore." When many people begin thinking about this difference, it is an "ah ha" moment for them as it helps them realize that one of the reasons they don't have love (noun) for their spouse is at least partly because they have been loving (verb) each other so little.

Another of the reasons we think it is helpful to focus on love as a verb rather than a noun is because it allows the theorizing to focus on variation where changes can be made. For example, Bahr and Bahr (2009) argued that the "type" of love they call family love is accepting, generous, enduring, other oriented, familial, and altruistic. We like their view of love, but prefer to change the conceptualization to focus on the verb aspects of love and its components. Therefore the issue is not that being generous, enduring, other oriented, or altruistic exists or is modal, typical, or even frequent in families. The issue changes to focus on variation in what happens, on how much the family members act in generous, other-oriented, and/or altruistic ways compared to reticent and self-oriented ways and how much they behave in altruistic or hedonistic ways. Even if love in families is generally, mostly, typically, or modally other oriented or altruistic, it is variation in the amount of these phenomena and how the variation influences other family processes and/or valued family outcomes that is important in our theory and research and in therapeutic, educational, and mass-media interventions.

Thus we think the phenomenon that ought to be a cornerstone in sacred theory is *variation in the amount family members are loving and unloving*. We view this as a continuous variable that can be different with different people, can be different in different times and settings, and can vary in subtle degrees or amount. It probably also varies in a number of qualitative ways, but thinking about these qualitative differences extends the thinking beyond where we have been able to go.

There is much that is still to be understood about this variable. For example, it may be that there is just one dimension, which varies between low and high in the amount of loving. Or it may be that loving is like some other aspects of family life in that there are positive and negative aspects. Orden and Bradburn (1968) and Fincham, Stanley, and Beach (2007) have made a persuasive case that there are positive and negative dimensions in several aspects of family life, and this may be one of the areas. If there are two dimensions, one positive and the other negative, it may be that family members can vary or change in the amount they are loving and also independently vary or change in the amount they are unloving. If there is just one dimension, family members who are highly loving are low in unloving behaviors, and those who are high in unloving behaviors are low in loving behaviors. If there are two dimensions, family members can be highly loving and highly unloving in the same family or relationships, or low in the amount they are loving and in the amount they are unloving. Questions such as whether there is one dimension or two separate dimensions are conceptual and empirical issues. They are questions that are not yet answered because we don't yet have research that helps us understand empirically how this plays out in families. These questions and many others about this conceptualization deserve more scholarly attention in the future, but we hope our attempt to describe how we prefer to define this term is clear enough that it is defensible to move to the theoretical ideas, and that it will help stimulate the needed additional research.

THE SCHOLARLY LITERATURE

In Bahr and Bahr's (2009) analysis, they argued that even though love is "'one of the most talked-about and longed-for of human experiences in the Western world' (Henslin, 1980, p. 3)," there has been an ambivalence among social scientists about studying love (pp. 70–71). Some prominent scholars such as Comte (Pickering, 1997), Goode (1959), and Sorokin (1967) have argued it is important, but "the scholarly neglect of love is a long-term pattern" (Bahr & Bahr, 2009, p. 87).

This pattern continued through most of twentieth century, but research about love has increased in recent decades. However, most of this emerging research, especially the study of "close relationships," which have been studied the most, focuses on romantic love, love as a noun rather than love as a verb, typologies, and descriptive and comparative analyses. This means that most of the emerging research is not very valuable in the type of theory construction we think is the most effective.

There is, however, a body of research that is more closely tied with loving as a verb than most scholars realize. The research team led by John Gottman for several decades provided a number of valuable insights about factors that are predictive of marital stability and adjustment. Most of the discussion of the findings by Gottman's group has stayed fairly close to their data. However, there is one instance where Gottman dealt with more abstract ideas by linking empirical observations with important theoretical ideas:

> In our study of long-term marriages we recruited couples from a wide range of backgrounds who had been married twenty to forty years to the same partner. Despite the wide differences in occupations, lifestyles, and the details of their day-to-day lives, I sense a remarkable similarity in the tone of their conversations. No matter what style of marriage they have adopted, their discussions, for the most part, are carried along by a strong undercurrent of two basic ingredients: love and respect.
>
> These are the direct opposite of—and antidote for—contempt, perhaps the most corrosive force in marriage. But all the ways partners *show each other love and* respect also ensure that the positive-to-negative ratio of a marriage will be heavily tilted to the positive side. (Gottman, 1994a, pp. 61–62)

The Gottman team focused most of their attention on concepts that are low in abstraction and close to their data. For example, they highlighted emotional flooding, ratios of positive and negative exchanges, and what they called the "Four Horsemen of the Apocalypse" (Gottman, 1994b, p. 72–77)—criticism, contempt, defensiveness, and stonewalling—but they recognized that these more specific behaviors are aspects of love and respect. We agree with this inference and believe this research is the most valuable so far in arguing for the validity and importance of the idea that loving in families has a powerful influence on other family processes and outcomes.

Even though there has been little research about the ways loving helps families, there have been a number of scholars who have theorized or written essays about the role of loving in family. Magoun (1948) focused on love as a verb and argued that it is important in helping families be successful. His volume was an analytic essay rather than an empirical study or review of empirical literature, but he provided persuasive arguments that loving others helps families thrive.

Fromm's (1956) volume *The Art of Loving* explores the nature of loving generally. His book focused primarily on the role of loving in mental health and in society in general, but part of his essay is about the importance of loving in families. His conceptualization and emphasis on loving rather than love is one of the reasons the focus in our theory is on loving as a verb rather than love as a noun.

Others who wrote essays about the importance of loving in families are Sorokin (1967), Jourard (1971), Boulding (1973), Powell (1974), and Guerney (1977). Each of them argued that loving is an important ingredient in family success, but they did not provide empirical data about these relationships.

As we have looked for literature that focuses on this principle, we find it interesting and intriguing that we have not discovered any literature where scholars have dealt with the sources of this idea. No one has bothered to discuss its basis or origins. It is as though those who have written about this idea assume it is so obvious and uncontroversial that it is self-evident.

The small amount of research about loving behavior means there is a great deal about the role of loving that is yet to be discovered by scholarly inquiry. For example, we have no information about whether this relationship is linear or curvilinear. We have little evidence about how powerful this relationship is, or how contextual factors or other contingencies influence the relationship in the principle. Hopefully, there will be considerable new research about these issues in the future.

New Research

Our observations in our extended families and our interviews have provided a few additional insights about this principle. We have observed many situations where loving behaviors help create successes and how unloving behaviors contribute to failures. The following examples from our families illustrate the advantages of being loving and the costs of being unloving:

> Being right was so important to my Dad. It didn't matter what was brought up or what was happening, he had to be right. Sometimes he'd hold on to things he said when it was obvious he was in the wrong. Everybody knew it, but he'd never admit it. Being right was a lot more important than being kind and thoughtful, and he alienated a lot of members of the family with his tenacious need to never be in the wrong—no matter what. Some of his grandchildren can't stand him and won't come to any family gatherings when he is there because they dislike him so much.

❖❖❖❖❖❖❖❖❖❖❖❖❖❖❖❖❖❖❖❖❖❖❖❖❖❖❖❖

> Sometimes our family kinda gets impatient with one another, and some will get in a foul mood, and everybody's kinda quarrelsome; and Eric will disappear, and he'll reappear later, and he won't say anything, and come to find out whoever was having a hard day will find that their bed has been made. It is usually the bed, and it is just a sign of compassion and love and helping someone who is having a hard time. This has helped us to be a close and loving family.

Our interviews and observations in classrooms, enrichment settings, and therapeutic settings also argue for the validity of this principle. For example, the following comments from interviews illustrate this idea:

> My dad was a very charitable man. Whenever we would go up to Idaho Falls to visit him, he would always have a pizza waiting for us waiting ready to go, or some French fries ready for us. It was his way of thinking about us and being thoughtful and trying to make things enjoyable for others. He would also always send us away with a little bag of goodies. He'd say "You can't open this until you get down to Shelly." That was his way of having fun with us. He always had something for the kids to take home with them, so we are all endeared to him because he was so thoughtful and gentle.

****

> My father was such a loving man. As I was growing up, he had two sisters who were widows, and he would call them every week. Every Sunday night he was on the phone with his sisters, finding out how they were doing. And when my grandmother was elderly and feeble he wanted to help her and care for her. Usually, daughters are the ones to bring them into their home, but my dad was the one to bring grandma into our home, and he cared for her for several years. My dad's love of family and his charity toward them has made me a different person. I'm not as charitable a person as he is. I'd like to be and try to be. It made me want to be like him more.

****

> My sister was in the kitchen and we were talking and telling stories and my little brother was at the dinner table, and my brother asked her to grab him a cookie. Without even thinking or hesitating, she went over and got it and gave it to him. In contrast, I was at a friend's house and the same situation happened. Her brother wanted something, and she said, "No. Get it yourself. You've got two good legs." Her response then led to some contention and arguing. I was impressed with how my sister was so kind and charitable. She was just living the Golden Rule. I think that sort of thing has helped the members of our family have a lot of love for each other. We're all best friends. We trust each other and enjoy being around each other.

****

> With my family, one of the things that stands out is the way my Dad is so loving to my Mom and to his family. He loves them more than anything. I've never seen my Dad and Mom fight or argue, and to me that is just amazing. A lot of the time the world teaches us about being the "man of the house" and my Dad is always willing to help with the chores. When my Mom asks him to do something, sometimes not in the nicest way, he always responds in a nice way. He doesn't think he has to be "the man" or the "big tough guy." This has really helped our family because the way he acts just takes any contention or fighting right out of the home, and we have a lot of closeness and love. I've learned from him to not ever say something that I'll regret.

WAYS LOVING IS HELPFUL

Thus there is a little empirical literature that argues for the validity and importance of this principle even though there are a number of essays that encourage family members to be loving. However, we have not found attempts to describe which aspects of family processes and outcomes are influenced by loving and unloving relationships. This is therefore a different situation than the chapters on forgiveness, asking, and sacrifice because there has been enough research about these other three principles that it is possible to begin theorizing about the aspects of family life that are influenced by differences or variation in them. This means that anything we say in this chapter about which aspects of marriage and family are influenced the most by loving behaviors is moving into uncharted territory.

We suspect that loving influences some aspects of family life more than others. For example, it is likely that variation in loving patterns makes more difference in the ability of family members and tendency of family members to listen to and appreciate differences in opinion and find constructive ways of dealing with conflict and disappointments than the parts of family life that have little to do with relationships, such as the rationality of economic decisions, but it may indirectly have some influence on them because it probably helps increase harmony and cooperation.

We suspect from our data that the amount family members are loving is one of the most powerful factors in influencing the probability of families finding successes and failures. We can't imagine anything that is more powerful. We have examined all of the theories that are widely used in family studies, and they identify many phenomena that are helpful. For example, systems theory argues that boundary maintenance and consistency in communication are helpful. Adler theorized that encouragement is helpful. Bowen theorized that differentiation is helpful, and symbolic interaction theorizes that consensus and effective role performance are helpful. All of these ideas and all of the other ideas in the existing theories are helpful, but we also believe that in most families the influence of these other factors on the probability of families finding successes and failures pales in comparison to the influence of variation in the amount family members are loving to each other.

To try to understand how loving and the lack of it influences other family processes and outcomes, we reviewed our observations of our own families and went through the notes and transcripts from our interviews. These reviews of our data reconfirmed our belief that both differences between people and changes in the amount of loving, especially when loving is absent and is replaced by other ways of relating, have an important impact on a large number of processes and outcomes in most families. Figure 5.1 summarizes the major patterns we have observed and that have been described in our interviews.

Loving is also so multifaceted and complex that there are many components or aspects to it. Chapters 6 through 8 discuss 17 of the less general components of loving, and they are all related to each other in complex ways. For example, when family members are forgiving, merciful, respectful, and patient, these qualities enhance and enrich other aspects. Also, conversely, when family members are not

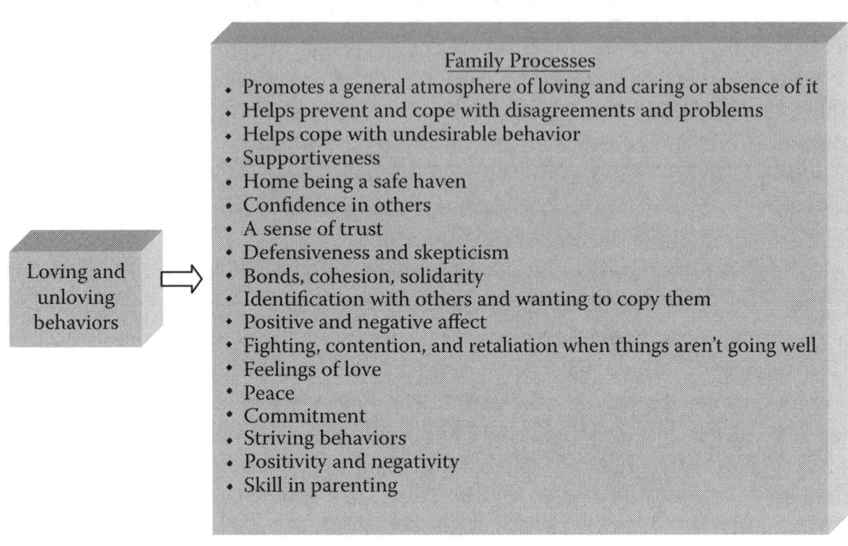

Figure 5.1 Family processes influenced by the amount of loving.

loving with any of the 17 aspects of loving, this undoubtedly interferes with the amount of loving in other aspects. For example, when family members have a pattern of impatience or lack of respect, these patterns interfere with other things such as forgiveness, trying to create unity, and kindness.

WAYS LOVING CAN BE HARMFUL

We mentioned earlier (p. 22–23) that there are at least four ways aspects of the sacred can be harmful. One of these is that aspects they sometimes simultaneously create desirable and undesirable outcomes. The second is that family members can misunderstand religious teachings or get carried away with them in ways that lead to excesses or extreme ways of behaving that are harmful. The third way is that some ideals and beliefs about the sacred can advocate ways of behaving that create harm.

We do not know of any previous literature that has focused on the ways loving others can be harmful in families. Also, we don't have any data about ways sacred teachings advocate unloving behaviors. However, it is likely that the first two ways aspects of the sacred can be harmful can and do create harm and problems in loving relationships.

We have little information about these negative aspects. But all human relationships are eventually disrupted and involve loss, and the greater the joy and beauty that has been involved, the greater the sense of pain and agony when the time of loss happens. Also, part of the reality and complexity of life is that there are problems, frustrations, and failures in even the best of relationships, and when these occur and there has been extraordinary joy and beauty, it is inevitable that there will be a proportionally greater sense of distress and anguish. The findings in the study by Krumrei et al. (2009) focused on divorce, but if the ideas are generalized beyond just what happens with divorce, it may be that these negative aspects of relationships are not entirely harmful because they also are an important part of living. They also can help in other ways by producing such things as growth, determination, and commitment, but all of the negative aspects of them cannot be avoided. It may also be that when relationships involve the sacred this provides an additional richness and perspective, which may help in coping with loss and failures. But the sacred also may make the negatives more intense when they occur, and it can't prevent them. These ideas appeared in some of our interviews and also are in the ideas suggested in some of the earlier literature (Krumrei et al., 2009; Mahoney et al., 2001, 2003).

SACREDNESS

There is variation in how much family members view loving as sacred. To some it is an integral part of the sacred, whereas to others it is a desirable way to live and relate but not particularly sacred. This raises the issue of whether loving is different when it is sacred and when it is not, and whether this makes a difference in families.

There is a growing literature about sanctification in families, and it provides evidence that when family members view any aspect of family life as sacred, it leads to benefits and also sometimes costs for individuals and relationships.[1] The first four propositions in sacred theory provide additional insights about these relationships because they theorize that when family members view loving as a part of the sacred, it has a unique salience and power. These propositions also provide insights about when the sacredness is helpful and harmful.

On the basis of the research about sanctification and the four general principles in sacred theory, we believe that when family members view loving as sacred, this increases the power and salience of the loving compared to those who do not view it as sacred. Unfortunately, we did not focus on this question in our interviews and observations. We were so involved in other aspects of loving that all of our attention was devoted to other issues. For example, we paid considerable attention to

[1] The main contributors to the research and theorizing about sanctification have been Mahoney et al. (1999, 2001, 2003); Mahoney, Pargament et al. (2005); Mahoney, Rye, and Pargament (2005); Murray-Swank et al. (2005); Krumrei et al. (2009); Pargament and Mahoney (2005); and Mahoney (2010). We like and use the ideas in this literature, but there are some problems with the conceptualization. We prefer a slightly different terminology that is less problematic. The word *sanctification* is a verb that means "to sanctify," and this means it describes the process of creating sacredness. A different view is that sacredness exists prior to family members discovering it and experiencing it, and, according to this alternative view, people do not sanctify. Pargament (2007) used this alternative view in his chapter about the discovery of sacredness because he described how people "discover" rather than create the sacred. Therefore we suggest that future scholarship in this area will be more precise and have fewer complicating problems that result from the terminology if the term sanctification is replaced with terms like sacred, sacredness, and sacred matters.

the ways loving is conceptualized, to creating and clarifying the proposition that loving is an influential powerful part of family processes, to identifying and clarifying the components of what it means to be loving, and to comparing the nature and effects of loving and nonloving ways of behaving. But we did not get to the question about how variation in sacredness makes a difference. This is therefore another of the many areas where additional research is needed.

APPLICATIONS

The ideas in this chapter can be applied in many ways. However, the main principle here has an intermediate level of generality. This is illustrated visually in Figure 1.1 on page 32. That figure shows that Proposition 5, the principle discussed in this chapter, is more general than Propositions 6–22, whose principles are discussed in the next three chapters—Chapters 6 through 8. What this means is that the ideas discussed in the next three chapters are the ways of applying the idea that loving relationships are helpful in families.

However, in addition to the more specific ideas about application that are discussed in Chapters 6 through 8, there are some issues about applying the ideas in this chapter that ought to be described in this chapter. One of these is that there are some ideas in modern cultures that advocate values, ideals, and lifestyles that are very different from the lifestyle advocated by the ideas in this chapter. These other philosophies compete with the philosophy that loving relationships in families are helpful. Some of these other philosophies are the excessive versions of individualism, materialism, a gain ethic, high concern with such aspects of the self as self-esteem, hedonism, and an exchange orientation in relationships. One way to apply the ideas in this chapter is to realize that these other philosophies are attractive in many ways, but they also contribute to the toxicity of the environment for effective family life. They interfere with what is important in creating effective families.

In some ways it would be desirable to discuss the role of these competing ideas in this chapter, but many of the ideas in Chapters 6 through 12 also deal with these competing ideas. Therefore it seems wise to defer the discussion of the competing ideas until Chapter 13 (pp. 213–231).

The application of the ideas in this chapter is challenging in another way, which is illustrated by the suggestion Bellah et al. (1985) made about applying these ideas—that is, that the solution to the problem of excessive individualism that leads people to behave in selfish rather than loving ways is to change what they call "the habits of the heart." Their proposal about the way to accomplish these changes is to change the social mores so there is a communitarian orientation wherein there is greater emphasis on civic responsibilities, citizenship volunteerism, and social involvement.

In Bellah et al. (1985) there is a chapter that discusses how more attention ought to be given to love and marriage, but there is an important difference in the way they use the term love and the way we are using the term loving in sacred theory. Their view of love is that love is a noun—something that is acquired, experienced, and felt—but not a verb.

The solutions suggested by the Bellah team have a certain appeal when they are viewed superficially and without attention to the differences between love as a noun and loving as a verb. Sacred theory suggests a slightly different view about the nature of the problem and the changes that are needed to moderate the excesses of the extreme versions of individualism. We think that trying to change the social mores that prescribe civic responsibilities, citizenship volunteerism, and social involvement is focusing on fairly superficial rather than fundamental aspects of the situation, and focusing on these communitarian goals will have little effect on excessive individualism or its consequences for society, freedom, or family life.

Individualism is qualitatively different from phenomena such as social mores, communitarian sensibilities, civic responsibilities, citizenship volunteerism, and social involvement. Individualism is a complex set of values that runs much deeper in the human mind and heart, and it is a multifaceted value system that is based on some of the most fundamental assumptions that are made about humanity. These fundamental assumptions that are the intellectual bedrock on which individualism rests deal with the nature of humanity—and in an ultimate sense, the meaning of life and existence—and sacred theory suggests that focusing on ways of changing the habits of the heart in family life so family members emphasize loving ways of relating with each other may be a more fruitful way to cope with the problems created by excessive individualism.

SUMMARY

This chapter discussed the difference between defining love as a noun and verb, and suggested that when love is defined as a verb it provides important insights about family processes. The main idea in the chapter is that loving relationships in families help them find successes and avoid failures, and unloving relationships decrease the probability of finding successes and increase the probability of failures. The next three chapters describe less general ideas that are derived from or components of the principle in this chapter and can help families thrive.

6

Aspects of Loving

As we try to understand the nature of loving and its role in families, our observations and interviews suggest that the concept is complex and multifaceted, and that loving also is a fairly general and abstract term. This means it includes a large number of less abstract components, facets, or aspects. For example, it includes kindness and concern for the welfare of others. It also includes respect for others and their ideas, feelings, interests, and wishes; and an interest in the welfare of others rather than just an interest in one's self. It includes thoughtfulness and integrity rather than hypocrisy, and a service orientation toward others. It also involves respect for the agency of others rather than trying to manipulate and control others for one's benefit. It includes trying to create unity with others and peacemaking rather than contention. It includes patience and cooperation, and bridling negative affect so it does not lead to aggressive, mean, and demeaning behaviors. It includes a desire to repent of mistakes that harm others and to forgive and seek forgiveness, and it includes mercy and compassion rather than rejection and condemnation. It also includes a desire to help those who are less fortunate and disenfranchised.

It is our experience that most of the time these many aspects of loving operate in a fairly unified or coherent way. This means that when individuals and/or families are loving, they tend to be loving in a number of different ways. For example, being kind, caring, considerate, respectful, thoughtful, gentle, and compassionate tend to go together; and when individuals and families are unkind, uncaring, inconsiderate, disrespectful, thoughtless, cruel and abusive, these ways of behaving also tend to occur as a set. It is as though these many aspects of being loving and unloving are parts of a larger philosophy or attitude toward life, and they tend to feed on and facilitate each other.

However, even though these many aspects of loving tend to go together, there are some families in which some of these components of what it means to be loving vary independently of the others, and when this happens it is important. For example, it is possible for some family members to be loving in many ways but not be respectful, patient, or forgiving. Because bad things tend to be more powerful than good things (as described on pp. 48–50), it is likely that when family members are not loving in one or two of these ways, it is disproportionately disruptive in families.

Because loving and unloving are such complex and multifaceted processes, and they have so many facets, it would take more than just one chapter or even a few chapters to be thorough. It would take many books and probably many lifetimes. Therefore the best we can do in this first attempt to describe sacred theory is to focus on a manageable cluster of the aspects of loving and try to expand and improve the theorizing about these aspects.

After thinking more than a little about the strategies we could use in this first attempt to integrate, expand, and improve ideas about the role of loving in families, and also talking with a lot of people about what they think is involved in loving, we decided to focus on a working list of 17 aspects of loving. The discussion of these 17 aspects is divided into three chapters. Six aspects are discussed in this chapter. They are (a) kindness and unkindness, (b) respect, (c) self-interest and interest in others, (d) integrity, (e) service, and (f) respect for freedom and responsibility.

Chapter 7 deals with five other aspects of loving that seem to be important in general but also seem particularly relevant when families are coping with disagreements. They are (a) trying to create consensus, (b) peacemaking rather than contention, (c) patience, (d) cooperation rather than competition, and (e) wise and unwise ways of dealing with negative emotions.

Chapter 8 discusses five more aspects of loving that we think are important generally, but that also are particularly relevant when families are coping with undesirable behavior. They are (a) repentance, (b) mercy, (c) compassion, (d) avoiding reciprocity, and (e) helping.

KINDNESS AND UNKINDNESS

Our observations and data suggest that *kindness* is one of the important components of loving, and *unkindness* is not just the inverse of kindness. It is a separate process that is one of the components of unloving ways of relating. Kindness can be defined as acting toward others in considerate and benevolent ways rather than mean and hurtful ways. It also means being gentle and compassionate rather than cruel or harsh. It is being humane and tender rather than aggressive and disparaging. It is being sensitive to the needs and desires of others rather than insensitive. It is being friendly and helpful rather than domineering and hostile. It is being charitable and altruistic, with the intention of benefit rather than profit, and it is motivated by a desire to do good. Unkindness is doing the opposite things.

The generalization we think is true and important and that summarizes the theoretical idea about kindness and unkindness is that *kindness helps families flourish, and unkindness is damaging in families.*

Evidence

There are three different sources of evidence about this principle. They are religious literature, previous research, and new data from our observations and interviews. We turn first to the religious literature.

The words *kindness* and *unkindness* are not used extensively in the literature of the major world religions, but the idea is pervasive. Also, kindness in this literature is mostly an individualistic idea, but it is also seen in family processes. For example, unkindness in the behavior of Esau's two sons caused devastating problems in that family. The resentments in their relationship were passed down to later generations, and have even became serious international problems for millennia. The unkindness of 11 of Jacob's sons toward the favored son Joseph (and perhaps his insensitivity to them) created serious problems in that family, and these problems too were passed down to later generations. The kindness and unkindness in the story of Ruth, Naomi, and Boaz illustrate ways kind behaviors also influence other aspects of family processes.

There is almost no research in the scholarly literature about the role of kindness and unkindness in families. The only research we have been able to find is a series of studies by Lee et al. (1997). When Lee and his colleagues revised the Family Profile instrument (Lee & Goddard, 1989), they separated the two concepts of kindness and unkindness and developed scales for each of them. The reason they separated these two concepts is because the factor analyses of their data consistently indicated that kindness and unkindness are separate factors that have considerable independence.

Their study also found that kindness and unkindness were both predictive in regression models of several different types of family success. They gathered data about family satisfaction, school performance, substance abuse, juvenile crime, and conflict; and "the strongest predictor across all areas was the Unkindness scale" (Lee et al., 1997, p. 470). This study provided evidence about two of the ideas in sacred theory: the independence of positive and negative family processes, and that kindness and unkindness are strongly related to the ability of families to find successes and avoid failures.

Our observations and interviews about the effects of kindness and unkindness lead us to theorize that these two variables have a number of beneficial and harmful effects in families. Our data suggest that kindness and unkindness influence how well families cope with disagreements and undesirable behavior, and the amount of confidence and trust in families. They influence the warmth and the amount of positive and negative affect. They influence the amount of defensiveness and skepticism, and the amount family members identify with and want to copy others. These patterns are seen in stories such as the following that have been shared in our interviews:

> My mother was the kindest person I ever knew. It didn't matter how bad the children or others acted, she was always nice. Even when she had to punish one of the children, she would explain that she loved them, and tell them it was what they had done that was bad, not them as a person. She was the greatest example of kindness I've ever seen, and we've tried to be just like her in our family. It hasn't always been easy, and we haven't succeeded as much as she did, but her ways of treating others have helped us cope with differences, solve problems, and find ways to be close to each other as we have faced a number of challenges.

Kindness also helps reduce negative behaviors in families such as fighting, contention, and retaliation when things aren't going well, as illustrated by the following example:

> Sometimes one of us gets bumped in the hall, and sometimes we bump the other person back or yell at them and it turns into a fight. Other times the one who gets bumped gives them the benefit of the doubt and everything blows away. Everything is fine, and you forgive each other. "Whatever" is a good word because it helps you just blow it off and not say anything. Also, when someone says something and you don't agree with it, you can say, "Oh whatever. I'll let you think that." Or, you could just blow it off because most things aren't a big deal and don't matter that much.

Some of the other beneficial effects of kindness are that it helps create bonds that have tenderness and beauty rather than bondage, as illustrated by the following situation:

> It was so enjoyable being around my brother, Harold. He was so gentle and was always interested in those around him. He didn't just ask how you were. He'd listen intently to what you had to say, nodding often and usually had his head turned just slightly and was looking right at you, like one does when they are concentrating and are raptly involved. He'd smile and comment and often asked questions to make sure he was understanding. [Also], if someone had a special talent or a problem that had been shared at an earlier time, he'd remember them and be interested in them. When I think about what Heavenly Father is probably like, he is the first one that comes to mind, soft and gentle, loving and kind, fair and thoughtful, accepting and understanding.

Figure 6.1 summarizes the best information we have about the ways kindness and unkindness influence family processes and outcomes. There is still only a small amount of evidence for these ideas, so they should be viewed as speculative, tentative, and preliminary at best. Hopefully, future research will provide more insights about these relationships and explore the likelihood that kindness and unkindness also influence other aspects of family processes and outcomes.

There is a little bit of evidence from the Lee et al. (1997) study that unkindness has more influence on family processes and outcomes than kindness; this is consistent with the truism that it is typically easier to destroy than it is to build. However, we do not know of data that provide information about ways kindness and unkindness influence different aspects of families in different ways. Therefore in Figure 6.1 we have combined kindness and unkindness. If additional research finds ways that they influence things differently, they can be separated in future summaries of these ideas.

Effects on Other Aspects of Loving

As we discuss the 17 aspects of loving, there is a pattern that we came to appreciate in our interviews and as we have analyzed our observations. It is that these 17 aspects tend to be interrelated in the sense that they are parts of a package that

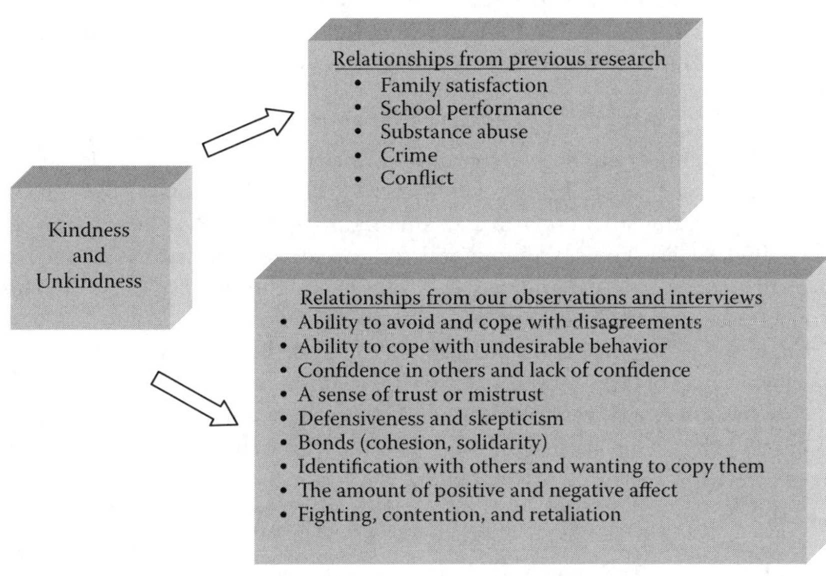

Figure 6.1 Summary of the evidence about ways kindness and unkindness influence families.

is fairly consistent and coherent. This means that even though there are situations where some individuals may not be consistent in how they act, most people are consistent with these 17 processes most of the time, and all of these aspects of loving tend to influence each other. Whenever family members become more loving with regard to any of the aspects of loving, such as becoming more patient or more forgiving, this tends to facilitate and help the other aspects or make them easier. And, conversely, whenever family members become less loving with regard to any of the 17 aspects of loving, this tends to interfere with the other aspects.

One way of thinking about this pattern is to generalize the law or norm of reciprocity a little. This law was developed by Gouldner (1960) and Deutsch (1973), and we mentioned it in our discussion of forgiveness (see p. 43), but the slight generalization of it is to conclude that behavior doesn't just lead to more and less of the same behavior. It also leads to more and less of similar behaviors. Because this pattern seems to occur for each of the 17 factors, we do not repeat this idea as each of the other aspects is discussed.

RESPECT AND DISRESPECT

The Abrahamic religions believe humans were created by God and "in the image" of God (Genesis 1:26–27). This belief in a divine origin and nature means that humans are different from other creatures and they deserve a type of respect that is qualitatively different. This respect can take many forms and has different meanings in different cultures and historical conditions, but it means that both the creation and taking of human life are serious matters, and people ought to interact with each other in ways that show high regard and reverence for others.

Some of the religions that originated in the Eastern cultures go much further than the Abrahamic religions with regard to respect for life generally. For example, the Buddhist concept of *ahimsa* encompasses "refraining from destroying life" of any kind, including such creatures as small animals and even insects (Palmer & Keller, 1993, p. 65). The Abrahamic religions are unique in that the divine origins of humans means they are uniquely different from other forms of life, but this has its roots in the traditions of several of the world religions.

When these religious ideals are applied to family life they suggest that respect is a valuable part of "the good life." Also, in addition to these ideals, our data suggest that the amount of respect family members show for each other is an important part of what it means to be loving. Dictionaries define *respect* as "esteem for or a sense of the worth or excellence of" something. When family members are respectful of each other, there is a certain type of reverence for the ideas, thoughts, and feelings of the other members of the family, and it helps relationships be enjoyable and pleasant. And, conversely, when family members are not respectful of others, many other aspects of family life tend to be more difficult. This pattern in the relationship between respect and family processes and outcomes can be stated in a generalization: *Respect among family members helps families flourish and disrespect disrupts and damages.*

Evidence About the Principle

There is considerable research about the role of respect and disrespect in education (Hajii, 2006) and in legal and political settings (Anderson, 1999; Emler & Reicher, 1995: Kennedy & Forde, 1999; Tyler & Huo, 2002). There is also considerable research about the role of respect in work settings (Tyler & Blader, 2000), negotiation (Cohen, 2002), and group membership and dynamics (De Cremer, 2002; De Cremer & Tyler, 2005). There also are analyses of the role of respect in medicine and in popular literature (Norville, 2009).

Hendrick, Hendrick, and Logue (2010) concluded in their recent review and theoretical essay that "the family science literature has not generally treated respect in any detailed way" and that the "neglect of respect in the study of the family is a significant shortcoming" (p. 126). It was mentioned by Gottman (1994b) when he concluded that married couples typically desire "just two things from their marriage—love and respect" (p. 18), but almost all of his research interests were on more specific behavioral patterns rather than abstract concepts such as love and respect.

Gaines (1994, 1997) studied respect in friendship and romantic pairs and found that reciprocity in respect-giving behaviors was helpful and that "the potential damage that reciprocity of respect-denying behavior may wreak upon many male-female friendships cannot be underestimated" (1994, p. 22). This is another example of how "bad" aspects tend to be more powerful than "good" aspects in relationships. Kline et al. (2008) studied East Asian and American students and found that respect was one of the top five qualities for expressing love in both groups. Feeney et al. (1997) found that respect was correlated with marital quality, whereas Vaux (1987) conceptualized respect a little differently by viewing it as a part of support rather than love.

Several studies have focused on measurement issues and methods. Frei and Shaver (2002) and S. S. Hendrick and Hendrick (2006) developed scales to measure respect in close relationships.

Because there is a limited amount of research about the role of respect and disrespect in families, we know little about their effects. Our observations and interviews, however, provide some impressive evidence in support of the principle. For example, the following situations illustrate several ways the lack of respect disrupts families:

> A couple invited [the husband's] parents to go out to dinner at one of their favorite restaurants. The father responded that they did not like to go out to eat. The mother looked a little sheepish as she said "I like to go out sometimes." The father looked over at her and said, in a fairly demeaning way, and with a look on his face and an attitude that communicated that he thought her comment was ridiculous, "No, you don't." She didn't respond. She'd learned long ago what she needed to do to avoid trouble. The subject was changed, and they didn't go out to eat.

****

> A couple was talking about one of their relatives, and the husband expressed his opinion that he liked one of the people involved. The wife shot back, "You couldn't possibly feel that way."

****

> We have some friends who don't get along very well in their marriage. She thinks he doesn't respect her and her ideas, and he doesn't. He ignores what she says all the time, and writes her off with a smirk and roll of his eyes, and she just hates it. And, it goes both ways. She never has anything nice to say about his opinions, and is just as disrespectful of him. And, what's interesting is they both see how the other one is not respectful, but they don't see it in their own behavior. They both think they are the one who is reasonable and kind doing the things they should, and they think their spouse is the one who is inconsiderate and thoughtless, but they both act the exact same way.

The difference between these examples of disrespect and the following illustration of respectful ways of interacting is dramatic:

> I know a family where the wife was converted to our church right after they were married, but he didn't convert. He stayed with his church. They are both active in their churches, and when one has an event they both go to support the other one. They are now grandparents, so they have lived their entire married life being members of two different churches. When they were in medical school, she worked, and she made donations to her church and they didn't

> make contributions to his, and after he finished medical school and began earning the money they made donations to his church and not hers because she doesn't make the money, and they both are comfortable with that arrangement. The children were all raised in the church the wife goes to, and he was comfortable with that.

Our observations suggest that when family members are respectful, it is usually part of a cluster of other ways of being loving, and that the effects of the respect are helpful but go largely unnoticed. However, when people are disrespectful it is powerful in more visible ways. For example, we have had people tell us in interviews that some members of their family are disrespectful when they are also generally patient, unselfish, and service oriented. In these situations, the disrespect seems to make a fairly unique difference in the family by creating negative emotional responses such as anger, resentment, and hostility and interfering with openness and effective problem solving.

Our observations and interviews also suggest that there may be something about respect that contributes to reciprocity being stronger with respect than many other parts of family dynamics. It is almost as though respectful and disrespectful behaviors are more than just permission to others to behave similarly. They also are an invitation to do so. Respect seems to foster openness to the ideas of others and willingness to compromise or surrender selfishness. Conversely, disrespect tends to stifle open communication and create defensive behavior as illustrated by the following comment:

> I think respect in families eliminates contention and defensiveness and creates feelings of safety, openness, and closeness. When there is disrespect there are feelings of being violated as a person, and respect creates confidence and trust.

One of the other issues that deserves attention in the future is whether the sacredness of respect and disrespect makes a difference in families. We suspect there are differences in how much respect is viewed as sacred or how much it is based on sacred beliefs, and our theory suggests it makes a difference. We do not have data about this question and it has not been addressed in previous research, but we hope future research will provide additional information about this question.

Figure 6.2 summarizes the ideas that emerged as we talked with people about this topic. It also adds the idea that sacredness may make a difference, but so far this is only a tentative and speculative idea that is deduced from the more general ideas in sacred theory.

SELF-INTEREST AND OTHER-INTEREST

The two concepts of *self* and *other* have a long history in religions, philosophy, and family studies. For example, they had a central role in the philosophy developed by Mead (1934). He focused on how the symbolism and meaning in interaction with significant others and generalized others create the mind and self; and his ideas

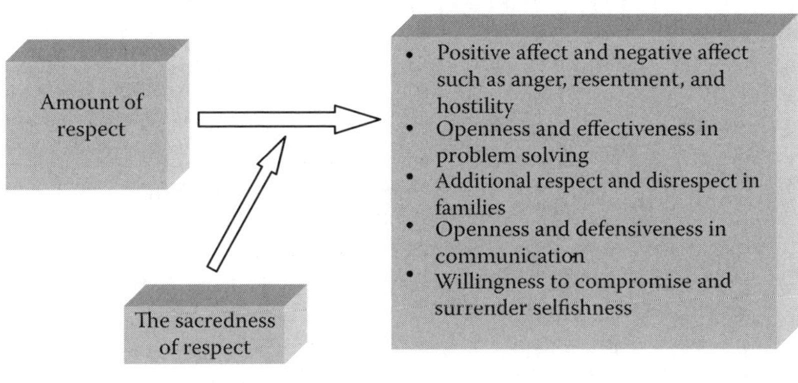

Figure 6.2 Summary of the emerging ideas about ways variation in respect influences families.

eventually became one of the major conceptual frameworks in studying family (Hill & Hansen, 1960; White & Klein, 2008).

More recently, Levinas has developed a different theory about the relationships between the self and what he called the Other and morality. He theorized that it is the face-to-face encounter with "the Other" that is the fundamental source of morality (Bauman, 1993; Peperzak, 1993). We prefer Mead's (1934) view that a society's versions of morality precede and help create the mind and self in interaction with others. According to Mead's philosophy, the symbolism and meaning in cultural phenomena already exist when an infant joins a society, and they are therefore more fundamental and help determine whether the symbolic interaction with generalized and significant others leads to moral or immoral responses. We agree with Levinas that the encounter with the Other can generate morality, but it also has the potential to generate immorality when the more fundamental cultural ideology promotes immoral behaviors and leads to valuing phenomena such as self, acquisition, and power more than it values others. When the cultural perspectives infants are born into are based on philosophies such as the ideas developed by Machiavelli (1531) or the more extreme versions of individualism, the encounter with the Other will lead to a very different morality than if the cultural ideology that precedes an individual is derived from a perspective such as Christian theology.

The aspect of self and other that seems to us to be an important part of loving others and therefore should be a part of sacred theory has to do with how much people are interested in themselves and how much they are interested in the welfare, needs, and concerns of others. There are dramatic differences in these patterns. Some people are so highly concerned about their own needs, feelings, and goals that they have little interest in the welfare and needs of others. A few go to the other extreme. They have great interest in the welfare and needs of others and little concern about their own interests and welfare. The main idea with regard to these differences is that *differences in the patterns of self-interest and other-interest influence the amount families find successes and failures.*

We will describe several aspects of this in more detail later, but first we need to spend some time defining the key terms because previous scholarship has created several different ways to conceptualize these differences. We find it helpful to think of these differences on the following three continuums.

Self-interest is at the left end of the top continuum. Another term for this end is selfishness. The extreme at this end is where people are highly interested in their own welfare and have no interest in the welfare of others. Other-interest is at the other end and is also called altruism. The extreme version at this end is where people are highly interested in the welfare of others and not interested in their own (Helgeson & Fritz, 1998; Horowitz, Rosenberg, & Bartholomew, 1993; Kunce & Shaver, 1994). The middle of this continuum is where people are concerned with self and others. The extremes on the continuum are, of course, rare, and there are many subtle differences in degree.

The middle continuum of these three shows how individualism is involved. Individualism is described in more detail on pages 219–222, but the extreme versions of it are the same as extreme self-interest and selfishness. Individualism, however, is not just one place on the continuum because people can be individualistic and vary in how much interest they have in the welfare of others. But as interest in the welfare of others approaches mutual or communal interest, it ceases to be individualism.

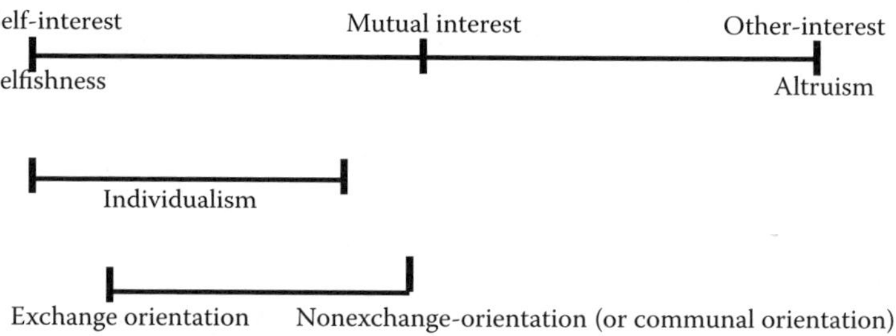

Exchange theory has another set of terms that conceptualize these differences. Exchange theories were developed by Thibaut and Kelley (1959), Homans (1950, 1961), and Blau (1964); and Murstein, Cerreto, and MacDonald (1977) introduced the terminology of exchange orientation and nonexchange orientation. They suggested that "individuals can be placed on a continuum according to the degree to which they believe equity of exchange should characterize their relationship" (p. 543). Those who view their relationships in this way believe positive or negative acts should be met by a similarly weighted action by the recipient:

> At the other end of the pole is the nonexchange-oriented (NE) person who is not at all concerned with keeping a mental balance sheet on just what he has done for others and what they have done for him. (Murstein et al., 1977, pp. 543–544)

Clark and Mills (1979) introduced the term communal to describe the nonexchange end of this continuum, and Clark and her colleagues conducted a series of studies over the next three decades that provide many insights about the role of exchange and communal orientations (Beck & Clark, 2010).

The Principle

The idea that it is good to be concerned about self and others has been a central theme for millennia in many religious traditions. For example, the Golden Rule is found in many forms and in all of the major world religions; and Christ taught, "Thou shalt love thy neighbor as thyself" (Matthew 22:39). When this idea is applied to family life, it yields the principle that a *mutual or communal orientation is helpful in families and is harmful when interests are dominated by concern for the welfare of self or others.*

This principle has several assertions. It asserts that when lifestyles emphasize self so much that it interferes with interest and concern for others, this decreases the probability family that members will find successes in their family life. Also, when their primary concerns are the welfare, goals, and concerns of others, and people do not focus on their own needs, this too is harmful. The probability of successes is highest when people focus primarily on the needs of others but also wisely attend to their own needs and interests.

Most people do not need to be encouraged to be interested in their own welfare. This seems to come rather naturally to most humans, whereas being concerned about others doesn't seem to come as naturally. The idea that the welfare of others is important is acquired only when people learn it as a part of their ideology or philosophy of life, and people need to be relatively mature to grasp this idea. Most people seem to need a certain level of empathy and understanding of abstract and complex ideas before they can understand this idea very well.

This principle originates in religious traditions, but there is a growing scholarly literature that also argues for its validity. The data in the Murstein et al. (1977) study found that an exchange orientation was negatively related with marriage adjustment. Also, the research program by Clark and her colleagues has considerable data that support the idea that communal relationships help marriages thrive (Clark & Lemay, 2010). Their data are so persuasive that they concluded that being responsive to others in a noncontingent manner that promotes the welfare of others may be the most important beneficial process in close relationships (Beck & Clark, 2010).

Our observations and interviews also provide additional evidence in support of this idea—as illustrated by the following comments by a husband:

> I made a macramé that was really cool, at least according to my seventh-grade teacher. I wanted to give it to my grandparents, and asked my parents if they would give me the money to make another one [so I could keep the first for myself]. They said they wouldn't and I needed to choose. Eventually I decided to give it to them, and I think that me choosing to give it to them without

> getting anything back helped me to learn some important lessons about the importance of service and lack of greed. That has helped our family because I learned to not be greedy and just concerned about myself.

There also are a number of scholars who have not reported empirical data but have developed rational arguments for the idea that it is helpful in families to have high interest in the welfare and interests of self and others. For example, this notion has been advocated in the writings of Magoun (1948), Fromm (1956), Sorokin (1967), Jourard (1971), Boulding (1973), Powell (1974), and Guerney (1977).

INTEGRITY AND HYPOCRISY

There is another set of behaviors that is important in sacred literature and has appeared again and again in our observations and interviews that seems to be another important aspect of loving. It has to do with whether there is integrity or consistency in what is said and done and the impressions family members try to create. The opposite of integrity is hypocrisy or duplicity. This part of loving is undoubtedly intertwined with the other parts of it, but our observations and interviews suggest it also is somewhat unique and makes a unique difference.

It is informing to examine the role of integrity in the teaching of Christ. The one thing he seemed to get the most upset about was the lack of integrity among the religious "elite" of the time. His most intense and passionate displeasure was with the hypocrisy shown by the scribes and Pharisees. His strongest words were not for the thief, the unbeliever, or the adulterer. They were for those who compromised their integrity (Matthew 23:27–33).

This same attitude toward duplicity and deceit is a theme in Buddhism. For example, the following comment is similar in tone to the biblical passages: "What is the use of platted hair, O fool? What of the raiment of goat-skins? Within thee there is ravening, but the outside thou makest clean" (Dhammapada 26: 394, The Brahmana, in Müller, 1901). Thus we believe another principle that should be included in sacred theory is that *integrity among family members helps families flourish, and hypocrisy tends to interfere with family effectiveness.*

The idea that integrity is important in families appeared as we searched sacred literature and began trying to organize our observations, and as we began to interview people about ways the sacred parts of their lives helped their families. As comments such as the following appeared in our interviews, they helped us realize that integrity and hypocrisy are important:

> To me being consistent or honorable is one of the most important things in marriage. It is important in raising children, but it is even more important in marriage.

❋❋❋❋❋❋❋❋❋❋❋❋❋❋❋❋❋❋❋❋❋❋❋❋❋

> When we started getting serious about our relationship, the first thing we found ourselves talking about very much was how much we could trust each other. We felt that being trustworthy is one of the most important features in a spouse, and we talked and talked about what we would do and want to do in situations where we could be deceptive or where misunderstandings could

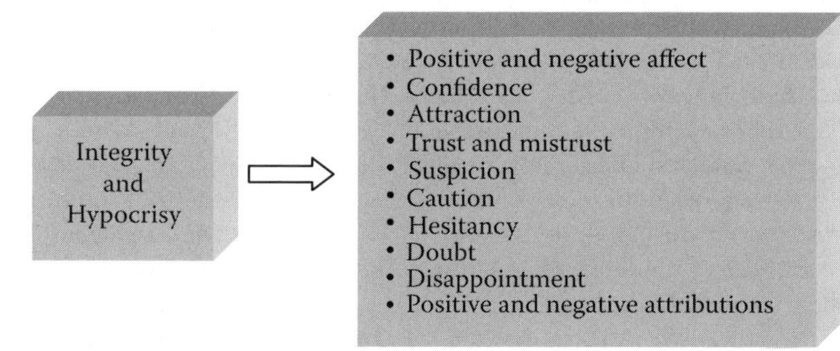

Figure 6.3 Summary of preliminary ideas regarding aspects of families influenced by integrity and hypocrisy.

> occur. We were both attracted to each other before we started taking about this, but our feelings of love and affection deepened as we felt we could both trust the other one.

We do not know of any attempt in the previous literature in family studies to identify the way integrity and hypocrisy are helpful and harmful in families. This means that these theoretical ideas are still very tentative and speculative. They are grounded on relatively few data, and the data are subjective, preliminary, and qualitative. Therefore there is a need for additional research that provides more evidence about the truth and importance of these ideas, and for revisions in these ideas. The ideas that have appeared in our observations and interviews about the effects of integrity and hypocrisy are summarized in Figure 6.3.

SERVICE

Both our reading of sacred literature and our data suggest there is another aspect of loving that is similar to some of the facets that have been described so far but also different in some important ways. It also seems helpful in family life in some unique ways. This additional aspect of loving has to do with the amount family members value *service* and how this valuing leads to a service-oriented way of relating to others.

The concept of service is similar to the concept of sacrifice that was discussed in Chapter 4 (pp. 69–85) because both of these terms deal with giving, but there seem to be some differences between them—even though they are fairly subtle and difficult to describe. Having a service-oriented lifestyle is where people have a general and pervasive pattern of reaching out, helping, assisting, and giving to others for the benefit of the others, but it doesn't have the same degree of giving up something, surrendering something, and/or losing something that exists with sacrificing. Sacrificing is more intense and more involved than service. Valuing service to others is more of an attitude toward life and others that deals with the whole of life as a lifestyle and way of relating to others rather than just with aspects of life where there is a relatively expensive or cost-oriented giving up or surrendering.

Valuing service, and having this value lead to a lifestyle of choosing to be of service to others, is very different from many other things that can be and often are highly valued. For example, valuing the acquisition of wealth and possessions and spending one's time and energy in pursuit of them is a lifestyle that is very different from a service-oriented lifestyle. A service orientation is also different from a receiving or getting attitude or selfish, exploitive, egotistical, conquering, exchange, abusive, competitive, domineering, or "I need to always be right" ways of relating.

We theorize that there is a principle that deals with these ideas—that is, *when family members have a service-oriented way of relating to each other this helps families flourish.* It is, of course, also wise to value many other things, such as safety, security, money, and possessions, enough to provide the necessities of life. But when a service orientation is minimized, replaced, or excluded by other values, this detracts from the ability of families to find successes and avoid failures.

The idea for this principle originates in teachings in sacred literature. Christ, for example, emphasized service as a good way to relate to others., as illustrated by his comment that "he that is greatest among you shall be your servant" (Matthew 23:11).

A substantial number of the people we have interviewed have described different ways serving others has been helpful in their families. The following examples illustrate this part of loving others:

> I think that service is really important. My mother and her brother both served missions for our church, and that service influenced them and who they are because, even though they were raised in the same environment as the other children in their family, and all of the brothers and sisters had relatively the same level of activity in the church throughout their lives, I see the time they spent serving on missions as making a big difference in the ways they lived their lives. It was really a differentiating factor that pushed them to be a little bit more concerned with others and putting a little more effort into a helping way of living in their homes. Their brothers and sisters that didn't serve missions were not quite as involved in these basic things. If you look at my cousins, the ones who have been the most successful in their families are from my Mom and her brother who served a mission. The other cousins vary in a wide degree, but they don't have the same kind of serving attitude or spiritual strength, even though they had the same grandparents. They separate out and the main thing, you know, that I would say is the separating thing is that my mom and her brother learned some special lessons by serving others on their missions.

❖❖❖❖❖❖❖❖❖❖❖❖❖❖❖❖❖❖❖❖❖❖❖❖❖❖❖

> When we lived in Tooele, I had my snow-blower and we had a lot of big snowstorms come through. Like, there were a lot of times we'd get a foot of snow at a time, and when I got the edge of my driveway, I just had to keep going because on both sides of us were widows, and I'd do one widow's house, and then realize there was a widow on the other side of us. The girls and the boys would get out and help, and sometimes we'd take care of the whole block. The key was to get them so they could get out of their driveways. It wasn't so much the walks but if somebody needed to get to the doctor's office or something,

> they needed to have their driveway cleared. There was a joy to doing it, but it also taught the kids that there are things that are more important than us. People can't deal with life situations sometimes, and it is important that we give that helping hand than just think of ourselves.

❖❖❖❖❖❖❖❖❖❖❖❖❖❖❖❖❖❖❖❖❖❖❖❖❖❖❖

> We've always tried to be helpful to others, and we're now seeing this same way of living with our married children. One situation that illustrates this is our oldest son and his wife recently learned of a student who had been flown by air ambulance from Rexburg to the hospital in Idaho Falls. The student, her name was Heidi, had collapsed in a social dance class as a result of a ruptured blood vessel in her brain and was in the intensive care unit. They live just 5 minutes from that hospital, and they hurried right over. They learned that Heidi's mother had not left her daughter's side in more than 5 days. They loaned the mother their spare car and made their home available to her as a place to stay. Our daughter-in-law went to the hospital every day, giving Heidi foot massages, providing her mother a few minutes' rest, and generally just giving whatever support and help she could. Their daughter, our granddaughter, Julie, works in a specialty hospital in Provo, not far from the home of Heidi's parents. Julie was able to help make arrangements for Heidi to be moved to a hospital closer to home, making things much easier for her and for her parents to be with their daughter.

We have not been able to find scholarly literature that has focused on the idea of having a service orientation in families. There is a great deal of literature in the family field that focuses on the role of a number of other ways of relating, for example, about the role of power. There is a massive literature about the role of communicating effectively, but we have not been able to find studies about service. We hope that future research will focus on this idea and provide new insights about how helpful and important this theoretical idea is.

We also believe that the tendency to have a service-oriented approach suffers when people value the extreme and unmoderated versions of individualism and materialism. This means that highly valuing individualism and materialism is another feature of modern societies that contributes to the cultural environment that surrounds families having toxic qualities for families, and wise families need to learn ways to avoid being seduced by the "Madison Avenue" mentality that is an inescapable part of the culture families exist in.

RESPECT FOR FREEDOM AND RESPONSIBILITY

Both sacred literature and our observations and interviews suggest there is another aspect of what it means to be loving that is different from the facets that have been described so far and that also can be helpful and harmful in families. There isn't just one term or word that describes this aspect, but two words used together work. They are *freedom* and *responsibility*. Neither of these terms is enough by itself, but when they are thought of as two parts of one idea they become an important concept. Before this idea can be described, we need to describe how we are using these two terms because scholars have debated for millennia whether human actions are free or determined by forces over which humans have no control.

This debate centers around two very different views about the existence and nature of freedom. One is known as *determinism* and the other as *indeterminism*, and there are mild and extreme versions of both of these views. The more extreme versions of determinism argue that everything in the universe, including human action, is entirely governed by causal laws. Advocates of this view believe that "every event in the universe is completely dependent on and conditioned by its cause or causes" (Honer & Hunt, 1987, p. 219). James (1947) called this view hard determinism and argued against it, but many social scientists, such as Skinner (1948, 1971), argue for it.

Less extreme views about determinism allow for some parts of reality to operate in deterministic ways and other parts to operate in indeterministic ways. Because deterministic thinking is focused on the parts of reality that operate in a completely predetermined way, the assumptions, conceptualizations, laws, propositions, and other truth statements of theories and research that use this approach are limited to the parts of reality where deterministic processes occur.

Indeterminism is a very different way of thinking. It is the belief that there are some aspects of reality that are not caused 100% by antecedent conditions. One way of thinking indeterministically is to think of phenomena occurring randomly or purely by chance. Another is to reject ideas such as randomness and chaos and believe there is a degree of freedom or unfettered choice when complex and creative mental processes such as volition, evaluation, analysis, choice, goals, and aspirations are involved.

A more extreme view of indeterminism is to believe that "some events, such as personal choices, are independent of antecedent events and are thus uncaused" (Percesepe, 1991, p. 457). The view we prefer is more complicated than the extreme versions of either determinism or indeterminism. We are comfortable with the idea that determinism occurs with the mindless and physical parts of reality, and that there are some limiting and qualifying conditions that operate in a deterministic manner with human thinking, emotions, choices, and behavior. For example, human behavior is constrained in deterministic ways by physical laws such as the law of gravity. Humans cannot use their "free" will to choose to jump to the moon. They also cannot choose to speak in a language they haven't learned, and they cannot choose to behave in charitable or merciful ways until they have acquired the necessary level of mental capacity and have experienced the learning that provides the ability to choose to behave in these ways.

We also believe humans have a fundamental degree of freedom or agency, and this means that deterministic thinking is not appropriate for the mental parts of human processes. Many scholars have used the term free will to refer to the aspects of human processes that do not operate in a deterministic way. We do not believe humans are ever completely "free" in their choices and actions, but they have considerable freedom, especially with regard to moral choices, and there are many subtle differences in the amount of their freedom.

There also are some aspects of mental processes that influence freedom that do not operate in a deterministic way. One example of these processes is that there are always preceding and succeeding phenomena that are taken into account in the complex mental processes of evaluating, assessing, imagining, considering, pondering, choosing, and deciding. People remember incidents in the past and anticipate future phenomena, and these components of mental processes limit the amount humans are free because their thinking and behavior are not completely "independent" of the preceding or succeeding events. Preceding events that are remembered have some degree of influence on the mental processes, but this is a matter of influence and consideration rather than thinking and behavior being either entirely free or entirely predetermined by previous necessary and sufficient causal events. Therefore the term *influence* seems to us to be the best way to conceptualize the indeterministic aspects of human processes. Others, such as Mahoney et al. (2001) and Beach et al. (2007, 2008), also use the term influence in similar ways in their theorizing.

Our view of the human mind is that it is a complex interplay of freedom, influences, limiting, and qualifying conditions. Freedom is not a dichotomous condition of either having no freedom or having total freedom. The amount of freedom varies and is a matter of degree. In some situations humans are fairly free to choose and act, whereas in other situations there are so many constraints, influences, and limiting conditions that there is less freedom. Many phenomena, such as knowledge, drug use, habits, and conditioned responses, can influence the amount of freedom in the human mind.

Thus we believe that determinism operates for some aspects of the human experience, including some genetic and biological processes. We also believe that the many indeterministic aspects of the human condition are so pervasive and relevant for the social aspects of the human experience that indeterministic parts of reality ought to be included in any model for studying family, and that these parts should receive a great deal of attention. We also believe that, even though there are many limiting and qualifying conditions that constrain human processes in deterministic ways, attempts to understand most human processes will be inadequate and fairly useless until indeterministic ways of thinking about human thought processes and behavior have a central role in scholarly inquiry.

Therefore one of our goals is to incorporate into sacred theory at least some of the indeterministic processes that seem to be important parts of family life. One of the results of trying to include indeterministic aspects of reality is that the assumptions, conceptualizations, laws, propositions, and other truth statements are very different from many of the prevailing theories in the social sciences.

Our use of the term freedom is also complicated by differences in religious traditions about whether humans have freedom. Calvin's theology argued for the idea of predestination—the doctrine that God has decreed every event that is to take place, including the final salvation of men and women, and that history is merely the working out of the sovereign will of God. This doctrine is also found in some of the literature in certain varieties of Judaism and Islam (Percesepe, 1991, p. 403).

For our purposes, we believe that the doctrine of predestination is not accurate. We believe that humans have freedom, and that this capacity is a very important part of the human condition because it makes phenomena such as responsibility, forgiveness, accountability, growth, sin, and repentance both possible and meaningful. Therefore in sacred theory, freedom is not only assumed, we believe it is an essential part of what it means to be human. Infants do not have the maturity to exercise complex freedom, but as they grow and mature, they acquire and expand in the ability to engage in the mental process of assessing and evaluating and then choosing and deciding.

The second term in the pair outlined in this section's heading is responsibility. It refers to the idea that when people have the freedom to make choices about their behavior, they are also accountable for what they choose. When children are too young to have freedom, they also are too young to be held accountable for their choices. However, as people mature and acquire the ability to have freedom, they also acquire responsibility for what they choose. Freedom without responsibility is inappropriate license, and responsibility without freedom is irresponsibility and indefensible (Frankl, 1984).

A Principle

There are many aspects of freedom and responsibility we could focus on, but many of them are so complex and involve such controversies and passions that they would subvert our goal of trying to identify ideas about sacred matters that are helpful in families. Therefore in the version of sacred theory described in this volume, we are limiting our concerns to just one aspect of freedom plus responsibility that our reading of sacred literature and our data suggest is important. It has to do with the idea that either family members can treat the other members of their family in ways that do not respect the freedom and responsibility others have, or they can relate to others in ways that do respect the freedom and responsibility others ought to have. The principle that summarizes the idea that we think is important is that *when family members are respectful of the freedom and responsibility of others in their family this increases the probability of families finding successes, and when family members are not respectful of the freedom and responsibility of others this increases the probability of experiencing failures.*

This idea asserts that when family members are cognizant of the fact that freedom and responsibility should exist in other family members and they are respectful of them, it creates an attitude toward them that influences how all family members feel and behave. When people are respectful of the freedom and responsibility of others, they treat the opinions, preferences, and wishes of others with respect. This allows others to feel they can be responsible for their own decisions, and it treats others and their wishes with gentleness, consideration, and understanding. It is, of course, also true that the amount of freedom given to others also should be consistent with their developmental level. For example, it would be unwise and irresponsible to allow young children to freely make their own decisions, and this means it is wise, moral, and helpful for parents to restrict the ability of children to use their agency. But even with small children there are benefits when the parents are considerate and respectful of the wishes and desires of their children.

There are many ways of behaving that are not respectful of the agency of others. For example, family members can forget about the freedom and responsibility others ought to have. They can try to force or coerce their will or wishes on others. They can try to manipulate, bully, or intimidate others rather than be considerate of others' wishes and preferences. Other disrespectful behaviors are being bossy, forceful, nagging, pressuring, and bribing—all of which are ways of relating that try to interfere with the ability of others to have responsibility for their behavior and freely make their own decisions.

A pattern in many marriages is that one or both spouses approach their relationship as though an important part of their marital goals is to make their spouse better. Furthermore, they often feel they know what their spouse ought to do to become a better person, and often are not shy about telling their spouse how he or she ought to behave and putting pressure on that person to do things their way. These ways of relating are not being respectful of the other person's agency, and frequently lead to various forms of marital distress.

Some people who are in this situation think their perception of what their spouse ought to do and be is "the" right way, and they set about the task of telling and pressuring the other person. They fail to recognize that their spouse is also an adult who has agency and that the other person's views or approaches may be as good as theirs. We believe it is a wiser approach to let the other person be what he or she is and wants to be; and to find ways to live with each other that allow each person to be the person he or she wants to be. This means it is wise to respect and love one's spouse for what they are rather than what one can help them become, and to try to help them change only when they want to change. This strategy tends to lead to successes in families.

Another aspect of this situation is that everyone is fallible and inadequate in some ways, and everyone falls short of their own ideals and the desires of others in their family. Everyone makes mistakes. Everyone sins and is inadequate and wrong in many ways, and a wise and loving spouse is respectful of the other person's freedom and responsibility and loves that person in spite of his or her limitations and inadequacies. Less wise spouses tend to be the first to tell the other person what he or she ought to be doing, and they often reject the other person as a person and put pressure on him or her to be better.

There are, of course, limits to this principle—for instance, a spouse who is doing severely detrimental things like being physically abusive and whose behavior is so inappropriate that it falls outside tolerable, humane, and legal limits. In these extreme situations, the wise and moral approaches are to limit the ability of people to exercise their freedom. The principle that is being described here is not very relevant for those situations, but does seem relevant and important for the daily, routine, and everyday interaction in families because there is a sizeable percentage of people who are so inconsiderate and disrespectful of the agency of others that their behavior interferes with the probability of finding successes in their family life. Our experience suggests that most of the time the harms that extend from disrespecting agency in families stem from matters of taste, preference, and style. In such issues, a formula for success may involve striving to make or help a spouse be happy, not better—unless the other person *wants* help to be better or is deviating so far from what is humane and legal that constraining is wise.

Our realization that humans have freedom and responsibility came from religious literature. Joshua's injunction to the Israelites to "choose" whether to serve their God would not have meaning without freedom (Joshua 24:15). Christ's plea to "follow me" (Matthew 4:19) recognizes this freedom and responsibility, and everything he did assumed people have freedom and responsibility and was respectful of these qualities.

Our data suggest that the usual pattern in American families is for most people to have little respect for the freedom and responsibility of other family members. This is seen in the way many people are quick to tell others how they ought to think, feel, and behave, and the variety of techniques they use to manipulate and entice others to do things their way. The result is that most families are used to a lifestyle where there is little respect, and this creates varying degrees of resentment, opposition, avoidance, and resistance. However, when family members do show respect for the freedom and responsibility of others, this helps create a different emotional climate in families, leading to more openness, understanding, gentleness, consideration, acceptance, support, and intimacy.

The evidence about this principle is preliminary and limited because we do not know of any previous scholarly literature where the idea of being considerate, patient, and respectful of the agency of others has been studied.[1] However, our observations and interviews provide enough evidence for this principle to suggest it is important and deserves more study.

APPLICATIONS

The application of the ideas in this chapter is not complicated, but it is difficult in modern cultures because the many prevailing values center around aims such as hedonism, fame, and fortune. Sacred theory suggests that the most important part of applying the ideas is to find ways to help people change their heart and values so they want to relate in loving ways rather than in the many other ways it is possible to relate. Our experience is that people rarely make these changes until the people they intimately associate with and identify with believe this style of living is desirable.

Being kind rather than unkind can be learned in our society because people need to be kind in public spheres to pass interviews for jobs and get along in the workplace. A typical pattern for many people is that when they get "off stage"

[1] There is a large literature about a process that is similar in some ways to the lack of respect for freedom and control. It is the literature on the effects of intrusive psychological control in families. However, the concept of psychological control is broader, and the way it is usually conceptualized and measured involves a number of other demeaning and aggressive behaviors such as invalidating feelings, constraining verbal expression, love withdrawal, and guilt induction (Barber, Stolz, & Olsen, 2005, p. 19). Having respect or a lack of respect for freedom and responsibility is a more subtle and delicate process.

and behind the closed doors of their home, they let down and are less kind to the people they live with. Indeed, most of the styles of relating that are illustrated in the mass media are unkind and disrespectful.

This is especially true when there are disagreements or other family members are not behaving as well as they should. The best way to help a spouse rise above her or his inadequate and less-than-perfect condition is to love and respect that person and accept them as a person, even though one may not like some of the choices she or he makes. If spouses think they have ideas that will help their inadequate spouse be better, it is more wise and sensitive to ask the other person, in a loving rather than pressuring way, if he or she wants ideas or suggestions and then allow that person to decide when and how he or she wants help before foisting the help on him or her. This approach allows for progressing and improving. It lets spouses be their own judge, and lets them set the agenda for what they want to do. It puts each person in the role of being supporter and helper in the process rather than a condescending judge, jury, whip master, or punisher.

The principle about respect has a number of practical implications for families and professionals who try to help families be successful. Many families pay so little attention to this principle that several expressions of disrespect toward others are viewed as normal and ordinary behavior. Some of these expressions may come into play as family members navigate issues that are matters of personal tradition and taste rather than objective realities. Indeed, many areas of potential conflict are based on differences regarding *subjective* beliefs rather than *objective* truths or ideas (e.g., When should the Christmas presents be opened?). Yet when family members express opinions about many things, especially those about which there are strong emotions, it is common behavior for others to respond with comments such as "You're wrong," or "That's not true," or "That's silly," or "Only an idiot would think that." Such comments assume the speaker has access to *objective* truth and that it is okay to respond to the ideas or feelings of others in ways that are not respectful of the ideas of the other people.

It is more respectful when people realize that others can be subjectively right even when they may be objectively wrong, and it is helpful to respect the subjectively right ideas or feelings and the person who holds the ideas or feelings. Therefore it helps grease the wheels of family life when family members are sensitive, considerate, and respectful of each other generally, but especially when there are differences of opinion and when emotions are intense.

SUMMARY

This chapter discussed six aspects or facets of loving others that our observations and interviews suggest are important in family life. The six aspects of loving all deal with how much family members are kind and unkind, respectful and disrespectful, interested in self and others, have integrity or hypocrisy, have a service orientation toward others, and allow others to use their freedom and responsibility. These 6 processes provide insights about what it means to be loving in families, and the next two chapters add 11 additional aspects.

7

Coping With Disagreements

Families always have both similarities and differences. Some family members are similar in age; and parents, grandparents, and children are a generation apart. Some want things one way, and others prefer other ways. Some personalities are similar to others, and some are as different as night and day.

This chapter focuses on one of the many ways that there are complex patterns in the ways family members are similar and different. It focuses on the ways family members are similar and different in their ideas, opinions, and preferences. Terms such as *consensus* and *conflict* are frequently used in the scholarly literature to refer to this part of family life, and the religious literature uses terms like *agreeing* and *unity*.

Even though there is a mythical belief that won't go away in our culture that "opposites attract," our observations and interviews suggest that a second idea should be added: Opposites attract *for a little while.* A large amount of scholarly literature suggests that for lasting and intimate relationships, the greater the similarity in ideas and opinions, the greater the likelihood things will move along smoothly. This ideal is stressed in religious literature as well. It is seen in the Old Testament in statements such as "Can two walk together, except they be agreed? (Amos 3:3), and in the New Testament in Christ's culminating prayer. It was not a prayer for people to have diversity and disagreement. It was a prayer that they would "be one, as we are . . . That they all may be one; as thou, Father, art in me, and I in thee, that they also may be one in us" (John 17:11 and 21).

The ideal of complete unity probably never exists in families, and the typical pattern is for family members to agree about some things and look at some things differently. Their individual development and new experiences are always introducing new and different ideas. Children continually bring unexpected ideas into families as they grow and mature. Therefore the presence of conflicting ideas is one of the inescapable realities of family life. The fact that disagreements are inevitable, unavoidable, and normal means they are not failures, but they do create challenges.

There are many different ways families can cope with disagreements. Family members can try to coerce and force others, put pressure on others, and intimidate others. People can also argue and fight. They can manipulate, deceive, distort, bribe, betray, punish, bicker, bully, compel, quarrel, and mislead. Strategies such as these are often successful for some people in the short term, but our data suggest that they usually lead to failures rather than successes in the long term and in the things that matter the most in families.

Our data suggest that coping with disagreements in loving ways is helpful and constructive, and this means all of the ideas in the last two chapters are relevant. This chapter discusses five additional aspects of what it means to relate in loving ways, and these strategies are particularly important when families are coping with disagreements. The five ideas deal with (a) peacemaking rather than contention, (b) patience rather than impatience, (c) cooperation rather than competition, (d) finding ways to keep negative emotions from being harmful, and (e) striving for consensus.

PEACEMAKING AND CONTENTION

Being a peacemaker in families is an aspect of loving that is similar to some of the other dimensions, but it is also somewhat unique and provides additional insights. It is particularly relevant when there are intense emotional feelings associated with differences. This dimension is also, undoubtedly, correlated with some of the other aspects of loving behavior, but it is also slightly different conceptually. It is a useful idea because it is a facet that can be changed in intervention programs. Also, as with so many of the aspects of loving that are discussed in these four chapters, we are not sure whether it is one dimension that has two opposites at its ends or two separate dimensions.

The best terms we have found to describe this aspect of loving are *peacemaking* and *contention*. Peacemaking is an attitude or approach that strives for calm and nonviolent ways of interacting when there are differences of opinion or other interpersonal problems. It promotes considerate, respectful, harmonious, and cooperative ways of relating and dealing with problems.

Contention, on the other hand, is a pattern that involves antagonism, fighting, and strife. It usually involves raised voices, anger, and negative feelings. It includes volatility and hostility, fighting and arguing, discord and combativeness, arguing and wrangling. It is a combative and confrontational rather than peaceful, caring, and gentle approach.

There is a great deal of literature in the world's religious traditions that advocates peacemaking and discourages contention. Christ taught, "Blessed are the peacemakers: for they shall be called the children of God" (Matthew 5:9). Paul told Titus that contention is "unprofitable and vain" (Titus 3:9), and a more emphatic statement is in the Latter-day Saint scriptures where Christ taught that "he that hath the spirit of contention is not of me, but is of the devil, who is the father of contention, and he stirreth up the hearts of men to contend with anger, one with another" (3 Nephi 11:29).

Families differ in the amount that their interaction is peacemaking or contentious, and our observations and interviews suggest that this idea is helpful in understanding family processes and in helping families be effective. The principle at work is that *peacemaking tends to help families flourish, and contention is disruptive in families.* The following comment illustrates the ways this relationship was often described in our interviews:

> We had some fighting among our kids, but it wasn't as much as some families have. I think it was partly because we had two peacemakers, and they were very helpful. They were in the middle, and when you have a peacemaker, they don't want to fight, so even though others are picking fights and doing disruptive things, they would sort of avoid the fights and smooth things over, and the result is you don't have so much fighting.

Scholarly Literature

There are several groups of researchers who have focused on ideas that are similar to what we are conceptualizing as peacemaking and contention. There have been some rather dramatic differences of opinion in this literature, some of which have been resolved, but other parts of this literature are still conflicting, confusing, and ambiguous.

One of the areas where the differences of opinion have been resolved fairly conclusively has to do with the value of aggressive, hostile, and belligerent behavior in marital and family relationships. A group of therapists advocated a few decades ago that it is helpful when family members overcome inhibitions and engage in fairly aggressive interaction (Bach & Wyden, 1968; Back, 1972; Berkowitz, 1973; Shostrom, 1967). Their advice included rather extreme statements such as "Don't be afraid to be a real shrew, a real bitch! Get rid of your pent-up hostilities! Tell them where you're really at! Let it be a total vicious, exaggerated hyperbole!" (Straus, 1974, p. 13).

Steinmetz and Straus (1974) reviewed related literature and concluded there was no defensible empirical or theoretical basis for it. Straus and his colleagues also completed a number of studies in the next several decades and found that violent or aggressive strategies consistently had negative relationships with several aspects of family effectiveness (Gelles & Straus, 1979; Straus, 1974).

One of the problems with the scholarly literature in this area is that much of it has ambiguity in the conceptualization. There is an extensive literature about the idea of conflict, but it is frequently not clear whether scholars are using the term conflict to refer to (a) the existence of disagreement or (b) contentious ways of trying to deal with disagreements. The findings from two different groups of scholars illustrate this confusion.

Cuber and Harroff (1965) interviewed more than 400 affluent American couples, and concluded from their data that there are several different types of marital relationships. They named one of their types "conflict habituated." These relationships had considerable tension and differences of opinion that interfered with the relationships, and they involved a continual struggle for power. These couples were relatively troubled and quite different from what they termed the "intrinsic" and "utilitarian" marriages. This study, therefore, argued for the validity of the principle that contention interferes with success and peacemaking helps families. However, the discussion of their data does not clarify how many of the challenges in conflict-habituated couples derived from differences and how many from an absence of peacemaking and a failure to resolve relatively mundane differences.

Gottman and his colleagues came to conclusions that in some ways are consistent with the principle proposed in this chapter, but in other ways are inconsistent with it. Gottman's team observed couples in their marriage laboratory and concluded that "there are three types of stable, happy couples, not just one. These three types—volatile, validating, and conflict-avoiding—have very different attributes" (Gottman, 1999, p. 88). On one hand, Gottman (1994b) argues that "there are couples whose fights are as deafening as the Honeymooners' yet who have long-lasting, happy marriages" (p. 32), and that volatile marriages "can require quite a balancing act considering the frequent storms these couples subject themselves to. But as long as they hold on tight, I think they are likely to experience many years of joy and positive intimacy" (p. 44).

On the other hand, Gottman also argued in other places that "no matter what style of marriage they have adopted, their discussions, for the most part, are carried along by a strong undercurrent of two basic ingredients: love and respect." There seems to be a fundamental inconsistency in the argument that "a strong undercurrent" of love and respect coexists with what he describes in other places as "deafening," "bickering," "fighting on a grand scale," "little interest in hearing the other's point of view," "the heat of an argument—and I do mean heat!," "don't try to understand and empathize with their partner," and "winning is what it is all about" (Gottman, 1994b, pp. 39–44).

In other research the Gottman group have argued that it is better for couples to bring their conflict into the open than to avoid and conceal it (Gottman, 1999). It seems to us that this issue is quite different from the one in the principle being discussed here. The issue here is not whether to avoid or deal with conflict but whether challenges are dealt with in peacemaking or contentious ways. We agree that it is good to have conflicts dealt with rather than avoiding or hiding them, but our data suggest it is usually best when they are dealt with in peaceful ways. This is particularly true in light of Gottman's research-based assertion that roughly 70% of all marital conflicts are irresolvable (Gottman, 1999). With these issues, resolution is not the core issue; what matters is whether the spouses take a peacemaking or contentious approach to the differences that cannot be resolved through conversation.

The complexity of the ways these issues are dealt with in the literature suggests there is a need for more research and better theory about them. Our observations support the idea that contention interferes with successes in marriages and families, but it may be that the Cuber and Harroff and the Gottman group also have identified important processes that should not be ignored. We suspect contention is generally disruptive in families, but it is possible there are contingencies or contextual factors that will eventually be identified that influence when and how it is harmful, as well as ways it is harmful in some situations but not others. Also, it may be that some of the couples Gottman described as volatile may have found ways to have long-lasting and relatively happy marriages because of many other aspects of their lives and relationships, but they might be more successful if they were to discover ways to avoid contention and find peacemaking styles of coping. In other words, we suggest that the levels of "understanding, honor, and respect," which are the components of what Gottman called emotional intelligence, would all be higher with peacemaking patterns and lower with contentious patterns. Thus until more scholarly study provides research findings and theory that are more helpful, we have more confidence in the research that argues for peacemaking being helpful and contention being harmful than in the rather confusing observations and conclusions of Cuber and Harroff (1965) and Gottman (1994a, 1994b, 1999), but these dynamics deserve more scholarly attention.

Effects

Our data suggest that this is also another area where the law of reciprocity described by Gouldner (1960) and Deutsch (1973) operates. Peacemaking tends to increase the amount of peacemaking and similar behaviors, and contention tends to escalate contention and similar kinds of behaviors such as arguing and fighting, striving to win, combativeness, resistance, and defensiveness.

Our observations and interviews also suggest that peacemaking tends to have a calming effect, like oil on troubled waters. It also tends to promote love feelings and other types of positive affect—especially when emotions are intense and there are interpersonal problems. Peacemaking increases the tendency to compromise, give in, and cooperate. Peacemaking also tends to keep the scope of problems and difficulties limited rather than escalating and including additional aspects of the relationships, as well as keep the problems confined to the issues rather than including personalities or persons in general instead of the issues or specific behaviors.

Our data also suggest that contention tends to inflame and escalate problems, and problems tend to expand to include personalities and individuals as persons rather than just be confined to issues, behavior, and specific situations. These ideas are summarized visually in Figure 7.1, and, as with all of the ideas that have been gleaned from our interviews, they are preliminary and theoretical and deserve more systematic and interpersonally replicable research.

PATIENCE

The *Random House Dictionary of the English Language* (1967) defined *patience* as "the bearing of provocation, annoyance, misfortune, pain, etc., without complaint, loss of temper, irritation, or the like." It refers to how quickly or slowly people express their displeasure, irritation, or annoyance in difficult situations, and includes the ability to retain composure and not react in an aggressive ways when difficulties such as aggravation, annoyance, and/or frustration are encountered. It is different from the components of loving that have been discussed so far, such as kindness, respect, and peacemaking, because they don't inherently deal with responding to a negative experience. Patience, by contrast, is inherently a response to something that is problematic or negative. Thus patience seems to be a slightly different aspect of what it means to have loving relationships with others.

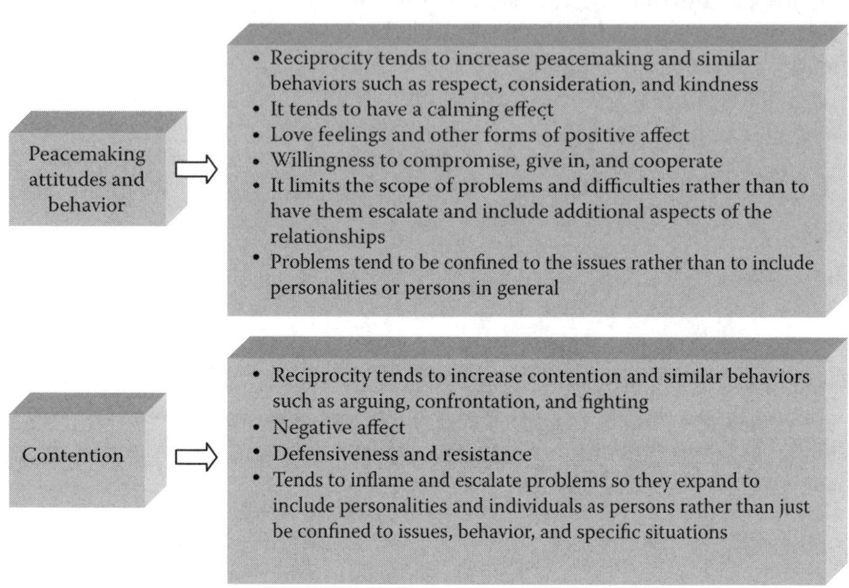

Figure 7.1 The influence of peacemaking and contention.

There are many times when it is difficult to be patient with family members. Things don't always go smoothly, and differences, misunderstandings, and undesirable behavior are unavoidable in families. Family members have so much they want to get done, and efficiency and productivity are so highly valued in our society that they often take over and make it difficult to be patient, especially when conflict appears. It would be nice if we could cope with differences quickly and efficiently. But we mortals aren't very efficient when it comes to our beliefs about what is important in our marriages and families, and it often takes more than a little patience to take the time that is needed to deal effectively and wisely with differences.

In our discussions with many people in a variety of settings and cultures about how aspects of the sacred are helpful in families, we usually didn't get very far into the discussion before people would bring up the idea that patience is helpful and important. The relevant principle is the idea that *patience tends to help families flourish, and impatience tends to increase the challenges and difficulties in family life*. In other words, when family members are able to be tolerant and long-suffering with each other, it helps families find ways to constructively cope with their differences and other difficult situations, whereas the lack of patience aggravates and inflames the negative and difficult aspects of family life.

For us, the most original source of the idea that patience is helpful is that it is a central theme in the Bible. It is taught in a variety of different ways in both the Old and New Testaments. Our observations and interviews have added additional evidence that it is important and helpful. The following comments illustrate the ways this principle was usually expressed in our interviews:

> My husband is so calm and patient. It doesn't matter what the kids do or what I do, he just never gets upset or angry. I've never seen him raise his voice or talk to anyone with an angry voice. I get mad and struggle to hold my temper and not say things I shouldn't say, but he doesn't even have to work at it. He's just Mr. Composed and Unruffled. His ability to calm the waters in our life has been a precious blessing.

❖❖❖❖❖❖❖❖❖❖❖❖❖❖❖❖❖❖❖❖❖❖❖❖❖❖❖❖

> I've always been fairly quick, impulsive and impatient, but having a handicapped child helped me learn, sometimes painfully, how to be patient. As I look back now, I'm amazed at how much this has blessed my marriage and ability to be a father.

Effects

We have never seen this principle operationalized in a study or included in a text or theory about family processes. This is, therefore, another area where we have little information about the effects of patience, and there is a need for additional research. We hope sacred theory will stimulate more scholars to include this aspect of family processes in future research.

There is an idea about effects that is suggested by a passage in the New Testament. In Paul's letter to the Romans, he says that patience leads to hope (Romans 5:4). This is therefore an idea that deserves attention in future research.

Our data also suggest that this is another area where the law of reciprocity tends to operate (Deutsch, 1973; Gouldner 1960). This law suggests that patience tends to lead to more patience in families and to similar kinds of behavior such as kindness, respect, peacemaking, compassion, cooperation, and consideration.

Our observations and interviews also added a few ideas about the effects of patience. A number of people suggested that patience helps people have hope and avoid regret and guilt. A number also observed that patience is similar to peacemaking in that it tends to have a calming effect when disagreements or undesirable behavior occur, whereas impatience tends to inflame and aggravate difficult situations. It influences the emotional atmosphere or climate in the family in that patience tends to create a warm, accepting, cooperative, and understanding atmosphere, whereas impatience tends to create tension and negative affect. Patience also tends to help disagreements remain limited to issues rather than expanding to include personalities, motives, entire relationships, and individuals as a whole, and these effects tend to help families cope effectively with disagreements and other problems. These ideas are summarized visually in Figure 7.2.

Patience does not seem to be a characteristic that is easily learned or practiced in our modern world. Most people have to consciously and deliberately tell themselves to be as patient as they need to be when other members of our families come up with what are viewed as weird ideas and beliefs. How well we succeed in dealing with the differences constructively and successfully is dependent on how well we discipline ourselves to be patient, to take the time to

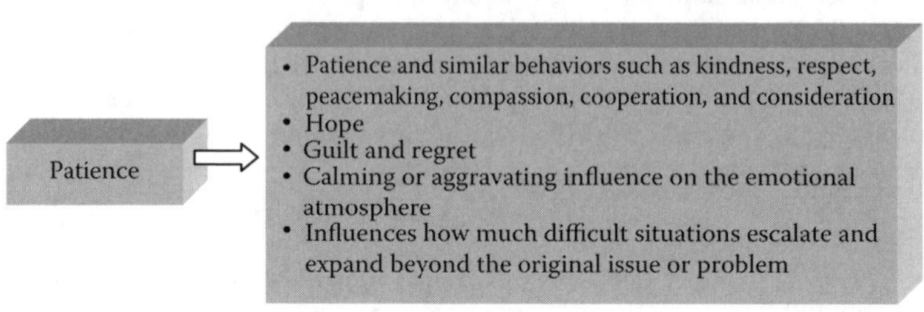

Figure 7.2 The influence of patience.

listen and try to understand, to explore possibilities and alternatives in trying to create unity.

COOPERATION AND COMPETITION

Our data suggest there is another aspect of "loving others" that is (a) slightly different from the aspects that have been described so far, (b) a part of the sacred, and (c) important in helping families find successes and avoid failures. It is the amount families have *cooperation* and *competition* in them.

A word search of the Bible reveals that words like *compete*, *competition*, *cooperate*, and *cooperation* never appear in it. They are apparently terms that have become popular in more recent times. However, the ideas that are described by these words are ancient and important in the sacred literature. It will probably help us describe their role in the sacred literature and family processes if we briefly review some of the historical evolution of these two terms.

The idea of people cooperating with each other has been a central ideal in all of the traditions of the world's religions we have seen, and there are many examples of it in their literature. The emphasis on loving, consideration of others, assisting, helping the downtrodden, assisting the poor and discouraged, forgiving, and praying for and loving enemies and those who oppose and hurt are pervasive. These ideas all suggest that the idea of cooperation is a fundamental and essential part of the traditions in the major world religions.

Competing with others, on the other hand, has become an ideal in most of the cultures in the Western world, but it is conspicuous by its absence in the traditions of the world's major religions. We have searched for it but have not found anything that advocates competition in the Qur'an, the Old Testament, the Jewish culture, the New Testament, or the traditions in the Eastern religions.

Competition was valued in the ancient Greek empire, and their values spread to the rest of the Middle Eastern world during the Hellenization of these other cultures at the time of Alexander the Great. Interestingly, competition seems to have caught on earlier and more in the Western cultures than Eastern cultures, but it is now valued in all of the major cultures in the world.

Competition has continued to increase in value in the Western world at the same time that Judeo-Christian values have also been a dominant cultural influence, which is paradoxical because the idea of competition is not only absent from anything that is Christian, it is an incompatible idea. There isn't a word, insinuation, or reference to anything that is even close to competition in Christian teachings other than Paul commenting that he had run a good race, and his point was about completion not competition. Yet competition has become a central and indispensable part of Western cultures.

Competition seems especially important in public areas such as economic and political systems, educational, legal and medical institutions, and the arts. And some scholars suggest that it is the best approach we know of in these public arenas (Edwards, 1973). However, when we are dealing with the familial part of life, the patterns and processes are fundamentally different from the public realms. For instance, there are a number of scholars who have argued that in the private or family areas it is intimacy, helpfulness, support, and nurturing that are important, and that competition is incompatible with these processes (Diesing, 1962; Kohn, 1986)—unless three conditions exist.

Deutsch (1973, 1985) identified the three conditions that mitigate the usual disruptive effects of competition in intimate relationships: (a) Winning is unimportant, (b) the rules are clear, and (c) participation is voluntary. The following situation shows how having clear rules helps:

> My brother and dad and I have played racquetball with each other for years, and we do it a lot for just fun, but we also play competitive racquetball in tournaments. When my brother was first deciding to work hard enough that he could get ready to play in tournaments, he started to get really competitive and he started to call a lot of things that we didn't usually call on each other when we were playing for fun. It got to the point that after three or four times in a row my dad and my brother didn't have any fun when they played. It was just an argument the whole time because my brother was being so competitive, and they weren't used to dealing with that. So they sat down and said, "Let's make some ground rules. The receiver always calls the serve. If he thinks it's short. No argument." After they made a few ground rules like that it helped.

Aristotle's Golden Mean is also relevant for this principle. Competition apparently does not disrupt intimacy when it exists in moderation. This means it is okay for families to play games such as Monopoly, Hearts, and one-on-one if the objectives are recreation, fellowship, and enjoyment. The more important it is to be better than the others, the more the competition will interfere with the intimacy and love in the relationships. Winning over others and loving them can both be important values in the human heart, but the more important they are, the less they can exist at the same time in one heart. When they are highly valued, we humans choose between these two incompatible values.

These patterns seem especially important in marital relationships. When couples are concerned with succeeding as a couple and helping each other have successes these patterns promote intimacy and love, and when they are concerned with being better than the other one they both lose.

Scholarly Literature

There are still debates in the scholarly literature about whether and when competition is better than cooperation. Some argue that competition is an inherent part of human nature (Caillois, 1961; Harvey, Heath, Spencer, Temple, & Wood, 1917; Huizinga, 1955). Others argue that competition increases striving and efficiency, especially in public realms such as industry, commerce, governments, and education. Some believe that competition facilitates productivity and innovation. Others such as Kohn (1986) argue that competition is always disruptive. The meta-analysis by Johnson, Johnson, and Tauer (1979) of 122 studies from 1924 to 1980 found mixed results.

Even though there are debates about the effects of competition and cooperation in public realms such as industry and education, there is no debate about the role of cooperation and competition in the family realm. Every scholar who has addressed this issue comes down on the side of competition being disruptive and cooperation being facilitating in family systems (Allred, 1981; Deutsch, 1985; Kohn, 1986). Diesing (1962) has argued that part of the reason for this is that the natural rules that govern interaction are different in the family and public realms. In the private or family arenas, intimacy and competition are like oil and water. They just don't mix (except under the three conditions described earlier), and the more important it is to excel over others, the more the competition tends to destroy intimacy.

To summarize, the previous research about cooperation and competition in families suggests that cooperation tends to increase intimacy, trust, closeness, openness, positive affect, warmth, and support. Competition, on the other hand, tends to reduce cooperative inclinations and creates distance, suspicion, reticence, spying, and so on. These patterns are summarized visually in Figure 7.3.

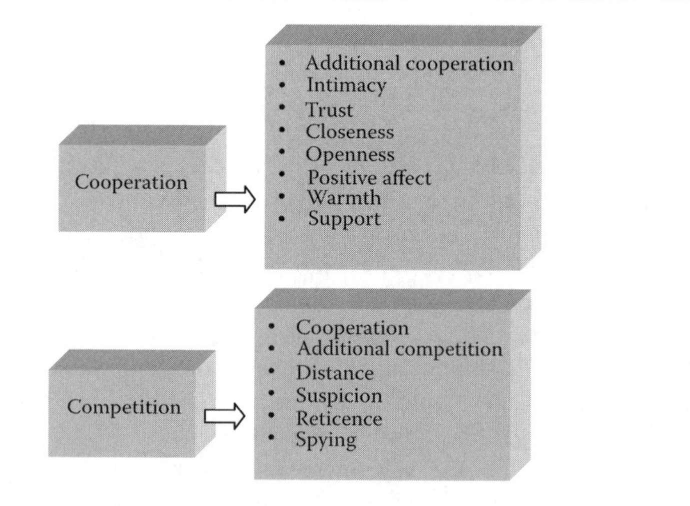

Figure 7.3 The influence of cooperation and competition in families.

COPING WITH NEGATIVE EMOTIONS

Because family life, to borrow a phrase from Dickens, is the best of times and the worst of times, there are many different emotions that appear in families. Some of them are positive, uplifting, and wonderful, and most people try to cultivate and enjoy them. They also add wonderful dimensions to the human experience. Other emotions are negative, and they are neither desired nor enjoyed. Therefore most people try to avoid them.

Some of the negative emotions that appear in families are fairly mild. For example, anger, annoyance, concern, exasperation, frustration, disgust, and anxiety are often minor and can be managed fairly easily. Others are more intense and challenging, and, unfortunately, there are a large number of them. Some examples are desperation, discouragement, abhorrence, antagonism, bitterness, enmity, hatred, hostility, infuriation, loneliness, panic, resentment, rage, revulsion, fear, worry, wrath, and a sense of victimization. These feelings are among the worst and most undesirable emotions humans ever experience, and some of them are extremely difficult to cope with.

Negative emotions appear in families for many reasons. They come when there are disagreements, when things don't go the way we hope and wish, and when we or others around us behave in undesirable ways. We can respond to these feelings in many different ways. We sometimes deny and run away from them. Psychiatrists differentiate between flight and fight responses. We sometimes rant and rave, yell and scream, hurt and abuse ourselves and others, argue and fight. In some circumstances, we also can sometimes use them as positive forces that lead us to constructive and helpful ways of behaving, and other times we respond to them in destructive and dysfunctional ways.

Our observations and interviews suggest that there are two important principles about how families cope with negative emotions, both of which rest on the idea in the New Testament that negative emotions are dangerous. Christ used the word *danger* three times in one sentence as he taught about the challenges of dealing with anger:

> But I say unto you, That whosoever is angry with his brother without a cause shall be in *danger* of the judgment: and whosoever shall say to his brother, Raca, shall be in *danger* of the council: but whosoever shall say, Thou fool, shall be in *danger* of hell fire. (Matthew 5:22, emphasis added)

Our theorizing identifies two principles that provide explanation and understanding about why anger is dangerous and how family members can deal with it constructively. One is the idea that *when family members find ways to deal with their negative affect in loving ways it helps them flourish, but when it is not dealt with in loving ways these emotions are destructive and harmful.*

Thus the existence of negative emotions, even some of the more intense and powerful feelings, is not necessarily disruptive or harmful. It is what family members do in response to these feelings that determines whether they help families flourish or flounder. Experiencing negative feelings is dangerous and risky because it is so easy and natural to do mean things when these emotions are experienced, but they are just dangerous and risky rather than disruptive and harmful.

The natural response when negative feelings appear is to be negative, reciprocate, and get even, and it takes deliberate effort to be loving. However, when people learn strategies of venting or releasing negative feelings in ways that are not harmful to others, and find ways to cope with these situations in healing and facilitating ways, these are constructive responses and help families accomplish the many things we seek in family life.

On the other hand, when members of families lash out and hurt, retaliate in aggressive and harmful ways, or abuse others physically or emotionally, these ways of behaving, which are driven by negative emotions, are destructive. Sometimes they are destructive in many ways, and often do damage that cannot be repaired for a very long time or even with great effort, Sometimes they can never be repaired. Hurtful words and actions that come from negative emotions are like the proverbial bushel of leaves spread into the wind. They can never be taken back.

Scholarly Literature

The research by the Gottman (1994b) group has provided several insights that are helpful in understanding and applying this principle. One of the ideas that emerged from their research has to do with what they call "the magic ratio" of positive and negative feelings and behaviors:

> Our research suggests that what really separates contented couples from those in deep marital misery is a healthy balance between their positive and negative feelings and actions toward each other . . . As part of our research we carefully charted the amount of time couples spent fighting verses interacting positively—touching, smiling, paying complements, laughing, etc. Across the board we fund there was very specific ratio that exists between the amount of positivity and negativity in a stable marriage, whether it is marked by validation, volatility, or conflict avoidance.
>
> That magic ratio is 5 to 1. In other words, as long as there is five times as much positive feeling and interaction between husband and wife as there is negative, we found the marriage was likely to be stable. (pp. 56–57)

The Gottman (1994b) team also identified an array of wise and unwise ways of dealing with negative affect. The five they focused the most on are complaints, criticism, contempt, defensiveness, and stonewalling. They argued that complaints are usually productive, but they called the last four of these methods the "Four Horsemen of the Apocalypse" (p. 72):

> On the surface, there may not seem to be much difference between complaining and criticizing. But criticism involves attacking someone's personality or character—rather than a specific behavior—usually with blame. When Pamela said, "You always do things like that—just think about yourself, of your needs," she assaulted Eric, not just his actions, and blamed him for being selfish and ignoring her sacrifice. For his part, Eric began to criticize Pamela as well. Why was she so negative? Why did she have to spend so much time chastising him over minor purchases instead of praising his all-around thrifti-

> ness? He told her she was the type of person who never had anything nice to say, who just wanted to give him a hard time.
>
> Since few couples can completely avoid criticizing each other now and then, the first horseman often takes up long-term residence even in relatively healthy marriages. One reason is that criticizing someone is just a short hop beyond complaining, which is actually one of the *healthiest* activities that can occur in a marriage. Expressing anger and disagreement—airing a complaint—though rarely pleasant, makes the marriage stronger in the long run than suppressing the complaint. (Gottman, 1994b, p. 73)

These conclusions seem valid as far as they go, but our data suggest that there is another ingredient that also is important: the degree to which these five behaviors are expressed in loving ways. It is possible to express anger and make complaints in both loving and unloving ways, and to express criticism and some levels of defensiveness in both loving and unloving ways. Our data suggest that the differences in the loving aspects of these behaviors are more important than their existence.

It may be that contempt and stonewalling are ways of responding to negative situations that are so far from loving that they are always destructive. This also ought to be studied in future research, along with the opposites of these patterns, which are respectfulness, openness to and acceptance of the negative phenomena, and a willingness to deal with them in constructive and loving ways.

Some of the reasoning behind this theorizing is that when the five behaviors in the Gottman (1994b) model are expressed in unloving ways, they include demeaning, aggressive, and mean side effects that tend to be destructive. Exhibiting components of loving others, such as the aspects of loving that have been described in previous pages—kindness, peacemaking, other-interest, striving for unity, and patience—are probably very helpful in dealing with negativity. As Mary Poppins would suggest, they help the medicine go down.

Emotionality

The second principle that provides insights into why anger is dangerous has to do with some of the patterns that usually happen when emotions become intense. When negative emotions are mild or moderate, most of the time people are able to control themselves. They continue to think rationally and usually are able to find constructive ways of dealing with their feelings. However, as emotions increase in intensity, there are some predictable patterns that tend to occur with most people. They tend to become less rational and have less control.

We first became aware of this pattern in Bowen's version of systems theory in families (1976, 1978). Bowen used the term "emotional fusion" (1976, p. 79) to refer to the process of self-control decreasing when emotions become intense. Kerr, a colleague of Bowen's, had a slightly different name for it. He called it "emotional reactivity" (Kerr, 1981, p. 237).

The theorizing by Bowen and Kerr about this process was closely tied to biological processes and what they called differentiation processes in families. However, others have theorized that these patterns operate fairly independently of the biological and differentiation factors that Bowen and Kerr thought were important, that the tendency for self-control to decrease when emotions become intense is situational, and that the intensity of emotions and self-control often changes in short periods of time as circumstances and conditions in family life change (Burr, Yorgason, & Baker, 1982).

This theorizing led to a principle that helps us understand one of the reasons intense emotions are dangerous and tend to become disruptive; and this principle also provides insights about strategies family members can use to help them be wise in the ways they cope with negative affect. Burr et al. (1982, p. 87) called this idea the "emotionality principle"; that is, *when emotions become intense, they decrease self-control.*

The Burr group theorized that the relationship in this principle is curvilinear rather than linear and there are thresholds in it. If it were a linear relationship, gradual increases in intensity would be accompanied with proportional decreases in rationality and self-control, but this is not the way this principle works. When emotions are in the mild to moderate levels of intensity, increases in intensity do not usually have any effects on rationality and self-control. However, when the intensity reaches a critical level or threshold, additional increases start having a meaningful effect on the ability of family members to think clearly, restrain themselves, and exercise self-control; and further increases have more dramatic effects.

Many times family members find themselves acting in ways that are quite different from their "normal" ways of being—humane, thoughtful, considerate, and helpful. Instead, they find themselves acting in mean, retaliating, rigid, defensive, resisting, and/or critical ways. If the emotions increase more in intensity or last for a long time, it is not unusual for people who are otherwise kind and cooperative to become very vicious and cruel, at first in subtle and hidden ways, and then in more open and dramatic ways. Many family members have little awareness of these changes in their behavior, and if someone were to accuse them of acting in these ways that are foreign to their personal code of conduct and usual ways of behaving, their tendency is to be defensive and deny they are acting these ways.

It is also helpful to realize that the emotionality principle operates the same way with both positive and negative emotions. With regard to positive emotions, as feelings of love and rapture become intense, rationality and self-control wane. One of the authors was so "out of it" mentally after a particularly enjoyable date that he once drove all the way home (about 15 miles) with his car in second gear the whole way. Sexual excitement responds the same way. Considerable research about the sexual response cycle shows that as sexual excitement becomes more intense, rationality and self-control diminish, and people find themselves doing a number of things they wouldn't do if their sexual feelings were calm (Masters & Johnson, 1966).

Our observations and interviews provide additional qualitative data that argue for the validity and usefulness of the emotionality principle, but we hope future research will provide additional tests of this idea. Comments such as the following in our interviews are persuasive evidence:

When I was a child I remember watching my dad get frustrated with a lot of things, but he'd especially get mad when our old pickup wouldn't start. He'd start swearing and slam the door and yell at it and kick it. Sometimes he would just lose control of himself and throw things and act like a mad man. When I was about 10 years old, I'd move a ways away so he couldn't see me, and I'd watch him and watch him, and I never could figure out why he'd get so upset and why he'd be so aggressive in taking it out on the truck and other things like the fence or tools or the wheelbarrow or shed. It just didn't make any sense. He never did hit any of us kids when he was so out-of-control or my Mom, but he'd hit and throw things at everything else. After a while he'd calm down and be nice and be himself again.

❋❋❋❋❋❋❋❋❋❋❋❋❋❋❋❋❋❋❋❋❋❋❋❋❋❋❋

My sister and her new husband are both "take charge" kinds of people, and they both like to be "in control." After they were married, they each struggled to get the upper hand in their relationship, and this led to frustrations and gradually they both became more and more frustrated about their marriage. This went on for several years, and their anger increased and their relationship became worse and worse. As their negative feelings became increasingly intense, they both started doing things to be mean and get even with the other one, and both of them thought the other one was the only one being mean. They went to several counselors, but they weren't able to get to the bottom of what was happening and solve their problems. When they were seriously considering divorce, they sought help from someone who helped them understand that both of them were trying to exert more control than was wise and that they had created some vicious cycles where their intense emotions were leading them to be cruel and mean in ways they didn't even realize. When they understood what was happening, they both decided to be less controlling, to be forgiving of the ways they had both been unkind, and to try hard to be kind to each other. It took them several months, but gradually they eliminated the vicious cycles they had been caught in and they have had a lovely marriage for the last several years.

❋❋❋❋❋❋❋❋❋❋❋❋❋❋❋❋❋❋❋❋❋❋❋❋❋❋❋

My dad had four children with his first wife, and his first wife died while the children were young and as a result of her death, two of the sons really struggled, and both of them got involved with alcohol, and both of them became alcoholics. When they'd be drinking and come home they would get upset and be angry a lot of the time, and when they did they became incoherent. They just didn't make sense.

The one son, even though he is still an alcoholic, has changed and we can interact with him, and he has stayed a part of the family although for some time it was hard when he was drinking regularly. It was difficult to stay close to the family, but now that he has changed he is very close to the family. With the other brother, his anger and alcohol have been dividing factors to keep him away from the family, and it made it very difficult.

I remember that when I was young one brother came around and tried to be around, and my dad reached out and tried to help him, but he'd still drink and get angry, and it was like a wedge in the family, in the relationship, and because of that he could not stay close to the family. Currently because of his

> addiction he is completely separated from the family. We don't really know where he is. It is interesting that it has grown because that wedge has split him further and further away from the family, almost to the point that it is very illogical. The last time I remember him coming by, he stopped by unannounced and we were there and before long he got really upset and it became a very illogical conversation, talking about things that happened when he was a teenager and he was home and his mom died, the time when he separated off, and he just continues to separate off, even to the point that now his interactions are very abnormal, almost unbelievable, you know threatening, in context with his interaction with the family, threatening that he is going to come back and get what is his, and threatening violence. He hasn't been around for many years since he has been separated, but he still has emotional ties back to his youth and back to things that he feels are his, that he deserves because he was part of the family. His addiction has separated him completely.

STRIVING FOR UNITY

Families can differ in how much they strive for consensus when they have disagreements. Some of the ways of coping with differences where there is little striving for consensus are when the powerful members of families, often the parents or males, try to impose their will on others. Another pattern is when it is important to some family members that they are "right," and they resist admitting they are wrong or that the ideas of others might be better than theirs. Some of the men we've observed and interviewed felt they would be "henpecked" if they were to give in to their wife very often, and they strive to dominate, coerce, force, and manipulate.

Some of the indications that family members are striving for consensus are when they make comments such as: "Let's see if we can work this out."; "Can we find some agreement here?"; "Can we come together on this?"; "Can we find some middle ground we are all comfortable with?"; "Can some of us change our ideas in ways that will help bring us together?"

Our observations and interviews suggest that striving for consensus makes a unique and valuable contribution in families. It releases or creates levels of ingenuity and resourcefulness that are helpful, and when there is a genuine striving most of the disagreements that appear in family life are solved by either finding ways to agree or finding ways compromises or alternatives that allow family members to live and interact comfortably even though their first choice would be to do something that is different from solutions that are the best for the whole family.

In some situations this striving for consensus means that the disagreements among family members are eliminated by some people changing their opinions or finding new ways to think about what to believe and how to act. This is usually the most ideal solution, but there are many situations where all of the differences cannot be eliminated. When this occurs it is helpful if family members try to create arrangements that are as close to consensus as possible or are respectful of differences and as accommodating as possible. This means that agreement is not a zero-sum situation. It is often a situation of more and less agreement, and agreement about some things but not others; and it helps if family members strive to get as much consensus as possible.

When complete consensus is elusive and family members are trying to find compromises or alternatives they can live with comfortably, it helps when family members feel that others have listened to their preferences and genuinely tried to find ways to come to agreement. This increases their willingness to compromise or live with alternatives that aren't their first choice. When family members do not listen attentively to each other and are not considerate of the opinions of others, this tends to create resistance and defensiveness and less inclination to be cooperative and adaptable.

In some situations the best solution that can be found is to have the family go along with one person's preferences in one area and another person's preference in another area. Another strategy is to do things the way one person wants for a period of time and then the way the other person wants for a period of time.

Part of American folklore is that diversity is good. This is seen in the often-used observation that "opposites attract." A theory was even developed in the 1950s by Winch (1955, 1958) that argued that people select spouses who are different from themselves. It was called the theory of *complementary needs*. It stimulated considerable research, but the findings eventually argued that people tend to select spouses who are relatively similar to rather than different from themselves, and that the more couples are similar rather than complementary, the happier and more successful they were. This suggests that when opposites attract it is usually attractive for only a little while, because before long sparks tend to fly in the relationships of opposites.

The scholarly literature deals with the relationship between the amount of similarity and family success, but it does not deal with the principle being proposed here that *striving* for consensus helps families. Our observations and interviews argue that trying to create consensus is helpful and productive in families, and we suggest that this idea will turn out to be a useful principle in family studies because it deals with something families can do to help increase their unity when there are disagreements. Comments such as the following illustrate the ways this idea appeared over and over again in our observations and interviews:

> The thing that attracted me to Beth was that we have the same values and believe the same about the important things. We discovered that we're different in some of our hobbies and leisure time interests, but we actually enjoy being different in those ways. As the years have passed, we've both changed about how we look at some things, and when it has been important we've tried to understand each other and find ways to agree through compromising or one of us changing, and that has been helpful in our marriage.

❖❖❖❖❖❖❖❖❖❖❖❖❖❖❖❖❖❖❖❖❖❖❖❖❖❖❖❖❖❖❖❖❖

> Joy and I look at most things the same. We disagreed some in the early years of our marriage about how to be parents, but we'd try to find a way to come together and be unified, and I think it has helped our home.

❖❖❖❖❖❖❖❖❖❖❖❖❖❖❖❖❖❖❖❖❖❖❖❖❖❖❖❖❖❖❖❖❖

> Having a lot of agreement in our family impacted my life as I was growing up. I am the youngest of eight children who grew up in an area of New Jersey where being religious meant that you were automatically different from neighbors and peers. The gospel my family chose to live by was not always the most popular or accepted, however they were principles where we were united as a family. Because my family tried to be unified by the gospel, it made it much easier for me being the youngest to follow my siblings' examples. The choices I made as a teenager and in my years at college were simplified because we had tried to come together and I had witnessed first hand my brothers and sister making the same difficult decisions before me. While I was in high school, everyone pretty much already knew someone in my family and knew the values and traditions we lived by, such as the word of wisdom, law of chastity, dedication to church, etc... These are difficult decisions that young people are faced with as they progress into adulthood. And, as I said before, since my family had made the decision to be unified on these principles my decision was simplified because of it.

Effects

The previous research in family studies provides no information about which parts of family processes and outcomes are influenced by trying to create unity. Our observations and interviews suggest that when the trying is genuine, it shows and promotes good faith, interest in others and their ideas, respect for others and their ideas, and openness and cooperation. These ways of interacting and relating tend to create positive affect and goodwill, especially in challenging situations, and they create expectations that these same supportive ways of trying will exist in the future. This helps create optimism in the present—as well as a hope for the future. It also facilitates and forms the kind of relationships that bring deeply felt security, joy, and love.

When family members do not genuinely try to create unity or oneness but have other objectives or strategies, such as getting even, manipulating the situation to their advantage, or forcing their ideas on others, these patterns undermine the trying, the effectiveness, the warmth, and the love feelings in the relationships. They tend to create negative affect, disrupt the positive expectations, decrease striving, and interfere with success.

Our understanding of the importance of striving for consensus was helped with an idea in the sacred literature of the Latter-day Saints: that decisions bring more "blessings" when there is unanimity (Doctrine & Covenants 107:27–29). When agreement cannot be reached, it is, of course, possible to find other methods of living and deciding, such as voting or going along with those who have the most authority or the most power, but when there is not agreement there will be fewer "blessings."

These ideas about the influence of trying to create unity are based on very little data and are fairly speculative. Therefore they ought to be viewed as tentative theorizing until additional research provides more evidence about them. These preliminary ideas are summarized visually in Figure 7.4.

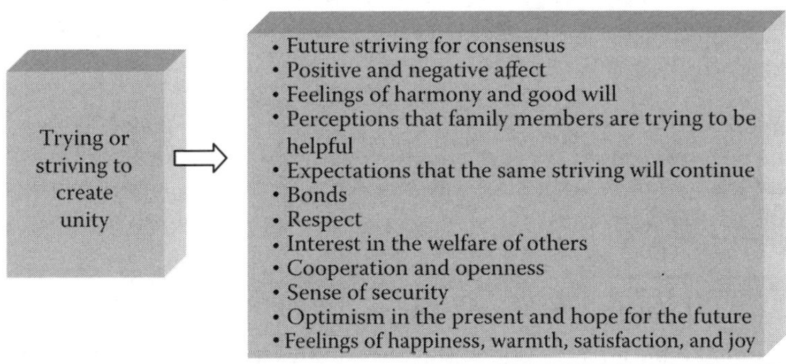

Figure 7.4 Summary of preliminary ideas about the influence of trying to create unity.

APPLICATIONS

The ideas in this chapter can be applied in families and by professionals in many ways. One way is to realize that it is helpful to "shift gears" between the competitive public realms and the family realm. One person we know kept a small radio playing calm music in his garage to remind him as he came home from work that he was away from the competition that was inevitable at work and ought to shift into the more "cooperative" style of living he wanted at home.

Four other skills that can help family members apply these two principles are: (a) Recognize when emotions are becoming sufficiently intense that they are becoming disruptive, (b) interrupt whatever is contributing to the emotions becoming intense, (c) find ways to decrease the intensity of emotions, and (d) create and re-create rapport.

Recognize the Intensity of Emotions

When disagreements or other problems occur in families, many people get so preoccupied with finding ways to solve the problems that they are not very sensitive to what is happening with the emotions. Also, it is likely that the more these people concentrate on the problems, the less aware they are of the emotions. The result is that many family members are not very aware of when emotions start becoming so intense that they contribute to people acting in unloving ways. This means it is a precious skill in family life for family members to have the ability and presence of mind to recognize when emotions are becoming so intense they are interfering with people being loving.

It is not all that difficult to cultivate this skill when people are aware of these emotional aspects of their situation, but it is not something that is widely recognized in American culture, wherein most people are so concerned with being rational and effective that they concentrate their attention on these unemotional aspects of what is occurring. It will help when more people become aware of the importance of the emotional parts of what happens in families, cultivate their ability to focus part of their attention on what is happening emotionally, and recognize when emotions are becoming so intense that they begin to interfere with the ability of family members to be loving. Comments such as the following illustrate how little of this skill some people have:

> I don't speak that language. I don't think about emotions, and don't have words for them. I don't know how to even think about those things. If it has to do with motorcycles or machines, I know what's going on, and can see what is needed, but the emotions you're talking about. They aren't a part of my life.

Deal First With Whatever Is Contributing to the Emotions

Recognizing that emotions are becoming intense and having the ability to interrupt whatever is happening are two different skills. The natural pattern for many people when emotions start to get intense is to focus less attention on the emotions and more attention on trying to cope with the problem or resolve the disagreements. They actually try harder and harder to solve the problem, and are more motivated to resolve the situation. They say things like "Let's not put this off. Let's take care of it right now." The result is that often when people become aware that they and others are getting upset, they are less and less inclined to stop whatever they are doing that is contributing to the emotions and deal with them. In other words, this skill is also not something that "comes naturally" to people, and the American culture tends to interfere with interrupting the situation and dealing with the emotions first. Comments such as the following illustrate this skill:

> The madder I get the more I try to get to the bottom of things and take care of the situation. I don't want to stop. I want to solve the problem.

❊❊❊❊❊❊❊❊❊❊❊❊❊❊❊❊❊❊❊❊❊❊❊❊❊❊❊❊

> When we are not upset we don't think about our problems. It is only when we get a head of steam up that we have the motivation to even talk about things, and if we stopped to calm down we would probably not want to start up again.

Find Ways to Decrease the Intensity of Emotions

A third skill in dealing with intense emotions is having the ability to know what to do to decrease the intensity of the emotions. In some situations, this is relatively easy. Sometimes it can be accomplished with short and simple things such as counting to 10, taking a short time-out, taking a few deep breaths, or stopping to get a drink of water.

In other situations it is more challenging to find ways to decrease the intensity of emotions. Emotions about the family part of life are sometimes deeply felt, not superficial feelings that easily come and go. Often they are complex and multifaceted, and often they deal with some of the most important parts of life. The result is that in some situations, it takes considerable time to find ways to help the emotions become calm enough that people can respond in rational, thoughtful, and loving ways. It seems to us that these are the situations where it is most important to back off from trying to solve a problem or disagreement and deal with the emotions first, and sometimes this takes considerable skill, empathy, and understanding. The following comments by people we have interviewed illustrate this skill:

> I just love what one of our grandsons does when he gets frustrated and angry. He gets up and walks out of the room and goes to his room. He's done it since he was a little guy. The family will be in the middle of something, and if he gets irritated or annoyed off he goes. After a little while he'll come back and join the rest, and he's calm and cool. I really don't know what he does while he's off by himself, but when he comes back it is like nothing is wrong. There are some other members of our family who are very different from him. They'll blow up and shout and yell or pout and be sour when things don't go their way, and it leads to some pretty loud arguments and ugly situations, but not him. He's off to his room all by himself, and then comes back in a while.

❊❊❊❊❊❊❊❊❊❊❊❊❊❊❊❊❊❊❊❊❊❊❊❊❊❊

> In my family as I was growing up, I learned to always deal with emotions first if there was a problem. For example, if we were planning a vacation, we'd sit around as a family and try to plan, and if my sister and I started fighting, the whole thing would get stopped, and wouldn't plan the vacation any more. We'd talk about "why are you mad" "how do you feel" and stuff like that, and we'd talk about the emotions with the ones who were upset, and once the emotions were taken care of and we weren't mad at each other, the planning would go super fast. Sometimes 90 percent of our planning was dealing with the bad emotions.
>
> Now I do the same thing with my kids. We talk about emotions, and I try to teach my kids how to deal with their emotions. We talk about it by saying things like "why do you feel that way" "yes, he said that and these are his words, but notice his tone of voice. Look at how he said it, not just what he said. What did he mean when he said it, and what does it tell us about how he is hurting? This helps us get along, and it helps us be a lot closer. And while we're talking about the feelings the topic or the content of what we were talking about becomes secondary, and usually pretty easy to deal with once you have the emotions happy.
>
> Stopping to talk about the emotions sometimes takes most of the time. It isn't the most efficient thing to do because it takes time away from other things, but it pays off in the long run because how we feel is an emotional thing, and helping the family members cope with the emotions, helping them label emotions, helping the learn how to handle emotions, change emotions, and express emotions helps the whole situation, and it bring people be closer in a family because you're not just doing things.
>
> If you wanted to be efficient you would just plan it and tell others, but for developing children and helping family members feel close to each other and help each other in tough situations, it is a valuable thing, to me really valuable.

Create and Re-Create Rapport

The dictionary defines *rapport* as a condition of connection having harmonious or sympathetic relations. When this concept is applied to the process of dealing with negative affect, it refers to how family members feel about communicating. When there is rapport, they feel comfortable, unthreatened, and safe.

When emotions are not intense, it is often easy to create a situation where family members have rapport by saying simple things like "Can we talk about something?" or "I have something I'd like us to talk about. Is now a good time?" It is more difficult to create rapport when negative emotions are intense, and family members may need to take more time to create rapport or wait until a later time when the negative feelings subside.

In emotional situations it is easy for the rapport to be lost. When anyone in the discussion becomes upset or feels threatened, these feelings may interfere with their ability to communicate freely and openly, and the rapport is lost. In these situations, it is often easier for family members to realize the rapport is lost than to realize that there are intense emotions, and the loss of rapport can be a clue that may help people realize the emotions in others are getting so intense that they are interfering.

There are many options when rapport is lost. One alternative that many people take is to persist in trying to communicate and solve the problem they have been discussing. When this happens, the situation often deteriorates more and becomes less productive. Another alternative is to use the skill discussed above and interrupt whatever has been causing the negative feelings by stopping the conversation. When this is done, the problem is not solved, but the situation does not deteriorate more.

A third alternative is to change the conversation and try to say things that will reestablish or re-create the rapport. This can be done sometimes with a simple apology such as "I'm sorry," "I shouldn't have said that," or "I didn't understand." In other situations, it may be helpful to describe positive feelings that may help. For example, comments such as the following can help: "I care about us and our relationship, and I want to be helpful"; "I didn't realize I was getting so carried away I was saying things that were offensive, and I'll try to do better"; "I love you and hope we can find a way to work things out." There are many situations where it is not possible to re-create the rapport quickly, and it is best to get away from the situation and try at a later time to solve the problem. In these situations, it is sometimes helpful to try to set a time to try again. This is especially helpful if some of the individuals are discouraged, highly concerned about the situation, and eager to solve the problem.

SUMMARY

This chapter discussed five aspects of loving behaviors that are particularly relevant when families experience disagreement. The five ideas are:

1. Peacemaking rather than contention helps families flourish.
2. Patience is helpful, and impatience tends to be harmful.
3. Cooperation tends to be helpful and most competition tends to be harmful. Competition that is engaged in for recreational purposes, where it is voluntary, and where winning is not an important part of life or tied closely with identities does not have the disruptive effects that flow from

competition that is personal, important, and involuntary, and where the rules are not clear.

4. Negative emotions such as anger are dangerous in families, and it helps when family members learn how to interact in loving ways even though they are experiencing negative affect, and to recognize when the intensity of the emotion begins interfering with their self-control and find ways to keep the emotion from being harmful.
5. Striving for consensus tends to be helpful in families, and strategies where family members strive to impose or force their will on others and are insensitive and disrespectful of the views of others tend to be harmful.

8

Coping With Undesirable Behavior

Another aspect of sacred theory deals with the ways families try to avoid undesirable behavior and how they cope with it when it cannot be avoided. Given the fallible and imperfect nature of we humans, it is inevitable and unavoidable that undesirable behavior will occur in families. And unfortunately, it doesn't just occur, it occurs frequently, even in families that are effective and successful. As children mature they try out many undesirable behaviors, and parents find themselves spending a substantial amount of time helping children learn which ways of behaving are desirable and which are not. Also, even after people are grown, as the old saying goes, "to err is human." Therefore all families find it necessary to deal with wrongs, and their ability to find constructive and facilitating ways of coping with these wrongs goes a long way toward being effective and successful or ineffective and unsuccessful.

In our search for ideas that seem to help in understanding which ways of dealing with undesirable behavior are helpful and which are harmful, our observations and interviews suggest that one of the most important and helpful ideas is to interact in loving ways. This chapter describes how six different aspects of this relatively general idea make a difference in families. They are (a) mercy, (b) compassion, (c) avoiding being judgmental, (d) avoiding reciprocity, (e) trying to be helpful, and (f) repenting.

Our data also suggest that the ideas that were discussed in Chapters 2 through 7 are also helpful in coping with undesirable behavior. Forgiveness, kindness, respect, interest in the welfare of others, service, dealing with agency wisely, peacemaking rather than contention, patience, cooperation rather than competition, and dealing with negative emotions wisely all help families to cope with undesirable behavior. There also are a number of other principles that help and harm, but we have limited our discussion to these ideas because it seems wise to build the theory in a gradual and manageable way, and other ideas can be added later.

MERCY

Christian teachings are one of the sources of the idea that mercy is important in human relationships. One of the beatitudes says, "Blessed [are] the merciful: for they shall obtain mercy" (Matthew 5:7). Christ also indicated that mercy is among the more weighty ideas in his teachings:

> Woe unto you, scribes and Pharisees, hypocrites! for ye pay tithe of mint and anise and cummin, and have omitted the weightier [matters] of the law, judgment, mercy, and faith: these ought ye to have done, and not to leave the other undone. (Matthew 23:23)

The idea that mercy is helpful when families are coping with undesirable behavior is one that we have observed, and it came up many times in our discussions with people about ways sacred matters are helpful. People described again and again how some family members are merciful and how some are not—and how those who do not exhibit this quality bring pain, suffering, and challenges into families, whereas those who are merciful in wise and appropriate ways bring healing, love, and growth, and help correct undesirable behaviors. The following two comments from our interviews illustrate these patterns:

> When my brother did not live up to what my father thought was right, my father thought the right thing for him to do was tell my brother how awful he was and be rejecting of him as a person. He'd criticize him in mean ways all the time and tell him he was "no good" and was an embarrassment and how ashamed he was of him. I'm sure he did it because he thought he was trying to hold up high standards, but the ways he rejected and condemned my brother created hard feelings all my brother's life. Even my brother's children couldn't stand their grandfather. They hated him because of how mean he was to anyone that didn't meet his high standards.

❖❖❖❖❖❖❖❖❖❖❖❖❖❖❖❖❖❖❖❖❖❖❖❖❖❖❖

> My father was not very tall, but he was really strong and worked in construction all of his life, and he even wrestled professionally for a while; but he also was soft and a gentle person. We called him our teddy bear. Whenever anyone was in trouble or did anything that was wrong he was the first one to reach out and try to help. He was so tender and gentle and understanding, and he always bent over backwards to find the positive side in everything. He was especially concerned about those who were being stepped on, and everyone just loved him. He was such a wonderful influence in our home.

One principle these situations illustrate is the idea that when undesirable behavior occurs in families it tends to be helpful if family members show mercy, and the absence of mercy tends to be harmful. Mercy is closely related to several other aspects of loving. For example, it is similar to kindness, forgiveness, and respectful patience, but it adds some unique qualities. These are subtle and difficult to describe and quantify, but they include a willingness or tendency to consider clemency, as well as an empathic and sympathetic concern for others that is prompted by an understanding attitude, softness, benevolence, tenderness, and gentleness. Mercy is a tendency to be lenient rather than harsh or strict, and it adds an extra measure to qualities such as tolerance, gentleness, and forbearance.

Low levels of mercy are evident when people tend to be stern, strict, and demanding; when people tend to be severe or cruel; and when they emphasize details or the letter of the law and tend to be callous and exacting rather than benevolent, munificent, and tolerant.

We do not know of scholarly literature that has focused on the role of mercy in family processes. Therefore the scholarly literature is not among the sources of this idea, and social science doesn't contribute evidence about the ways mercy influences family processes or outcomes. The reasons mercy has not been studied likely include the challenge that because it has such a subtle quality, it would be difficult to observe and quantify. Therefore it is probably better studied and understood through literary and artistic lenses rather than scientific inquiry. It will be interesting to see how much it is studied as a result of including it as a part of sacred theory.

One issue that deserves attention in future research is whether mercy has one dimension or two. There is evidence that some concepts, such as kindness and unkindness, have two dimensions,[1] but mercy seems to be different. Being merciful and merciless seem like the opposite ends of one dimension rather than separate phenomena.

Some of the people in our interviews commented that they thought mercy tends to create some of the more delicate, noble, and gracious parts of what it means to be human—that it tends to foster other gracious, decent, noble, and fine qualities such as gentleness, patience, tenderness, appreciation, and love. Conversely, the lack of mercy tends to move relationships and conditions toward more inconsiderate, intolerant, and base qualities—toward the more baneful, ignoble, and base. Thus mercy seems to have an ennobling, enriching, and enhancing quality to it that helps families develop some of the more beautiful, inspiring, elevating, and decent qualities. However, these ideas are based on the ideas of relatively few people, and much more research is needed.

The principle that mercy ennobles life probably ought to be qualified with the idea that mercy is helpful when it is used *wisely*, because there are some circumstances and conditions where mercy is wholesome and uplifting and others when it is neither helpful nor loving. In the absence of research that helps us understand when it is wise and unwise, we are left to speculation to try to understand these differences. However, it seems reasonable to posit that mercy is helpful when family members exhibit undesirable behavior unintentionally or in ignorance, and when family members are trying to exhibit desirable behavior. Conversely, mercy does not seem wise when family members are intentionally evil, exploitative, or abusive, or when they continue to exhibit undesirable behavior for long periods of time. In these situations, it is probably wise to give more emphasis to justice than mercy and to have these individuals face and deal with the consequences of their behavior. One way of doing this is to resort to the less merciful but helpful and effective strategies that have been described as "tough love" (P. Neff, 1982). The bottom

---

[1] The literature about aspects of family life having one or two dimensions was discussed in Chapter 2 on pages 36–37. Orden and Bradburn (1968) and Winch and Blumberg (1968) introduced the idea that some aspects have two dimensions, and additional evidence has been provided by Gray (1987), Fincham (Fincham, 2000; Fincham & Beach, 2002; Fincham, Davila et al., 2007; Fincham et al., 2004), and Gordon et al. (2009).

line is that there is a need for more study of the nature and role of mercy in families to help us understand the circumstances in family life that enable us to better see when mercy is wise, when it is unwise, and when it becomes a destructive and "enabling" part of the undesirable behavior.

COMPASSION

Compassion is another quality that is similar to some of the other principles about loving. It bears similarities to concepts such as mercy, forgiveness, and kindness, but also seems to have some unique features. The principle here is that *compassion tends to help families cope with undesirable behavior and the lack of it tends to be harmful.*

The idea that compassion is important is another central idea in many of the world religions. It is elevated to the status of the key virtue in the Mahayana branch of Buddhism (Smith, 1991, p. 126). Christ also exhibited compassion and taught that others should follow him (Matthew 18:33), and Peter pled with his followers that they show compassion to each other (1 Peter 3:8).

Dictionary definitions of compassion are helpful in understanding how it is different in subtle ways from similar terms such as mercy and forgiveness. The *Random House Dictionary of the English Language* (1967) defined compassion as a feeling of sympathy or sorrow for another who is stricken by suffering or misfortune, accompanied by a strong desire to alleviate the pain or remove its cause—and it often includes a desire to help. Thus compassion is an attitude that means family members have a desire to respond to undesirable behavior and to the individuals who misbehave with gentleness, tenderness, care, kindness, consideration, hope, softness, empathy, and *help*.

Some of the ways of responding to undesirable behavior that are not compassionate are to demean and shame, or to show indifference, coldness, and harshness. Other ways of relating that are not compassionate are to be condemning and rejecting of the ways others behave. A lack of compassion is also exhibited when people think they know what is right or proper for others, and are demanding and critical in stern and severe ways.

We do not know of any scholarly literature that has specifically focused on the role of compassion in families. It is likely that some of the reasons it has not been studied are similar to the reasons mercy has not been a part of scientific research. Both of these aspects of loving are so subtle and delicate that they are difficult to define, observe, and quantify.

Our observations and interviews provide a little related evidence. We have seen some family members exemplify compassion whereas others have not, and we have watched the difference this has made in several families. Also, some of the people we have interviewed have commented on the presence and absence of compassion. Our data suggest that when compassion is a lived quality, it is a "table setter" for many of the beautiful and noble traits and actions that characterize flourishing families. More specifically, compassion tends to promote sympathy, empathy, warmth, understanding, mercy, kindness, consideration, patience, and gentleness, whereas the lack of it tends to produce distance, rejection, negative

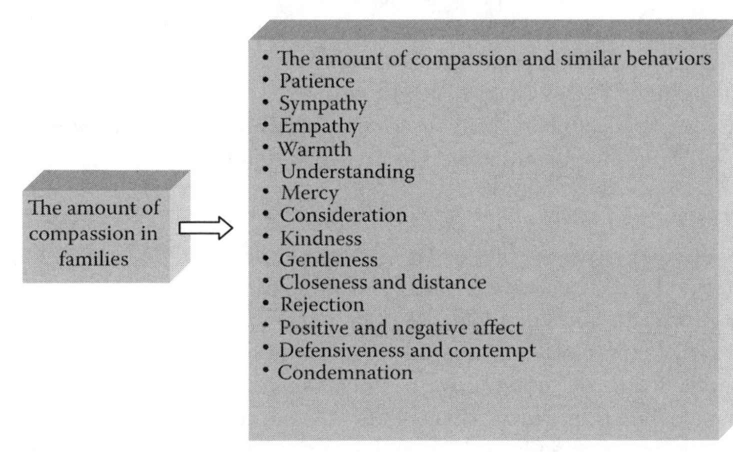

Figure 8.1 The influence of compassion.

affect, defensiveness, contempt, and condemnation. These outcomes are visually summarized in Figure 8.1, and are illustrated in the following comments:.

> Laura is critical of Fred in about every way. It doesn't matter what he does, she reads into it that he is just being selfish, inconsiderate, and egotistical. He takes it and takes it, and she never lets up. It is especially bad when she is upset about something, because then she's just like a buzz saw or machine gun peppering him with how stupid and immature he is. I've seen the pain in his eyes and the way he responds by withdrawing into a shell to protect himself, and her attitude also drives her away from him. They don't have much that is beautiful left in their relationship.

The compassionless example above contrasts sharply with the story of Megan, the young child who was fighting leukemia, as told in Chapter 4, page 73.

We find it significant that in the above narrative, compassion not only is beautiful in and of itself but also seems to beget compassion in others. Our data do not provide much additional information about how different aspects of family life are influenced differently by variation in compassion so we need to wait for future research to provide insights about these differences. Another issue that future research will help with is whether it is useful to distinguish between aspects of being loving that are very similar—such as compassion, mercy, kindness, and forgiveness. It is possible that it will be best to combine some or all of these aspects conceptually.

BEING JUDGMENTAL

Our observations and the patterns in our interviews suggest that the biblical ideas about judging are another part of coping with undesirable behavior in loving and unloving ways. A few of the people we interviewed suggested that the best approach is to follow the injunction in the Sermon on the Mount and "judge not" (Matthew 7:1), but most people believe this issue is more complicated than this and that judging can be wise, appropriate, and helpful, or unwise, inappropriate, and harmful (John 7:24; Leviticus 19:15; Luke 7:43).

The idea that seems to best summarize when judging is helpful and harmful deals with how much family members are "judgmental." The relevant principle is that *when family members avoid being judgmental it tends to be helpful, and when they are judgmental it tends to be harmful.*

It is challenging to define the differences between judging and being judgmental, but our discussions with a variety of people helped clarify these differences and their effects. Our data suggest that people are judgmental when they have a pattern of being condemning and critical in a conclusive way that allows little opportunity for those being judged to change, repent, or reform. People are less judgmental when they are cautious, tentative, and sensitive, and when they confine their judgments to specific acts or behaviors—as opposed to casting the person as holistically "bad." People are more judgmental when they are quick to make negative conclusions about the motives, intentions, and character of others—and when they make negative judgments about others as whole personalities. They are judgmental when they emphasize the mistakes, inadequacies, and limitations of others—and when they are quick to attribute malevolent motives and intentions. Family members can observe acts and behavior, and it is often necessary to make judgments about these actions (i.e., teaching children that hitting their siblings is wrong). However, family members cross a line and become judgmental when they make negative conclusions about the inappropriateness of motives, intentions, and the goals of others. This tendency crosses a line because they are making (harmful) inferences about things that are largely inaccessible to them. In the words of one person, "We only know where people hit. We do not know where they aim." Being judgmental involves emphasizing, paying attention to, assuming, and even creating negative aims and motives for others' undesirable behaviors. Those who are less judgmental tend to emphasize and pay attention to the positives around them. People are less judgmental when they look for and emphasize benevolent aims and goals and are willing to give others the "benefit of the doubt."

As the ideas about being judgmental became clearer to us, we did a number of searches in the scholarly literature to try to find previous research that focuses on these processes. We did not find any literature that deals with judgmentalness, but there is research about several topics that are similar. One of these is blaming. A number of studies have data that support the idea that intrafamily blaming is positively correlated with problems in families.[2] These studies provide some evidence in support of the principle, but blaming is sufficiently different from being judgmental that this research is only partially relevant. A key part of blaming is removing responsibility from one's self to others, and this can be done in both judgmental and nonjudgmental ways. Another complication with this research is

[2] Illustrative studies in this area are Montada (1992); Furlong and Young (1996); Schüutz (1999); Friedlander, Heatherington, and Marrs (2000); Wolpert (2000); C. Bowen, Madill, and Stratton (2002); Bowen et al. (2005); Stratton (2003); and Kim and Miklowitz (2004).

that most of it deals with other issues such as the role of blaming in therapeutic settings and the study of correlations that deal with antecedents of blaming. There is so much ambiguity and complexity in this research that it is limited in the inferences that can be made about the role of judgmentalness in families, and "there is no consensus about how patterns of blaming may causally influence the development of psychological problems" (Bowen, Stratton, & Madill, 2005, p. 310).

A second topic where there is research that is relevant for this principle deals with negative attributions in families. There are a number of studies that have found a correlation between negative parental attributions and child conduct problems,[3] but the inferences that can be made from this research are also limited because the concept of negative attributions is slightly different from the concept of judgmentalness. Negative attributions are more of an optimism–pessimism issue than a propensity to be judgmental, and these attributions can be made in a judgmental way or in a cautious, thoughtful, considerate, and reluctant way. Also, the research about negative attributions has so many complexities about measurement and directions of influence that it is "unclear how child conduct problems and parental attributions influence each other over time." (Wilson, Gardner, Burton, & Leung, 2005, p. 111).

The bottom line is that research about topics such as blaming and negative attributions provides some evidence in support of this principle, but it is very limited and there is a need for additional and better research. The data in our interviews and discussions provide some of this additional research, but it too is very limited and only a beginning. Our data suggest that when family members are judgmental, it tends to produce negative affect, defensiveness, discouragement, resistance, and alienation. Our data also suggest that being judgmental may be less contagious than many other harmful things in families. If this is the case, it is probably partly because there are social norms in our culture that discourage the negativism and pessimism that are associated with being judgmental. These ideas are based on relatively few data, and they should be viewed as highly speculative until additional research provides more evidence about the existence and importance of these ideas.

AVOIDING RECIPROCITY

The law of reciprocity is an asset in families when things are going well and there are positive feelings and helpful ways of behaving. However, when there is undesirable behavior, the law magnifies the undesirable processes and interferes with success. These patterns lead to the insight that avoiding reciprocity by doing good to those who wrong us is another insight about being loving that is valuable when families are coping with undesirable behavior. This reasoning leads to the principle that *responding in loving ways rather than in reciprocal or contingent ways when there is undesirable behavior helps families thrive.*

---

[3] Illustrative studies in this area are Baden and Howe (1992), Johnston and Freeman (1997), Johnson and Patenaude (1994), Nix et al. (1999), Hastings and Rubin (1999), and MacKinnon-Lewis et al. (2001).

The idea that it is helpful to return good for evil is a major theme in the New Testament (Matthew 5:43–47), and the law of reciprocity helps us understand that this principle goes against human nature. It is healing and constructive when we are able to resist our natural tendencies of returning evil for evil and wrong for wrong. It helps relationships endure and even thrive, in spite of challenging situations. It helps avoid and break vicious cycles. It helps avoid and quell tendencies toward vengeance and retaliation that are so destructive and disabling.

There is considerable classical literature that also takes its cue from the tension between the above ideas of vengeance and "returning good," including Dumas's *Count of Monte Cristo*, who insists on premeditated and ultimately unfulfilling revenge on one hand, and Victor Hugo's priest in *Les Miserables*, whose merciful refusal to call for justice proves to be the echoing impetus for change in the life of erstwhile thief Jean Valjean. The idea that "turning the other cheek" can be a transition toward the wise use of positive reciprocity is also seen in the following example:

> The more he treated her as though she were really very nice, the more Lotty expanded and became really very nice, and the more he, affected in his turn, became really very nice himself; so that they went round and round, not in a vicious but in a highly virtuous circle. (von Armin, 2007, p.152)

A least a portion of these ideas address the notion that the demand for an "eye for an eye and a tooth for a tooth" eventually leaves us all blind and toothless. There is, as these examples from literature contend, a better way to live as individuals and families.

There is a large literature that argues for the validity of the norm of reciprocity, but there is very little scholarly literature that focuses on the idea that "turning the other cheek" is helpful in marriage and family relationships. One study that deals with these ideas was conducted by Murstein et al. (1977), who measured the amount of "exchange orientation" people reported in their relationships. An exchange orientation Is the tendency to keep track of the positives and negatives in a relationship (i.e., "tit for tat") in an effort to be equitable and fair. In some ways, this idea is a reciprocity orientation where individuals try to behave in reciprocal ways. This study found that an exchange orientation is positively related to the quality of relationships in friendships but negatively related in marital relationships. This suggests that marital relationships tend to thrive when people behave in loving ways—whether the other spouse is behaving in loving ways or not. This conclusion is a rather substantial inferential leap from the data, but it seems reasonable. This is another area that needs more research, but in the meantime, the meager extant evidence seems to argue in favor of the idea that turning the other cheek is usually helpful in marriage and family relationships. This is particularly evident when the reciprocity cycle is negative. *Someone must break the cycle* if positive reciprocity is to ever commence, or recommence.

Our observations and interviews provide a little evidence that turning the other cheek is helpful in families, and the following comment illustrates one way this appeared:

> There were some ways our marriage was wonderful right from the start, but in other ways we struggled in the first years of our marriage. Whenever one of us did something that wasn't very nice, the other one would usually respond in the same way. Sometimes this led to some long periods of time when it would escalate and we didn't even speak to each other. We tried several counselors, but it didn't really help until about three years ago. We learned from one counselor that the natural pattern is to reciprocate, and that is ok when things are going well; but it is helpful when things aren't going well to suck it up and try to be nice even if the other one isn't. It took us a while to break our old habits, but eventually we did, and it has made a world of difference in our marriage. And, one of the nice things about it in addition to avoiding the vicious cycles we used to get into is that both of us find it easier to be nice more of the time.

Next, we turn from the concept of avoiding negative reciprocity to the importance of trying to be helpful when there are challenges and difficulties in families.

HELPING

A theme that is given considerable emphasis in the New Testament is that people ought to pay attention to "the lost." One place this is emphasized is in the 15th chapter in Luke, where there are several parables that focus on various aspects of seeking and helping those who are lost. Some of the people we have interviewed mentioned that an aspect of this idea has been helpful as they have tried to cope with undesirable behavior in families. It has to do with the ways members of families respond to others in their family who are wandering, struggling, misbehaving, or "lost" in other ways.

When there is undesirable behavior in a family, there are many ways the members of families can respond. They can reprimand, censure, or criticize the undesirable behavior, and they can put pressure or demands on those who are deviant. Other negative ways of responding include being rejecting, judgmental, and condemning, and in more extreme situations family members can shun, ostracize, and even disown those who behave in undesirable ways.

The message in the New Testament is that the moral and noble way to respond to those who are inadequate or struggling is to give special attention to them, and to have the attention involve kind, loving, and noncondescending ways of trying to assist and be helpful. The best ways to respond involve more than just being disappointed, sad, angry, or distressed when things aren't going well. And merely having feelings of mercy and compassion for the less fortunate is not enough. It is important to translate feelings of concern into positive and loving behavior and actively try to do what one can to be helpful. These teachings in the New Testament are about human relationships in general, but this idea seems especially relevant and helpful when things are not going well in family relationships because relationships in families tend to be among the most intimate and enduring relationships for most people.

The principle that summarizes these insights is the idea that *actively trying to be helpful in loving and positive ways to family members who exhibit undesirable behavior is helpful in families, and negative patterns of relating in unloving ways are harmful.*

This is another area where we do not know of any scholarly literature that has focused on this idea, but it is an area where it would be relatively easy to get qualitative and quantitative data that are relevant. Our observations and interviews provide a little evidence that is persuasive, but there is a need for more research. The following comments illustrate this principle in the families of the people we interviewed:

> When members of our family, especially the sons-in-law, did not behave the way my mother thought they should, she was very rejecting. She didn't say much to them, but she would snub and ignore them, and she would tell others in the family how they weren't worthy of her daughters and [that] her daughters ought to divorce them. I never did think that the way she responded was very helpful or constructive, and I think it created a lot of pain and hurt in the family.

❋❋❋❋❋❋❋❋❋❋❋❋❋❋❋❋❋❋❋❋❋❋❋❋❋❋❋

> When I was young I can't count the number of whippings I got from my Dad. He'd take his belt off and let us have it until the cries of my mother would make him stop. I was about 15 when he started coming after me one day, and I knew what was coming, so I took off running. I easily cleared the gate of the corral and just kept on running, and stayed out in the field for about an hour—until I knew he would be cooled off. He never tried to spank or whip me again, but he also never ever sat down with me and talked with me in a calm, helpful, and loving way about what I was doing wrong. It wasn't that I was all that bad as a child, but I did a lot of dumb things that I wish I hadn't done, and I'll bet that if he were more helpful rather than just punishing I may have avoided some of the trouble I got into later.

The story on pages 28–29 of a brother who spent 50 years doing many things he knew he shouldn't is an example of helpful ways of responding to those who are struggling or misbehaving. A year or so after he turned his life around at age 65 he was asked by several of his siblings what prompted him to change. His response was: "You guys just kept on loving me. It didn't matter what I did, you just kept on loving me."

There is another valuable message in the parables about "the lost" (e.g., the lost coin, the prodigal son, and the lost sheep). In our efforts to help rescue family members who are profoundly struggling or "lost," a dangerous self-righteousness can creep in. A human tendency, like that of the scribes and Pharisees Christ explicitly condemned, is that we frame ourselves (i.e., in the parable of the lost sheep) as being among "the ninety and nine" or as the dutiful brother of the prodigal son, and we think we are doing well whereas our brother, sister, or wayward child is obviously "lost." We fail to catch the implicit and masterfully nuanced idea in these teachings that the "ninety and nine" are those who have "no need for repentance" (Luke 15:7). A closer look reveals *there are no* "ninety and nine," except for those of us arrogant enough to cast ourselves in that role. It appears that as elsewhere, Christ is subtly drawing on and referencing the words of the prophet Isaiah: "*All* we like sheep have gone astray; we have turned *everyone* to his own way; and the Lord hath laid on Him the iniquity of us *all*" (Isaiah 53:6; emphasis added). Therefore as we conclude this section on recognizing, reaching out to, and redeeming "the lost," we note the emphasis this sacred literature places on a commencement point—ourselves.

REPENTING

Another principle that can help families cope with undesirable behavior is for people to turn from undesirable behavior and behave in more desirable ways. In religious teachings this is called repentance. The principle is that *repenting is helpful in families, and the lack of repentance is harmful.* This principle is illustrated in a delightful way in the comments of one of the mothers we interviewed:

> One of our boys was always in trouble because he was so curious and had so much energy, but he was a world-class repenter. He was always repentant, instantly, as soon as realized what he was doing, and it was very helpful in our family.

There are a few ideas in the scholarly literature that provide insights about this idea. One is the idea in systems theory that family systems tend to have an inclination for morphostasis—which is stability or a lack of change. Repentance involves change, and this means there is a tendency in families to resist repentance and to expect that family members will continue to act the way they have in the past. Sometimes the desire for predictability and order is so strong that it even appears as pressure on people to not make changes that would generally be viewed as positive and constructive. This tendency to resist change is illustrated in the way Inspector Javert absolutely refuses to believe that Jean Valjean has genuinely repented in Victor Hugo's *Les Miserables*.

There is an aspect of Christian teachings that seems especially valuable in helping family members repent. According to Christian beliefs, Christ is the Redeemer or Savior, and one aspect of his saving ability is that he has the capacity to remove the undesirable aspects of sin and allow people to start over with a clean slate. When this idea is coupled with the idea that mortals ought to readily forgive others, those who believe in these ideas have some unique resources that can help families resist the natural tendency for morphostasis and move toward genuine change or morphogenesis.

APPLICATIONS

In this chapter, we have emphasized mercy, compassion, helping, repenting, avoiding harmful reciprocity, and not being judgmental as six powerful principles/qualities/efforts that help families cope with undesirable behaviors. Given the aforementioned dearth of empirical literature on these six principles in family life, we again turned to other sources including classical and religious wisdom literature as we highlight some potential applications of these principles.

First, we emphasized Aristotle's notion of a golden mean—a prudent and effective balance of opposing forces—in connection with applying each of the six identified principles. For example, mercy must be balanced with justice. Avoiding being judgmental and being tolerant should not be stretched so far that we embrace undesirable behavior and abandon sacred core values. Compassion must sometimes include punishment and tough love. Helping (which by definition tends to be done by one in a stronger position) must be gracefully laced with the quality of humility and be devoid of condescension, or it can do more harm than good. Indeed, it may be that no other principles in this book are more complex to balance and apply effectively than those listed above—and yet they are all vital in coping with undesirable behavior.

A second point, drawn from the classical German playwright Johann Wolfgang Goethe, states, "Treat a man as he is and he will remain as he is. Treat a man as he can and should be and he will become as he can and should be." This single statement integrates several, if not all, of the preceding principles for coping with (and indeed transforming) negative behavior. Similarly, social scientists have long been aware of the "Pygmalion effect" or self-fulfilling prophecy whereby the *expected* outcome is unwittingly made more probable through subsequent behavior (Covey, 2001). It may be that this holds especially true in families, for good or ill, depending on whether we counter and cope with negative behaviors by meeting them with increased negative behavior (and implicit expectations for more of the same) or with a behavior that has the potential to disrupt negative reciprocity and promote family strength.

> Treat a man as he is and he will remain as he is. Treat a man as he can and should be and he will become as he can and should be."
>
> Goethe

A third recommended application for integrating the above principles into a productive model for coping with undesirable behavior is drawn from LDS religious literature:

> Influence . . . ought to be maintained . . . only by persuasion, by long-suffering, by gentleness and meekness, and by love unfeigned; By kindness . . . without hypocrisy, and without guile—Reproving betimes with sharpness, when moved upon by [God]; and then showing forth afterwards an increase of love towards him whom thou hast reproved, lest he esteem thee to be his enemy; That he may know that thy faithfulness is stronger than the cords of death. (*Doctrine & Covenants* 121:41–44)

Like Goethe's earlier gem, the above statement encapsulates several of the principles needed to successfully cope with undesirable behavior. These two highly integrated statements lead us to our final point of application.

In coping with undesirable behavior across time in families, we previously drew on Aristotle's rule of the golden mean to emphasize that mercy must be balanced with requisite justice, and each of the other principles with their respective counterbalance. There is an additional point that comes into play as well. Although it has been pragmatically difficult to deal with six different principles for coping with undesirable behavior in the same chapter, part of our intention in doing so is to emphasize not only that balance is crucial with individual principles (i.e., mercy and justice), but that these six principles must all be applied in a synergistic union to optimally cope when a family member really blows it. In such cases, resisting the urge to refuse to hurt in return (reciprocity) is critical, but it is only an initial step. Mercy (even well-balanced mercy) is rarely enough alone. Compassion and a lack of degrading judgmentalism are also important, but again, still more may be needed. Help may be offered—help of the best possible quality—but still more is needed. True, heartfelt repentance is requisite to fully put the pieces back together, as is repentance's twin sister, forgiveness.

Another idea that helps apply the ideas about reciprocity is that it is helpful to think about two different aspects of it, which have been called the *ripple effect* and the *restoration effect* (Burr et al., 1982, p. 33). The ripple effect is that the ways of behaving expand out from a person like the ripples in a pond when a pebble is thrown into it. This is seen when a person "gets up on the wrong side of the bed" and their grumpiness tends to spread through the family. The restoration effect occurs when the ripples hit the side of the pond and eventually return to the place where the pebble is thrown in. Thus when people are kind and thoughtful or mean and hurtful, the influence of these behaviors tends to spread out to others and then return back to the person who was the point of origin.

In conclusion, the energy, effort, and almost dizzying complexity required to successfully cope with undesirable behaviors serve as a testimony that, typically speaking, we are far better off as family members to behave in desirable and considerate ways in the first place. Even so, individuals in successful families must learn to cope with the undesirable behaviors of those they love, as others learn to cope with theirs. This is perhaps the most complex and challenging exercise in family life and, as many family scholars have observed, the surprising thing is not that some families fall apart but that any of them miraculously choose to stay together. In our own work we have defined strong families *not* as those without "storms and stresses" but as those who find ways to weather life's inevitable storms well and together (L. D. Marks et al., 2006, 2008).

SUMMARY

This chapter discussed six concepts and accompanying principles that are aspects of being loving and are helpful in avoiding and coping with undesirable behavior. Those concepts and principles included:

1. Mercy: When undesirable behavior occurs in families it tends to be helpful if family members show mercy, and the absence of mercy tends to be harmful.
2. Compassion: Compassion tends to help families cope with undesirable behavior, and the lack of it tends to be harmful.
3. (Not) Being Judgmental: When family members avoid being judgmental it tends to be helpful, and when they are judgmental it tends to be harmful.
4. (Avoiding) Negative Reciprocity: Responding in loving ways when there is undesirable behavior helps families thrive.
5. Helping: Actively trying to be helpful in loving and positive ways to family members who exhibit undesirable behavior is helpful in families, and negative patterns of relating in unloving ways are harmful.
6. Repenting: Repenting is helpful in families, and the lack of repentance is harmful.

Our discussion of these principles was primarily grounded in sacred and classical literature, but there is also some evidence for these principles in our observations and interviews.

We also argued that there may be a conceptual justification for studying these principles for coping with undesirable behavior in an integrated way because all six principles seem to be necessary and interconnected. There is a need for much more research that provides additional evidence about whether, when, and how these principles are helpful to families as they cope with undesirable behavior.

9

Loving God

We suspect that some of the ideas in sacred theory are relevant only for people who believe in the spiritual-divine-sacred-religious parts of life, and that others are relevant for believers and nonbelievers. For example, when family members are loving, kind, respectful, forgiving, and merciful, this probably helps families of believers and nonbelievers; and, when people act in the opposite ways, it probably hurts in the families of believers and nonbelievers. But asking and seeking spiritual help may be helpful only in the families of those who believe the spiritual-divine-religious parts of life are real and important. Research has not focused on these differences, so this is merely a working hypothesis; but it seems like a reasonable difference and is one of the many research questions that are raised in this book where future research will hopefully provide new insights.

Another aspect of the sacred that is probably more relevant for believers than nonbelievers is the relationship family members have with the divine. Mahoney (2010, pp. 819–820) theorized that the relationships family members have with the divine is one of the important ways the sacred influences families, and this chapter focuses on one aspect of these relationships that our observations and interviews suggest is important. It has to do with how and how much family members love God.

PRINCIPLE

The principle that is the central idea in this chapter comes from one of the common aspects of the Abrahamic religions. These religions all believe that loving and following God is *the* most important and fundamental ideal. This is seen in the first four of the Ten Commandments in the 20th chapter of Exodus and in the teachings in the Qur'an. It is also seen in the following exchange in the New Testament:

> Then one of them, which was a lawyer, asked him a question, tempting him, and saying, Master, which is the great commandment in the law? Jesus said unto him, Thou shalt love the Lord thy God with all thy heart, and with all

> thy soul, and with all thy mind. This is the first and great commandment. (Matthew 22:35–38; also in Mark 12:28–30 and Luke 10:25–28)

The lawyer and Christ in this exchange were interested in commandments from God, and they were probably also interested in the commandments' implications for salvation in the next life. In sacred theory we are not interested in loving God as a commandment or imperative or for the implications it has for what happens in heaven. Our interest is in whether loving God helps families during mortality, and as we focus on this issue, our first concern is with trying to understand the principle that underlies the injunction. It seems to us that the general principle is the idea that *the amount family members wisely love God influences family processes and outcomes*.

There are several aspects of this principle that deserve elaboration. One of these is that most of the ideas in sacred theory are so broad, fundamental, and widely shared in many of the world religions that they are relevant for many different religious traditions. The ideas in this chapter are slightly different in that they derive from and are more relevant for the Abrahamic religions and other religions that view God(s) as something that ought to be loved. Many of the religions that originated in Eastern cultures do not view God(s) as something that has a unique existence and identity and ought to be loved, so the ideas in this chapter are probably not very relevant for those who are part of these traditions. Rather, they seem relevant only for those who view God(s) as having an existence and presence where love for God(s) is appropriate.

There are four other aspects of this principle that seem important in creating sacred theory. We have chosen to discuss them in the following order, framed as questions. First, when is loving God helpful and when is it harmful? Second, what do our data suggest about the effects loving God has in families? Third, what evidence do we have for the idea that loving God makes a difference in families? Fourth, how do contingencies or contextual factors influence the effects?

WHEN IS LOVING GOD HELPFUL AND HARMFUL?

What is sometimes called the "law of opposition" says that when anything has a potential for good, it also has a potential for bad and the amount of potential is proportional. The proportionality means that a phenomenon that has the potential for great good also has the potential for great harm, and a phenomenon that has the potential for only a small amount of good tends to have the potential for only a small amount of harm. We think this idea is relevant for the principle about loving God because our data suggest this principle is an idea that has the potential for great good and therefore also the potential for enormous destruction.

If we were using deterministic and mechanistic assumptions about the role of the sacred in family, we would be seeking propositions about how some parts of reality cause other parts in a necessary and sufficient manner, but such an approach would ignore the reality that humans have at least some degree of independence and agency in the ways they define, perceive, and behave. Humans are always in the process of perceiving what is happening around them and responding in ways that are at least partially creative, unpredictable, spontaneous, indeterministic, and innovative. They frequently choose from a range of possibilities and an almost infinite variety of alternatives and variations as they respond to what they perceive and try to realize their aspirations.

This means that when people love God this can lead them to act in many different ways. They can act wisely and unwisely. They can do things that are compatible with the needs of families and engage in actions that are helpful, moral, and constructive. And it is also possible to do things that are incompatible with the nature and needs of families—things that are destructive, immoral, and unwise. There are some views of God and philosophies about loving God that are vindictive and cruel, and some of these views lead to exploitation and abuse. Some of them lead to immoral activities such as taking the life of other humans in sacrifice them to appease God(s), disfiguring people, and participating in cruel rituals. These ways of showing love to God(s) are incompatible with the nurturing, caring, and helping behaviors that are necessary for peaceful, loving, and effective family life.

There are many examples of the dark side of loving God. More than a few people have murdered prostitutes with the perverted view that their behavior is showing their devotion to God and that God wants them to act in these destructive and immoral ways. Spouses and parents can use their love of God as the justification for being unbelievably cruel to and punishing and rejecting family members they believe are doing wrong.

Much of the greatest good and the greatest art, music, and literature that have ever been created arguably exist because of and derive from the love of God. The most beautiful peace and rapture that are known exist because of the love of God; on the other hand, the love of God also has led to some of the greatest pain and evil that has ever been known. One example of this is the ideological and cultural struggles between some of the Middle Eastern cultures that have existed for over three millennia. These conflicts have spawned numerous wars, revolutions, and unbelievable cruelty. They also are at the heart of what is called "terrorism" in our contemporary world. This is because the driving force behind and most fundamental cause for the contemporary spate of terrorism is a perverse "love" of God.

We suspect there is a natural harmony between what most people want to do with the spiritual and the needs and goals in families, but it is possible to twist and deviate from the moral and humane ideals advocated in the major world religions and adopt ways of relating that exploit and abuse others in the name of the sacred beliefs. It is also possible to use values based on the sacred as the basis for seeking power and domination over others in evil and destructive ways, sometimes in ways that are cruel and brutal. If people choose to turn to the dark and evil ways of using the sacred, it can lead to disastrous consequences, as illustrated in several case studies in Arterburn and Felton's (2001) book-length study, *Toxic Faith*.

Our analysis of a wide variety of the world's religious traditions suggests that most of the ideas and ideals in the widely used perspectives are an influence for good. However, this is not always the case, as some of the teachings do not translate into healthy ways of relating in families, but these deal with specific areas where there are problems rather than the general pattern.

There are many examples in different historical periods where people have twisted and perverted the behaviors that result from loving God in ways that have been harmful to families. Cultures have assembled armies and used military might to conquer in the name of God. The armies that marched thousands of miles and fought to dominate others during the Crusades undoubtedly created enormous harm to many families. Some of the ways people have expressed their obedience to and love of God have led many males to exploit, abuse, demean, and dominate women and children in the name of God. These examples have neither wisdom nor ethics.

The analysis by Griffith (2010) of ways religion can be used to heal and harm provides many additional insights into how the love for God can be constructive and destructive. He discussed how pathologically seeking a parent in God or seeking security in religious communities can be destructive, and how people can use their love of God only to protect their own family or possessions rather than to be concerned about larger communities or moral issues. Others who have elaborated on the many ways the love of God can be destructive are Ellis (1980), Walls (1980), and Pargament (1997, 2007).

Pargament et al. (1998) also developed several scales to try to measure ways people can use sacred phenomena in undesirable ways. They created scales for neglect, apathy, self-worship, punishment, passivity, vengeance, denial, conflict, and anger. The research about the relationships these scales have with other factors has focused primarily on individualistic aspects of coping and mental health, but these scales also can be used to study family processes.

EFFECTS

Our observations of marriages and families, the comments of our students and people we have tried to help, and the observations of people we have interviewed have led to some insights about some of the ways aspects of family life are influenced by loving and not loving God. Our data suggest that two of the ways variation in the love of God influences families are through *values* and *hearts*. These two concepts therefore are important parts of sacred theory, and the way we are using these terms deserves clarification.

Values

We use the term *values* the same way it has been widely used in scholarly inquiry for decades, but it seems wise to describe the way we are using it. Each wedding creates a new family, and when two individuals are married they bring with them complex sets of ideas and feelings in their minds and hearts. Some of their ideas are about specific and concrete parts of life, such as how clean and neat their home ought to be, how often they should visit relatives, how close they ought to be to their relatives, and whether muffins should be buttered on the top or broken in half and buttered inside—or whether they think it doesn't matter how muffins are buttered. Each cluster of ideas also has beliefs about what is important, and some of these beliefs are about specific and tangible things like cars, rings, and prized possessions.

Some of the ideas about what is important relate to intangible and abstract parts of life such as loyalty, freedom, beauty, achievement, fairness, cruelty, and abuse; and some of these abstract and general beliefs are about the things that are extremely important. The important and abstract beliefs are about the parts of life people think are the most fundamental, precious, and worthwhile; and social scientists have a term for these ideas. They are called values. The more specific and concrete beliefs are not values, even though some of them may deal with the monetary value of items and some of them may be important.

Values define which parts of life are the most basic, essential, central, and esteemed parts for us. Though everyone has some values that are similar to the people who are their personal and intimate associates, it is likely that they hold some values that are unique and different from those of many who are close to them (including family members). By the time we reach adulthood and perhaps are ready to wed and create a new family, most of us have some extremely strong emotional feelings about some of our values, and these parts of our ideology or beliefs are deeply revered and venerated.

There are a few things that are valued so highly that family members build their lives around them. Some value achievement, independence, or their career or profession more than anything else. Others value truth, learning, music, or physical fitness more highly than anything else. Some value the adrenaline rush that comes from dangerous and life-threatening experiences. Others value fame, power, or the economic parts of their life more than anything. Indeed, there is an almost infinite variety in human values.

It is not possible to value all of the many aspects of the human experience so much that everything is the most important. Therefore we all make choices about which parts of life are central and which parts are less important, peripheral, or devalued.

The term values is reserved for the beliefs that are highly general, abstract, and important. The love for God is important with regard to values because when people genuinely love God, this is such a fundamental and basic process that it has a profound influence on the other values people cherish. It leads them to value the sacred, religious, and spiritual parts of life, and has a profound impact in ancient and modern societies. Research indicates that 60% of Americans report that religion is "important" or "very important" to them (McCullough et al., 2000). However, levels of involvement in religion and religious influence in family life vary profoundly. Indeed, many Americans are only nominally or moderately religious, or are spiritual but not religious. Even so, Miller and Thoresen (2003) reported that religion *is* "the single most important influence in [life]" for "a substantial minority" of Americans (p. 25).

Hearts

We find it interesting that the term heart is not a central concept in any of the prevailing theories that are used in studying family (White & Klein, 2008). The term is not even in the index of Christensen's (1964) or Sussman and Steinmetz's (1987) handbooks. It is not in the two volumes of *Contemporary Theories About the Family* (Burr et al., 1979); nor is it in the Boss et al. (1993) or Bengston et al. (2005) sourcebooks. It is an important concept in the volume by Bellah et al. (1985) titled *Habits of the Heart*, and in Warner's (1995) model, and they use it the same way we are using it in sacred theory. But other than these exceptions, the term is not even a peripheral part of existing theories. This is another way sacred theory is different because the term heart is a central idea in the principle being discussed in this chapter and in many of the principles described in the other chapters in this volume.

We think it is no accident that the first descriptor Christ used about how people ought to love God is that they should love with all their "heart" (Matthew 22:35–38; also in Mark 12:28–30 and Luke 10:25–28). We think this word was used because it describes an unusually vital and important part of what is involved in this type of love, and this means that the concept of heart is also an essential component of sacred theory.

It is difficult to provide a rational definition of the term heart, and even more difficult to create operational definitions. It certainly isn't the organ that beats about 60 times a minute in our chests. However, as with most primary concepts in scholarly models, along with it being difficult to define them, it also isn't all that necessary to provide careful definitions because the concepts are fairly well understood by most people. For example, it is neither possible nor necessary to define a "dot" in geometry, and it isn't necessary to define behavior in behaviorism.

The concept of heart is widely used in the English language, and most people have a fairly good understanding of what it means without a precise definition. We refer to someone losing their heart, being pure in heart, the desires of the heart, hardness of the heart, and the bottom of the heart. The heart is partly mental, partly emotional, partly intentional and motivational, partly experiential, partly spiritual and divine. It is also more than each of these aspects, and none of these parts of it describe or define it well or capture its full essence. They don't get to the "heart" of what it is. It is, in a sense, the center of the soul or total personality. It is a group or cluster of desires, motivations, and inclinations that are deep inside the human spirit; and the heart is so central and important that humans tend to build their lives around what is in their hearts. It is therefore a crucial part of humans, as illustrated with this comment in the Bible: "For where your treasure is, there will your heart be also" (Matthew 6:21). This means the most precious and important values, choices, and behaviors derive at least partially from (and are consistent with) this cluster of emotions, thoughts, desires, experiences, aspirations, connections, and so forth.

Thus when humans set their hearts on something, it becomes a central and guiding part of their lives that helps determine what they are devoted and committed to and influences how they behave. Also, hearts can change in a number of ways. For example, we speak of being hard hearted and soft hearted, and we talk of opening or closing our heart. These changes are more than just cognitive or emotional changes. They are ways of being and living, ways of responding in a fundamental way as a whole person.

To summarize our ideas about the role of values and hearts, we theorize that variation in the amount people love God influences values and hearts in important ways. These three phenomena have an important influence on a number of the behaviors and family processes that are discussed in Chapters 2 through 12. Subsequently, these behaviors ultimately impact the probability of families encountering successes or failures. This means that loving God (and the effects this love can have on values and hearts) is one of the fundamental and basic concerns in sacred theory—and one that is related to many of the other parts of the theory.

Our data also suggest that what happens with this particular type of loving and with values and hearts probably does not have its greatest influence by *directly* changing important family outcomes like marital quality, marital stability, meeting important emotional needs, and effective socialization. Rather, it probably has its greatest influence indirectly rather than directly. By indirectly, we suggest that loving God tends to influence values and hearts, and they in turn influence an array of other family processes that influence desirable and undesirable family outcomes. When the love of God is strong enough to impact values and hearts, this love sets in motion and influences processes that open many doors and prompt family members to follow through with other ideas and ideals such as loving neighbors, forgiveness, mercy, peacemaking, patience, helping those who are less fortunate, returning good for evil, and avoiding being condemning and judgmental. As described in Chapters 5 through 8, these more specific ways of behaving have an influence on whether families flourish and flounder.

Valuing the Sacred

Our data suggest that one of the ways loving God influences values and hearts (and then other family processes) is that those who love God tend to value, appreciate, cherish, and use the sacred parts of life. In biblical terms, they seek first the kingdom of God (Matthew 6:33), and this leads them to: "Lay up for yourselves treasures in heaven, where neither moth nor rust doth corrupt, and where thieves do not break through nor steal. For where your treasure is, there will your heart be also. (Matthew 6:20–21).

Those with these values tend to seek and are involved with the spiritual, holy, or religious parts of life and use them as a resource. Those who do not have these values tend to ignore, avoid, and do not participate in or get involved with these sacred parts of the human experience. This difference is important because those who avoid and ignore sacred phenomena do not find the spiritual parts of the human experience helpful, but those who value, seek, and turn to the sacred may acquire an array of resources that can be helpful because many of the world's religious traditions provide a wide range of ideals and beliefs, prescriptive and proscriptive norms, aspirations and dreams, hopes and fears, and meaningful perspectives that tend to be consistent with the needs of family life. These aspects of the sacred "shape many individuals' core assumptions about ultimate goals, suffering, and good and evil behavior" (Mahoney et al., 2001, p. 585).

Valuing sacred phenomena probably makes little difference in families when it is a minor value or just one among many other things that are also valued. When the spiritual parts of life are just one among many things that are valued, the spiritual phenomena are so abstract, subtle, and elusive that they are easily crowded out by more the immediate, visible, and overtly powerful parts of life and the parts that provide more immediate and tangible benefits. It is only when the spiritual parts are valued so highly that they are an important and salient part of the heart that they exert much influence on what happens in families.

One of the practical consequences of this idea is that when the study of family gets sophisticated enough to quantify the relationship between valuing sacred phenomena and family successes, it is likely that the relationship that will be found will be curvilinear rather than linear. It will probably be an exponential curve, and it may have an identifiable threshold.

When people value the sacred in ways that are consistent with any of the world's major religious traditions, this is more than just consistent and harmonious with the nature of family and the needs of family. There are many aspects of this type of valuing that can actively help families thrive. It adds a perspective and vision that emphasizes allegiance, devotion, and commitment—as well as ways of relating to others that are almost always helpful and facilitating, especially to the weak and those not able to help themselves. It adds ways of approaching the challenges, tasks, and transitions of life in stable and nurturing ways. It adds ways of defining joy and fulfillment, ways of perceiving events and processes in life, and ways of meaningfully placing humans and family in a grand scheme that helps families cope, adjust, and endure. It adds ways of experiencing what it means to be human in interaction with others and the many aspects of the environments around families. Conversely, when significantly differing approaches to valuing and integrating the sacred exist within a family, challenges arise. This phenomenon can be intergenerational, intragenerational, or marital and has been called family *di-vision*—literally, two divided ways of viewing family life (Marks, 2004). When a spiritual family vision is *shared* there are several related benefits, as described by the following Jewish father of two young daughters:

> Being Jewish within a family of Jews was really important and marrying Jewish was real important to me. I wanted to be married to someone who had as much in common with me as possible. . . . There's a certain framework for life and marriage in Judaism. . . . I look at the dynamics of a happy family, and it's just all part of it.

Revering the sacred tends to create a cluster of attitudes and orientations, a direction and emphasis, and an overall philosophy of life that leads people and families to try to be moral and obedient, devoted, and responsible—and, when this center is shared, it also promotes unity. Family members may be more inclined to be forgiving and to ask and seek help from spiritual sources. They tend to view their lives and their family life as parts of a large and meaningful whole, which prompts them to behave in ways that are helpful in family life. They tend to have an openness in their minds and hearts, which helps them seek ideas about ways of behaving that will help their family life. Also, Chapters 5 through 8 discuss how being loving to others helps families, and those who value the sacred tend to encounter many ideas and admonitions that promote loving ways of relating.

Avoiding High-Risk Conditions

Our data also suggest that another of the ways loving God influences family processes is that it leads family members to create and maintain boundaries between their family and a number of lifestyles that involve high-risk behaviors where the probability of failures is high. This love can be a protective factor and help families avoid these undesirable conditions.

For example, theistic religious traditions encourage people to avoid immoral and illegal lifestyles. These traditions tend to encourage lifestyles that proscribe violent behavior, sexual promiscuity, and drug abuse. They tend to steer people into love and service-oriented lifestyles that avoid excessive greed, materialism, hedonism, and irresponsibility. They tend to direct people into lifestyles that encourage people to care for and love their children and make permanent commitments to provide, protect, and assist their children rather than abandon them for lifestyles that focus on fame, accumulation, adulation, and social prestige. Most of these alternative foci do not facilitate and promote a healthy and flourishing family life, and we believe that loving God helps people avoid these undesirable conditions.

Rationale for Moral Beliefs

Our data suggest that another of the ways loving God helps families is it provides a rationale for a moral code or philosophy. Family members in our modern world are bombarded with complexities and subtleties wherein different groups try to entice them to act in various ways. It is helpful to have a moral code or philosophy of life they can rely on to make choices and decisions in these situations, and loving God helps provide a moral code.

There are many things other than loving God that can also be the basis for moral codes. For example, they can be based on cultural traditions: "It is the way I was brought up"; "It is what everybody is doing"; "It is the latest trend"; "It is what experts, philosophers, historians, or charismatics say." Moral perspectives that are based on things that are this superficial and transient provide less stable and defensible beliefs.

Other Effects

Our data also suggest there are several other ways loving God tends to help families. One of these is that when people love God and realize that they are loved by God, this helps them understand God's desires, goals, and purposes. It helps them realize that God's work and glory, God's very purpose, is to love and help humans in their journey through mortality and toward salvation. These insights help provide a sense of meaning and purpose in life generally. They help provide a sense of dignity, value, and significance, and help people avoid a sense of meaninglessness, emptiness, disillusionment, discouragement, and nihilism. When people have a sense of meaning and purpose within an environment that emphasizes caring, loving, and helping others grow and develop, this rich combination of conditions helps family life flourish.

Another effect is that loving God helps people be aware of the limited, inadequate, and finite nature of their own selves, including the fallibility of their personal opinions and judgments. This way of thinking and feeling about one's own abilities helps cultivate a type of humility, teachableness, healthy deference, and openness to the ideas and opinions of others rather than a know-it-all attitude. Such ways of relating to others in families helps people understand others with empathy and cope effectively with differences and challenges.

Another effect is that loving God probably tends to create a conventional and obedient lifestyle rather than a rebellious, defiant, or distant way of living and relating to others, and these ways of behaving are consistent with the nurturing, helping, and loving needs in family life. Also, believing in God and loving God are acts of faith rather than certainty, and faith cultivates other good things, such as hope, optimism, and striving, and helps people avoid despair and emptiness. These qualities are so consistent with the widely shared goals described in Chapter 1 (pp. 18–21) that they probably help families thrive.

Another way loving God helps is that it tends to lead to the realization that God loves, which leads to feelings of being loved and loveable—not just loveable by other mortals but loveable to God and being loved by God. This helps provide such benefits as feeling accepted and worthwhile, and having an important degree of comfort with self and others—even in our struggling and imperfect wmortal condition—and these conditions help families thrive. These beliefs and feelings lead people to behave in ways that are consistent with God's love and God's wishes and commandments, and all of the major religious traditions strive to lead people to behave in their family life with love, care, nurturing, commitment, patience, and so on. Then, as the law of reciprocity suggests, these wholesome behaviors that are consistent with the needs of families tend to be reciprocated by others, and beautiful and productive cycles grow—increasing the probability of families finding successes and decreasing the probability of failures.

EVIDENCE

The sacred literatures in the Abrahamic religious traditions treat loving God in an individualistic way, but we have generalized the idea to family processes. The religious literature asserts that individuals ought to love God, and the implications are that individuals will be blessed if they love God. However, we have not found anything in these bodies of literature that connects loving God with family processes. Yet we are suggesting not only that there is a connection but that the connection is important for understanding the phenomena that help families flourish and flounder. Why do we make this connection? What is the basis of it? What are the sources of this extension or modification of this idea?

The individuals we have interviewed have described many situations where most of those who deeply love God and have organized their family around this love have flourished, and most of those who live differently have found more failures. The individuals in the following example are now great-grandparents, and they have a deeply felt joy in the family part of their life:

> From the very beginning, we were committed to creating a worthy family. We tried to put the Lord first in our lives and to organize our family life with God at the center. I don't know that we ever wrote out a "family mission statement" but if we had, it might have been expressed thus: This family is founded upon faith in the Lord Jesus Christ, and service in the Kingdom of God. We will obey the Lord's prophets and we will serve whenever and wherever we are called. We love one another and serve one another . . . Because of our faith in the atonement of Jesus Christ, we had faith in His prophets and we chose to be obedient to their counsel. . . .
>
> Since each of us is still a "work in progress" we might have to qualify the idea of success, or at least try to define it within some measurable parameters. Even then, I am not sure I am completely comfortable with the designation "successful," but I am willing to say that I believe we did some things right enough and long enough that we didn't ruin the absolutely wonderful children that the Lord entrusted to us . . . We are blessed beyond measure. Our cup runneth over.

The tragic side of these patterns is seen in the family of another father interviewed by one of the authors. He recounted the life of his brother as follows:

> You know, people tend to isolate themselves from the rest of the family [when they are in a state of depression], which is stressful for the rest of the family [meaning both "church family" and biological family]. I think one of the worst things that they do is, *they give up on faith*. In this particular case, he [my brother] stopped going to church, probably stopped praying. The worst thing that people could do is stop going to church, lose contact with their faith, not staying in contact with those people that would normally be like a support mechanism for them, and then, [instead turning to] things like drugs and alcohol, and violence. [My brother eventually drank himself to death.]

In addition to these examples, the authors have more than a little experience trying to help troubled marriages and families, and our observations of the marriages and families in these settings are consistent with the principle that is the thesis of this chapter. As families move through the therapeutic process, the nature of the changes couples and families make or do not make and the consequences of the changes are also consistent with this principle.

We also emphasize that we have known strong families who did not believe in God, much less claim that a love of God was central in their family life. We have also seen families who professed a love of God that was *not* manifest in their family relationships. We have also seen families where a deep and apparently authentic love of God was not enough to counter the destructive behaviors and decisions of some members. However, even with these caveats, the majority of our data suggest that the principle of loving God above all else was a central force in family life for many families. We could provide many more examples of the stories people have shared about how experiences tend to be different in families where loving God is a central part of life and where it is not, but we will limit ourselves to one more example from a father of four who shared his thoughts on this point:

> There's something that . . .when as a family your hearts are pointed together toward the same thing, and it's God, then parenting and economics and space and food and disagreements and hassles and joys and celebrations and all that other stuff . . . it works different, it seems different, it feels different. . . . Our family are all oriented in the same way. Christ is king. He's center. He's what it's all about. . . . I don't know how to convey to you that . . .yes, our faith informs our relationships and everything about us.

As seen in these narratives, the sources of these ideas are not quantitative scientific data. They are from our observations and qualitative data in interviews and discussions that are personal and subjective. This provides a depth and richness that is not usually found in quantitative data, and this description of the principle and the evidence for it makes this idea part of the literature in family studies, which means that now there is a need for more quantitative research about this notion that provides systematic and interpersonally replicable scholarly inquiry. This future research will be helpful in seeing if other kinds of data from other sources are consistent or inconsistent with the principle, and it also may help in refining and improving the idea. We describe some of these and other research needs and opportunities in Chapter 14, but next we shift to several other insights provided by our data about some of the ways loving God wisely helps families.

CONTINGENCIES

Our data suggest there also are several contingencies that influence when and how the expected relationship in the principle about loving God exists and doesn't exist. We do not know of any quantitative or systematic research that has addressed these issues, but our observations, interviews, and inputs from students and clients suggest there are several contingencies that are important.

One of these contingencies has to do with how consistent or harmonious other aspects of life are with the love of God. The ideal pattern is for people to behave so the other parts of their lives are consistent with their love of God. When this happens, people tend to love their neighbors and be honest and upright. They tend to be merciful and forgiving, live in accordance with the Golden Rule, and the like. When this type of harmony and authenticity exists, the principle probably operates in the expected way.

However, it is also possible for people to love God but live other parts of their lives in ways that are not consistent with this love. For example, they may act in ways that are dishonest, take advantage of their neighbor, or be condemning, judgmental, or cruel. When inconsistencies such as these exist, they probably negate or diminish the expected relationship between loving God and blessings in family life. The blessings that would be created in more harmonious situations tend to not happen as much or as often, and a variety of undesirable conditions probably tend to appear.

There is another contingency that also seems to influence how and when the relationship in this principle operates in the expected way. It is easy to understand that a deficit of love for God is less desirable than moderation, but what about an excess? Could an excess of this type of love lead to harm? James (1902) offered several extreme case studies in *The Varieties of Religious Experience* that indicate it is possible to have such an overabundance or excess of devotion or love that it can become pathological or fanatical. Also, Griffith (2010) identified a number of ways excesses can be harmful. These excessive conditions are probably rare, but they are possible, they exist, and they undoubtedly influence when loving God is helpful and harmful.

APPLICATIONS

Modern societies have so many persuasive, seductive, and attractive alternatives to loving God that it is not an easy matter to use or apply the principle in this chapter. Those who choose to use it need to exert considerable concentration, dedication, and ingenuity. One aspect of this application is that the principle makes a difference in families only when it becomes more than just a mental ideal. If it is to make a positive difference, it must become sufficiently salient and important that it shapes and influences *values* and changes *hearts*. When it is powerful enough to genuinely change hearts and to mold fundamental ideals it, then it can become something that helps families. This suggests that when people want to apply this idea, they might want to begin by examining how committed they are to this ideal and how much they are willing to forgo many aspects of modern society that compete with this ideal.

When people are sufficiently committed to the ideal of loving God that it changes their hearts and values, one of the next issues that is then relevant is finding ways to translate the ideal into behavior. Even when minds, hearts, and values are changed, if people do not find ways to translate this abstract ideal into how they act, then it will have little influence in their families. Intent and emotion are indispensable but insufficient.

There is a great deal of literature that suggests that people are the most successful in learning these skills when they find ways to surround themselves with intimates who share their values and help them practice and learn these skills.[1] This involves bridging and bounding—building bridges with those who share these desires and having the desired skills and abilities and boundaries to keep out the influence of those who do not share these ideals.

Another aspect of applying this principle has to do with a closely related idea in Christian thought. Christ taught that the two most important commandments are to love God and to love "thy neighbor." No "neighbors" are closer than one's immediate family. If these two commandments to love both God and neighbor are viewed as an inseparable pair and strived for in families, this effort commands attention and concern. If, however, these commandments are not sanctified through loving

---

[1] This is a central theme in several branches of the social sciences and has been well documented for decades. It is a thesis in symbolic interaction theory created by Mead (1934), Blumer (1938, 1969), and Rose (1962). It also was a major finding in a series of studies by Zimmerman and Broderick (1954, 1956) and Zimmerman and Cervantes (1956, 1960). It is also a central idea in a series of influential studies by Hyman (1942), Festinger (1954), Kelly (1955), Charters and Newcomb (1958), Siegel and Siegel (1957), Sherif and Sherif (1967), and Sherif, Sherif, and Nebergall (1965).

action and application, they are not very useful ideals. Another way of summarizing the application portion of this chapter is to emphasize that the ways of applying this ideal are more contingent on *behavior* toward our closest neighbors than they are on stated beliefs. This strong behavioral emphasis has many implications for clinicians, family life educators, and others who try to help families.

SUMMARY

This chapter described the principle that loving God can help families in a variety of ways—when this ideal is converted into sincere behavior and action. Loving God helps individuals and families value sacred phenomena, and can change values and the deepest desires of hearts. Loving God helps families avoid a number of high-risk behaviors that increase the probability of personal and familial failures. A love of God also provides a rationale for a moral code and philosophy that is harmonious with the needs of families, and contributes to a variety of other family processes that help families flourish.

With all of the above possibilities noted, there is another aspect of the principle in this chapter that also seems important. The principles about loving God and valuing the sacred do not suggest that a lifestyle where family members love God is the only way family members can find successes and avoid failures. They merely argue that loving God and valuing the sacred are *helpful* and *assist* families in increasing the probability of finding successes—when the ideal is converted into home-based action.

10

Generations

In some ways our attempt to describe a conceptual framework and theory about how sacred matters influence the quality of family life is like putting a puzzle together. Some of the pieces are simple to convey and easy to identify and put in the puzzle. Others are complex and subtle, and it is challenging to describe and integrate them. This chapter is about one of the more subtle ideas that appeared in our observations and interviews, and it is not as widely known or appreciated as many of the other ideas.

The central idea in this chapter is that *when hearts are turned wisely to predecessors and posterity, it helps families find successes and avoid failures.* This idea originated in several religious traditions. In the Judeo-Christian tradition, it is described in the last two verses of the Old Testament:

> Behold, I will send you Elijah the prophet before the coming of the great and dreadful day of the LORD; and he shall turn the heart of the fathers to the children, and the heart of the children to their fathers, lest I come and smite the earth with a curse. (Malachi 4:5–6)

A portion of this "curse" is outlined a few verses earlier. It includes "burning as an oven" that "shall leave neither root nor branch" (Malachi 4:1, KJV). In some unfortunate situations, individuals make decisions that sever ties with their parents and grandparents ("roots"), whereas others, most often fathers, sever ties with their children ("branches").

A similar version of this idea is one of the four main themes in Confucius's teachings about morality. It is the theme of *hsiao*, which is usually translated into English as filial piety or filiality. In Chen's (1990) description of Confucius's teachings, he describes reverence, respect, and appreciation for preceding generations as "the root of all virtues, which serves as the moving force for action in accordance with moral standards. It permeates all virtues, and gives life and strength for their translation into actions" (p. 275–276).

It is, of course, possible for people to be wise and unwise in the way their hearts are turned to their ancestry and posterity, and when these relationships are wise they are helpful. Also, our data suggest that wisely turning one's heart to ancestry and posterity influences some aspects of the human experience that are deeply important and very meaningful. It influences the ways people think and feel about themselves and others in their family and outside their family, the ways they relate to others, and what they value. It also provides a resource that helps people learn, grow, and develop effectively.

RELATED LITERATURE

There are ideas in four rather different bodies of literature that deal with parts of this principle: Erikson's theory of human development, Nagy's contextual theory of family processes, the literature on generational alliances, and the "roots" phenomenon created by Alex Haley. Each provides evidence for this idea and have contributed to and expanded our understanding of it.

Erikson's Theory

Erikson's (1950, 1959, 1968; Erikson & Erikson, 1997) theory of psychosocial development argues that humans move through eight stages, and they face dilemmas or struggles between opposing conditions in each stage. During the stage he calls middle adulthood, the primary challenge is to find ways to cultivate what he calls *generativity* rather than what he calls *stagnation*.

Generativity is a concern for establishing and guiding the next generations. According to Erikson's model, people who are in the middle adulthood stage of their life cycle and have been moving through their life in healthy ways have previously resolved challenges concerning their ability to have trust, autonomy, initiative, industry, identity, and intimacy; and they are ready to focus less on themselves and more on nurturing the next generations. In other words, their hearts turn to the welfare of those who follow them—which includes their own posterity and others.

According to Erikson's theory, if people are able to cultivate generativity, it helps them and others around them grow and experience in successful ways rather than stagnate and focus on aspects of life that are unhealthy or more superficial or irrelevant. Thus this part of Erikson's model is similar to the part of the idea that is the thesis of this chapter that deals with hearts being turned to posterity. Erikson's idea does not focus on the part of the idea in this chapter that deals with hearts being turned to relatives in earlier generations, but it provides rich insights into what happens when hearts are and are not turned to the next generations.

Some of the ideas that were developed in literature that appeared after Erikson developed his ideas suggest that some of Erikson's ideas ought to be modified in several ways. However, three other streams of literature need to be described before it is meaningful to describe the changes that should be made in Erikson's ideas. One of these is Nagy's model.

Nagy's Theory

Böszörményi-Nagy (1987; Böszörményi-Nagy & Krasner, 1986; Böszörményi-Nagy & Spark, 1973) and his colleagues developed a theory that focuses on what they call *invisible loyalties*, a complex web of intergenerational loyalties that permeate and are central to family systems. Their main thesis is that a sense of appreciation and respect for what earlier generations have provided is helpful in families. Their model focuses on more than just what parents and grandparents do. They argued as well that a sense of appreciation for and loyalty to the things that earlier ancestors provide is also important and helpful. Their theory also suggests that stories that are handed down through the generations are helpful in cultivating this sense of appreciation and loyalty.

One of their central ideas is that when the earlier generations of families are treated with respect and appreciation, this creates balance within the intergenerational relationships, and a sense of depth and meaning in the contributions of the earlier generations contributes to the healthy development of individuals and family systems. Conversely, when there is a lack of invisible loyalties and sensitivity to them, or when there is an imbalance in them, such as when the sense of appreciation and obligation to earlier generations is ignored, this detracts in important ways from the quality of family life.

What they called the "transgenerational accounting of obligations and merit" (Böszörményi-Nagy & Krasner, 1986, p. 46) is an important part of the relationships between generations, and it is important that this accounting is in balance and is an important and valued part of what people care about. Although Nagy and his colleagues emphasized the balance more than the importance of the relationships between family members and preceding generations, and the relationships with the preceding generations more than the succeeding generations, their ideas provide some of the basis for the principle in this chapter.

The Nagy group argued that the relational ethics in intergenerational relationships are not just a set of prescriptive norms, nor simply psychological phenomena, perspectives, or constructions. Rather, they have an objective ontological and experiential basis by virtue of being derived from basic human needs and from meaningful relationships that have concrete consequences. This is consistent with the thesis in this chapter that the turning of hearts in intergenerational relationships is profoundly important and partly a spiritual phenomenon.

The Nagy group theorized that a sense of connection with earlier ancestors creates a sense of rootedness and bonds and also meaning and purpose that help individuals and families cope with the daily and routine challenges of life as well as the more overwhelming disruptions that occur with such things as serious illnesses, accidents, and premature deaths. Thus the intergenerational bonds help provide resilience and strength, which help families prepare for and make developmental transitions and cope with expected and unexpected challenges.

There is a lot we don't yet understand about these processes, but they have considerable potential. Hopefully, future research will provide more insights into how, why, and when these processes make a difference in families.

Generational Alliances

A third body of literature that provides several different and important insights about the role of hearts in intergenerational relationships is that about generational alliances. Scholars such as Lidz (1963), Framo (1970, 1976), Minuchin (1974), A. Haley (1976), and Palazolli et al. (Palazolli, Boscolo, Cecchin, & Parata, 1978; Palazolli, Cirillo, Selvini, & Sorrentino, 1989) have demonstrated that healthy generational alliances contribute to success in families, and unhealthy generational alliances are detrimental to the social, emotional, and mental health of parents and children.

One of the main ideas in this literature is that it is important that intergenerational alliances do not interfere with intragenerational alliances. This means that families tend to be the most healthy when parents are able to work together in a cooperative way with each other in the ways they relate to their parents and other ancestors and to their children and later posterity. This is consistent with the later position of Gottman and Silver (2004) that one of the best gifts a parent can give their child is a strong marriage.

Conversely, when parents have a difficult time cooperating with each other, and one or both of them form close, influential, and enduring alliances with one or more people in another generation, this tends to undermine the intragenerational alliances. These cross-generational alliances tend to create challenges and difficulties that disrupt and harm families, and if the dominance of the intergenerational coalitions persists, it decreases the probability of families finding successes.

In healthy families, the alliances among children change and move around in different situations, but the parental alliances tend to be relatively consistent over time. These ideas are related to the ideas in the principle in this chapter because part of what is usually involved in alliances is affection, caring, and power; and they help us understand which aspects of relationships are the most effective and helpful in intragenerational and intergenerational relationships. It is helpful to have caring, helping, and bonding relationships between generations and have the power and authority aspects of alliances be strong and enduring in the intragenerational relationships—especially among people who are married.

The literature on generational alliances provides valuable insights, but its main emphasis is also a little different from the main thesis in this chapter. The generational alliances literature tends to emphasize and provide ideas about the importance of intragenerational rather than intergenerational alliances. Our data suggest that both of these alliances are important and make a difference in families, but the emphasis in this chapter is on the role of the heart in the intergenerational alliances.

Roots

A fourth body of literature that provides insights about the ideas in the principle that is the thesis of this chapter is the literature and the social movement that was created by the writings and experiences of Alex Haley in the 1970s. Haley is a descendant of enslaved people who were brought from Africa to the United States, and he became so interested in learning more about his ancestry that he traveled to Africa to see if he could learn more about them.

What he learned changed his life and the lives of many others. His story was serialized in *Reader's Digest*, published in a book titled *Roots*, and made into the first week-long television mini-series. It generated phenomenal and almost unprecedented interest and appeal, and was viewed by an estimated 130 million people (Haley, 1976).

There are probably several different reasons for the interest in the *Roots* phenomenon. Some of the reasons are that people in the United States were struggling at that time with several different aspects of race relations. Many were trying to cope with guilt about racial injustices, and were trying to find ways to improve these relationships. Another reason was probably because the insights provided by Haley's relationships and experiences struck a chord in many that related to some deeply held and at least partially unfulfilled desires for connections and relationships with their own roots and ancestry.

Another aspect of this "turning" of hearts to ancestry has to do with the vast amount of time and energy that is devoted by many people to genealogical research. Millions of people find themselves fascinated, intrigued, and captivated by their interest in learning who their ancestors were and what their lives were like. Many are unaware that after personal correspondence such as e-mail, Facebook, instant messaging, the viewing of videos, and e-commerce, *genealogical research* is one of the leading Internet activities, particularly among older populations.

Another aspect of these phenomena has to do with the yearning so many adoptees have to learn about their biological parents. There seems to be a deeply felt and only partially understood desire on their part to learn about their predecessors and be connected in some way to their biological roots.

We don't understand much about what it is that creates and maintains these desires in the hearts of so many humans, but there is something that is very real about these connections. Apparently, there is something about the human "heart" that seeks meaningful connections to ancestry and posterity, and it seems to run very deep in the human species. These feelings are, of course, more meaningful to some than others, and they make more difference in some families than others, but they are widely experienced and important to many people.

Another reason turning hearts in this way helps families be more successful than they would otherwise be is because there are a limited number of things that hearts can be turned to, and when feelings are turned toward ancestry and posterity, they are probably not as focused on such things as fame, fortune, power, and possessions. The diversion from these more fleeting and seductive parts of the human experience that are not as conducive to family effectiveness probably helps families turn their focus, attention, and concerns from things that divert attention from or interfere with the familial and helps them focus instead on things that help lead to family success.

These four different bodies of literature are based on different kinds of research, and they are each a part of larger perspectives that have little in common and little to do with the principle about hearts being wisely turned to progenitors and posterity. The way these four are related to the ideas in this chapter is that each of them deals with an aspect of what it means to have hearts turned and ways this has an influence in families. Therefore when they are viewed as a set, they provide persuasive support of the principle in this chapter. We now turn to some ways some of the ideas in these four bodies of literature can be integrated and several additional insights we gleaned from our observations, interviews, and discussions.

NEW RESEARCH

As the ideas in this chapter became clearer in our minds, we devoted some time to discussing them with a number of individuals and families. These discussions provided additional insights into how, why, and when the various ways turning of hearts to ancestors and posterity make a difference in families. They also helped convince us that this idea taps into a helpful part of family processes that provides insights that none of the other ideas provide.

The data from our interviews suggest that several of the ideas in the four bodies of literature can to be integrated. One of the central issues in the “roots” phenomenon created by Haley deals with identity, and identity development was also a core concern in Erikson’s theory regarding the adolescent stage. The development of identity is grounded in, among other elements, satisfactory answers to existential questions such as “Who am I?” and “Where did I come from?” A strong and healthy sense of intergenerational loyalty, appreciation, and connection helps provide insights into these interests and dilemmas—thereby aiding healthy individual-level and familial coping, development, and identity formation, and a wholesome evolution of identities over the life cycle.

Another insight that can be gleaned by integrating the ideas in these bodies of literature is that some of the aspects of Erikson’s ideas need to be modified. He argued that aspects of generativity become issues and are salient in middle adulthood. Nagy’s theory, Haley’s insights, and our data all suggest that the turning of hearts to ancestors and posterity is relevant not just for people in the middle adult parts of their life but also for individuals and families in many of the stages of the life cycle. It is important in the search for identity in the adolescent stage, in the attempts by young adults to create intimacy, in the struggle to be effective parents, and in the attempts to avoid despair, emptiness, and a lack of meaning and purpose in the later stages of life.

Our data also provide a few insights into which aspects of family processes are influenced by hearts being turned to predecessors and posterity. For example, the following comments by a 55-year-old lawyer illustrate how hearts being turned to predecessors helps create feelings of joy and being connected. He also illustrates how these intergenerational connections help create a sense of being a part of a larger scheme and how this can soften hearts, help people feel integrated with aspects of life that are larger than themselves, and help them feel complete as a person:

> I took a genealogy class when I was young, and got into it. And, it started me on writing my history, and later I took a class on family histories at the university and got into it even more. Later, we had a series of family reunions where we were able to put each family on a big cardboard tree and add everybody’s names to it. And, we interviewed our aunts and uncles and got their stories written down about their growing up, and you can hear their voices as you read them. I left the salty language in there, and didn’t correct it grammatically, so

> it is just like talking to them. They loved to tell stories and laugh, and it was great to be able to hear their stories. The blessing of that was the joy and feelings it brought into my life, and I think it softened my heart. It helped me feel connected and like I was a part of something that is bigger than me that is comforting, and it helps me feel more complete as a person.

Some of the aspects of family life that are influenced by these generational relationships are powerful but also subtle, complex, elusive, and difficult to describe. The comments by the following mother illustrate several of these characteristics as she talked about how the "feelings" helped create a sense of "connection" and "foundation," but that it was also "hard to put into words" how and why the generational connections made a difference, yet at the same time she was aware she "liked" what they brought into her home:

> As I was growing up I learned from my parents that "family comes first," and we try to live that way now that we are raising our family. Part of it is a kind of reverence and respect for the heritage provided by the earlier generations, especially those that were pioneers, and we share some pioneer stories and lessons to learn from them all the time. It also even goes back to some ancestors who were Pilgrims on the Mayflower. We still tell the story about Pricilla Mullens and John Alden; and it even goes back to England. One of my Dad's ancestors was King Richard and one of my Mom's ancestors was King John, and they tease and have fun all the time with stories about how Grandpa Richard was gone all the time and Grandpa John was an evil king. These feelings about our ancestors provide a kind of connection and foundation that is hard to put into words, but I like what it brings into our home. Our children are all teenagers now, and we are trying to help them have these same feelings.

Several other themes that appeared in our data are that when people care deeply about where they came from and their posterity, these sensitivities seem to help them keep their priorities in line. They don't get so carried away with worldly things. Their multigenerational focus helps provide a sense of meaning and purpose, and helps them avoid problems such as drug abuse and crime.

SACREDNESS

It is likely that people differ in how much they view generational relationships as sacred. Some religions pay considerable attention to these relationships and emphasize that they are sacred, whereas others pay little attention to them and don't seem to view them as sacred or particularly important.

The first two propositions in sacred theory suggest that this variation in sacredness influences the power and salience of this part of family life. According to these two theoretical ideas, the variation in whether hearts are turned to progenitors and posterity makes more difference in families in which these parts of their lives are viewed as sacred, and less in families in which they are not viewed as sacred.

Figure 10.1 is an attempt to summarize these theoretical ideas about how turning hearts to predecessors and posterity tends to help families. The figure shows how variation in whether hearts are turned to ancestors and posterity influences

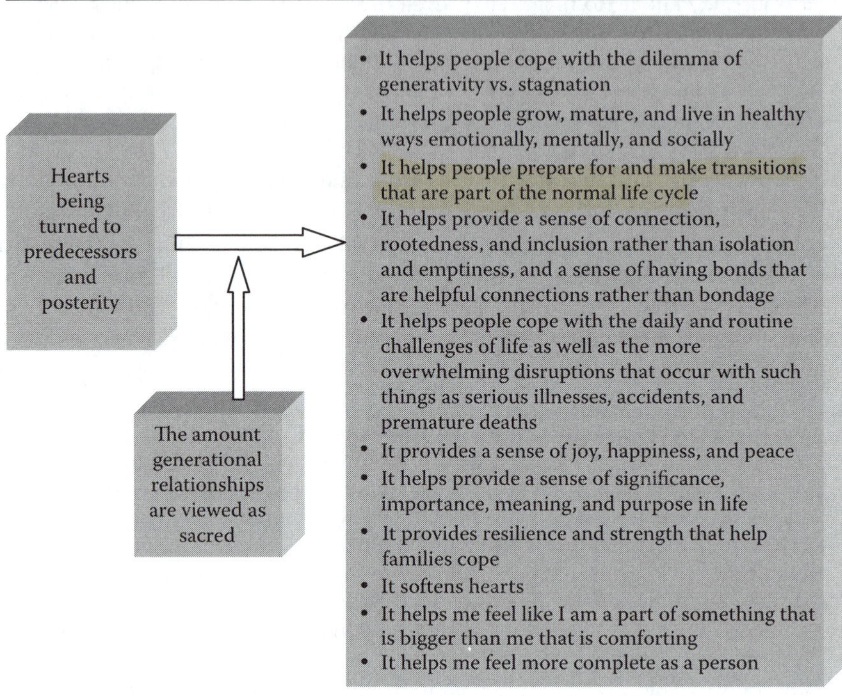

Figure 10.1 Ways turning hearts to predecessors and posterity influences families.

nine different aspects of family processes. It also shows that the amount generational relationships are viewed as sacred influences these patterns of influence. All of these ideas are based on relatively little data, and they therefore should be viewed as tentative and provisional rather than conclusive and proven. There is a need for additional research, but there is enough evidence for them that it is meaningful to think about ways they can be applied.

APPLICATIONS

The ideas in this chapter can be applied in a number of ways by families, educators, and professionals. For example, it is relatively easy to make genograms that show the families of several generations, and these can provide insights and help people find new ways they appreciate the heritage provided by earlier generations. Another way is to do Internet searches about one's grandparents and great-grandparents, and much information can be acquired quickly through Internet sites such as Ancestry.com.

More in-depth and meaningful information can be obtained through conducting life history interviews with predecessors—interviews that the descendant/interviewer audio-records and later transcribes. We have enjoyed engaging in these generational activities ourselves, but as family life educators we have also seen the significant impact they can have on university students who are in late adolescence and emerging adulthood. Perhaps because so many within this developmental group are struggling with identity formation and a sense of self, activities such as completing a genogram, a family history, or a life history interview with a grandparent can help them gain insight regarding the existential question of "Who am I?" by learning more about where they came from. In-depth experiences with preceding generations can also have a humanizing effect on the younger generation's view of the aging—a heightened awareness that in spite of technological changes, many domains of life and experience are strikingly similar across time. "Us" and "them" may begin to blend into "we" (Myerhoff, 1978).

Another interesting effect of family history work is that virtually every family has, both literally and figuratively speaking, the blood and influence of both nobility and criminality—family narratives that alternatively evoke pride and shame. As we learn about our dualistic family heritage and history, we learn more about our own potential. We may more closely resonate with Viktor Frankl (1984), who recorded, "We watched and witnessed some of our comrades behave like swine while others behaved like saints. Man has both potentialities within himself; which one is actualized depends on decisions" (p. 134). Indeed, many of the influences of engaged family history work quickly lead us to sacred ground where we are implicitly asked a question that pushes us beyond the "Who am I?" identity question to the defining query "Who will I become?" In the context of the sacred and the familial, this question is infused with relational implications.

In the LSU family studies curriculum, students conduct an intensive family history project that includes constructing genograms and doing life history interviews. In a succeeding family studies course, the focus turns from the past to the future. Journal reflections in this course include entries on topics such as "A Letter to My Future Child," "Qualities I Am Looking for in a Coparent," and "Things I Need to Work On." A capstone journal entry in this class challenges students to project 60 years into the future and to write their own obituary, including reflections on their legacy and lived values (Covey, 2001). There are often some subtle changes that happen inside people as they do these kinds of things that are difficult to explain, but they are sometimes life-changing experiences. These activities are versatile and can be tailored to fit clinical, educational, or personal/family settings.

In this application section we have offered some specific ideas and techniques, but the central principle at work is that when we turn our hearts toward our mothers, fathers, and other predecessors in healthy and humble ways, we can obtain wisdom and experience that will help us in our efforts to be generative to our children, grandchildren, and the generations that accompany them (see Malachi 4:5–6). For many, these processes are at the heart of family life and at the core of much that is deemed sacred.

SUMMARY

This chapter is built around the idea that when hearts are turned wisely to predecessors and posterity, it helps families find successes and avoid failures. This idea originated in sacred literature, but four different bodies of scholarly literature have created additional insights about several aspects of this principle. These are Erikson's theory of human development, Nagy's theory about contextual aspects of family life, the literature about generational alliances, and Alex Haley's study of his roots. Several ideas in these different bodies of literature were integrated, and interview data were used as the basis for theorizing that when the hearts of family members are turned to their ancestry and posterity, it creates bonds, loyalties, and connections that help people focus on the needs of others in their families in helpful ways. These relationships also help provide meaning and purpose, help provide a number of positive emotions, and help family members make developmental transitions and be resilient when faced with challenges.

11

Morality

The study of morality has an interesting and complex history in family studies. It has had a central role in some ways, and in other ways it has been ignored. It is a central concern in feminist theory where the emphasis is on emancipating women from the inequitable "one down" and immorally oppressed position they have had in most societies. The idea of morality also has a central role in psychoanalytic and neo-analytic theories, but in these theories it tends to be used in a negative way most of the time because the superego is viewed as a constraining and inhibiting part of the mind that uncomfortably binds rather than uplifts. In most of the general theories that are widely used in family studies, the idea of morality is virtually absent (Bengston et al., 2005; Christensen, 1964; Doherty, 1995; Sussman & Steinmetz, 1987; White & Klein, 2008).

In contrast, religions tend to have high levels of concern with ethical or moral issues. Indeed, a concern over moral issues is one of the universal characteristics in religious traditions. These traditions provide the basis for most systems of morality and codes of ethics, and many of the beliefs about what constitutes the moral are similar in many of the religious persuasions. One of the general principles in many of the traditions is that positive outcomes (blessings) follow when behavior is moral, whereas undesirable consequences (curses) follow when behavior is immoral, and these blessings and curses may be individual, familial, societal, or all of the above.

Another difference in the ways religion and the social sciences frame and focus on the moral lies in their different conceptions of morality. From most social science perspectives, morality is (if it is of concern at all) purely "horizontal" in nature. Culture and the human psyche are the sources of morality. Therefore moral beliefs are social constructions, just as fashion is—the skirts run long this year and short the next. In juxtaposition, many religions hold morality to be "vertical" in nature. The origin of moral truths is not cultural but divine, and the corresponding applications of these truths are divinely revealed and mandated. For example, the Ten Commandments were given to Moses by God.

Stark has theorized and documented how, across time, revelation-based religions claiming to possess some vertical, absolute truths almost universally tend to move from a position of high tension with broader social mores toward positions of less tension where cultural accommodation and even assimilation eventually occurs (Stark & Finke, 2000). Even so, the claim of "vertical" (as opposed to cultural) religion is a claim to truths that are believed to be absolute and require the believer's moral adherence, and these are qualitatively different from moral imperatives that originate in culture. For example, Christ's plea, "If you love me, keep my commandments" (John 14:15), Islam's five pillars, Buddhism's eightfold path, and Mormonism's law of chastity are viewed within these faith traditions as absolutes that require obedience, and are therefore qualitatively different from cultural mores (Dollahite & Marks, 2006; Mawadudi, 1988; H. Smith, 1991).

The sacred and vertical concepts of morality are usually viewed individualistically in the sense that they focus on (a) how individuals ought to behave and (b) benefits that come to individuals when they obey. However, our data and some previous research in family studies suggest that what family members do with the moral can influence family processes and outcomes. To clarify, our purpose is not to preach a vertical conceptualization of morality but to note (a) that the idea that some aspects of the moral have vertical origins has typically gone unacknowledged in the social sciences, and (b) that to understand families who accept a vertical conceptualization of morality, scholars cannot exclusively use a horizontal lens. To be transparent, we hold each of these lenses to be both appropriate and useful in studying families.

This reasoning led us to include morality in sacred theory, and this chapter focuses on that idea. The guiding idea in this chapter is *morality matters in families*, and we discuss several less general ideas about how, why, and when it matters.

A PRINCIPLE

There are large bodies of literature about some aspects of morality. For example, philosophers have discussed for millennia the nature of morality and ethics, they have argued over what is the highest good, and they have debated whether morality is even possible. These analyses have led to many complex ideas, opposing points of view, different typologies and categories, divergent lines of cleavage, different frames of reference, and little consensus. This means there are many different ways to conceptualize what is moral and immoral, and how these terms are similar to and different from several closely related pairs such as right and wrong, good and bad, ethical and unethical. For our purposes, the differences between most of the ideas in the various schools of thought are not important, and we view these four sets of terms as sufficiently similar that they can be used interchangeably.

Social scientists have rarely shown interest in the conceptual and ontological issues surrounding morality, but they have created large bodies of literature about issues such as how moral capacities and behaviors evolve and change, how they develop in children, gender similarities and differences, and the role of morality in education. In our theory and research, we are not overly concerned about these areas of inquiry because our focus is on a fairly narrow set of issues.

The principle in sacred theory that deals with how morality influences family processes and outcomes is the idea that *the more family members live in ways that are consistent with their moral beliefs, the higher the probability of successes and the lower the probability of failures.* This idea has been a central tenet for millennia in a wide range of religious traditions, and there also is some scholarly literature about it.

Christensen's Research and Theory

The scholarly study of the ways the morality of behavior influences family processes began when Christensen gathered data about premarital pregnancy and divorce for his master's thesis. He then devoted his entire career to studying these relationships in a number of research projects that gathered cross-cultural data, and toward the end of his career he integrated the findings into what he called "normative theory" (Christensen, 1969).

Christensen's operationalizations of morality focused on values about premarital sexual behavior, and his studies compared couples who were premaritally pregnant with those who were not. He gathered data in Utah, Indiana, and Denmark because the norms about premarital sexual behavior were so different across these three cultures. The norms were the most proscriptive in Utah and the least proscriptive in Denmark. Indeed, Christensen found that the negative consequences of premarital pregnancy were stronger in his Utah samples, and the fewest negative consequences were in his Denmark samples. He generalized from these findings the idea that the more behavior deviates from cultural values, the greater the negative consequences of the behavior.

Christensen measured differences in values that were part of cultural norms, and thus moral beliefs and behavior were relative to cultural contexts. Therefore his research focused on a solely horizontal view of morality. He did not discuss in his professional publications his beliefs about the vertical origins of the moral beliefs because the professional norms at that time dictated that scholarship ought to be as impersonal and "value free" as possible (Christensen, 1964), but Wes Burr talked with him several times about these ideas, and in these personal conversations Christensen indicated that he appreciated both the vertical and horizontal aspects of morality.

Warner's Model

Another body of literature that focuses on the role of morality in families was developed by Warner (1995). His model is similar to Christensen's in some ways but also different in several ways. Warner's theory describes ways a variety of immoral behaviors lead to a number of undesirable effects, and also identifies ways moral behavior tends to be liberating and productive. His thesis is that when behavior is not consistent with people's personal moral beliefs, their approach to life and relationships is characterized by a rather long list of unfortunate conditions such as doubt, feelings of anger and resentment toward self and others, blaming and deceptiveness, destructive collusion, hypersensitivity, self-justification, false ways of being, bondage, collusion, twisted understandings, misperceptions, self-condemnation, fear, anxiety, anger, and self-righteousness. On the other hand, when people behave in ways that are consistent with their moral beliefs, they experience positive conditions such as peace, harmony, wholesome bonds, a sense of fulfillment, and love.

Warner's work is both conceptual and ontological. It is conceptual in that he invented several concepts, and ontological because he assumed and articulated a view of being human that makes the moral fundamental. According to his model, moral beliefs are more fundamental than cultural norms or majority practices regarding right and wrong, and they are not necessarily congruent with them. His view of morality is an implicitly vertical approach.

At first glance, Warner's emphasis on living consistent with one's personal beliefs calls to mind the reference by Bellah et al. (1985, pp. 221, 235) to a post-modern, narcissistic form of religion they called "Sheilaism," but Warner's direction is quite the opposite. His concluding lines are, Books are lifeless inscriptions on sheets of paper, but your living connections with others and with God speak to you the living truth (p. 316). Truth in Warner's view has socially constructed elements that emerge though our living connections with others, but it also has a vertical dimension—God speaking the living truth—and this lies at the core of his model.

Warner's model is impressive because he sought to account for a wider range of moral and immoral behaviors, and he made a person's "moral way of being" fundamental to whether they would experience relationships, feelings, thoughts, and behaviors of high (beneficial) or low (destructive) quality. In his model, it is neither skill nor knowledge that comes first in navigating the circumstantial minefields of mortal living, but whether one is living true or false to conscience. In his model, every aspect of human experience is tied to moral issues, ethical calls, and doing right or wrong, and is set in motion by whether people are honoring their personally held moral beliefs.

We view Warner's model as creative and thought provoking, and it deserves further study. But it also has several limitations. For example, his model is more of a philosophical essay than social science, and he provided so little information about the basis for his ideas that it is difficult to know how much confidence to place in the ideas. Also, he seemed to frame the outcomes of immoral behavior as all-or-nothing conditions that are fully present when immoral behavior exists and not present at all when people are moral. According to his model, even minor moral improprieties create full-blown undesirable conditions in the outcomes, and it seems to us that immoral behavior and the family processes influenced by it have many levels or degrees and that slight changes may lead to minor effects. Therefore we prefer to think of changes in the probability of processes and outcomes rather than just the presence and absence of desirable and undesirable conditions. Even so, Warner provided substantial food for thought in connection with morality in personal and family life.

New Theorizing

We like the ideas developed by Christensen and Warner as a beginning point in understanding the role of morality in families, and our data provide additional evidence for their theories. However, our data also suggest that the role of morality in families may be more complex than their ideas imply. We therefore theorize that there are at least four contingencies that influence when, how, and why immoral behavior influences family processes. These contingencies are (a) the *sacredness* of immoral behavior, (b) the *seriousness* of the misbehavior, (c) the *duration* of inappropriate behavior, and (d) the *resilience* of families.

Sacredness Proposition 2 (on page 16) asserts that when aspects of family life are perceived to be sacred, this gives them a unique, unusually powerful, and salient influence in families, and our data suggest this is frequently true for misbehavior as well. When things are perceived to be sacred, the benefits from living in accordance with the ideals and adverse consequences of misbehavior are magnified. One person we interviewed described these differences in the following way:

> When our mother walked out on our family to do her own thing, she went against obligations and commitments that were holy, and that made it so much worse. It just hurt. I have a friend whose mother also left their family, and they don't think about their family life as holy, and it was hard for them, but it wasn't as hard as it has been for us.

As we see here, this individual struggles to articulate that this betrayal of something sacred (an "eternal" family bond) was more than just nonnormative or disappointing—it was a desecration.

Seriousness Some ways of misbehaving are more serious than others, and our interviews and observations suggest that the consequences of immoral behavior are usually more harmful as the seriousness increases. Sociologists have created concepts such as folkways and mores to describe these differences, but this is merely a dichotomy, and the severity and salience of moral beliefs are considerably more complex than just a dichotomy. For example, there are many levels of seriousness of physical abuse or violence, and scales have been designed to measure this variation (Straus & Gelles, 1978). Hitting someone with a slap and an open hand is less serious than hitting someone with a closed fist. Hitting with an object such as a stick or club is more severe, and attacking with a knife is even more serious. Attacking someone with a gun or explosives is even more serious, and there are a lot of data that show that these more serious forms of abuse have more detrimental consequences in families (Gelles & Straus, 1979).

There also are many gradations in the severity of misbehavior with regard to sexuality. Sexual behavior with a minor is usually viewed as more serious than the same sexual behavior with an adult. Sexual behavior that is forced on others is a more serious wrong than inappropriate consensual sexual behavior. Talking about sexual matters is less severe than behavior, and so forth—with many gradations. Also, as we have talked with people about inappropriate sexual behavior, our data also suggest there is something about this particular type of misbehavior that is qualitatively different from other behavior that deviates from moral beliefs. Misbehavior with regard to sexuality somehow deals with aspects of life that are so core and central to the human spirit that the consequences seem to be more dramatic, long lasting, disruptive of other family processes, and difficult to cope with. Even one inappropriate sexual encounter can be emotionally, mentally, and spiritually devastating for a long period of time. The comments from individuals in two families we have known illustrate the unique nature of sexual misbehavior:

> Her uncle was the one who did it, and it only happened once, but it has influenced [her] ever since, and our whole family is different. We're more suspicious and find it harder to trust. We don't do anything with his family at all. They are just not welcome at all in our home, and we will never be the same. We all have a hurt that just won't go away.

❊❊❊❊❊❊❊❊❊❊❊❊❊❊❊❊❊❊❊❊❊❊❊❊❊

> When I was about 7 one of my brother's friends made me undress, and he touched me in ways he shouldn't, and it has been over 30 years and I can't let go of the uncomfortable feelings. I've tried to put it out of my mind, but it is not like other things. There is something different. I don't understand it very well at all, but in ways I still feel invaded and abused as a person; and now I have three daughters. I wish I could put them in a cocoon and protect them, but I know that's not possible. I wish so much there were something I could do or some way I could make it go away.

As with sexual abuse or misbehavior, there are also many different levels of severity with regard to other types of behavior such as dishonesty, emotional abuse, addiction, and violating family rules. Our data suggest that with all of these forms of inappropriate behavior, the more severe the misbehavior, the more likely it is to lead to undesirable consequences in what happens in families.

Duration In addition to the issues of desecration and seriousness involved in misbehavior, our data also suggest that the *duration* of misbehavior can influence the effects it has in families. Sometimes misbehavior happens only once or infrequently, and is usually less harmful than when the misbehavior lasts for a long time. Generally, the longer family members persist in their misbehavior, the more the harmfulness of the behavior increases. Therefore the ideal when misbehavior occurs is for people to reform, repent, and apologize quickly.

Our data suggest that when misbehavior continues over a long period of time and is repetitious or constant, there is a subtle balance in how much it is wise to be patient, merciful, and forgiving. The longer misbehavior continues, the greater the value of (a) replacing mercy with justice, (b) replacing patience with accountability, and (c) replacing forgiveness with natural and logical consequences that are not pleasant. And, conversely, the greater the inclination on the part of the person who is misbehaving to admit the inappropriateness of the behavior, apologize, and change the behavior, the greater the wisdom in being patient, merciful, compassionate, and forgiving.

Resilience Our data also suggest that *resilience* is a fourth contingency that influences the effects of misbehavior in families. Walsh (2006) defined resilience as "the capacity to rebound from adversity strengthened and more resourceful" (p. 4).

Misbehavior is one type of adversity, and when families respond to it in constructive ways it can help the consequences of undesirable behavior be more growth producing and less harmful than if a destructive approach was taken. The loving ways of behaving described in Chapters 5 through 8 (i.e., being kind, patient, merciful, and compassionate, and trying to help family members) can help turn situations that involve undesirable behavior into times of learning and growing. In colloquial terms, resilience involves finding ways to make lemonade out of lemons rather than just living with the natural consequences of an undesirable situation, as in the following example:

> It is often easier to be resilient with the misbehavior of children than adults because children are still learning the basic aspects of morality, and this process is illustrated with an example from the life of one of the authors. When one of our [Ruth and Wes'] sons was in the second grade he came home one day with a handful of the tokens that were used in the school to reward achievement. He knew the tokens were not his, and he knew it was wrong to take them, but, for whatever reasons, he had put them in his pocket and brought them home. Wes viewed this immoral behavior as an opportunity to help his son better understand some of the more subtle aspects of right and wrong, and to increase his son's motivation to behave in moral ways. The discussions and interaction that followed in the next several days as we tried to be supportive, nurturing and helpful were a valuable time in our home and were constructive and bonding as we tried to help our 7-year-old son.

It is easy for most people to recognize that the misbehavior of children can be turned into constructive situations, but our data also suggest that this type of learning is important throughout the entire human life cycle. Adults never outgrow the need to refine, improve, and expand their understanding of what is moral and immoral, and of the various ways moral and immoral behavior make a difference. This suggests that the ideas in Chapters 5 through 8 that discuss being loving to others continue to be important in relating to adults whose behavior falls short of their ideals. When family members respond to the misbehavior of others in judgmental, condemning, rejecting, and punishing ways, these ways of relating are not as helpful and productive as being loving, merciful, patient, understanding, supportive, and nurturing.

We humans can learn a great deal about morality and the importance of behavior being consistent with moral beliefs by teaching, modeling, and sharing examples and stories. However, our data suggest that this type of learning is never enough to learn all of the intricacies and aspects of morality. Some parts of this learning can occur only when family members go through the personal and painful experiences of misbehaving, and then experience the emotional, mental, spiritual, and interpersonal consequences of their misbehavior, gradually learning how to behave in moral ways. This is an experiential type of learning that seems to be essential for everyone. Some things can be learned from others, but some things can be learned only by living and experiencing, by falling down and learning how to get up in the school of hard knocks. And, unfortunately, most of us need quite a bit of this type of learning. This means that all families have to cope with more than a little undesirable behavior, and they therefore have many opportunities to turn potentially unfortunate situations into growth-producing moments.

APPLICATIONS

We see several applications for family scholars and practitioners in connection with morality. As we noted earlier, Warner added a sacred, vertical morality to Christensen's socially constructed horizontal morality. This is a relatively new idea to the social sciences, but in religious thought it is at least as old as the Abrahamic faiths. Whether engaged in intervention, education, or empirical study, family professionals will better understand and interpret morally laden family processes as a result of this additional vantage. The utility of both the horizontal (socially constructed) and vertical (absolute/Divine) notions of morality lies in the reality that many families likely integrate *both* types of moral concepts into their thinking and action. As a result, the complexity of morality is better captured through an awareness and use of both.

Another meaningful addition to the discussion of morality that religion brings to social science is an emphasis on sins of *omission*. Christensen's foundational work centered on violations of sociocultural sexual mores that might be categorized as sins of commission (e.g., actively doing something morally or socially unacceptable). Warner's (1995) conceptualization adds, and indeed emphasizes, that "*not doing right when we know what's right is doing wrong*" (p. 219, emphasis in original). By implication, particularly in the context of family, the aim of simply not doing significant harm is not a lofty moral standard. Warner added that we must also actively do that which is right—paraphrasing an idea from his faith's literature that "men should be anxiously engaged in a good cause, and do many things of their own free will and bring to pass much righteousness" (Doctrine & Covenants 58:27). We find this conceptualization to be of value for families where so much needs to be actively done—dishes, food preparation, laundry, care for children, provision, forgiving, supporting, and loving.

An additional application of the vertical view of morality takes us back to the Jewish Psalm referenced at the end of Chapter 9 that exhorts those wishing to "ascend into the hill of the Lord" to have "clean hands *and a pure heart*" (Psalm 24: 3–4, emphasis added). Clean hands and clean actions are vital—but purity of heart and intent is equally essential. In short, sacred, moral actions must be motivated by sacred, moral intent. Cognitive-behavioral approaches have much to offer, but to be fully effective and transformative we believe efforts must include the heart.

Moving to the fourth contingency of family resilience, we note Pauline Boss's (2002) observation that the Chinese character for *crisis* also means "opportunity." For the family life educator, counselor, and clinician—and perhaps most of all, for families—it is important to realize that one of the richest contexts and opportunities to develop and live morally lies in our personal and familial response to immoral behavior. We see in this idea one of the more significant application opportunities of sacred theory.

The ideas in this chapter have many implications for families and professionals who work with families. They suggest that it is helpful to not just pay attention to the legal issues or the social propriety of undesirable behavior, but to also take into account the moral aspects. This is difficult because there are so many different views about morality, but the complexity and challenges in paying attention to the moral dimensions should not prevent families and professionals from recognizing and dealing with morality because it has an independent and poignant relevance in family relationships.

SUMMARY

This chapter discussed the role of morality in families. The theories of Christensen and Warner were reviewed. They argued that it is helpful in families when behavior is consistent with moral beliefs, whereas it is harmful when behavior is inconsistent with values and beliefs. We also identified from our data four contingencies that influence this relationship. The desecration of the misbehavior, the seriousness of the misbehavior, the duration of the misbehavior, and the resilience of families all influence how much a given misbehavior harms families. The greater the desecration, seriousness, and duration of the misbehavior, the more the misbehavior tends to be harmful. The less desecrating, the less serious, and the shorter in duration the misbehavior is, the less it tends to be harmful. A fourth contingency of family resilience can be a buffering influence—and, ideally, even a transformative one that helps to convert trials into times of learning and unification.

12

Psychosocial Aspects

One of the contributions of the influential work on religion by Mahoney et al. (2001) is that they differentiated between *psychosocial* and *substantive* aspects of the sacred, and then suggested there are two questions about these aspects that deserve attention. First, "What are the substantive and psychosocial aspects of religion in family life? The other question to address is, What are the potentially helpful and harmful roles religion may play in family life?" (Mahoney et al. 2001, p. 586). Our goals in this chapter are to examine the previous literature for ideas about which aspects of the psychosocial are important and how these aspects influence family processes and then to bring our data to bear on this issue. As we reviewed the previous literature, we discovered there has been almost no research in this area other than the Mahoney et al. paper.

This led us to examine their article more carefully, and we discovered an interesting pattern. When Mahoney et al. (2001) focused on substantive elements of religion and marriage, they had two full pages of ideas and 14 references to other literature, but the section on psychosocial functions was quite different. It was only a half-page, and there were no references to other literature. Also, the ideas were only about aspects that "may" and "might" be relevant. When they discussed substantive elements and parenting the same pattern appeared. There were two pages of ideas about the role of substantive elements and 12 references to other publications; but for the psychosocial parts there was also only a half-page, and there were no references to other literature. Also, the ideas were appropriately tentative speculations about what "may" or "might" be relevant.

Also, as we examined our data to try to identify psychosocial aspects that make a difference in families, we realized there was little in the data that provided information about the role of psychosocial aspects. These experiences led us to several conclusions. First, there is little, if any, previous research about the role of psychosocial aspects, and there is also little related theorizing. Also, it is apparently more challenging to identify, describe, and theorize about the psychosocial aspects than the substantive aspects.

These insights prompted us to focus for a period of time on trying to identify psychosocial aspects that seem to make a difference in families. We discussed this question with a number of colleagues, individuals, and families, but these discussions did not identify very many psychosocial aspects. However, they did lead us to consider two other notions: first, that the distinction between substantive and psychosocial aspects may not turn out to be as fruitful a distinction as we initially thought and, second, that it may help if we examine more carefully the questions being asked and explore the possibility that some different theoretical questions may turn out to be more fruitful. This second alternative seemed to be promising, so we pursued it further.

The ideas developed by Mahoney et al. (2001) about the role of psychosocial aspects of religions in families dealt with the theoretical question of how "psychosocial elements of religion could benefit or harm family adjustment," and their goal was "to facilitate more conceptually and methodologically sophisticated research" (p. 559). Unfortunately, there has been little theorizing or research since then that has taken advantage of these more complex conceptual and theoretical ideas. Virtually all of the research about the role of religion in families has continued to focus on the role of religion-in-general—as measured by affiliation, beliefs, and activity in churches.

We eventually concluded that part of the reason the theorizing by the Mahoney group did not lead to "more conceptually," "methodologically," and theoretically sophisticated scholarship is because the question they focused on has the same limitations as the previous research on global religiosity that we discussed on pages 2–4. Namely, the question focuses attention on how psychosocial elements of religion-in-general "could" or "may" influence families, and there is so much variation in the ways family members use the psychosocial aspects that it may not be helpful to focus on these aspects in general or in a global sense. It may be more fruitful to focus on variation in the ways family members use or participate in the psychosocial aspects than on the way these aspects make a difference in general. This change in the theoretical question alters the theoretical and research concerns so the focus is on *variation in what family members do* and ways this variation influences relatively specific family processes and outcomes.

As we discussed these slightly different theoretical questions with colleagues and families, two aspects of the psychosocial emerged wherein variation in what family members do seems to make a difference in family processes and outcomes—namely, what family members do with the *social networks* around families and what they do with sacred *rituals*. It may be that more psychosocial aspects will be identified later, but these are the only two that clearly appeared in our data.

SOCIAL NETWORKS

Richly Interconnected

We have not found the religious literature very helpful in providing insights about the role of social networks in families, but there is some theorizing and research in the scholarly literature that seems helpful. Research about families and their social networks began in the 1950s with a group of scholars led by Zimmerman (Cervantes, 1965; Zimmerman & Broderick, 1954, 1956; Zimmerman & Cervantes,

1960) and a monograph by Elizabeth Bott (1957). The Zimmerman group published a series of studies on urban networks, and one of their key findings was that one of the most helpful things families can do is surround themselves with families who are successful in the ways they want to succeed (Zimmerman & Broderick, 1956). Further, according to Broderick (1993):

> The effectiveness of these networks is enhanced if the members are richly interconnected with one another, which provides more coherence and focus to their influence . . . Socially isolated parents tend to be far less effective in their parenting skills, more likely than others to be involved in incest and child abuse, and to have children who drop out of school or become delinquent, even when socioeconomic factors are controlled. They also are more likely to indulge in spouse abuse, to experience stress and depression, and, eventually, to divorce.
>
> But one also can be overly involved with the members of one's network to the detriment of relationships inside the family. Also possible is that high levels of network involvement are correlated with antisocial behavior such as violence and incest if the core values of network itself are antisocial. (p. 147)

This research provides two insights that seem valuable: first, that it is helpful when family members are "richly interconnected" with the parts of their social network they want to emulate and, second, that this is another aspect of life where Aristotle's golden mean is relevant because family members can have a deficiency, moderation, or excess in their bounding and bridging. This leads to the generalization that *it is helpful when family members have moderation rather than deficiency or excess in the ways they are interconnected with their social network.*

Reasons the Sacred Parts of Social Networks Are Important

There are several reasons why family members' interactions with the religious parts of their *social networks* influence the ways psychosocial processes help and harm families. One is because the sacred parts of life do not occur in a social vacuum. They are always intricately intertwined with larger communities. Whether Buddha, Mohammad, Moses, or Christ is the central figure in a religion, the ideal social pattern is similar among those who believe their teachings. Adherents learn sacred and social patterns from others, they share them with others, and they become parts of the social networks around families and in communities.

This means that whenever we try to understand the role of religion in families, it is vital to pay attention to the complex web that is larger than just individuals or families. As we do research and theorize about how religion helps families, some of the ideas in these theories and research ought to deal with the connections and interactions families have with the environments around them.

Taylor's (1991) following analysis of these relationships is individualistic rather than familial, and he emphasized more than just the religious parts of these networks. But his way of summarizing the importance of the larger contexts around individuals and families is helpful:

> The agent seeking significance in life, trying to define him- or herself meaningfully, has to exist in a horizon of important questions. This is what is self-defeating in modes of contemporary culture that concentrate on self-fulfillment in *opposition* to the demands of society, or nature, which *shut out* history and the bonds of solidarity . . . Otherwise put, I can define my identity only against the background of things that matter. But to bracket out history, nature, society, the demands of solidarity, would be to eliminate all candidates for what matters. Only if I exist in a world in which history, or the demands of nature, or the needs of my fellow human beings, or the duties of citizenship, or the call of God, or something else of this order *matters* crucially, can I define an identity for myself that is not trivial. (pp. 40–41, italics in the original)

It is likely that involvement with the religious parts of social networks makes more difference than involvement with most of the other parts of social networks such as the workplace, friends, neighbors, and the like. Granovetter's (1983) differentiation between what he called *strong-tie* and *weak-tie* networks provides some insights about how and why. Broderick (1993), in connection with this conceptualization, explained:

> Strong ties involve those kin and close friends who are most trusted and most relied upon in time of real need. This network never constitutes a large number of persons, and in some cases may be limited to only one or two—or even *no* outsider who will qualify. Weak-tie networks, on the other hand, are those extensive and amorphous collections of casual associates and acquaintances who know us and whom we know with varying degrees of intimacy. Included in this category are our more distant relatives and in-laws, present or former college roommates, neighbors, co-workers, classmates, members of the same congregation, business acquaintances, and friends of friends. (p. 141)

Granovetter (1983) viewed involvement with the religious parts of the environment around families as part of the weak ties. However, there are several aspects of the connections with the religious parts of social networks that seem to make them more relevant and powerful than the interaction with most of the other weak-tie aspects of the environments. Further, for some people our data indicate that "church family" qualifies as a strong-tie network—as indicated by reports of financial and emotional support such as the following:

> [When it looked bad for us] another church member stood right behind me and said—basically he let me know that he would be there to help us out if our house ever [was at risk] . . . I knew that he would take care of us and nothing would happen as far as our home. . . . [You want to] talk about feeling like God put you in the place to [have someone] take care of [you]!

One of these aspects is that connections with the religious parts of social networks deal with the sacred parts of life, and, as described on pages 12–16 in Chapter 1, when aspects of life are perceived to be part of the sacred this gives them an unusual salience and power. Mahoney et al. (2001) emphasized that:

> Religion is unique because of its focus on the nature of the sacred (e.g., God, Higher Power) and transcendental phenomenon (e.g., miracles, afterlife). Theological beliefs shape may individual's core assumptions about ultimate goals, suffering, and good and evil behavior. (p. 585)

The ties with the religious parts of social networks are also unique and powerful because the interaction with the nonreligious parts of environments is based on empirical observations with the five senses and with fairly unambiguous aspects of reasoning. But the beliefs that are central to the religious parts of the network are based on personal, private, and spiritual experiences that are subtle and elusive, and on faith rather than clear-cut observation and reasoning that can be more conclusively grounded or demonstrated in observations that are interpersonally replicable. When family members are richly interconnected with others who have similar beliefs and experiences, this provides a valuable resource that helps create and maintain faith-based beliefs and the behaviors that flow from these beliefs.

The connections with the other weak-tie parts of the environment, such as the workplace, schools, athletic events, and neighborhoods, deal mostly with the more superficial, public, and transient aspects of life. They do not deal with and sustain such fundamental and core aspects of reality as the nature of the cosmos, basic beliefs and values, the purposes of life, and preparation for life after death. These differences make the connections with the religious parts of social networks a profound and helpful resource.

Bridging and Bounding

Broderick (1993) also theorized that there are two different processes in the ways family members create and maintain connections with the various aspects of their social networks. One of the processes is creating and maintaining boundaries between a family and the various aspects of its environments. These boundaries need to be strong enough and rigid enough to keep undesirable people, ideas, and products out of the family, but permeable enough to allow desirable things such as food, relatives, and representatives of social agencies in. Broderick called this regulation of boundaries *bounding*.

The other process is *bridging*. It is finding ways to manage the process of connecting and using aspects of the environments that families want or need. This involves such things as exchanging goods, services, and information with other families and institutions.

In the process of acquiring these, families must send their members out into the world—to the workplace, marketplace, school, church, theater, hospital, polling booth, and so on. They are likely also to both need and want to permit selected outsiders into protected family space: close friends, relatives, and children's playmates; not to mention various delivery, repair, or salespersons, social workers, pastors, and the like (Broderick, 1993, p. 140).

The Nature of Networks

Our data also suggest that the nature of the parts of the social network where there is involvement also makes a difference. People become like the parts of their social network they associate with intimately, and groups differ in how much they advocate values and lifestyles that are compatible with the essential processes in families. Some groups advocate transient, superficial, highly individualistic, hedonistic, exotic, and materialistic values and lifestyles. Other parts of social networks advocate violent, criminal, deviant, and drug-oriented values and lifestyles, and involvement with these groups likely decreases the probability families will be successful.

Most of the religious traditions we are familiar with strive to advocate values that are consistent with the essential processes in families. They also generally strive to advocate lifestyles that are loving and nurturing, forgiving and healing, helping and stable; and this means that those who choose to be moderately involved with these religious communities have a resource that is usually helpful in family life.

Our data also suggest, however, that there are some religious traditions that are not very consistent with the essential processes in family life. For example, some religious traditions advocate punitive and rejecting ways of coping with undesirable behavior in children. And more extreme examples are those religious traditions that advocate mutilation and disfigurement of bodies—even human sacrifice. This suggests that wise families will examine the nature of the various aspects of their social networks and build bridges and boundaries that will exclude the undesirable parts and use the desirable parts.

Benefits of Involvement With Religious Networks

Some of the other advantages of involvement with religious parts of social networks are that they can provide social support, a sense of belonging, and "socially sanctioned, structured avenues to engage in pleasurable activities and spend time together" (Mahoney et al., 2001, p. 588). A study by Abbott et al. (1990) found that the social support families received from their involvement with the network in their church had the highest relationship with family satisfaction in their sample. The aspects of social support they identified in their study included doing recreational activities with friends in their religious congregations and being helped by these friends.

Abbott and colleagues' work does not argue that involvement with religious networks is helpful and involvement with nonreligious networks is not helpful, but rather that it is helpful for family members to be moderately interconnected with meaningful networks that provide interaction and activities that are consistent with the needs of families, and some religious networks provide these types of resources. Some nonreligious networks provide a similar type of resources, and they also are helpful to families. But many nonreligious networks also provide values and activities that are quite inconsistent with healthy family life, and many of these tend to be harmful.

Bronfenbrenner's (1979) bio-ecological theory of human development, especially the later versions of it (Bronfenbrenner & Morris, 2006), provides additional insights about the ways social networks can help families. Bronfenbrenner theorized that optimal development takes place through three progressively more complex reciprocal interaction processes he called *proximal processes, contexts,* and *time.* Networks involving the sacred are only one part of this web, but they are an important part.

As Putnam (2000) has illustrated in his influential work *Bowling Alone,* U.S. culture has moved steadily in the direction of dis-integration. In short, more and more of our hitherto communal activities have become increasing isolationist (e.g., choosing to watch a DVD at home instead of a play at the theater; bowling alone instead of on a league team, etc.). In connection with fathers, Marks and Dollahite (2007) stated:

> Compared with men of previous generations, today's fathers are far less likely to be engaged in community clubs, fraternal organizations, sports leagues, or other contexts that promote meaningful social and personal ties outside of work. Further, a variety of modern forces combine to make stable employment with the same colleagues the exception rather than the rule. These changes have served to leave many contemporary fathers without deep and supportive personal relationships, including relationships with role models and mentors for fatherhood and family life. [In our study], active faith community involvement was reported as profoundly important in filling these needs that are increasingly difficult to fulfill elsewhere. (pp. 347–348)

As involvement in civic clubs and organizations has waned, social networks have similarly waned and weakened. An obvious consequence of this tendency is that both the quantity and quality of an individual or family's social networks will decline. However, a final and often overlooked functional element of religious communities as social networks links closely with our discussion of generational relationships in Chapter 10 (pp. 175–184). In short, the faith community is likely the best (and perhaps the only remaining) context that meaningfully and consistently unites nonrelated persons across several generations.

These changes in modern societies are probably unique changes that are happening because of unique cultural and historical conditions. Therefore it is likely that part of the reason the religious parts of social networks are helpful to families in the United States at this particular historical era is characterized by unique cultural, technological, and historical conditions that have weakened most other nonreligious networks. Hopefully, future research and theorizing will help us learn more about which of these processes are unique historical conditions and which are more general and enduring processes that are relevant in a wide variety of historical and cultural situations. We now move from a focus on the psychosocial context of social networks to a discussion of another rich psychosocial phenomenon—sacred rituals.

RITUALS

The study of *rituals* has been an important part of scholarly inquiry for well over a century. It began in the fields of anthropology and sociology and became a part of family studies with Bossard and Boll's (1950) groundbreaking volume. Since then there have been numerous improvements conceptually, theoretically, and empirically (Doherty, 1999; Fiese, 2006; Grimes, 1995; Imber-Black, Roberts, & Whiting, 1988); and evidence is accumulating that rituals constitute a psychosocial part of religion that can help and harm families. As with all parts of sacred theory, one of the first steps is to define the key terms; but this is especially challenging with rituals because it is such "an elusive concept, on the one hand transparent and conspicuous in its enactment, on the other, subtle and mysterious in its boundaries and effects on participants" (Wolin & Bennett, 1984, p. 401).

Definitions

Bahr and Bahr's (2009, Chapter 7) review and analysis of the large and complex body of literature about rituals demonstrates how challenging it is to define this elusive but important concept. They described 17 different ways scholars have defined this term (pp. 264–266) and seven different typologies (pp. 269–270); and their lists are merely illustrative arrays that serve "as a basis for discussion" rather than exhaustive lists or the basis for a definition or typology. The conceptual chaos is further illustrated by the variety in solutions that have been suggested.

Boyce, Jensen, James, and Peacock (1983) and others said it is not useful to try to distinguish between rituals, celebrations, and traditions, and suggested we use the term routines for all of them. Curran (1983) and Meredith (1985) argued that all of the routine and ritualized parts of family life should be called family traditions. Wise (1986) preferred to divide them into routines and rituals, and a recent group of scholars suggested we use the term ritual to refer to all of these events because "while these terms—rituals, celebrations, and traditions—may have subtle differences, they all appear to refer to the same general collection of family-oriented activities" (Meredith, Abbott, Lamanna, & Sanders, 1989, p. 76; see also Burr, Day, & Bahr, 1993, p. 325).

Some of the reasons for this conceptual complexity are that rituals are studied in a number of different disciplines. Each discipline has a slightly different perspective; and each of them focuses on different aspects of rituals. Therefore we agree with those who believe it is not possible to provide a precise definition for the many ways to study rituals (Collins, 2005; Parkin, 1992). However, as Bahr and Bahr (2009) suggested, it is possible to create "a 'soft,' flexible working definition" (p. 264).

"Working" definitions are desirable because our data suggest that rituals are different in several important ways from routines and traditions, and that they influence family processes and outcomes in ways that are different from and more powerful than the effects of routines and traditions. The definitions we find the most useful are those that view customs and traditions as the broadest category of patterns in behavior, so broad that they include rituals and routines. Rituals are a subset of routines, and they are similar in several ways.

They are similar in that rituals and routines involve more than one member of a family. They involve multiple members, and involve both overt behavior or action. Thus just thinking about something is not a family ritual or routine. There also is repetition in the form and content of what is done. The form refers to how things are done, and the content refers to what is done. Both of them also always have morphostasis and morphogenesis. These two terms refer to stability and change, and they mean that rituals and routines both have some continuity over time, and that both are also always evolving and changing as individuals and families develop and as the environment around families changes.

Rituals and routines are also similar in the ways they originate. Some are part of cultural traditions that are handed down from one generation to the next. Others are new creations that are invented. Some of the rituals and routines that are handed down over generations change little over time, but others change and evolve in many ways as families add, modify, and remove parts of them.

Even though all rituals are routines, some routines are not rituals; and there are at least four ways they are different. They differ in the amount of symbolism and meaning. When activities have little symbolism and meaning they are merely routines. The greater the symbolism and meaning, the more they become rituals. The symbolism means that some components refer to abstract ideas or beliefs that are complex, widely understood, and shared; but they are so subtle and elusive that they are difficult to put into words. Rituals provide tangible representations of these intangible, multifaceted, and hard-to-pin-down ideas.

A second way routines and rituals are different is in the amount of emotional significance associated with them (Doherty, 2001; Wolin & Bennett, 1984). There is a great deal of emotion associated with rituals such as weddings, births, funerals, children leaving home, a bar mitzvah, and other important celebrations. Even frequent rituals that aren't very elaborate and don't take very long, such as saying goodbye in the morning or saying a prayer before a meal, have more emotion than less ritualized activities such as talking about the events of the day, sitting at the same place at the table, taking the dog for a walk, helping children with homework, and patterns that are repeated in the morning and at bedtime.

A third way rituals are different from routines is in how practical and ordinary the routine behaviors are. Rituals tend to include some behavior that is relatively unusual or extraordinary. For example, when family members bow their heads and are quiet while they say a prayer in a reverent manner before eating a meal, these are impractical but significant behaviors. Even though some of the special aspects of these behaviors occur fairly frequently, they still have a certain "uniqueness" or lack of routineness in them.

A fourth way rituals are different is that many of them have three phases, and routines have just one. "Ritual is not just the ceremony or actual performance, but the whole process of preparing for it, experiencing it, and reintegration back into everyday life" (Roberts, 1988, p. 8). Even rituals that are fairly frequent have a preparation phase and a back-to-normal phase. The preparation and follow-up activities tend to be fairly elaborate for rituals such as weddings and funerals, and the preparation activities for less elaborate and more frequent rituals can be simple things such as kneeling, bowing heads, and folding arms to prepare for a prayer. Routines do not have the same phases, no transitions "into" or "out of" ritual, because routines are just a continuation of the usual ways of behaving.

Sacredness

Some rituals have little about them that is sacred. For example, Valentine's Day is a romantic day that has little if any sacred meaning for most people. The Fourth of July in the United States and Cinco de Mayo in Mexico have little about them that is sacred to most people. Also, birthday celebrations, anniversaries, and graduations have little that is sacred.

Some rituals are complex combinations of the sacred and secular. Christmas and Easter involve both the sacred and secular. The more Christmas is a celebration of the birth of Jesus Christ, the more it tends to be a sacred experience; and the more it is a time for tinsel, shopping, and Santa Claus, the more secular the experience. When the emphasis at Easter is on the resurrection of Christ it is more sacred, and when the emphasis is on the Easter Bunny and beginning of spring it is more secular. Funerals and weddings also can be primarily sacred or secular—or a complex mixture of the two.

Our data suggest there are several important differences between sacred and secular rituals. There seems to be more morphogenesis in secular rituals and more morphostasis in sacred rituals. New rituals can emerge with both of them, and old ones can change and sometimes decay, but there seems to be more stability with those that have religious significance. Further, the changes in sacred rituals tend to be with minor rather than major aspects, whereas changes in secular rituals often involve major aspects.

Our data also suggest that sacred rituals tend to be more powerful and have more influence on family processes and outcomes. This idea ties back to the principle at the heart of sacred theory that was discussed on page 14 in Chapter 1. It theorizes that the parts of the human experience that are perceived to be sacred have a unique, unusually powerful, and salient influence in social and cultural conditions generally—and in family life in particular.

Contingencies

There is a sizeable body of scholarly literature that suggests rituals can be beneficial in families (Bossard & Boll, 1950; Fiese, 2006; Imber-Black et al., 1988; Meredith et al., 1989; Wolin & Bennett, 1984). For example, Wolin and Bennett concluded that "family rituals are vital to the life of the healthy family" (p. 407). Loser et al. (2009) gathered data from 224 members of 67 families to try to learn more about the benefits that were perceived by these families, and they found that the benefits of "religious rituals included greater spiritual growth, happier daily life, more focus and direction, and better personal behavior. Familial benefits of religious rituals included strengthened relationships, more family togetherness and unity, increased communication, less contention, more kindness, and better parenting" (p. 345).

There also is literature that suggests that rituals are sometimes harmful. For example, Lee et al. (1997) found that when family worship is "compulsory" it can be counterproductive. Families also can try to have so many rituals that it can be overwhelming. Similarly, rituals can be too rigid or too flexible, with so little structure that they are chaotic and confusing. Also, some family members can try to enforce rituals in ways that are not consistent with the developmental needs of children or adults. Religious rituals also can be used to promote inappropriate, immoral, and unhealthy ways of living. For example, they can be used to create or promote abuse and exploitation. They also can be used to dominate other family members—especially those who are young or have less power. They also can be used to mutilate, create disfigurement, and even cause death.

This suggests that the effect of religious rituals in families is not just a simple relationship wherein the presence of religious rituals is beneficial. It is apparently a more complex relationship with a number of contextual factors, circumstances, or contingencies influencing when rituals are helpful and harmful. Fortunately, some of the previous research has information about these contingencies, and one of our goals as we try to improve and expand the theorizing and research in this area is to learn more about their role in ritual. Three contingencies that have been described in previous literature are the amount of (a) *stability and change*, (b) *moderation*, and (c) *distinctiveness.*

Stability and Change Wolin and Bennett (1984) introduced the idea that balance in the amount of stability and change influences whether rituals are helpful or harmful. They argued that flexibility is required if rituals are to be relevant and effective in families, and they described examples such as children reaching an age where their opinion ought to carry more weight in the home, as well as families needing to accommodate the children's evolving views in the way they carry out their rituals. Another of their examples is that as families add or lose members through marriage, divorce, remarriage, and death, there is a need to adapt aspects of rituals.

The ability to adapt and modify ritual observance—ranging from important holidays celebrated to the rules for routine family dinnertime—applies to both the types of ritual as well as their level of practice (Wolin & Bennett, 1984, p. 416).

Too much stability can occur when families get stuck in one developmental stage and try to maintain rituals after they have outlived their usefulness. Also, families can have too much stability when they try to maintain rituals in rigid, repressive, and degrading ways to preserve the status quo when they experience problems such as incest or abuse and hope that rigid rituals will keep their secrets from getting out.

Moderation The three-generation study by Meredith et al. (1989) found Aristotle's golden mean helpful in understanding another condition that influences when rituals are helpful and harmful. They found that moderation in the amount of ritualization is desirable, and that both underritualization and overritualization are problematic. The number of rituals can be overwhelming when young couples try to incorporate all of the rituals from both parental families and also try to include the rituals that are encouraged by various cultural, civic, religious, and fraternal groups.

There also are some conditions where there is underritualization and sometimes no ritual to help families deal with events such as miscarriages, stillbirth, rape, transitions from childhood to adolescence and adolescence to adulthood, divorce, early retirement, and old age. An example of this is the absence of rituals for dealing with the end of nonmarital relationships. As Imber-Black et al. (1988) explained, "The end of a nonmarried relationship not only has no healing ritual, but also often is not acknowledged as a loss by family and friends, or is considered 'less serious' than a divorce" (p. 58).

This lack of confirmation with rituals makes healing in these situations more difficult. When families are able to create rituals that allow for the expression of pain and sadness and provide mechanisms for coping with losses, it can be helpful.

Distinctiveness Research about the generational transmission of alcoholism found another condition that influences the helpfulness of rituals (Wolin, Bennett, Noonan, & Teitelbaum, 1980). When families have undesirable characteristics such as alcoholism, it helps to keep the rituals distinctive from (separated from) the problem. Apparently, if family rituals can be separated from family problems, there tends to be less generational transmission of the problems. For example, if families are able to keep the alcohol problems separated from their holiday celebrations, it decreases the likelihood the alcoholism will be passed on to future generations.

So far this process has been demonstrated only with the generational transmission of alcoholism, but it may also occur with other problems such as physical abuse, fighting, aggressiveness, excessive competitiveness, and the lack of intimacy. Future research is needed to find out if separating these problems from rituals decreases the generational transmission of them.

Effects

Another goal in the study of rituals is to identify how the wise use of rituals influences family processes and outcomes, and there is considerable and increasing evidence that they influence many things in families. Most of the literature about these effects deals with rituals in general, rather than just sacred rituals. Therefore we know little about the unique effects of rituals that involve the sacred—other than the idea that we think rituals that involve the sacred tend to have relatively more salience and power.

Imber-Black et al. (1988) have argued that rituals help families cope with membership changes that come with birth, death, children leaving their family of orientation, marriage, and divorce. For example, weddings help families make the adjustment of creating and integrating a new family unit. Announcements, christenings, and other baby-naming rituals help new members be assimilated, and funerals and wakes help families cope with death. Bar mitzvahs and bat mitzvahs redefine membership in families in the Jewish community.

There also are some major changes in membership wherein families sometimes lack the rituals that would help them make the necessary symbolic and emotional adjustments. For example, there are few rituals that help families cope with divorce, adoption, and forming stepfamilies. Weddings are used to create the marital part of stepfamilies, but the children seldom have a role in the wedding, and sometimes are even excluded. One consequence is that often the marital part of the new stepfamily is formed symbolically and emotionally, but the family system is not formed as clearly and effectively. Imber-Black et al. (1998) described a clinical situation where this was important. A couple in a stepfamily came for therapy due to stepparent–stepchild conflict, and they were moving toward extruding a child. Their wedding had been celebrated with extended family and friends, but "their five children from their prior marriage, ages six to twelve, were barred from attending. The wedding ritual had publically affirmed the new couple, but not the new stepfamily" (p. 52). Ultimately, a ritual that "helped" some members harmed others. As a result, everyone is likely to harmed over process of time. Family rituals should, ideally, benefit and unify *all* family members.

Rituals also help family members create, maintain, and change identities. Weddings, for example, do more than just redefine membership. They transform identities, as a member of each family becomes a spouse and others become in-laws. Also, ways of dressing and even the presence of specific foods during rituals help people gain a sense of their identity and locate themselves in their larger cultural groups (i.e., wedding cake for newlyweds, or breaking the fast with traditional Islamic foods during Ramadan for Muslims).

Another way the wise use of rituals helps families is that rituals can promote healing. Many religious and cultural groups have rituals for remembering and honoring family members who die. For example, Catholic survivors may request that Mass be said to commemorate the anniversary of the death of a loved one. "In Judaism, a special ceremony is held to place the headstone on a grave a year following a death, and family members recite the Kaddish prayer both on anniversaries of the death and on certain holidays" (Imber-Black et al., 1988, p. 54). Such rituals are time and space bound, and this allows for the expression of grief and loss in a manner that simultaneously facilitates the ongoing life.

Religious rituals also can help family members cope with undesirable behavior, conflict, and other stressors (Pargament, 1997). Three of these rituals that can help violators and others in their families are acknowledgment of personal transgressions (confession), reparations for misdeeds (repentance), and "cleaning of the slate" accompanied by divine acceptance (reconciliation) (Pargament & Mahoney, 2002).

Another benefit that has appeared in a number of studies is that rituals help promote a sense of belonging in individuals—and integration, cohesion, solidarity, and bonds in families and societies (Durkheim, 1915; Meredith, 1985; Schvaneveldt & Lee, 1983). Meredith et al. (1989) summarized some of the reasons the wise use of rituals helps families in these ways: "Family rituals, first and foremost, encourage contact between family members, usually in a relaxed, enjoyable setting. Family conflicts and problems are temporarily set aside. This may lead to increased communication and cohesiveness" (p. 77).

Meredith and colleagues (1989) also suggested that rituals can help bridge the intergenerational gaps that separate family members by providing meaningful interaction between parents and children and extended family members. They explained: "A major theme of most family rituals is appreciation of one another and the enjoyment of life together; therefore commitment to the family may be renewed by the regular observation of family rituals" (p. 77). Thus family values and beliefs may be learned and perpetuated through a variety of rituals that foster feelings and beliefs that create unity and oneness.

Rituals have a complicated and reciprocal relationship with beliefs. Durkheim (1915) argued that rituals are influenced by or stem from abstract and complicated beliefs; and they also help create, maintain, and refine beliefs. This is particularly important for families and societies when threatening, unanticipated, or stressful conditions exist, because rituals can help promote stability, predictability, and order.

As mentioned earlier, the Loser et al. (2009) study found that rituals can promote spiritual growth, happiness, focus and direction, better personal behavior, strengthened relationships, family togetherness and unity, communication, less contention, more kindness, and better parenting (p. 345). They also help individuals and families by offering rites of passage that help create and maintain meaning and purpose. Rituals can also help provide a sense of completeness, value, and integration. Doherty (1999, 2001, 2004) has repeatedly argued and demonstrated that one of the greatest dangers to marital and family closeness and meaning is the dis-integrating influence and pace of daily life. If Doherty's point is valid, and our research also argues that it is, meaningful and sacred rituals seem key in restoring and maintaining a sense of purpose and unity in "a world that pulls us apart."

There are many different aspects of rituals, and it is possible that some aspects have different effects than others. One example of this was suggested by Fiese and Tomcho (2001). They argued that the *meaning* and *routine* aspects of rituals are different and tend to have different effects. The routine component involves the way roles and routine practices are assigned. The meaning component involves expectations for attendance, how important various acts are, the symbolic meaning and significance of acts, and a role of commitment to continue practices into the future. As Fiese and Tomcho (2001) noted, "These two components have been found to be reliably distinct from each other across several laboratories and study populations (Baxter & Clark, 1996; Bush & Pargament, 1997; Fiese, 1992; Fiese & Kline, 1993; Markson & Fiese, 2000; Poch, 1994)" (p. 598).

Fiese, Hooker, Kotary, and Schwagler (1993) and Fiese and Tomcho (2001) both found that the meanings associated with family rituals were related to marital satisfaction. They also found that the marital satisfaction of husbands was more closely linked to ritual meaning, and wives' satisfaction was more closely associated with routine practices. Thus there is a little evidence that there may be gender differences in the ways religious rituals influence family processes, but more research is needed before we know what to do with this finding.

Our data also provide additional information about a number of ways the wise use of rituals helps families (Marks, 2004). Rituals facilitate communication in a variety of ways, help families create effective relationships, and also help to create a sense of shared history. They provide examples for children and help families be effective in building bridges and boundaries with desirable and undesirable aspects of contemporary culture without segregation. They promote prosocial behaviors such as empathy, patience, gratitude, and discipline. Rituals provide sources of change outside the family and realm of personal influence. They foster a sense of relaxation and a sense of personal relationship and connection with God, and provide the ability "to breathe." They offer structure, provide a "rhythm to life," and give a sense of comfort (Marks, 2004).

Rituals also help families transmit religious beliefs to the rising generation and teach the new generation moral ways of living. Some of this learning deals with beliefs and attitudes that are abstract and complex, which would be difficult to teach to new generations with less ritualized and purely rational ways of behaving. Two examples from our interviews illustrate these patterns. One of the rituals among members of the Church of Jesus Christ of Latter-day Saints is to have a "family home evening" on Monday evenings, and the following comments by a mother of four illustrate how this ritual provided opportunities to promote love in their home and help their children learn to support and encourage each other:

> The simple things we did in home evenings were not remarkable, nor unique nor particularly creative. We just tried to be consistent and to have a variety of fun things to do as we taught gospel principles. We often began home evenings when the children arrived home from school on Monday afternoon. We went bowling or played tennis or played racquetball or went swimming. It may have been in those settings where we first began to teach them to support and cheer for one another as a way of showing our love for each other. I can still see our youngest struggling to hold a bowling ball with both hands, dropping it with a thud, and then all the family cheering as it v-e-r-y slowly rolled down the alley, and occasionally knocked down a few pins.
>
> One of the best parts of family night came at the end. Each week we held interviews with each child, my husband interviewing two and I the other two. The following week, we switched, so that every two weeks we had one-on-one time with each child. Of course, there were many other one-on-ones during those weeks, but Monday nights were special. Many years later, when he had children of his own, I asked our oldest son what he remembered about those interviews. He admitted he couldn't remember any specifics. He just remembered feeling that he was important and that he was being listened to.

The following comments from a mother of five similarly illustrate that when rituals become an established tradition in a family, it helps new generations learn the values and ideals of a family:

> My grandmother and her brothers homesteaded some land in Arizona, and they had a place where we could go and have reunions. So, they started holding reunions every year, and as a result I got to know my cousins and my second cousins and even some third cousins. This last year we had a reunion where there were 1,000 people there. It was almost too many, but it was so nice to see the ones we know. And, they had family members act out things my grandparents had done. Like, for example, they had a chair-making operation and we acted it out. Each year there was something that focused on our ancestors and it was fun to learn about them, and it helped us be close to them as well as being fun. In some families it is so hard to get teenagers to come to

> reunions, but we did it right from the time we were little, and it became an established tradition, and we got to know our cousins, and it helped us support each other; and then helped our children feel that they are a part of a larger loving family.

APPLICATIONS

This chapter described ways religious social networks and rituals influence family processes and outcomes. The applications of these two psychosocial elements are quite different and need to be addressed separately.

In connection with religious social networks, we encourage families and those who work with them to have sensitivity to the capacity of religious organizations to both unite and divide families. Shared attendance and worship, shared service in church-related outreach, shared enjoyment of "church family" or religiously based social events, and other family-level involvement may all have personal, marital, and family-level benefits—but there is more to the story.

As one of the authors has reported in previous research, the challenges and blessings of faith community involvement on marriage seemed to be symbolically captured by an Orthodox Jewish Sabbath service he attended. Namely, "men and women, husbands and wives, took their respective places on separate sides of a central partition. Following readings from the sacred Torah and an accompanying worship service, husbands and wives joined each other in the foyer" (Marks, 2005, p. 106).

We see this format of worship as symbolic of the voluntary service many religious mothers and fathers give to their faith communities. Namely, for many couples in the above study, volunteer service to the faith community seemed to serve as a temporal partition between husbands and wives. At first glance, these heavy sacrifices seem to "pit religion against marriage and family in a struggle over limited time and energy" (Marks, 2005, p. 106). However, these couples shared a mutual commitment to their faith and tended to value the contribution the other was making as a mutual and necessary sacrifice for which the couples believed their marriage and family were blessed. Even so, this study led to a conclusion that "a key challenge for faith communities may be to avoid turning the temporary partition of volunteered time into a formidable wall between wives and husbands"—and, we would add, parents and children (p. 106). A concluding application of this piece posits: "Clinicians, especially pastoral counselors, may be beneficial in encouraging couples to avoid constructing such walls while remaining *secondarily* sensitive to faith community needs" (p. 106).

Faith communities have been identified as important and perhaps uniquely potent social networks, given the strong kinlike ties that exist in some "church families." We briefly highlighted this idea early in the present chapter, and our own research has repeatedly supported this point. However, in application there is an important counterpoint drawn from a series of qualitative studies by Dollahite and colleagues. These studies found that fathers gave specific narrative accounts of how their faith communities had offered social, emotional, spiritual, financial, and temporal support (including transportation and housing) in times of need. However, when the parents' faith communities failed them "it was both disappointing and hurtful in ways that seemed to elicit deeper frustration and pain than failures by secular agencies and institutions" (Marks & Dollahite, 2001, p. 636). Thus for some persons, faith community seems to be a unique and profoundly important social network that qualitatively differs from other groups, in both positive and negative ways. Next, we turn from the psychosocial element of religious social networks to the phenomenon of sacred rituals.

As we conclude this chapter's application section with a brief note on sacred rituals, such as the shared study of holy texts, bar and bat mitzvahs, Ramadan fasts, and family prayer, we note that these family rituals may need little discussion in an application section because *religious family rituals are lived applications and expressions of the sacred.* Because a wide array of clinicians and family professionals are well aware of the application value of family ritual, we turn to a forthcoming edited volume (Hoffman, 2011) that invites *researchers* to more carefully consider the potency of ritual. This volume includes the following relevant passage:

> Humans, according to William James (1902), have a powerful innate desire to believe. A host of psychiatrists, psychologists, and family researchers have argued that there is no other group that infuses us with such a craving for belonging and acceptance as family (Pruett 2001). With these two fundamental human hungers posited, we turn to sociologist Douglas Marshall's conclusion that: "The practice of ritual produces two primary outcomes—*Belief* and *Belonging*" (2002: 360, emphasis in original). If the above experts are correct in asserting that we: (a) long for something to believe in, (b) long for something to belong to, and (c) can satiate both of these craved, primary longings through sacred ritual practice—then family ritual (especially religious family ritual) seems a promising phenomenon for social researchers to examine. (Marks, Dollahite, & Barker, 2011, p. 190)

It is our hope that additional research responding to the above call will more precisely delineate how, when, and why sacred ritual can strengthen families—and how imprudent applications of it can damage and weaken families.

SUMMARY

This chapter discussed ways social networks and rituals can help and harm families. Being richly interconnected with the religious parts of social networks is helpful when the involvement is moderate and avoids the extremes of deficiency and excess. Bridging and bounding are both important parts of this management, and wise families are careful to be involved with networks that are consistent with their goals and needs.

Rituals involve unusual or extraordinary behaviors, and they tend to have the three phases of preparation, enactment, and return to normal life whereas routines are merely the continuation of normal life. The best data available suggest that rituals can be both helpful and harmful in families, and three contingencies were described that provide insights about the conditions that influence their effects in families. They tend to be helpful when there is a balance of morphostasis and morphogenesis, when there is moderation in the amount of ritualization so there is neither under- or overritualization, and when problematic behavior is separated from rituals.

Rituals influence many aspects of family processes and outcomes, and rituals that involve the sacred tend to have more influence than secular rituals that are otherwise similar. When family members are wise in the ways they use rituals, they help families cope with membership changes, help with healing, and help provide meaning and purpose—especially with abstract beliefs and ideas that are difficult to describe and teach. They also contribute to cohesion, solidarity, integration, unity, and bonds, and help families cope with stressful situations, conflict, and problematic behavior. They promote spiritual growth, happiness, focus and direction, better personal behavior, strengthened relationships, communication, less contention, more kindness, and better parenting. They also help individuals and families make rites of passage, and they help create order and predictability. They also help provide a sense of completeness, value, and integration.

13

Relationships With Other Perspectives

In this chapter we describe three ways sacred theory has relationships with broader issues and ideas. The first part of the chapter describes ways the ideas in the theory are related to a number of ideals and beliefs that are advocated by theories and philosophies that are very different from sacred theory. Many of these other philosophies advocate ideas that compete with the ideas in sacred theory, and some of them promote ideas that are harmful in families. We compare these competing ideas with the ideas in sacred theory in the hope this will help more family members better understand the differences, and choose ways of behaving that are helpful rather than destructive. This part of the chapter concludes with some ways to apply these ideas. The second section in this chapter discusses ways sacred theory is related to the conceptual frameworks and general theories that have been widely used in studying families, and some of the ways of integrating ideas in different theories. The last section describes some of the implications sacred theory has for several nonfamily institutions such as government, law, and education.

COMPETING IDEAS

There are many aspects of modern societies and cultures that are helpful and wonderful for families, but there are also several philosophies that advocate ideologies, values, and behavior that are very different from the lifestyle advocated by sacred theory. Some parts of these alternatives are often in conflict with the ideas in sacred theory, and some of them are so inconsistent with the widely shared goals in families that they contribute to the toxicity in the cultural environment around families.

There are several reasons it seems important to describe these differences. One is because some of the alternative ideas are attractive and seductive—especially in the short run. Another reason is because the destructive aspects of some of these alternative ideas are not readily apparent, and many of them do not appear quickly. Another is because being aware of the consequences of the competing ideas can help family members make wise choices and not be seduced in subtle ways by the attractive but destructive ideas. A final reason is because these philosophies are such broad, inclusive, abstract ideologies, perspectives, or philosophies that they lead to an infinite number of specific ways of behaving. It is not practical to identify, focus on, or even try to remember all of the specific ramifications of the philosophies, but it is helpful to focus on the abstract values, ideals, or philosophies and the ways they lead to harmful patterns in families.

We have grouped these competing philosophies into seven areas. They are (a) secularism, (b) unmoderated liberating values, (c) the role of the individual, (d) acquisition, (e) ways of relating, (f) epistemological issues, and (g) hedonism; and most of these seven areas include several different clusters of ideas.

Secularism

Secularism is the philosophy that argues against the idea that the sacred matters. This means it is diametrically opposed to the main thesis of this book. There are many different versions of secularism, some of which are more extreme than others, but all of them argue for separating the sacred from the important parts of the human experience. The more extreme versions view the sacred as an unwise, indefensible, and illegitimate source of ideas that is not justified by reason or experience, and they advocate that beliefs about such things as Gods, heavens, and the divine should be eliminated. The softer versions merely argue for separating the sacred from other parts of life, but even the softer versions are usually opposed to the idea that aspects of the sacred are helpful. And most secularists argue that family life will be the most effective when it is separated from sacred ideas and traditions (Taylor, 2007). This philosophy has become an influential perspective in modern societies, especially among philosophers and educators, those who are highly influential in the media, and leaders in entertainment, government, and law.

The term secularism was coined in the middle of the nineteenth century by Holyoake (1896), but the philosophy has been around for millennia. Plato (1979) was the first scholar we are aware of who argued against the idea that aspects of the sacred are helpful in families. He argued in *The Republic* that religion should be tolerated for the uneducated masses, but that it should not have a role in the lives of the elite, educated, and leaders. Marx and Engels (1964) called religion "the opium of the people," and Freud (1927, p. 88) argued that turning to the sacred and using ideas derived from and about it is an obsession and neurosis that people should try to overcome. Ellis (1980) argued that "religiosity . . . is in many respects equivalent to irrational thinking and emotional disturbance" (p. 637).

The secular philosophy argues for removing many of the ideals advocated in this book. For example, it argues that asking for and seeking divine help through activities such as prayer and meditation should not be a part of family life. It also argues that sacrificing for others should not have sacred aspects to it, and that commitment in marriage should be a matter of personal commitment and God should not be a part of it. It advocates that the sexual part does not have sacred aspects, and this means that beliefs and practices about sexuality can be changed easily. This is the philosophy scholars have used to argue that sexual behavior should be separated from marriage. It also argues that the responsibility for rearing children is not a divine activity, and that morality is all relative.

The word *desecration* means to remove something from the consecrated or sacred, and is usually used to refer to a violation of something that is viewed as sacred. This is an accurate description of the result of the ideology promoted by secularism because, according to sacred theory, it is a desecration of a part of the human experience that benefits from viewing the sacred as important.

We are among those who believe in the noumenological and phenomenological reality of the sacred and also the reality of the unholy that is also spiritual. Therefore we also believe that those who create ideas and answers that do not include the sacred will eventually and inevitably come up with many ideas that are empty, inadequate, and less meaningful as they cannot "put it all together" because they ignore an important part of reality. Those who believe the sacred is not important may be satisfied intellectually for a while that they "have it all" and know what "the good life" is, and some of their ideas may even last for a generation or two. But while they are trying out ideas that are incompatible with the needs and goals in families but that they think are wise, they will also bring a great deal of harm to many families.

Some secularists advocate that family processes have traditionally not been a part of the public marketplace, and that they ought to be rationalized and bureaucratized because they think the emotional and bonding patterns that have been parts of family life are unwise. Some of these ideas are incompatible with the widely shared goals in families, and adopting them as widespread patterns or policies would have devastating consequences for family life. Dialogue and scholarly analysis of ideas such as these are needed, but our data suggest that reducing the role of the sacred while examining and evaluating radically different strategies is dangerous and would be unwise. There are probably some ideas about the sacred that are widely believed that are unwise and ineffective, and the scholarly community ought to debate and analyze these possibilities, but ideas about the sacred ought to be respected and included in these debates rather than excluded, ignored, or rejected. Further, ideas about the sacred should be discarded only with great care. It also would be nice if these analyses could be conducted in ways that are more respectful of the individuals who have different points of view than has traditionally been the pattern. Indeed, we have personally witnessed incidents where there was a lack of respect by both some who advocate the secular approaches and some who advocate the sacred approaches.

The differences between secular and sacred views are important for several reasons. One is because sacred perspectives provide reasons and motivation to try to create effective and successful families. Secularism eliminates these reasons, and one of the effects is that family life in secular perspectives has less priority, and people have fewer reasons to be motivated to create effective families. It is likely that one of the effects of this is that as secularism becomes more dominant in a society, it leads to decreases in the quality of family life.

Another reason the difference between the secular and sacred perspectives is important is because it leads to very different assumptions and strategies for improving social conditions. The secular perspectives argue that marriage and family life are merely one way to organize humans, and those who prefer secularist perspectives have little reason to be apprehensive about exploring new and creative alternatives they think might be better than patterns that have existed in the past. This leads secularists to be relatively creative and uninhibited in exploring ideas and possibilities that are designed to create changes in the current patterns in marriage and family life. They also pay little attention to conserving aspects of the patterns that have existed in the past. Some of the alternatives they are willing to consider would merely be modifications of the past patterns, and one of the more extreme possibilities is to eliminate marriage and family life.

Many who appreciate the sacred believe that at least some of the existing patterns in family life were instituted by God and that God has a better understanding of the needs and nature of humans. Therefore they often feel threatened by alternatives suggested by those who prefer secular perspectives. Also, those with sacred perspectives are motivated to preserve the patterns that were instituted by God and are essential for the welfare of humans. One problem with this is that people who believe in sanctification have a difficult time determining which parts of family life are essential and which parts are not, leading to ambiguity and controversy about many issues. But generally those with sacred perspectives tend to be resistant to many of the innovations proposed by those who prefer secular perspectives.

Holyoake (1896) argued over a century ago that when secularism is wisely used, it need not be an argument against the sacred as it can be an argument for ideas that are independent of it. It need not question the value or beliefs about the sacred, and it is the most useful when it advocates ideas that are valuable that are created in nonreligious ways. Unfortunately, this view of the role of secularism is more idealistic than realistic because the tendency among those who advocate secularism is to react against that which is sacred rather than think of independence. The best solution for dealing with the challenges of secularism is to use this distinction and appreciate both sacred and secular phenomena.

Unmoderated Liberating Values

Some of the perspectives that advocate ideas that compete with the ideas in sacred theory are excessive or extreme versions of wholesome values that grew out of the Enlightenment. The Enlightenment was a trend in Western philosophy and cultural life that had its roots in the Renaissance, the Protestant Reformation, and the scientific revolution; and it became a widely advocated ideology in the seventeenth and eighteenth centuries. The ideas in the Enlightenment began and were emphasized first in Europe, and then migrated quickly to the colonies in America.

The Enlightenment was, in many ways, a reaction to the domination of the Catholic Church and the ruling elites in medieval Europe and the Middle East. The Renaissance and scientific revolution provided new ways of creating knowledge and new ways of thinking and valuing that were strongly opposed to the subjugation and oppression of the masses during the previous millennium. The dominating forces during the Middle Ages were based on religious authority, guild-based economic systems, and censorship of ideas.

There were a number of ideas and values that became increasingly cherished as the Enlightenment grew. Some of them were values such as freedom, liberty, autonomy, independence, and the rights of individuals. Part of the reason these values were championed was because they helped provide an intellectual rationale or philosophy that opposed the earlier patterns of the supremacy, dominance, and tyranny of the traditional institutions that had been so oppressive and coercive in medieval Europe; and the new ideas and values opened the door to alternative ways of organizing societies and living that seemed very attractive.

As these innovations became ascendant in the eighteenth century, they led to a sea change in what people believed in and what they thought was possible; and this led to dramatic improvements in social conditions. The innovations helped societies move toward an era of rational discourse, increased freedom in many areas of life, appreciation for personal judgment, liberation from tyranny and oppression, appreciation for science, modernity, and self-governance, and an emphasis on the rights of individuals.

New forms of government based on democracy and republicanism were fashioned, scientific knowledge exploded, and new approaches were created in industry, finance, and commerce. Undreamed of technological innovations appeared, and these social, scientific, and technological successes led to an increasing emphasis in the twentieth century on the liberating values that had fueled the improvements—freedom, liberty, the rights of individuals, independence, and autonomy—and these gradually became the unquestioned undergirding intellectual pillars of a culture that has since spread around the globe.

Unfortunately, these desirable developments also have some unintended, unanticipated, and largely unrecognized side effects, some of which have become increasingly problematic for the quality of family life. One is that the increasing appreciation and dominance of the liberating values has led to some other ideals being given much less attention, so much less that they have receded dramatically in importance in the eyes of many people. The result is that some of the values that are different from and complementary to the liberating values, and that tend to moderate the liberating values, are getting less and less attention and priority. Some of these values deal with obligations and responsibilities, commitments, interdependence, restraint, and bonds. A few scholars have focused on the value of this more complex array of values rather than giving such exclusive attention to the value of freedom as in volumes such as Fromm's *Escape From Freedom* (1965) and Frankl's *Man's Search for Meaning* (1984). For example, the latter noted and criticized the tendencies during a post–World War II visit to the United States. He stated:

> Freedom . . . is not the last word. Freedom is only part of the story and half of the truth. . . . In fact, freedom is in danger of degenerating into mere arbitrariness unless it is lived in terms of responsibleness. That is why *I recommend that the Statue of Liberty on the East Coast be supplemented by a Statue of Responsibility on the West Coast.* (p. 156, emphasis in the original)

As a Jewish survivor of the Nazi concentration camps, Frankl surely had a more profound appreciation for freedom and liberty than most. However, his wisdom regarding the critical balance between liberty and responsibility is timeless. A similar theme is evident in the family relationships addressed in this volume.

Because many of the liberating ideals of the Enlightenment were spawned by secular perspectives, as time has passed and the technological, social, and scientific advances have become more impressive, secularism and rationalism have been seen increasingly as desirable philosophies. This has led to further decreases in appreciation for and value of sacred phenomena among large segments of the population.

One effect of these patterns that is continuing in a fairly unabated way with many people is that increasingly extreme versions of many of the liberating values have been appearing. The extreme versions are appearing partly because these values have not been moderated by alternative theories (one of the goals of this book), competing philosophies, or values that complement the liberation by emphasizing aspects of life that are limiting and constraining. This pattern of valuing the relatively extreme and unmoderated versions of the liberating values has been especially prevalent among the intellectually elite, governing leaders, opinion leaders, those in the legal system, and those who dominate the media. As Peter Berger quipped, "If India is the most religious country on our planet, and Sweden is the least religious, America is a land of Indians ruled by Swedes" (Smith, 2001, p. 103).

One of the results of this situation is that large segments of modern societies now value freedom without limits and restraints, and liberty without responsibility, and this has several problems for family life. One is that when these values are unbridled and excessive, they are not moderated by other ideals that also ought to be viewed as important, leading to many different ways of behaving that are inconsistent with the goals and needs in family life. As Aristotle's golden mean suggests, excess and deficiency tend to be unwise, ignoble, unethical, immoral, and harmful; and moderation with most things tends to be wise, noble, and moral. As some of the liberating values have become excessive and unmoderated, and as the constraining and obligating values have become deficient, this has created a problematic situation in some of the most fundamental and foundational parts of contemporary cultures, and with some of the pillars upon which many social conditions rest. As a result, certain excesses and deficiencies have contributed to the toxicity of the environment around families. There is, therefore, a need to moderate the extremes of the liberating values and the deficiencies of the constraining values.

For example, an immoderate emphasis on liberation from the constraining aspects of churches, governments, traditions, and other social institutions can lead to familial failures. When individually liberating values are valued at the expense of wise constraint, this context tends to produce individuals who undervalue and distort the ways of relating to these other aspects of reality. Governments are viewed as oppressive rather than helpful. Churches are viewed as constraining rather than facilitating. Traditions are viewed as rigid, harsh, and irrelevant. Employers are viewed as tyrannical and unfair rather than supportive and caring. The reality is that whereas churches, governments, traditions, and other social institutions can be evil and harmful, they also can be helpful and facilitating; but these positive aspects tend to be ignored, undervalued, and underappreciated when the liberating values are unmoderated by complementary ideals and values.

There are many aspects of this unmoderated situation that deserve attention, but when these insights are applied to sacred theory and the ideas in this chapter they provide several insights about loving God and valuing spiritual phenomena. They help us realize that one of the important parts of the solutions to these problems is to be sure to give appropriate value to the spiritual parts of the human experience. In more colloquial terms, it is important to not throw out the baby with the bath water—to not throw out valuing the spiritual because of the limitations, excesses, and inappropriate oppression of the patterns and the dominating forces in the Middle Ages.

Individualism

Another group of philosophies that contributes to the toxicity in the cultural environment around families has to do with the role of the individual. One of these philosophies is usually described as *individualism*. It is a moral stance, a political philosophy, an ideology, or a perspective that gives priority to the importance and legitimacy of individual rights. It emphasizes the rights of individuals and argues that collectivities such as state, government, or religious institutions should defer to the rights of individuals. According to an individualistic perspective, the goals of individuals and their independence and self-reliance should take priority over communal, group, societal, or national goals and aspirations. Individualism therefore tends to emphasize self-interest rather than interest in, much less responsibility to, others. Beliefs that emphasize the opposites of individualism include collectivism, communitarianism, communalism, and socialism.

The dominant pattern in the world before the fifteenth century was for collectivities, especially governments and religions, to give little priority to the rights, independence, and autonomy of individuals. The rights of the masses were sacrificed by the elite and powerful for what they perceived as the good of the larger group—or more accurately, for the things that would preserve the power, wealth, and rights in the hands of the powerful and elite in ways that promoted their interests.

Cherlin (2009) has suggested that the Protestant Reformation was one of the changes that helped create individualism. The thinking of reformers such as Luther and Calvin argued that the road to salvation was a personal matter between individuals and God. The Catholic Church had argued that the sacraments and rites of the church were necessary to help people toward salvation. But the reformers viewed the role of the church as less central and important, and believed that the individual's personal relationship with the divine was more crucial than it was viewed by the Catholic Church.

The Protestant Reformation was only one of a number of important changes that were occurring at the same time. The invention of the printing press made literature more available to the masses, and the Enlightenment (see pages 216–219) helped rearrange the values and priorities in ways that gave greater emphasis to individuals generally and less emphasis to the interests of the powerful elites. This transferred some of the power in societies from royalties, dictators, and religious leaders, and more fully legitimated the right of individuals to have more control over their own destinies. The new ideology emphasized the rights, freedoms, and liberties of individuals, and placed less emphasis on their responsibilities and obligations to collectives.

The concept of individualism has gradually become a mature and well-established value system over the last several centuries, and many believe Western cultures are becoming increasingly individualistic. The culture in the United States is viewed by many as the culture that prizes individualism the most, and this is partly because the American culture places such high value on ideals such as freedom, liberty, independence, and individual rights.

The trend toward emphasizing individual rights created a great deal of good, and in many ways it has promoted levels of morality and justice in some areas that have never been seen before in the history of the world. It helped provide the intellectual perspective and motivation for the creation of democratic forms of government that paid attention to human rights, liberty, and freedom. It has been a driving force that has helped eliminate abuses such as slavery, discrimination, and oppression. It has helped to correct historical patterns of governments, churches, oligarchies, and other social collectivities having excessive and inappropriate power and control over individuals.

Unfortunately, however, when the emphasis on the rights and freedom of the individual became so important that it became the prime emphasis, this created a philosophy that is having a number of undesirable effects in modern societies. One of the patterns as individualism increases is many people pay great attention to finding ways to satisfy their individual interests, especially their hedonistic and selfish inclinations, at the expense of loyalties, duties, obligations, and responsibilities to others. Given the extent to which individual rights were suppressed in earlier historical times, considerable change in this direction was justified, appropriate, desirable, and moral. However, as the emphasis on the individual became the prime and dominating value, this created a new set of problems.

One of the analyses of the undesirable effects of individualism was Bellah et al.'s (1985) *Habits of the Heart: Individualism and Commitment in American Life*. The theme in their analysis is that:

> [Individualism has] marched inexorably through our history. We are concerned that this individualism may have grown cancerous—that it may be destroying those social integuments that Tocqueville saw as moderating its more destructive potentialities, that it may be threatening the survival of freedom itself. (p. vii)

Neither we nor the Bellah group argue that individualism is inherently and entirely evil and inappropriate. Individualism in moderation has been and continues to be a valuable and desirable part of the American culture. However, when individualism becomes excessive and is not moderated by other constraining values, it creates too much of an emphasis on the self and too little emphasis on others.

Individualism grew out of several developments in the Enlightenment. The intellectual developments that emerged from these changes led to increasing appreciation for ideals such as freedom, rights, liberty, equality, and reason, and gradually these ideals became deeply cherished. These values led to a wholesome appreciation for the worth and importance of individuals and the importance of their control over their own destinies, allegiances, and forms of government. It became problematic when the emphasis on the individual became more important than other ideals.

The philosophy underlying individualism opposes the idea that humanity is a part of an eternal, spiritual, or heavenly schema or plan. When this philosophy of life is the driving force, the kind of individualism it creates doesn't visualize anything as more important, moral, or profound than the rights and freedoms of the individual. The ideas in sacred theory are different from this philosophy in several fundamental ways. Sacred theory argues that the human experience is a part of a larger plan and scheme that involves many things that are greater than the rights of individuals. In this view, humans are not primarily communitarian or biological beings who have occasional spiritual experiences. They are fundamentally spiritual beings who are part of a noble and grand plan that extends beyond mortality.

In our version of sacred theory, we suggest that the most important component of an effective antidote for extreme individualism is not increased concern about civic responsibilities or citizenship or attention to political or economic concerns. Also, it is not merely turning to love and marriage and family—if we are conceptualizing love as a noun. Those ways of thinking sell well in America, and they are helpful ideas, but we do not think they focus on the most important or helpful solutions for the excessive individualism or the many ills it leads to in modern societies.

The solutions lie partly in beliefs about the nature of human existence. When humans are viewed as having an existence that only begins with conception and ends with death, they have little inherent value and are not fundamentally different from other forms of life such as protozoa, amoeba, or sunflowers. When humans are viewed as having divine and spiritual components that exist and are important before conception and after death, there is then a basis for the realization that loving other humans is more important than mere individualistic dreams and aspirations.

Another part of the solution to the problem of hyperindividualism lies in the realization that this is another situation where Aristotle's golden mean is relevant. He argued that the greatest good usually comes from moderation rather than extremes. The dominant pattern in modern society is to emphasize individualism and the ideals and values that are so closely allied with it such as freedom, independence, liberty, autonomy, and human rights. We ought to continue to cultivate these basic values and also the complex set of values that will moderate the excesses that come with extreme individualism. This is not just a cosmetic or superficial change, but one that creates balance in the most fundamental values in the human experience, and one that will create a lifestyle that will avoid excessive self-interest and create interest in self and others in a balanced manner.

Doherty (1995) has also argued that the trend toward excessive individualism has unfortunate consequences. His concerns are mostly about the ways psychotherapy has emphasized self-interest, and his suggestion for improving the situation is to give more emphasis to moral responsibility in psychotherapy. His emphasis on morality seems like a wise way to correct an inappropriate emphasis in therapies, but the problem and solution in family are different. Morality is important, and it deserves a central role in family, but there also are many different views about what is moral, some of which advocate ways of relating that emphasize excessive individualism or high levels of control and domination rather than loving ways of relating. Therefore even though morality is important, valuable, and necessary, having a loving way of relating is the particular form of morality that is needed in families.

The conditions that are suggested by this reasoning are important for marriage and family in several ways. Individualism leads to spouses caring primarily about their own needs and gratifications, and loving is valued less and less. The individualistic philosophy moves people beyond an appropriate emphasis on the rights, desires, and self-interest, and interferes with the inclination to engage in loving, caring, and attentive ways.

Another philosophy that deals with the role of the individual and competes with the ideas in sacred theory is the belief that the self should be given emphasis and priority. This philosophy grew dramatically in the twentieth century, and some have described that century as the century of the self. An example of the ways this philosophy is pathological is the widespread idea in modern societies that "you can't love others until you learn to love yourself." This belief leads therapists, educators, and people to focus their attention and concerns on beliefs and feelings about the self, and many programs have been developed to enhance self-esteem as a strategy to improve the life and social conditions of people.

This emphasis on the self tends to create a rather unfortunate form of selfishness. Burr and Christensen (1992) argued that the widely used programs designed to enhance self-esteem usually exacerbate rather than help the problems people are trying to solve. Stated differently, when people focus on "the self" and on enhancing self-esteem to solve personal and social problems, it tends to make them even more self-centered and less aware of (and less in tune with) others than they were before, thereby complicating and multiplying their existing problems.

A more wise strategy is to focus simultaneously on the worth and dignity of all people, and to cultivate kind and respectful beliefs, feelings, and behaviors toward all people, including the self, without focusing exclusively or even primarily on the self or others. But this balanced approach is not the norm in contemporary society. Such a strategy would help people see themselves as part of a larger picture, and it would be a wholesome contribution to intimate relationships. Conversely, inordinate attention toward the self first, without regard to the larger human context, tends to create an unbalanced, unwise, and unhealthy approach that interferes with the flourishing of marriages, families, and other intimate relationships.

Acquisition

Another group of ideals or philosophies that compete with the ideas in sacred theory and contribute to the toxicity in the cultural environment around families has to do with acquisition. One of these philosophies is usually described by the term *materialism*, but the word has two very different meanings. One is a part of metaphysics, and when it is defined in this context it is the idea that everything that exists is fundamentally matter. This is not the way we are using the term here.

The way we are using *materialism* here has to do with ethics rather than metaphysics. The ethical definition of materialism is the belief that it is good to emphasize material objects, needs, and considerations, and this is usually with a correlated disinterest in or rejection of the sacred parts of the human experience. Defined this way, materialism is an attitude or philosophy that stresses the acquisition of material possessions. The popular inscription on the front of T-shirts that says "The one with the most toys wins" is an example of this way of using the term materialism.

Valuing the material and economic aspects of life is not inherently harmful, but only when materialism is so highly valued that it crowds out the values that complement and moderate it, such as concern for God and other aspects of the sacred, concern for the welfare of people, and creating loving, compassionate, and merciful relationships. The problem exists when the emphasis on materialism escalates and is accompanied with less emphasis on values that compete with materialism.

There are several values that are slightly different from materialism that often cluster with it. They are a *gain ethic* and an emphasis on *greed*. Myers (1983) developed the idea that a greed-oriented or gain ethic is becoming an increasingly pervasive part of the morality in modern societies. He argued that the morality of social relations among kindred folks has traditionally been governed by a "morality characterized by kindness and a predisposition to love and care" (p. 4), which involves a propensity to sacrifice for others and the welfare of one's family. This morality includes a willingness to not "count the cost" in sacrificing for members of one's family.

He contrasts this morality with a different basis for morality that dominates in nonkin relationships. It is governed by a less confining morality that is based on ethics grounded in personal gain and the market. As the gain ethic becomes increasingly powerful and dominant, it justifies and creates what can be called a greed-oriented ethic. Because it is centered in the acquisition of wealth and material possessions, this view of morality is a powerful opponent of an ideology that argues that loving, helping, and sacrificing are valuable.

Many believe the economic chaos that became a worldwide problem in 2008 was created by excessive greed in many places. There was a high level of greed as thousands of people invested in housing to get a share of the profits that were being made in the appreciation of house prices. There was a high level of greed among those in the banking and financing parts of the economy as they changed the criteria for mortgages and international investments in the bundling of mortgages. And when the inevitable time came that housing prices began to moderate, it began a series of events that created chaos in the international monetary system and ultimately in all aspects of the economy. The levels of greed that were the precipitating factors in the resulting recession illustrate how powerfully and pervasively greed is viewed as an important moral ethic, and it undoubtedly contributes to decreasing emphasis on sacrificing—except when it is used as a means for further gain that is driven by greed.

Myers (1983) argued that in modern societies there is a tendency for the nonkin, gain-oriented, market morality to become the more dominant perspective and to replace kinship morality, and that this pattern among "liberators" tends to "free those who would be responsible for children and parents . . . to pursue personal gain in one form or another" (p. 11)

It is important to understand the ways these different values compete because they lead to lifestyles in families that are very different from the lifestyles that are created by loving others and valuing the sacred—resulting in very different consequences in the ability of families to flourish. Also, these values are such dominant forces in modern societies that it is easy for family members to be seduced by the less spiritual ideals and get so carried away with the liberating values and/or materialism and an emphasis on gain and greed that these values interfere in serious ways with the ability of families to meet the more subtle and emotional goals and needs in family life.

Ways of Relating

There are several philosophies that advocate ways of relating with people that compete with the ideas in sacred theory that human relationships should be loving. One of these philosophies advocates the market-oriented and exchange-oriented relationships that have been created by modern economies and commercial and industrial systems. These perspectives view people and relationships with them in terms of efficiency, profit, and loss, and as instrumental in the larger purposes and functions in an economy. People are viewed as objects to be used for market and exchange purposes, and they are to be controlled, conquered, manipulated, and used. Often this means also being exploited and distant in authoritarian, critical, harsh, demanding, demeaning, and cruel ways.

These ways of relating are very different from the demands created by the essential processes in families. Many people find ways to shift between the relatively temporary and instrumental relationships in the public spheres and the more personal, caring, and helpful ways of relating in their family; but others do not understand these differences and don't even try to behave differently in the two spheres. The result is that a sizeable percentage of people, especially males, develop skills and lifestyles that are effective in the public spheres and never learn how to relate effectively in their families.

One of the major theoretical perspectives in the twentieth century was exchange theory. The newest version of this theory is called rational choice theory (White, 2005), which assumes that the market-oriented and exchange style of relating is "the" way humans relate and interact. Clark and Mills (1979) introduced the term *communal* to describe a nonexchange style of relating, and Clark and her colleagues have assembled an impressive body of evidence that a communal rather than exchange orientation is helpful in families (Beck & Clark, 2010).

One of the ways of thinking about these differences is to realize that some ways of relating are more noble, moral, humane, and uplifting. The ideal of loving others is a way of relating that lifts and elevates humans to be the best and most noble they can be. It tends to lift and help people be humane and decent. The philosophies that urge styles of relating that emphasize market-oriented and exchange relationships tend to degrade and debase people and bring out the parts of humans that are less noble. These ways of relating are incompatible with the needs in family life for nurturing, caring, and helpful ways of relating; and philosophies that emphasize these less noble ways of relating decrease the probability of families finding successes and increase the probability of failures.

Another philosophy that is incompatible with the style of relating advocated by sacred theory is built on the underlying ideology that "everything is political," a theme that is prevalent in feminist perspectives and theories (Osmond & Thorne, 1993). Adopting a loving lifestyle emphasizes the need for humans to experience care, compassion, mercy, patience, help, and nurturing, and creates the kind of relationship where people try to assist and help others with devotion, service, and sacrificing for each other. Viewing relationships as political leads people to be adversarial and confrontational against those who try to eliminate discriminations that create and maintain inequality; and they try to maximize their advantages and position relative to others, to conquer and out-vote others, and to eliminate problems with force, manipulation, and coercion rather than love, service, and helpfulness.

Sacred theory argues that the most ideal patterns in family life are to create loving rather than political relationships, but the tendency of the privileged to maintain their privileged conditions makes this difficult. This means that the immorality and injustices created by the inequalities cannot be corrected with loving ways of relating, and it becomes necessary to resort to less noble ways of relating. The resulting struggles make equality, loving, and success in family life difficult to attain. The ideal pattern is to move toward equality and justice because they create a climate where the more noble, humane, and loving patterns can be created.

Part of the reason some people resort to political relationships is because the ideologies that maintain male dominance are so difficult to eliminate. The widespread belief that males ought to be dominating in their relationships with females is illustrated in the style of relating portrayed by John Wayne in movies. It advocates that males ought to be dominating and controlling physically, mentally, and emotionally, and that it is also part of the good life to do it in demeaning and debasing ways. Another example is that many males believe it is important for their manhood that they are always "right." These styles of relating mean that being "right" is more important than being considerate, respectful, and kind, and that it is acceptable, even preferable, for males to behave in unkind ways when they are in situations where they may be in the wrong. In short, this view of what it means to be "a man" puts males in the egocentric trap of choosing to fight to be right, rather than gracefully admitting wrongs to help get along.

These ways of relating are very different from the loving styles that are encouraged by sacred theory. The following example illustrates this type of situation and shows how it can interfere with family successes:

> It's a lot more enjoyable to be together when we're not fighting all the time. It's easier if everyone is working together, to just be patient and not fight. I remember when Sue was trying to give that really spiritual lesson, and she asked a question, and wanted it to be really meaningful, and George answered in a funny voice, and it just ruined it. It was like he was just trying to just be mean and make her mad, and he wanted to be the one who was in control. He always

> had to be right all the time. And Jessica was the one who smoothed things over so we could get back to the lesson. She just did that all the time; sometimes saying something funny, or just listening or being calm or something. She knew when to say something funny or make a joke to help somebody.

Gender inequality and domination by males was one of the factors that contributed to the feminist movement, and the literature in this movement has argued persuasively that these patterns are incompatible with other values such as equality, liberty, and freedom. Fortunately, the traditional pattern has become less of an ideal in recent decades, and is gradually being replaced with more equality in gender relationships (Gallagher, 2003; Wilcox, 2004). However, even though cultural ideals have arguably changed, there are still many situations where there are gaps between beliefs and actual *behavior* (LaRossa, 1997; Marks & Palkovitz, 2004).

Hedonism

There are several philosophies that are grounded in a hedonistic perspective that advocate ideas that compete with the philosophy in sacred theory. Hedonism is the idea that the greatest good comes from seeking and finding personal pleasure and satisfaction while also avoiding or minimizing pain or costs. Some of the more extreme versions of this philosophy argue that humanity's most important pursuit is sensual self-indulgence and that pleasure is the only good. Hedonism is therefore the antithesis of some of the ideas in sacred theory such as the notion that sacrificing for the benefit of others, loving others, and having an interest in the welfare of others are beneficial.

One version of hedonism is when people turn to drugs and other forms of stimulants and hallucinatory agents such as alcohol to seek pleasing mental conditions. Many of these sources of pleasure are so addicting that they divert attention and concern from other parts of life such as family relationships and obligations. They also often contribute to exploitive rather than helping relationships, and contribute to violence and other forms of abuse—patterns that are often tragically harmful in families.

There are many other ways hedonistic philosophies can play out, many of which are not as disruptive as addictions, but some of which divert attention and concern from family life. For example, some people get so involved with such activities as athletics, careers, hobbies, fitness, nutrition, virtual realities, and Internet involvement that they ignore commitments and responsibilities that are important in family life. These patterns are another situation where Aristotle's golden mean is relevant, because moderate involvement in these activities can be productive and contribute to family life but excesses and extremes can lead to destructive patterns.

Another way hedonistic philosophies can compete with the ideas in sacred theory is in the emphasis on and value of the public display of sexuality and sensuality. A number of leaders in the entertainment industry try to "push the envelope" as much as possible to increase the emphasis and display of public sensuality, and these patterns may be more disruptive in families than is generally recognized. We are still working on clarifying the ideas about sexuality that ought to be included in sacred theory, but the emphasis on the public display of sexuality and sensuality is so inconsistent with the ideals in all of the major world religions that this pattern is probably inconsistent with the dominant perspectives in every version of sacred theory that can be imagined.

Most people in modern cultures do not advocate the more extreme versions of hedonism, but the idea is pervasive enough that it probably interferes, at least so some extent, with the inclination of some to give up their pursuit of personal pleasures and self-interests. Also, we suspect this philosophy is the most disruptive when it is combined with other ideas such as individualism, materialism, and a gain ethic; but this idea is merely a speculative possibility. We hope that research about these possibilities will increase in the future.

Rationalism and Empiricism

Rationalism and empiricism are two very different epistemological perspectives. Rationalism is the belief that knowledge is acquired through reasoning. In the more pure or extreme versions of it, scholars believe that reason alone, unaided by the senses, is sufficient for obtaining reliable knowledge by examining ideas and the relationships of ideas. Philosophers who advocate this way of getting knowledge are known as rationalists. Plato (427–347 BCE) was one of the first to advocate this approach, and even went so far as to "argue that sense experience contributes nothing to genuine knowledge" (Percesepe, 1991, p. 19). Even though Descartes was a dualist metaphysically, he was one of the more extreme rationalists epistemologically as he argued that all knowledge could be attained by reason alone. Some other well-known rationalists were Spinoza (1632–1677) and Leibniz (1646–1716).

Aristotle (384–322 BCE), a student of Plato's, rejected his mentor's approach and began a different approach that later came to be known as *empiricism.* This approach argues that knowledge is acquired through the five senses. Many empiricists argue that the five senses are the most reliable source of knowledge, and some purists who advocate this perspective go so far as to "claim that all knowledge is ultimately derived from sense experience" (Percesepe, 1991, p. 19), and that "knowledge has its source and derives all its content from experience. Nothing is regarded as true save what is given by sense experience or by inductive reasoning from sense experience" (Honer & Hunt, 1987, p. 220). Freud was an advocate of a rather pure version of empiricism, as he argued that "there are no sources of knowledge of the universe other than carefully scrutinized observations—in other words what we call research—and along side [*sic*] it no knowledge derived from revelation" (Jackson, Fischer, & Dant, 2005, p. 143).

Few, if any, modern scholars rely purely or exclusively on rationalism or empiricism. Most follow the lead of Kant and believe that reason and experience are both valuable and necessary for human knowledge. Some rely more heavily on one more than the other or give more emphasis to one over the other, but virtually everyone appreciates and uses both.

We couldn't care less about the philosophical arguments over whether reason or observation is the more ultimate, fundamental, or first. We assume both are useful and valuable, and when they are used in combination they are both more valuable than when they are used separately. One of the limitations or problems with rationalism and empiricism is they exclude sacred sources of knowledge—sometimes known as mystical sources. We assume that the most defensible approach is to use a broad range of epistemological sources, and to not limit the search for knowledge or insights to reason and observation. We believe, and there is accumulating scholarly evidence in support of this position, that it is helpful to ask and seek ideas from sacred sources, and that those who rely only on rational and empirical sources of knowledge are so limited in their strategies for acquiring knowledge that they underappreciate a valuable source.

These two philosophies promote ideas that compete with the ideas in sacred theory because they both exclude or demean sacred sources of knowledge. We believe, and the evidence assembled in Chapter 3 suggests, that it is helpful in families to ask and seek help from sacred sources in addition to using reason and the five senses, and families who do not avail themselves of this source of ideas, comfort, integration, and help are missing out on an aspect of the human experience that is enriching and enabling.

Applications

General theories are valuable because they can be applied in a variety of ways in different situations, and they provide insights and understanding about a wide range of less general phenomena. One of the many areas where sacred theory can provide new insights has to do with the changes that have been occurring in marriage in recent decades in the United States. Census data and a number of surveys show there have been major changes in the proportion of adults in the United States who are married and the number of people living in nonmarital arrangements such as cohabitation and polyamorous relationships.[1] For example, between 1960 and 2009 the percentage of people age 35–44 who were married in the United States decreased from 88% to 66%, and between 1976 and 2009 the percentage of young adults who believe it is a good idea to live together before getting married increased from 32.3% to 63% for females and 45% to 69% for males (Wilcox, 2010, pp. 64 and 103).

The best explanation of these changes so far is that they are a result of "shifts in marriage mores, increases in unemployment, and declines in religious attendance" (Wilcox, 2010, p. ix). This explanation is plausible when the changes are viewed from the widely used perspectives in the social sciences. But there are also some limitations with this explanation, and sacred theory provides some additional insights about these processes and changes that are fundamental, defensible, and helpful—and provide further explanation.

One of the limitations with the theory that unemployment, religious attendance, and changes in attitudes are creating the changes in marriage is that there were dramatic changes in unemployment during the economic depression of the 1930s but there were only minor decreases in marriage rates. During the decades when the marriage rates changed dramatically, there was considerable stability in

[1] These changes are documented in studies such as Amato, Booth, Johnson, and Rogers (2007), Hymowitz (2006), Cherlin (2009), Pew Research Center (2010), and Wilcox (2010).

unemployment rates (they remained fairly low). Unemployment increased during and after the 2008 recession, but the major changes in marriage rates happened well before 2008.

A second limitation is that religious attendance is correlated with marriage rates, but the analyses by Mahoney et al. (1999, 2001) and the data reported in Chapter 14 in this volume suggest that distal factors such as religious attendance are correlated but not as powerfully as more proximal and specific factors such as the ideas in sacred theory. A third complex limitation is that norms usually change in response to other events, rather than serving as causes of change in and of themselves.

Sacred theory provides an additional, and in some ways different, explanation. Our theory suggests that the decreases in the marriage rates are the third phase in a sequence of three changes. The first phase was evolution in values and behavior with regard to the competing ideas and sacred matters. These changes occurred during industrialization and the emergence of modernity, and they were so gradual they happened over several centuries. Some of them were obvious, but others were subtle and almost imperceptible, and they transformed the American culture by the middle of the twentieth century. These changes were that a substantial number of Americans, especially the elite and leaders in government, education, law, science, and entertainment, gradually came to value high levels of secularism, individualism, acquisition, materialism, greed, gain, rationalism, hedonism, and competition, and liberating values such as autonomy, independence, and freedom. There also were increases in how much relationships were viewed as exchange, market, and/or political processes; an increase in the emphasis on self-esteem and other forms of selfishness; an increased reliance on science and technology; and a decrease in the value of sacred matters.

Many of these shifts were very helpful in public sectors such as government, commerce, industry, education, and law. Further, when these ideas were valued in moderation they also probably helped many aspects of marriage and family life. However, a sizeable percentage of Americans, especially among the elite and opinion leaders, began to value more excessive, unmoderated, and extreme versions of these ideas; and as these extreme views found their way into family life, they created a second phase of changes. The second phase was a cluster of new problems in marriages and families that were unintended, unanticipated, and largely unperceived side effects of the changes in the competing ideas. Even though the increased appreciation for the extreme versions of the competing ideas along with decreased appreciation for sacred matters were helpful both in making governments more effective and humane and in scientific and technological innovation, they were a formula for disaster in marriage and family life.

By the middle of the twentieth century, the new values and behavior had enough of an adverse influence in marriage and family life that there were dramatic increases in a number of problems that are part of (or closely related to) marriage and family life. These included an unprecedented increase in divorce between 1960 and 1980, as well as substantial increases in other problems such as violence, infidelity, illegitimacy, desertion, crime, social unrest, deterioration in the educational system, various forms of abuse such as physical, sexual, and substance abuse, and a number of other undesirable conditions associated with a general decrease in many aspects of morality, civility, and a sense of community.

Most of the problems in this second phase of changes are widely recognized, but the primary response to them by the elite in America has been to view them as primarily economic, educational, law enforcement, and government problems. Most of the attempts to cope with them have been economic because the main strategy has been to allocate more money to governmental programs, law enforcement, and the military. In the educational system, the problems are usually viewed as inadequacies in math and science. According to sacred theory however, these strategies are ill-advised and will probably have little effect on the problems because they focus on visible and easily observed symptoms, consequences, and results rather than the phenomena in the first phase of the changes that have contributed to the problems and will continue to exacerbate them.

The third phase in this series of events is the decrease in marriage rates and the escalation of alternatives to marriage—which are a small part of the larger cluster of problems. These changes are occurring because a large number of people who became adults in the last half of the twentieth century grew up in dysfunctional families and with high levels of divorce—and they experienced an enormous amount of pain and loss. Because of the problems in their parents' marriages and their family life as they grew up, a sizeable number of these people are searching for ways of relating and living that are more effective than what they experienced and observed as they grew up. Unfortunately, many of them have never seen a healthy marriage or family and have no idea of what it takes to create an effective marriage and family. They do not understand how or why the excesses in the competing ideas are disruptive in family life, and they are searching for helping, loving, and intimate relationships. Unfortunately, many of them are guided in this search by the excessive versions of the competing ideas—which means they find few successes in their search. Many of them believe marriage and family are the source of their problems, as they do not understand the destructive effects of the extreme versions of the competing ideas or how sacred matters can be helpful. As a result they marry less and are trying, largely in vain, to invent or create alternatives they hope will be more effective. This leads to increases in cohabitation, serial relationships, relationships with little commitment, impersonal relationships, single lifestyles, communes, turning to careers for meaning, sexual exploration, same-sex coupling, a variety of polyamorous arrangements, and increases in the use of mind-altering substances. Unfortunately, the new generations of children who are growing up in most of these arrangements face the probability of less stability than children with married parents.

Thus sacred theory suggests that the most defensible and helpful explanations for the decreases in marriage and increases in alternative lifestyles are not unemployment, changes in norms, and less involvement in religion. They are a result of philosophies that compete with the ideas and ideals in sacred matters that are considerably more disruptive than is realized by the elite and masses in America.

Sacred theory also provides insights into strategies for coping with the problems that will be more helpful than putting money in governmental, educational, and law enforcement programs. Improvements will begin when more people realize that some aspects of the extreme versions of the competing ideas and ideals disrupt long-term intimacy, loving, helpfulness, bonding, and commitment. There will be additional improvement when values are changed so there is more balance, moderation, and harmony in the areas where the extremes are disruptive. Some of the ways of valuing and behaving that are disruptive in family life are helpful in the more public, low-intimacy, impersonal, economic, industrial, scientific, and market areas; and it will be helpful when more people find ways to keep the disruptive ways of behaving from being parts of family life. This means people may need to change what they value and the ways they act as they move between the public and family parts of their lives. The idea that it is wise to behave differently in different parts of life is obvious to most people in some areas. For example, people generally understand that it is wise to act differently at athletic contests, in church, and on the job. What many do not yet realize is that many of the innovative ways of valuing and behaving that are wise in the public sectors are destructive in marriage and family life, and the ideas and ideals provided by sacred matters can be more helpful than many have believed.

There also are lessons that can be learned by examining the historical patterns in attempts to eliminate or revolutionize marriage. Plato tried for decades to implement his idea in *The Republic* that marriage ought to be eliminated among his philosopher-kings, but his attempts were unsuccessful. The attempts by the Israeli revolutionaries a century ago to eliminate marriage and family life in the kibbutz lasted less than a generation; and the attempts by idealists in the Communist revolutions in Russia and China to eliminate marriage proved futile in less than two decades.

The dialectical pattern in historical evolution is also helpful in understanding these patterns. Many people have been distressed by problems in marriage patterns (the thesis), and they have tried to create different and innovative ways of coupling (the antithesis). Eventually a synthesis emerges that retains the essential features that have proven so effective in meeting the widely shared goals that are described on pages 18–21, and the revolutionaries find themselves making minor modifications. In simple terms, they find themselves reinventing the wheel—with a few relatively minor innovations. This pattern will undoubtedly appear again and again in the evolution of marriage.

RELATIONSHIPS WITH OTHER THEORIES AND CONCEPTUAL FRAMEWORKS

Sacred theory also has implications for and relationships with the other general theories and conceptual frameworks that are widely used in family studies. At the most general level, if the idea that "the sacred matters" was included in the other theories, they would each be enriched and expanded. In addition to this broad generalization, there are a number of other ways parts of sacred theory can be integrated with parts of other theories.

Integrating Ideas in Different Theories

Some people view theory building as a search for "truth" in an objective and ultimate sense, and believe that only one theory or view about a topic can be true and that others need to be rejected. We have a different view. We view theories as socially constructed linguistic tools that provide explanation, understanding, and useful ideas, and believe there can be multiple perspectives about a topic that can all be true and useful. There are two analogies that are helpful in understanding this view of theories.

It may be helpful to think of each framework as constituting a set of eyeglasses, with each set having a different prescription. When people wear one theorist's glasses, they see the world as that theorist sees it. Each framework, each prescription, involves seeing the world differently, with a different focus. What is seen clearly, in sharp focus, with one set of eyeglasses may be blurred using a different theorist's "correction." Each framework also focuses on a different dimension of reality. Because reality is so complex, we cannot take it all in simultaneously. Thus these coexisting theories concentrate on a different aspect of the real world (Winton, 1995, p. 2).

The other analogy is an ancient Indian tale about six blind men and an elephant. We have modified John Godfrey Saxe's version of this fable to apply it to scholarly inquiry rather than theological arguments.

> It was six men of Indostan to learning much inclined,
> Who went to see the Elephant, though all of them were blind,
> That each by observation might satisfy his mind.
>
> The First approached the Elephant, and happening to fall,
> Against his broad and sturdy side, at once began to bawl:
> "God bless me, but the Elephant is very like a wall."
>
> The Second feeling of the tusk cried, "Ho! What have we here?
> So very round and smooth and sharp?
> To me 'tis very clear, this wonder of an Elephant is very like a spear!"
>
> The Third approached the animal, and happening to take
> The squirming trunk within his hands, then boldly up he spake:
> "I see," quoth he, "the Elephant is very like a snake."
>
> The Fourth reached out an eager hand, and felt about the knee.
> "What most this wondrous beast is like, is oh so plain," quoth he:
> "'Tis clear enough the Elephant is very like a tree!"
>
> The Fifth, who chanced to touch the ear, said, "E'en the blindest man
> Can tell what this resembles most. Deny the fact who can?
> This marvel of an Elephant is very like a fan."
>
> The Sixth no sooner had begun, about the beast to grope,
> Than seizing on the swinging tail that fell within his scope,
> "I see," quoth he, "the Elephant is very like a rope."

These six blind men of Indostan disputed loud and long,
Each in his own opinion, exceeding stiff and strong.
Though each was right in how he thought, they all were partly wrong.

And all who try to use their mind on tasks both large and small,
Would best themselves and others too if they would but recall,
One view of things can help the mind, but will not give it . . . all.

We view theories as intellectual perspectives that are like using different eyeglasses and like the ideas of the six men of Indostan. Our theories help us "see" intellectually and understand complex parts of the reality inside and around us, but it is neither helpful nor possible to use all lenses at the same time or to think in an integrated way about all the parts of elephants. One idea that can be gleaned from these analogies is that even though the ideas about the various parts of the elephant are all different, they also all can be true—as long as we remember that each of them is only about a part of truth and not all truth.

Another implication of these analogies is that it ought to be possible to back off a little and think about more than one part of the elephant at one time, but it is never possible to have a comprehensive or holistic theory. Some believe it is possible to have a theory that is comprehensive or holistic, but we believe this is neither possible nor useful, and that the search for a holistic theory is similar to searching for a fountain of youth, Holy Grail, or pot of gold under a rainbow.

One reason it is never possible to have a completely holistic theory is because theories are just tools we use in our minds, and there are so many different aspects of "the elephant," and so many models that have such different assumptions and ideas that no human has a mind that can deal with the complexity of a completely holistic model. Also, the tools in our scientific toolbox are so limited that it is not just our minds that can't assimilate and integrate enough. Our computers and methodologies also can't deal with a truly comprehensive model. In short, each theory offers an incomplete but intellectually manageable view of the world—and each of the views give us permission to minimize or ignore certain aspects of life, while inviting, if not demanding, that we focus on other aspects.

As scientific knowledge has expanded, it has become increasingly necessary to focus at any one time on ever-decreasing parts of reality because of the complexity of the parts that are studied. Said more simply, we are not ready for a theory about everything about elephants, let alone a model about *all* reality.

There is another limitation in the amount of integration that is possible, a limitation that moves well beyond which part of the elephant we are thinking about. This limitation has to do with the incompatibility of the assumptions that underlie theoretical models and conceptual frameworks. Some of the assumptions that are made in some models are incompatible with some of the assumptions of other models. For example, the behaviorist perspective has traditionally assumed it is best to focus on observable behaviors and not on cognitive processes in the mind that cannot be observed directly. This is incompatible with the assumptions in cognitive models that argue that the most fruitful place to focus on is the unobservable cognitive processes in the mind. The behavioral approach is also incompatible with the assumptions in the psychoanalytic and symbolic interaction schools of thought because both of these other perspectives assume that the most fruitful parts of the human experience to focus on are complex mental processes. These differences are so incompatible that these perspectives cannot be integrated in the form they were suggested by the scholars who developed these models.

Another reason it is impossible to create a completely holistic model is because many of the theories were developed for different purposes. The psychoanalytic theory was designed to do a certain type of therapy with patients who have certain types of mental illness. Behaviorism was designed to intervene with a different type of social problems, challenges, and strategies, and—by extension—it would be impossibly confusing and useless to try to combine all of the approaches into one perspective.

Even though it is not possible or practical to meld everything in social science discourse into one integrated model, it is possible and helpful to do some integrating of different theories if we remember that, for practical purposes, we can't integrate very many at once. When we want to integrate theoretical ideas or theories, there are two strategies that can be used. One of them is to be *eclectic*. This approach is to select parts of different models and integrate them in our minds into a coherent approach in a research project, an educational program, or a clinical setting. This strategy is widely used by researchers, educators, and clinicians. In fact, there is some evidence that this is done much more than trying to use just one theory in its pure form (Richards & Bergin, 2005, p. 17; Taylor & Bagdi, 2005).

A second strategy for integrating theories is to *merge* two or more theories together and view them as one integrated approach. This is also possible and useful when it is tried with a limited number of perspectives. This is the strategy White (2005) used as he integrated four theories into two theories. This strategy has also been used fairly widely, and is seen in the trend of viewing the cognitive-behavioral approach as one perspective.

There is a rather complicated aspect of social science models that is important to understand when we try to integrate ideas from different models. Some of the concepts and ideas that were created in theories can be separated from some of the assumptions scholars made when they created the concepts. For example, Watson and Skinner made a number of assumptions when they developed ideas in behaviorism. One of their assumptions was that it is not helpful to pay attention to cognitive processes. However, just because these scholars made this assumption does not mean that everyone who wants to use some of the concepts and principles they developed must make the same assumption. If we are careful to be consistent, it is possible to make different assumptions and still use their concepts and theoretical ideas.

Some other ideas that are helpful when we try to integrate ideas that originated in different theories are to focus on only a limited array of phenomena and temporarily ignore other parts of reality. We even have a Latin term for this. It is *ceteris paribus*, which means "other things being equal." As Marshall (1961) said:

> We reduce to inaction all other forces by the phrase "other things being equal"; we do not suppose that they are inert, but for the time we ignore their activity. This scientific device is a great deal older than science; it is the method by which, consciously or unconsciously, sensible men have dealt from time immemorial with every difficult problem of ordinary life. (p. xiv)

We believe that some aspects of sacred theory are compatible with some of the notions in other theories, and that it is useful to integrate them in either an eclectic or hyphenating way. We also believe that some of the ideas in sacred theory are not compatible with some of the thinking in other ideas. Therefore it seems useful to describe some of the things we think are compatible and incompatible and some of the ways theories are complementary.

Systems Theories

Systems theories grew out of research on cybernetics (Wiener, 1948) and communication (Bateson, Jackson, Haley, & Weakland, 1956; Bertalanffy, 1968) during the middle decades of the twentieth century. The systems approach gradually found its way into the social sciences in the 1950s and 1960s (Buckley, 1967), and gradually became one of the main models in studying marriage, family, and human development (Broderick, 1971; Burr et al., 1979; Holman & Burr, 1980).

Systems theory moved away from individualistic approaches by focusing on patterns in relationships, and this proved helpful in the family field because family life is inherently systemic. One of the other contributions of this school of thought is that it stimulated and expanded thinking about reciprocal relationships rather than just linear causality.

One of the ways systems theory is different from sacred theory is that it emphasizes ways systemic processes contribute to, or are responsible for, outcomes. For example, one of the ideas in systems theory is that feedback in systems leads to cycles. One type of cycle is sometimes called a vicious cycle. This occurs when one individual observes something in the system, defines it as a negative thing, and reacts to it with more negative behavior, whereas another member of the system observes this reaction, defines it as negative, and responds in another negative way, which leads to another negative response from the first individual. The vicious cycle is then fully under way. Interestingly, this cycle about negative things is called a positive cycle in systems theory because it is a pattern of systematically increasing certain types of behavior. These cycles are maintained by systemic processes, and can lead to increasingly desirable or undesirable outcomes.

Sacred theory has a different set of ideas. The emphasis in sacred theory is on the role of sacred processes rather than systemic processes and on ways individuals contribute to or are responsible for outcomes. This isn't an incompatibility but rather a matter of emphasis and focus. The systems models don't rule out the role of individuals also being responsible, and sacred theory does not rule out systemic phenomena from being influential, but the two theories focus on different parts of reality. Furthermore, the approaches are similar in that they use the same strategies to break cycles and move creatively toward conditions that will lead to desirable outcomes. Both assume that individuals have the ability to take initiative and choose to act in noncyclic ways that facilitate healthy cycles and interrupt unhealthy patterns.

All of the differences we are aware of between systems theories and sacred theory are matters of emphasis and focus rather than incompatible assumptions or conceptualizations. Therefore the ideas in systems approaches can be combined with sacred theory in either an eclectic or merging way, and the two together focus on a larger set of ideas than either approach alone.

Scholars have begun the process of integrating sacred and systemic ideas. For example, Butler and Harper (1994) and Butler et al. (1998, 2002) described several different ways couples can triangulate with God when they are not well differentiated, and they described healthy ways of relating to God when people are well differentiated. The latter strategies assist couples in dealing with marital discord, reconciliation, and inspiration in problem solving. We suspect that future research and theorizing will find more ways to integrate the conceptualizations in systems theories and sacred theory.

Cognitive-Behavioral Theories

The behavioral approach is different from sacred theory in some fundamental ways. The behavioral approach was created by scholars such as Pavlov, Watson, and Skinner, who focused on observable phenomena and avoided less observable processes such as cognition. Sacred theory takes a different approach by emphasizing processes that are less observable than cognition and behavior. Those who cling to the purist versions of behaviorism will probably dislike sacred theory even more than cognitive theories because it emphasizes sacred processes, which are even more difficult to observe and quantify than cognitive processes.

Yet even though many of the scholars who have contributed to the behavioral approach have avoided dealing with cognitive and affective processes, many of the concepts and ideas that have been developed in behaviorism are compatible with sacred theory, although some of the assumptions that have been made by some behaviorists are not. Ideas such as reinforcement and punishment as well as contingencies that influence these relationships are all quite compatible with sacred theory.

A number of theories that focus on cognitive processes were developed in the middle decades of the twentieth century. Ellis's (1961, 1975) rational therapy led the way and was followed by Beck (1975), Lazarus (1958, 1971), and many others. Their models were a reaction against psychoanalytic theory and focused on ways of changing conscious perceptions and beliefs as a strategy for coping with problems.

Initially these cognitive theories were fairly independent of behavioral models, but by the 1980s a number of scholars were ignoring the assumptions about *tabula rasa* and the exclusive emphasis on observable behavior, and began integrating behavioral and cognitive ideas and strategies. The result is what is now called the cognitive-behavioral approach.

When scholars ignore some of the assumptions made by several of the earlier behaviorists that led to incompatibilities with beliefs about human freedom and dignity (Skinner, 1971), they find that many of the ideas in the cognitive-behavioral approach are compatible with the ideas in sacred theory. Scholars such as Ellis had little appreciation for the sacred, but argued that the ideas in their model were still relevant for those who had religious perspectives. This means that when a few changes are made in some of the nonessential, preference-based assumptions that some of the early behaviorists made, it is easy to appreciate and use many ideas from the cognitive-behavioral approach and sacred theory, and it can be done with either an eclectic or hyphenated approach.

Symbolic Interaction

Some of the ideas in the symbolic interaction framework were in the writings of James (1890, 1892), but it didn't emerge as a unique and widely appreciated school of thought until the ideas were more fully developed by Cooley (1902, 1909), Mead (1934), Blumer (1938), Goffman (1959), and Rose (1962).

Mead made the largest contribution to this perspective. He was a social philosopher at the University of Chicago who was so unhappy with the Watsonian version of behaviorism that he developed many of the core ideas in this school of thought in reaction to, and as an alternative to, behaviorism. One of the unique aspects of this approach is that it argues against the determinism in behaviorism. Mead argued that humans had complex mental processes that involved the I and the me aspects of the self, and that the I is a creative and spontaneous part of the self rather than a deterministic part.

This indeterministic aspect of symbolic interaction is compatible with sacred theory, but it focuses on aspects of the human experience that are not central to sacred theory. The basic questions in Mead's scholarship focused on how the human mind develops and works and how interaction with others contributes to the social self. The result is that this is another perspective where the ideas can be integrated in an eclectic way or hyphenated with ideas in sacred theory when scholars want to deal with the concepts, theorizing, or interventions they both provide. This compatibility is illustrated in the Baker et al. (2009) study of covenant and standard marriages because they used symbolic interaction theory as part of the intellectual foundation for their study and focused specifically on sacred processes that deal with covenants.

Transition Theory

Duvall and Hill (1948; see also Duvall, 1957) used the developmental approach created at the University of Chicago in the 1940s to create what is known as family development theory (Hill & Rodgers, 1964), a model that focuses on predictable patterns, stages, transitions, and processes in the family life cycle. The model was expanded and refined by Rodgers (1973), Aldous (1996), Falicov (1988), and White (1991). These later developments placed more emphasis on transitions and careers, dealt considerably more with the role of rituals in transitions, and paid more attention to family diversity and complexities in developmental processes (Carter & McGoldrick, 1989).

One of the interesting aspects of this approach is that Wes Burr talked several times with Reuben Hill about the origins of Reuben's ideas about family development, and Reuben perceived that the idea of development and progress, sometimes conceptualized as "eternal progression" in his Latter-day Saints religion, was the main source of his interest in developmental processes. This means that some of the roots of the family development approach were at least partially inspired by ideas about and from the sacred even though Reuben did not make this connection explicit in his published work or in his teaching.

The fact that Hill separated the religious roots of his ideas from the academic sphere was consistent with dominant perspectives at that time. The postmodern approach that emerged later allows for more candor about these relationships, and one of the effects of these connections between Hill's religious ideas and family development theory is that this theory is more than just compatible with the philosophy and principles in sacred theory. There is a fundamental harmony in them.

White (2005) integrated the ideas in family development theory with ideas from several perspectives that had previously been viewed as different approaches, such as Elder and Hareven's life course perspective (Bengston & Allen, 1993) and Breunlin's (1988) oscillation theory, and suggested that the theory be called transition theory. These insights about the origins and nature of some of the ideas in transition theory demonstrate that it is compatible in a number of ways with sacred theory, and that the ideas in these different approaches can also be integrated with eclectic or hyphenated strategies.

Humanistic Theories

The humanistic models that became widely used in the middle decades of the twentieth century have their roots in ancient Greek and Asian philosophies and in the writings of more recent philosophers such as Rousseau (1762, 1763). They also are reactions to the pessimism of psychoanalysis and the dehumanizing and one-sided nature of behaviorism (Crain, 1985, Chapter 16). Scholars such as Maslow (1943, 1954, 1962, 1966, 1971) and Rogers (1951, 1961) were the main architects of the modern versions of the humanistic perspective, and the main thrust in their theory is to argue that humans are inherently noble and wholesome in their search for growth and fulfillment and it is subjective experience that is the final arbiter of morality. They assumed that the primary motivating force in humans is a drive toward a type of actualization they defined as good. These perspectives also rest on assumptions that individualism and self-interest are the highest and most noble good.

There are similarities between the humanistic views and sacred theory, there are ways they are different, and there are some incompatibilities. For example, they share the view that humans deserve dignity and freedom, and they share a belief in the importance of the moral. But their views of the role of the nature of humans and the role of the divine are quite different from the dominant views in many Christian traditions. The Calvinist view about the nature of humans is either that they are inherently evil or, in a revised view, that they change from innocent to fundamentally evil as they mature and can rise above this condition only with faith, works, and/or grace. To the humanists, the striving for good exists fundamentally even when social conditions repress and diminish it, and all that needs to be done to improve the human condition is to find ways to allow the basic striving to reassert itself.

According to the humanist perspectives, people need to be freed from the restraints of religious injunctions or political or social authority to reach the actualization they seek. In sacred theory the sacred parts of life can be used in ways that constrain and are unwise, but when they are wisely used they provide help and assistance in changing the nature of humans and helping them rise above the carnal.

Different and Complementary

Another issue that is important in understanding the relationship sacred theory has with other perspectives has to do with whether sacred theory is different and complementary or just a part of another theory. It is different from the widely used theories in family studies in several ways. All of the prevailing theories began with and rest on secular assumptions about the cosmos; but sacred theory uses a cluster of ideas that are faith based and rest on assumptions that sacred phenomena are real and important. Even those who do not believe that the sacred parts of life are real noumenologically must admit they are real phenomenologically. We are among those who believe they are real noumenologically and phenomenologically, but there are many who have perspectives that are different from ours. We suggest that even those who do not believe in the noumenological reality of the spiritual will benefit from having a theory that deals with ideas about and from the sacred that are phenomenologically real.

Sacred theory is also complementary with the existing theories in several other ways that we think are important. One way to view this complementarity is to examine the phenomena that are the primary explicantia in the widely used theories. In philosophical terms, *explicantia* are the phenomena that provide explanation, and *explicanda* are the phenomena that are explained. The existing theories in family studies and sacred theory all have the same general explicanda because they are trying to explain various aspects of family phenomena. Where they differ is in what they turn to for explanation and understanding. All of the existing theories turn primarily to some combination of cognitive, affective, behavioral, biological, or relationship processes as their explicantia. None of them turn to the sacred and transcendental parts of the human experience as an important part of their explicantia.

Table 13.1 summarizes the centrality of the role of these six processes in the theories that are widely used in studying family. The categories of high, medium, low, and none are a rough description of the authors' view of how central or important each of the six explanatory aspects is in each theory. High means something is a central, fundamental, and emphasized part. Medium and low mean something is a part of the theory but has little emphasis as an explicans. The differences between the high, medium, and low are debatable. In fact, they can be debated endlessly, but these differences are not the important

TABLE 13.1 The Role of Six Areas in the Major Theories in Family Studies

Theories	Cognitive	Affective	Behavior	Relations	Biology	Sacred
Cognitive-behavioral	High	Low	High	Low	Low	Low
Conflict theory	High	Medium	High	High	Low	Low
Critical theory	High	Low	Low	Medium	Low	Low
Bio-ecological	Medium	Low	Medium	High	High	Low
Feminist theory	High	High	High	High	Low	Low
Hermeneutics	High	Low	Low	Low	Low	Low
Transition theory	Medium	Medium	Medium	High	Medium	Low
Psychoanalytic and neo-analytic	High	High	Medium	High	Medium	Low
Phenomenology	High	Low	Low	Medium	Low	Low
Rational choice/exchange	High	Low	Medium	Medium	Low	Low
Functionalism and neo-analytic	High	Medium	Low	Medium	Low	Low
Symbolic interaction	High	Low	Medium	Medium	Low	Low
Systems theory	High	Medium	Medium	High	Low	Low
Interdependence theory	High	Medium	High	Medium	Low	Low
Sacred theory	Medium	Medium	Medium	Medium	Low	High

point that is made in Table 13.1. The important point is that whereas sacred phenomena are not a central component in any of the other theories, they are the primary explicantia in sacred theory. This is the main way sacred theory is different from and complementary to the existing theories that are widely used in the study of family.

There are four other aspects of sacred theory that illustrate why it is different from and complementary to the theories that are widely used in family studies. First, in sacred theory we seek or look for ideas about and from the sacred that we think make a difference in family processes and valued outcomes. All of the perspectives that have been widely used in the field have systematically ignored ideas about and from the sacred parts of the human experience.

Second, there has been some research in the last several decades about several of the ideas in sacred theory, but, with one exception (Butler & Harper, 1994; Butler, Stout, & Gardner, 2002; Butler et al., 1998), this research has not derived from or been tied to any of the widely used perspectives. Some of the research has used the interdependence theory developed by Thibaut and Kelley (1959), and expanded by Kelley and Thibaut (1978), but that perspective is typically not included in any of the lists of the theories that are widely used in family studies (Ingoldsby et al., 2004; White & Klein, 2008).

Third, we also make a number of suggestions about future needs and possibilities for research and theorizing, and none of the suggestions we make originates in any of the existing frameworks. They all derive intellectually from a view of reality that is quite different from the existing perspectives.

Fourth, sacred theory introduces a number of innovative ideas about ways families can use the ideas, and ways professionals can apply the ideas in therapy, education, and the mass media. These innovations also do not originate in the existing theories.

RELATIONSHIPS WITH OTHER INSTITUTIONS

The ideas in sacred theory have a number of implications for other social institutions. One example is that there is a widespread belief that governments are more effective when they are secularized and ignore the sacred. A large number of people in the United States and France take pride in the way their governments have become secularized. Sacred theory, on the other hand, suggests that governments are the most effective when they have a balanced concern with the secular and sacred.

There is an unfortunate and long history of religions being abusive and unwise when they are closely tied to governments, but a wise concern with the sacred is a broader perspective than sponsoring a particular denomination or religion, and concern with the sacred does not contribute to the unwise abuses and constraints. It is beyond the scope of this volume to deal very extensively with the implications of sacred theory for governments, so all we can do here is briefly identify several issues and their implications and hope others who study governments in greater depth will increase their concern with the role of the sacred.

Sacred theory also has important implications for social institutions such as education, law enforcement, the judiciary, industry, commerce, the economy, and entertainment. The idea that "the sacred matters" is relevant in a number of ways for each of these institutions. Educational institutions were dominated several centuries ago by religions, and this domination has gradually been removed. However, in the process of elimination, the educational system in the United States has, unfortunately, moved so far away from the sacred that it has also lost wholesome connections with the sacred. We suggest that education is the most effective and wise when there is a balanced concern with the history and contributions of the sacred and secular. For example, there are some who would have schools avoid the different ways of thinking about evolution, but it seems wiser to help students understand all of the issues, controversies, and widely shared perspectives.

It is equally true that the study of other institutions such as law enforcement, the judiciary, and entertainment would be more effective if there were a balanced concern with the sacred and secular rather than either of these dominating and excluding. Also, there would be serious undesirable consequences if the bases for morality provided by the sacred were excluded from industry, commerce, and economics.

It is beyond the scope of this volume and the expertise of the authors to explore these implications in depth, but we hope others will recognize the needs and seize the opportunities for greater attention to the role of the sacred.

SUMMARY

This chapter described ways sacred theory is related to a number of broader issues and concerns. The chapter began with a discussion of seven ideas that compete with the ideas in sacred theory. The middle part of the chapter discussed relationships the theory has with other general theories and conceptual frameworks. We argued that the ideas in sacred theory can be integrated with some of the theories in either an eclectic or hyphenating method, but they are incompatible with some of the ideas and cannot be integrated with them. The theory is different from and complementary to the other theories because it has different assumptions and focuses on different parts of reality, but there is compatibility and complementarity with most of the existing perspectives. The chapter concluded with a brief summary of implications the theory has for a number of other institutions.

14

Researching Sacred Matters

The primary goal in this chapter is to move the theoretical language about sacred theory into the realm of verification, validation, and refinement. As we have noted, we view the process of theory building as ongoing and developmental. By developmental we mean the theoretical ideas within any theory should not be thought of as stationary. Instead, theory-building processes are ongoing and dynamic. For example, reading Bronfenbrenner's (1979; Bronfenbrenner & Morris, 2006) ecological systems theory, one is immediately struck with the evolving and developmental nature of the emergence of his key ideas (Tudge et al., 2009). In like manner, Boss's (1999, 2006) theory of boundary ambiguity has evolved for several decades as it has been refined and tested. In each case (and in many others that could be cited), a germ of an idea was created, and through multiple iterations a more refined and useful theory emerged.

Ultimately, theoretical progress relies on verification, validation, exploring, and rethinking. Sometimes the verification process is achieved through polemics, argumentation, and logic exploration. Such was the case with much of what Freud initially wrote and proposed. Other theorists and social philosophers gather observational and clinical data to enrich and bolster their positions, a strategy used in many disciplines. Still others attempt to tell a different story through qualitative and thematic-based research from which common themes are extracted from dialogue and behavior.

In our case, we relied primarily on qualitative data while generating the ideas in the theory, and we turn to quantitative data in this chapter to begin the process of testing the story line of sacred theory. Even though our examples are based on an empirical approach, there is plenty of room for a variety of approaches as we, collectively, attempt to verify, substantiate, and corroborate the concepts, propositions, and hypotheses in the sacred theory framework. It is also important to note that the data used in this chapter were gleaned from the Flourishing Families Project (FFP). That project began in 2005 (as will be discussed later) and was a research effort independent of the formation and development of the ideas within this book. In other words, these data were not collected as a way to confirm or even refine the sacred matters theory construction effort. Fortuitously, however, as the ideas about sacred matters began to emerge, we realized that there were several parallel constructs within the FFP that could shed some light on how sacred-living principles operate in a familial context.

Thus our purpose in this chapter is to demonstrate ways some of the ideas in sacred theory can be tested, expanded, and revised by more empirical research. The thrust of this chapter, therefore, is to test, revise, and demonstrate rather than create a statement of theoretical finality. We hope by beginning the testing process that others will want to jump in and test—and retest—the ideas in sacred theory.

Our method in this chapter is to (a) introduce a data set that contains several measures of sacred-living constructs; (b) explore what the relationships among a number of variables are and how they provide a basis either for confidence in the ideas in the theory or for revisions and changes, (c) determine if the sacred-living constructs are more predictive in understanding variation in family outcomes than only assessing religious attendance or participating in faith activities; (d) see if findings from a quantitative research project can improve and expand the theory; and (e) describe ways insights from the research can spawn future research and theory construction efforts.

THE FLOURISHING FAMILIES PROJECT DATA SET

As mentioned, while we were generating the ideas in sacred theory, we began dialoguing with a group of colleagues who were building an important family process-based data collection effort that would have quantitative data that could be used to begin the process of testing the ideas in the theory. As we began to work together, it became clear that it would be instructive to try and test some of the ideas, principles, and hypotheses in the theory. Clearly, another strategy would have been to develop an ongoing research project that more directly and specifically emerged *from* sacred matters theory. However, in some ways working with an existing ongoing data effort that was not designed to test the theory also has its advantages: For example, it may be that the scholarly independence of the two projects actually provides a bit more objectivity. In this case the FFP was designed to examine the trajectory of key processes over time and how the dynamics of inner family life impact children's well-being. As such, there is much less worry about the project and data analysis design biasing outcomes that advantage the proposed theoretical principles.

With that limitation in mind, we decided to include an analysis of some of the data from the FFP to see how some of the constructs assessed in that project map onto the theoretical ideas in this book.

The FFP began in 2007 and is a longitudinal survey and observations of 500 families in a large northwestern city. For each of five years (2007–2011), family members were administered questionnaires about a host of constructs centering on inner family life. Additionally, each family was videotaped in their homes while performing certain set tasks. We describe a short version of our research methods here. More detailed versions can be found in Day and Padilla-Walker (2009), Carlo et al. (2010), Carroll et al. (2011), and Harper and Dome (2011).

Sample

During 2007, 500 families with a child between the ages of 10 and 14 were identified using a national telephone survey database. Families were selected representing the population distribution of census tracts in Seattle. The city was chosen for its overall economic and ethnic diversity. All families with a child between the ages of 10 and 14 living within target census tracts were deemed eligible to participate. Eligible families were subsequently contacted directly using a multistage recruitment protocol. Through recruitment efforts, a total of 1,068 potentially eligible families were identified. Of those, 692 families reported having a child within the target age range, and 423 of these agreed to participate (61% participation) in Wave I. Additionally, we continued sampling and recruited an additional 77 families to be more inclusive of lower socioeconomic status (SES). The final sample of 500 families became the base sample of the project.

At Wave II (2008), 488 (97.6%) families remained in the study, with 94% and 95% of the original families agreeing to continue participating at Waves III and IV, respectively. Both boys and girls in the sample average slightly over 11 years of age at Wave I. Average family size was 4.41 including parents and children at Wave I, and the range was 2 to 13 people in a household. The median combined yearly income for our sample by Wave IV was $83,000. Seventy-three percent and 74.5% of boys and girls respectively were Caucasian; 12.8% and 11.1% were African American, and 14.3% of daughters and 14.4% of sons were of other races or multiethnic. Families received $200 for participation in each wave of data collection.

Outcomes and Hypotheses

For the purposes of this chapter, we have selected a few of the constructs in the FFP database that serve as our target outcomes. To keep our analysis manageable, even though the FFP data set contains information from mothers, fathers (where possible), and a child, for the purposes of the present analysis we use only the mother's report of the target constructs. This choice was made purely because of space limitations. We also present data here that model change over time. Our independent assessments (such as religious attendance, forgiveness, and kindness) were assessed in 2009 (Wave III), and our outcomes (such as depression, marital quality, and marital intimacy) were measures gathered in 2010 (Wave IV).

Outcomes were chosen for the demonstration element of this chapter that represented commonly assessed important outcomes central to effective daily family life. The theoretical foundations of our analysis follow from the core messages of this book—that sacred matters are helpful in understanding family life. Said slightly differently, when family members employ strategies and ways of interacting that are derived from sacred ideas (such as loving, forgiving, sacrificing, and being kind to one another) they are using a sacred-living approach. We reemphasize that this type of approach is not tied to any one religion in particular, but reflects, instead, the adoption of sacred-living approaches that emanate from a variety of sacred movements (be they Christian, Jewish, Muslim, Buddhist—to name but a few) that have emerged over the last several thousand years.

Further, we suggest that when family members use a sacred-living approach to attain goals in family life, they will be more successful than if they ignore these ideas. By success we usually think in terms of family systemic-level goals, which can include such outcomes as martial stability (staying married and not divorcing), marital and family quality (the family members enjoy and relish being in those relationships), avoiding conflict (when conflict is high emotions are high and problem-solving attempts are less effective), and being more involved as a parent (we assume that positive parent involvement has payoff in seeing children do better in life). It is also hypothesized that when family members employ sacred-living strategies in their everyday interactions that children and parents both will be personally advantaged: These advantages, we hypothesize, should be less depression, less anxiety, and a greater ability to perform and excel at the tasks of life.

For our demonstration here, we chose outcomes that represented different elements of successful well-being in family life. First, we chose three outcomes that identified couple strengths: They are marital instability, marital quality, and marital intimacy. Marital instability was assessed using items from the RELATE assessment battery (Busby, Holman, & Taniguchi, 2001). Using a 5-point Likert scale ranging from 1 (*never*) to 5 (*very often*), respondents answered questions such as “How often have you and your partner discussed ending your relationship (or marriage)?” and “How often have you broken up or separated and then gotten back together?” The higher the score, the more instability was associated with the marriage or relationship. For this variable and each of the ones to follow, Table 14.1 provides descriptive statistics such as means, standard deviations, and variable range results.

Second, we selected marital quality as assessed using a 5-item modified version of the Quality of Marriage Index (Norton, 1983). The responses were based on a 6-point Likert scale ranging from 1 (*very strongly disagree*) to 6 (*very strongly agree*). The items included “My relationship with my partner makes me happy” and “My relationship with my partner is very stable.” Higher scores indicate higher perceived marital quality. Marital quality has a long well-developed research track record in family science, and we have chosen to use this measure because of its recognizability and connection to so many research efforts over the years.

Marital intimacy was assessed by asking the respondent’s desired frequency and actual frequency of sexual intercourse with their partner, two items taken from the RELATE test (Busby et al., 2001). Participants were asked questions such as “About how often do you currently have sex with your partner?” and “How often do you desire to have sexual intercourse with your partner?” Response categories ranged from 0 (*never*) to 7 (*more than once a day*) on a 7-point Likert scale.

Next, we selected three outcome variables that provide information about how (or if) sacred living by the parents has an impact on child well-being. These were children’s report of feelings of shame and guilt, childhood depressive symptoms, and child integrity. Shame and guilt were assessed using a self-report measure of eight items taken from the Shame Profile Scale (Harper & Hoopes, 1990), a measure of interpersonal/intrapersonal feelings of shame. Participants responded to items asking how often they experienced certain thoughts or feelings. The response options were based on a 5-point Likert scale ranging from

TABLE 14.1 Descriptive Information About the Variables Used in the Analysis

Variables	*N*	Mean	*SD*	Min	Max
Monthly family income	335[a]	7024	5341	900	7000
Occupation	335	8.4	6.5	1	22
Race	335	.7	.9	0	1
Religious activity					
Religious attend	335	2.6	2.5	0	20.5
Faith activities	335	1.25	1.3	0	6
Sacred living					
Kindness	335	3.9	.56	2	5
Sacrifice	335	5.1	1.0	1	7
Forgiveness	335	5.5	1.16	1.5	7
Unkindness	335	1.8	.81	1	5.5
Commitment	335	6.2	.82	2	7
Outcomes					
Marital instability	335	1.7	.61	1	5
Marital quality	335	5.2	1.1	1.8	6.6
Sexual intimacy	335	2.4	1.15	0	5
Family function	335	3.3	.42	2.1	4
Mother involvement	335	3.7	.58	1	5
Marital conflict	335	2.3	.51	1	4
Child shame	335	1.7	.77	1	5
Child depression	335	1.6	.52	1	3.5
Child integrity	335	3.6	.35	2.6	5
Mother depression	335	1.4	.28	1	3.5
Mother anxiety	335	.4	.36	0	3.6
Mother stress	335	1.07	.75	1	4.3

[a] Less than 1% of the data were missing for all variables. When missing, a multiple imputation procedure was used to retain all cases. Only couples were used in the analysis; single parents were eliminated.

1 (*never*) to 5 (*almost always*), with higher scores representing higher levels of shame. The items included "I feel like I am never quite good enough" and "I think that people look down on me." Cronbach's alpha reliability coefficients were found to be .919 in this sample.

We also selected children's depression as a key child outcome. This construct was assessed using the 20-item self-report CES-DC (Center for Epidemiological Studies Depression Scale for Children; Weissman, Orvaschel, & Padian, 1980). Participants responded by rating the degree to which they have experienced each item in the past week, with a Likert-type response scale ranging from 1 (*not at all*) to 4 (*a lot*). Higher scores indicate greater depressive symptoms. The items included "I was bothered by things that usually don't bother me," and "I felt lonely, like I didn't have any friends." For the current sample, the Cronbach's alpha reliability coefficient was found to be .907.

Children's integrity, as perceived by the child, was assessed using a six-item adaptation of the Values in Action survey (Peterson & Seligman, 2004). The items included "I am someone who keeps their promises," and "I am someone who others can trust." Participants responded using a 5-point Likert scale ranging from 1 (*very much unlike him/her*) to 5 (*very much like him/her*), with higher scores representing higher levels of integrity. Although no previous reliability data exists for this version of the measure, for the current sample Cronbach's alpha reliability coefficients were found to be .81.

For our third group of outcomes, we chose variables that represented more general familial functioning. These elements included reports using the McMaster Family Assessment Device (FAD; Epstein, Baldwin, & Bishop, 1983). A revised version of the FAD was used consisting of 20 items, including the entire General Functioning and Affective Responsiveness subscales and 2 items from the Affective Involvement subscale. Respondents answered how much they agreed or disagreed with statements about their family, such as "We are reluctant to show our affection for each other" and "We confide in each other." Responses ranged from 1 (*strongly disagree*) to 4 (*strongly agree*). Higher scores indicate better family functioning.

Parental involvement in their child's life and their view of their partner's level of involvement in the child's life were measured using items adapted from the Inventory of Father Involvement (Hawkins et al., 2002). Additional items were based on ideas taken from Pleck (2010). Participants responded to 24 questions based on a 5-point Likert scale ranging from 1 (*never*) to 5 (*always*) about the frequency of their involvement in various aspects of their child's life. Twelve questions were self-report (regarding the respondent's parental involvement), and the other 12 were questions regarding the respondent's partner. The questions included "[Do you] help your child with homework?" and "[Do you] read books or magazines with your child?" A higher score indicates a greater degree of mother or father involvement in the child's life. For this sample, the Cronbach's alpha for the overall 12-item version was .86.

Our last assessment of family-level functioning centered on conflict. To assess conflict, participants addressed eight common problems experienced in family relationships by responding to how often each problem occurs. Items were selected from the RELATE assessment battery (Busby et al., 2001), including things such as "rearing children," "intimacy/sexuality," and "financial matters." Responses were based on a 5-point Likert scale ranging from 1 (*never*) to 5 (*very often*). The reliability for this sample (Cronbach's alpha) was .70.

Our next three target outcomes focus on the well-being of the parents. Parental depression-related symptoms were assessed using 11 items from the Center for Epidemiologic Studies-Depression Scale (CES-D; Radloff, 1977). Adults responded based on a 3-point Likert scale ranging from 1 (*never*) to 3 (*most of the time*). The symptoms included "I felt depressed," "People were unfriendly," and "I could not get 'going.'" Symptoms 5 and 8 were reverse coded so that higher scores indicate higher levels of depressive symptoms. For this sample, reliability was .810.

Parental anxiety was assessed using an 8-item self-report measure, based on the Burns Anxiety Inventory (Burns, 1989). Participants responded to items using a 4-point Likert scale asking how often they experienced thoughts or feelings with response options ranging from 0 (*not at all*) to 3 (*a lot*), with higher scores representing greater anxiety or anxiety symptoms. The items included "feeling that things around you are strange, unreal, or foggy" (Anxious Feeling subscale) and "racing thoughts or having your mind jump from one thing to the next" (Anxious Thoughts subscale). Cronbach's alpha reliability coefficients for the current sample were .76.

The severity of chronic stress in the parents' lives was assessed focusing on various types of role- and health-related stressors (Umberson, Williams, Powers, Liu, & Needham, 2005). The 10-item measure asked respondents to note how stressful issues were, including "not enough money for housing" and "feeling stressed by work." Parents responded on a 6-point Likert scale ranging from 0 (*did not occur*) to 5 (*occurred, extremely severe*) with higher scores indicating higher levels of chronic stress. Reliability coefficients (Cronbach's alpha) for this sample was found to be P1 = .84.

FINDING VARIABLES THAT OPERATIONALIZE SACRED MATTERS

As we employed the FFP, we searched for measures in the data set that would operationalize constructs described earlier in this book. For example, we found that the FFP had data on forgiveness, kindness, unkindness, sacrifice, and commitment. Fortunately, the FFP also assessed both religious attendance and a measure of religious faith practices such as praying and reading sacred texts.

Forgiveness

One of the ideas in sacred theory argues that forgiveness is important in family life, and considerable evidence for this proposition was discussed in Chapter 2. To measure forgiveness across the family's relationships within the FFP, participants responded to 12 questions based on McCullough et al. (1998). Items assessed the respondent's ability to forgive both partner and child and the ability of the partner and child to forgive the respondent. The 7-point Likert response categories ranged from 1 (*not at all true for me*) to 7 (*very true*) with items such as "I can forgive him/her [partner] pretty easily" and "He/she [partner] can forgive me pretty easily." The higher the score, the more forgiveness there is within the couple or parent–child relationship. Previously, the reliability coefficient was found to be .88 (McCullough et al., 1998). Reliability tests for this sample indicated a Cronbach's alpha of .891 for our sample.

Kindness and Unkindness

As with many constructs, something sounding like the opposite of an idea or construct may not, in fact, clearly be its true opposite. Such is the case of kindness. Some may assume that unkindness is the opposite of kindness, but research by Lee et al. (1997) and Baumeister et al. (2001) suggests these are different constructs with different influences. Baumeister et al. (2001) reviewed considerable research that argues that bad things tend to be stronger than good things in a variety of settings including family life. Apparently, it does not take much of the "bad" to leave deep marks. Unkind, harsh, vitriolic, nasty, and venomous relationships where the adults (or children) are acerbic, caustic, and hurtful have tremendous power to cause harm and detract family members from achieving or even wanting to participate in family ideals and goals. Gottman (1994b) suggested that even one caustic retaliation delivers enough venom that as many as five or more soothing, kind, and inviting comments may be required as antidote.

Rather than simply asking couples if they were unkind to one another, we decided to assess unkindness in relationships using the Covert Relational Aggression Scale (Carroll, Nelson, Yorgason, Harper, Ashton, & Jensen, 2010). This is a relatively new scale developed to assess the amount of love withdrawal and social sabotage each partner employs with the other. Social sabotage is a covert form of aggression toward one's partner that involves social isolation, spreading rumors, and blackmailing. Love withdrawal means that the partner withholds sex or gives the other person the "cold shoulder" for a time. These behaviors have been examined in numerous studies of child aggression, but Flourishing Families is the first project to examine these behaviors in marriage. Relational aggression was measured using an adapted version of the Self-Report of Aggression and Victimization in Marriage (SRAV-M; Nelson & Carroll, 2006). Based on the original Self-Report of Aggression and Victimization (Linder, Crick, & Collins, 2002), the SRAV-M was modified in language for committed couples where respondents were instructed to respond about their current relationship. This subscale includes six items measuring the degree to which partners feel that their spouse utilizes socially aggressive behaviors in times of conflict and difference. The items included "My partner has gone 'behind my back' and shared private information about me with other people" and "My partner tries to embarrass me or make me look stupid in front of others." Scales are measured on a 7-point Likert scale ranging from 1 (*not at all true*) to 7 (*very true*). Higher scores indicate higher perceived relational victimization. Reliability tests for this sample produced a Cronbach's alpha of .905 for mothers (.904 for fathers) for the overall scale.

In like manner, we assessed the level of kindness experienced in the family setting. Rule-focused aspects of daily family life were assessed using the Family Implicit Rules Profile (Harper, Stoll, & Larsen, 2010). We selected a subscale for our analysis here that measures kindness. This subscale asks questions like "How important is it that family members stand up for one another?"; "How important is it that family members be kind and sensitive to other family members?"; "How important is it that family members be gentle with others?"; and "How important is it that family members not blame others unfairly?" Responses were based on a five-item Likert scale that ranging from 1 (*never*) to 5 (*most of the time*). The Cronbach's alpha for this scale is .84.

Again, it is important when developing items and scales related to sacred-living constructs that one think carefully before using the deficit of one scale to represent a separate construct. In our case here, a low score on our Unkindness subscale is clearly not the same measure as a high score on the relational aggression measure that assesses a harsh version of specific unkind behavior.

Sacrifice and Commitment

The FFP data set has information about sacrifice and commitment because it includes some of the items from the instrument developed by Stanley and Markman (1992). The research by Stanley and Markman viewed sacrifice as a component of commitment, whereas the research by Wieselquist et al. (1999) viewed sacrifice as a component of commitment and trust. However, there are a number of reasons to suggest that sacrifice and commitment should be viewed as two separate processes in families. The research by Van Lange, Rusbult et al. (1997), the analysis by Fincham, Stanley, and Beach (2007), the analysis by Bahr and Bahr (2001, 2009), and the qualitative data we used in Chapter 4 as the basis for the idea that sacrifice is important all argue that these two factors ought to be separated.

Fortunately, the Stanley and Markman (1992) inventory includes items about sacrifice and commitment, and they can be treated as separate subscales. The commitment items assess the degree each partner is willing to always work things out, the degree of commitment to their current partner, and each person's desire to stay in the relationship. The sacrifice items ask about willingness to give up something for one's partner. Couple commitment was assessed with six items, and satisfaction with relational sacrifice with four. Responses were based on a 7-point Likert scale ranging from 1 (*strongly disagree*) to 7 (*agree*). The items included "Giving something up for my partner is frequently not worth the trouble" and "I may not want to be with my partner a few years from now." Higher scores on the Commitment subscale indicate higher levels of commitment to one's partner, and higher satisfaction on the Sacrifice subscale indicate higher satisfaction/willingness in sacrificing for partner. Stanley et al. (2006) found the reliability to be .74 for the Sacrifice subscale and .88 for the Commitment subscale. The reliability (Cronbach's alpha) for this sample was .804 for P1 sacrifice (.830 for P2) and .862 for P1 commitment (.865 for P2).

Distal and Proximal Factors

Mahoney et al. (1999) found that "distal" factors were less powerful in families than "proximal" factors. Distal factors are activities that are more distant from the core of inner family life, and are operationalized with variables such as religious affiliation and attendance. These differences seem important because sacred theory argues that sacred-living behaviors such as forgivingness, kindness, commitment, sacrifice, and unkindness are more powerful in understanding couple and family outcomes than attending religious services or even participating as individuals in daily religious faith activities like praying and reading scripture.

Our data included several measures of distal and proximal factors. We used items from the Santa Clara Strength of Religious Faith Questionnaire (Lewis, Shevlin, McGucklin, & Navrtil, 2001). Part of this questionnaire asks about religious affiliation and attendance, and these questions were our measure of the more distal factors.

Parents also responded to four statements based on a 4-point Likert scale ranging from 1 (*strongly disagree*) to 4 (*strongly agree*). The statements included "I pray daily" and "My faith impacts many of my decisions." Higher scores indicate greater perceived religious influence on identity, meaning, life decisions, and religious behaviors. Lewis et al. (2001) found reliability to be .93 for the overall scale, and the Cronbach's alpha coefficient was found to be .960 in this study for the reduced scale. Activities such as prayer and religious discussion seem to be intermediate between the distal and proximal factors. They are more proximal than affiliation and attendance, but central to family life and therefore less proximal than being a forgiving person, kindness, unkindness, and sacrificing.

RESULTS

Table 14.2 shows the raw correlations of all the variables in the present analyses. We have organized the variables around three groups of independent variables. Group 1 represents our control variables or covariates. The controls employed are income, occupation, and/or race disparity. Occupational status was coded based on occupational codes developed by the Bureau of Labor and Statistics (BLS; 2003). In the FFP, we have reports from both mothers and fathers: The higher occupational status of the two was used in these analyses; a higher value means their occupation is rated higher by the BLS. Income levels used in these analyses were the combined income of both parents, and the value shown in Table 14.1 is a combined monthly income of the couple. Only couple data were analyzed here, and only the mother's reports of the independent and dependent variables were used. Income, however, was calculated from the reports of both parents. It is important to also note again that only intact couples were used in this analysis because several of the key indicators we are using require a partner present for appropriate response.

Correlation Results. We found that those with higher incomes were more likely to also report higher levels of forgiveness; those with lower incomes were more likely to report more unkindness or relational aggression in the relationship. Not surprisingly, those who reported attending religious activities were also more likely to say they had daily prayers, read scripture, and prayed together as a family. In like manner, those who attended religious activities reported more sacrifice in their family relationships and more commitment to the couple/marital relationship. Interestingly, those couples reporting more religious attendance also had children who reported more depressive symptoms and increased reports of self-shame. Increases in church or other religious attendance also correlated highly with increased levels of sexual intimacy. This finding probably connects with the finding that increased marital intimacy is also highly correlated with increased levels of commitment (which is correlated with religious attendance) and marital quality. These are not new findings, but they replicate past research and lend some legitimacy to data collected within this project. In like manner, reporting higher frequencies of daily prayer, scripture reading, and other faith-based activities correlates with increases in sacrifice, forgiveness, commitment, marital quality, and marital intimacy. Increases in faith activities are negatively correlated with marital instability, conflict, and unkindness.

Hierarchal Regressions. The more important questions for the theory, however, are whether these correlations continue to be strong even when the effects of

TABLE 14.2 Zero-Order Correlations of the Variables in the Analysis

Predictor Variables	1	2	3	4	5	6	7	8	9	10	11	12	13	14	15	16	17	18	19	20	21	22
Covariates:	1																					
1. Income	—	2																				
2. Occupation	.15	—	3																			
3. Race	.14	.08	—																			
Religious predictors:				4																		
4. Attendance	.10	.04	.00	—	5																	
5. Faith activities	.17	.04	.06	.59	—																	
Sacred—living predictors:						6																
6. Kindness	.03	.00	.01	.01	.05	—	7															
7. Sacrifice	.06	.03	.08	.22	.27	.26	—	8														
8. Forgiveness	.13	.06	.05	.07	.11	.26	.54	—	9													
9. Unkindness	.10	.08	.04	.05	.07	.26	.37	.49	—	10												
10. Commitment	.09	.01	.05	.17	.22	.27	.55	.62	.56	—												
Outcomes:											11											
11. Marital instability	.09	.08	.04	.09	.18	.25	.38	.51	.52	.60	—	12										
12. Marital quality	.06	.06	.08	.08	.16	.28	.45	.55	.49	.65	.67	—	13									
13. Marital intimacy	.03	.09	.07	.14	.19	.05	.26	.29	.02	.37	.24	.40	—	14								
14. Family functioning	.06	.05	.05	.00	.04	.39	.33	.42	.42	.46	.35	.54	.20	—	15							
15. Parent involvement	.09	.02	.06	.04	.08	.24	.31	.30	.25	.32	.31	.40	.10	.34	—	16						
16. Conflict	.12	.13	.02	.08	.09	.36	.31	.44	.53	.53	.56	.60	.28	.47	.42	—	17					
17. Child shame	.00	.04	.08	.01	.00	.10	.05	.00	.01	.06	.16	.17	.02	.14	.06	.11	—	18				
18. Child depression	.07	.11	.15	.02	.02	.10	.07	.04	.03	.08	.17	.13	.02	.13	.12	.12	.66	—	19			
19. Child integrity	.06	.01	.00	.01	.00	.00	.07	.02	.02	.04	.04	.00	.02	.09	.14	.03	.06	.04	—	20		
20. Parent depression	.20	.07	.10	.12	.05	.22	.14	.26	.26	.25	.36	.28	.02	.34	.24	.29	.16	.18	.05	—	21	
21. Parent anxiety	.14	.08	.03	.08	.01	.19	.11	.18	.27	.24	.37	.26	.06	.27	.20	.33	.18	.18	.07	.68	—	22
22. Parent stress	.28	.14	.08	.11	.03	.13	.11	.16	.26	.26	.36	.26	.08	.21	.26	.42	.11	.18	.04	.54	.53	—

control variables and of religious attendance and faith activities are accounted for. To answer these questions, a series of hierarchical stepwise regressions were computed. During the analysis, variables were entered into the analysis beginning with the control covariates followed by the attendance and faith activities (as a block), and then each of the sacred-living measures where entered individually—not as a block. This strategy allowed us to examine how much attendance/faith activity counts toward explaining variance within each model and how much each of the sacred-living constructs matters net of the other sacred-living measures and net of covariates and attendance and faith activity.

Table 14.3 shows the effects of the covariates, religious attendance and faith activities, while comparing the effects of each of the target sacred-living measures on three measures of couple strength: marital instability, marital quality, and marital intimacy. In all three cases, the covariates and attendance/activities did little to explain the outcome measures: Only religious attendance seemed to have an impact on reported levels of marital instability, quality, and intimacy. On the other hand, sacred-living constructs, generally, had a significant and systematic impact on explaining differences in each of the three outcomes. The statistical relationships between faith activities and outcomes were significant but much weaker in power compared to the impact of sacred-living measures. Still, these results indicate a possible connection between couples' religious attendance and activities, and fewer reported thoughts of getting divorced or being interested in extramarital love.

TABLE 14.3 Effects of Hierarchically Regressing Religious Attendance, Religious Activity, and Sacred Living on Couple Strength Outcomes

	Marital Instability			Marital Quality			Marital Intimacy		
	R^2	Δ	β	R^2	Δ	β	R^2	Δ	β
Step 1 Covariates[a]	.06*	—	—	.02	—	—	.02	—	—
Step 2 Religious attendance	.03	.00	.09	.02	.00	.14	.04	.02	.01
Step 3 Faith activities	.06**	.03	.12	.05*	.03	.16	.06*	.02	.10
Step 4 Kindness	.11***	.05	.09	.11***	.06	.03	.06	.00	.09
Step 5 Sacrifice	.20***	.09	.02	.25***	.14	.05	.11**	.05	.06
Step 6 Forgiveness	.32***	.12	.18	.36***	.11	.09	.14**	.03	.11
Step 7 Unkindness	.39***	.07	.18	.40***	.04	.20	.15	.01	.00
Step 8 Commitment	.46***	.07	.40	.51***	.11	.26	.18***	.03	.27

[a] Controlling for occupation, SES, education, and race.

$^{*}p < .05$. $^{**}p < .01$. $^{***}p < .000$.

To be specific, marital instability is predicted more by sacrifice, higher levels of forgivingness, and commitment than by religious attendance or faith activities. Looking at the standardized betas, one can also see that the three largest predictors of decreases in reporting marital instability were higher levels of commitment and forgiveness and lower levels of unkindness. The same pattern held true for increases in marital quality with the addition that higher levels of kindness also predicted less marital instability. Although sacrifice was significant in these models, the small standardized beta scores tell us it had much less predictive power than commitment.

Marital intimacy is best predicted when there is less kindness, more commitment, and higher levels of forgiveness. In this particular model it is interesting to note that unkindness (relational aggression) was not connected to sexual intimacy.

With regard to unkindness, Table 14.2 shows that it is strongly related to several key outcomes. There seems to be a "toxic" bundling of processes occurring in these troubled families. Relational aggression is high, marital stability is low, quality is low, family functioning is lower, parent involvement in children's lives drops off, and depression significantly increases along with anxiety and stress. We raise this issue here for two reasons. First, we want to reemphasize that kindness and unkindness as measured here are two different processes. Unkindness seems to be reported hand in hand with relationship destruction and disengagement. Second, we acknowledge the tenuous nature of causal statements that are based only on cross-sectional data, but sacred theory was built primarily with qualitative data, and it provides a basis for inferring causality. The analysis of the quantitative data here shows that the relationships predicted by the theory are generally consistent with the theory. Further, they are consistent in a powerful way and thus provide additional evidence for the ideas in the theory.

Table 14.4 provides a window into how sacred living is related to child well-being, and we chose three kinds of outcomes. First, we note that shame is an important emerging outcome in the developmental literature. The research on shame indicates that children who experience a great deal of shame may also report higher levels of psychopathology with attendant symptoms such as depression, anxiety, eating disorders, and lower role-taking ability (Tangney, 1990, 1991, 1994; Tangney, Wagner, & Gramzow, 1992). To our knowledge the connection between family processes in general and shame is not well established. Moreover, there have been no attempts to assess how shame may be specifically connected to sacred living.

We also gathered data about depression in children, an area of growing concern. We hypothesized that when parents embrace sacred-living interaction styles, their children tend to be less likely to report depressive symptoms. In other words, living in a home within which the climate is one of kindness and forgiveness, parents are committed to the relationship, and the sacrifice for each other should have a net effect of decreases in childhood depression.

Unlike shame and depression, the emergence of positive psychology in recent years has been dramatic (Seligman, 2001). In short, this new disciplinary focus examines how a person learns and implements values such as persistence, hope, gratitude, and integrity. We asked if sacred living by parents (net of religious

TABLE 14.4 Effects of Hierarchically Regressing Religious Attendance, Religious Activities, and Sacred Living on Child Outcomes

	Child Shame Time 4			Child Depressive Symptoms Time 4			Child Integrity Time 4		
	R^2	Δ	ß	R^2	Δ	ß	R^2	Δ	ß
Step 1 Covariates [a]	.01	—	—	.01	—	—	.01	—	—
Step 2 Religious attendance	.04	.01	.21	.02	.01	.14	.01	.00	.04
Step 3 Faith activities	.08*	.04	.15	.03	.01	.11	.01	.00	.02
Step 4 Kindness	.08	.00	.11	.04*	.01	.14	.01	.00	.03
Step 5 Sacrifice	.08	.00	.01	.04	.00	.06	.02	.01	.03
Step 6 Forgiveness	.08	.00	.03	.06*	.02	.17	.02	.00	.02
Step 7 Unkindness	.08	.00	.04	.06	.00	.13	.03	.01	.01
Step 8 Commitment	.08	.00	.11	.07**	.01	.19	.03	.00	.01

[a] Controlling for occupation, SES, education, and race.
*$p < .05$. **$p < .01$. ***$p < .000$.

attendance and faith activity) has a carryover effect into the positive-values world of the child. We target only one element of possible values—that is, integrity. We hypothesized that when the home climate exuded a more positive outlook that included forgiving, kindness, decreased unkindness, and higher levels of commitment and sacrifice, children would also be more likely to report increases in other sacred values such as integrity.

Table 14.4 shows that, first of all, the sacred-living measures were not nearly as powerful in predicting the target child outcomes as they were in predicting familial level or parent outcomes. None of the sacred-living measures were significant in predicting changes in child's report of feelings of shame. The two assessments of attendance and faith activity did, however, predict changes in shame. Religious attendance was significant: As religious attendance increased, so did the level of reported shame. In contrast, as families reported more prayer, reading, and other faith-based activities, shame significantly decreased. This finding is somewhat difficult to explain given that attendance and faith activities are highly correlated. We suggest researchers in the future explore this connection aggressively. It could be that religious affiliation may account for this unusual finding.

Children's depression was more responsive to increases in sacred living–based concepts. When mothers reported more couple kindness, forgiveness, and commitment, depressive symptoms reports dropped significantly for children. Again, however, the amount of variance in these models is quite low overall and does not provide a great deal of insight about how these processes may be unfolding. Having said that, future researchers should pursue the connections among child mental well-being, couple strengths, and sacred living. Future research should include explorations into how sacred-living constructs may be moderating or mediating the impact of parent and couple well-being on children's outcomes.

Our least predictive set of outcomes can be found in trying to predict changes in child integrity. Neither sacred living nor religious activities of any kind, proximal or distal, matter in these analyses. This is an area for more research and exploration. One would think that claims of church attendance, reading scripture-based texts, and parents living a more sacred-oriented life would have some impact on children's sense of right and wrong and other integrity-based virtues. This finding will be difficult for religious leaders and parents to grasp. It may be that the relatively young age of the children in the FFP data set is part of the reason these relationships are lower than expected.

On the other hand, sacred living seems to be powerfully tied to measures of general family functioning, parent involvement, and levels of conflict. Table 14.5 shows that, in each case, sacred-living measures were significant and powerful whereas attendance and faith activities had virtually no predictive power.

One of the new insights from our quantitative data is that the sacred-living predictors matter differentially. That is, different elements of sacred living mattered

TABLE 14.5 Effects of Hierarchically Regressing Religious Attendance, Religious Activity, and Sacred Living on Family Outcomes

	Family Functioning Time 4			Parent Involvement Time 4			Conflict Time 4		
	R^2	Δ	ß	R^2	Δ	ß	R^2	Δ	ß
Step 1 Covariates [a]	.00	—	—	.00	—	—	.02	—	—
Step 2 Religious attendance	.0	.00	.01	.01	.00	.00	.03	.03	.00
Step 3 Faith activities	.01	.00	.01	.02	.01	.00	.03	.00	.01
Step 4 Kindness	.16***	.15	.26	.12***	.10	.22	.15***	.12	.19
Step 5 Sacrifice	.21***	.05	.02	.18***	.06	.18	.19***	.04	.05
Step 6 Forgiveness	.26***	.05	.09	.19***	.01	.00	.26***	.07	.10
Step 7 Unkindness	.30***	.04	.14	.20***	.01	–.04	.34***	.08	.25
Step 8 Commitment	.33***	.03	.25	.22***	.02	.15	.38***	.04	.28

[a] Controlling for occupation, SES, education, and race

*p < .05. **p < .01. ***p < .000.

differently for different outcomes. For general family functioning, kindness was a significant predictor with a generous level of variance accounted for (.16) and with a powerful standardized beta score (.26). All of the three outcomes in this table share a similar story line about the effects of kindness. Sacrifice seems to be a more powerful predictor with regard to parent involvement—yet less influential in predicting conflict or family functioning. In like manner, forgiveness matters substantially in family functioning and conflict reduction, but hardly at all in parent involvement. Unkindness has a dramatic impact on family functioning and the level of conflict but is less powerful in explaining parent involvement. We were concerned here about issues of colinearity. A simple variance inflation factor (VIF) was calculated for these and several other measures for our analyses, and the VIF scores indicated that, in this case, conflict and unkindness were orthogonal within acceptable range. None of the independent measures in our analyses here failed the VIF test.

Commitment is a strong and powerful predictor for many of the models we ran in these analyses. In Table 14.5, family functioning, parent involvement, and conflict are all predicted by level of commitment net of covariates—religious activity, faith activity, and the other sacred-living constructs. Notably, commitment seems to best predict reduction in conflict and increases in family functioning whereas sacrifice, as was mentioned, best predicts mother's involvement with her children.

One of the more important findings in our demonstration here is that elements of sacred living have differential impacts on different outcomes. To our knowledge, no one has explored this idea. For one thing, there are few if any studies that gather a buffet of sacred-living measures together and test their relative strength on family and personal outcomes within one series of models. This is an important idea and one that needs a significant amount of research attention.

Finally, we asked if sacred-living measures would predict adult outcomes within a family context, and the results are in Table 14.6. Again, we chose outcomes that have a plethora of research with which researchers could connect. These commonly researched parent/personal outcomes are known to have important impacts on family life.

Our first model in this table shows how sacred-living measures map onto parent report of depressive symptoms. Religious activities including even more proximal activities like prayer have very little impact on decreasing parent depression, but having a kinder couple relationship has a significant and moderately powerful impact on reducing depressive symptoms. Likewise, vitriolic relational unkindness appears to generate significant increases in depression, and higher levels of commitment seem to ameliorate reports of depression.

Parent anxiety is most impacted by higher level of couple kindness and also seems to be increased significantly by unkindness. None of the other sacred-living measures appear to have a significant connection to anxiety.

Decreases in parent-reported stress are responsive to more couple kindness and commitment and less unkindness. Again, it is important to note that, at least for our analyses, not all sacred-living measures have the same impact. They do seem to bundle together in predicting marital quality, stability, and intimacy much more than they do individual or general familial attributes.

TABLE 14. 6 Effects of Hierarchically Regressing Religious Attendance, Religious Activity, and Sacred Living on Parent Outcomes

	Parent Depression Time 4			Parent Anxiety Time 4			Parent Stress Time 4		
	R^2	Δ	ß	R^2	Δ	ß	R^2	Δ	ß
Step 1 Covariates [a]	.00	—	—	.01	—	—	.05**	—	—
Step 2 Religious attendance	.00	.00	.03	.02	.01	.05	.05	.00	.04
Step 3 Faith activities	.00	.00	.03	.02	.00	.09	.05	.00	.03
Step 4 Kindness	.08***	.08	.22	.06***	.04	.15	.07**	.02	.14
Step 5 Sacrifice	.08	.00	.05	.06	.00	.05	.07	.00	.02
Step 6 Forgiveness	.09	.01	.02	.06	.00	.04	.07	.00	.13
Step 7 Unkindness	.11**	.02	.14	.09***	.03	.20	.11***	.04	.16
Step 8 Commitment	.11*	.00	.08	.10	.01	.07	.13**	.02	.18

[a] Controlling for occupation, SES, education, and race.
*p < .05. **p < .01. ***p < .000.

SUMMARY

The quantitative data analyzed here provide the basis for several more general conclusions, and also provide a number of ideas for future research. First, the central premise in this book is that sacred matters are helpful in understanding inner family life. The data support this claim and offer some ideas for continued development of the theory. Of course, a single research study by itself does not present the power necessary to substantiate or refute a theory. However, our findings here are viable, powerful, and have enough validity that continued research is called for.

Second, Mahoney et al. (1999) recommended that we examine the effects of religion using a proximal–distal orientation. Our data corroborate and extend this idea and suggest that the interactive personal/proximal elements of sacred principles are far more powerful than more distal activities such as affiliation or attendance. We should not dismiss the power of sacred practices such as attending, praying, and understanding the concepts of religious ideals, but we ought to view them as a good starting place. The take-home message is that unless the "ore" found in religious activity and concepts is transformed into the "precious metal" of sacred living, the power of ritualistic attendance or even faith activities will be muted at best. It is also the case that one can find sacred-living concepts and principles outside of church, mosque, or synagogue walls. The same effect stands. However, unless the concepts are turned into practice, their effect will be seriously minimized.

Third, our data corroborate that just because a concept seems to be connected to religious tradition does not mean it will find equal predictive weight with other similar concepts in understanding a variety of outcomes. The concepts matter, the outcomes matter, and the reporters matter. The limitations of time and space kept us from more complex analyses of the FFP data, but more research is needed that provides information about how the responses of other family members make a difference. For example, we need similar and more extensive statistical analyses for men in families. From their viewpoint, there are even further different profiles of measures that matter depending again on outcome. As future researchers build and test statistical models based on sacred theory, it will be important to take into account the nature of the construct, its connection to the theory, who is reporting, and what outcomes are being considered. Surely there will also be suggested models within which multiple reporters within one family are considered simultaneously.

Fourth, we ignored earlier in this book the idea that commitment ought to be included in sacred theory. Our quantitative data, however, posit that it is more powerful than our qualitative data suggested. In the spirit of the theory being a *developing* theory, the data in this chapter suggest that future refinements of the theory give commitment a more prominent place. This also opens the door to other possibilities. The theory in this volume focuses on the role of four general propositions and 25 less general ideas. We believe there are a number of other aspects of the sacred that are also important, and we hope later generations of the theory expand the ideas.

Fifth, more research is needed about the role of contextual factors such as ethnicity, stages in the individual and family development, race, age, education, and nontraditional family styles. Our research is based on secondary data analyses of data in one sample from one city. The FFP was not designed to be a study of sacred living in family life. As such, the findings in this chapter are only a beginning. They do not give us much of a window into how families in a variety of disparate settings use sacred-living ideas and how they make a difference. We have not analyzed data about single-parent families, and most of the FFP families are not challenged with children having disabilities. Most of the parents are moderately healthy, the vast majority of them are middle-income families, and most are Euro-American. As research is acquired that studies other family types, contexts, and SES levels, we should be vigilant in our theorizing to be inclusive and generous in searching out how the sacred matters in those families' lives.

Sixth, we were somewhat puzzled by the lack of predictive power in explaining the impact of parent sacred living on children's outcomes. Future research and theorizing ought to pay more attention to how sacred-living constructs may reflect either moderating or mediating influence in statistical models. Our simple analysis here left much to be desired, only pointing the way and taking a few steps down a very long road. As researchers examine these constructs using multiple respondents and employing structural equation modeling and advanced hierarchical linear modeling approaches, the intricacies of moderating and mediating influences will be better addressed.

Within that vein, future research also ought to use profile- and threshold-based analyses. Profile analyses will allow researchers to identify ways sacred matters make a difference in different groups of couples as taxonlike indicators are created. Our guess is that latent profile analyses will reveal that there are several types of couples and/or family groups who employ different aspects of sacred-living elements in their relationships with differing levels of outcome success.

Seventh, more research is also needed about thresholds, nonlinear relationships, and how variation on the tails of distributions makes more difference than variation around the mean. For example, we have little insight into how much kindness is necessary to result in a given impact with regard to a given target outcome, or how much toxic relational aggression is required to tip the scales and result in measurable drops of family and/or couple functioning. It is probably the case that many of the ideas generated so far in sacred theory are not linear in their effect, and finding the shape of these relationships will be as important as finding if they are important.

Finally, we offer a reminder. The theory and research in this book is neither comprehensive nor final. It begins the third generation of research and theory, and it improves on what was done in the first and second generations, but there is a need for many additional generations. A top priority for developing and advancing this theoretical story will be for researchers to rethink the measures currently available. Sacred-matters theory will require new measures, reworked constructs, and innovative statistical analysis. To that point, we also recommend that both qualitative and quantitative research efforts be used, even in concert, to further this approach. The FFP has moved toward also using objective video-recorded task analyses to more clearly assess constructs that are not easily seen behind closed doors, and innovative methods such as these are needed as we try to understand the intricacies of inner family life and the role of sacred matters in family life.

15

Methods

Our goal in this chapter is to describe the methods that were used in this project. One aspect of these methods is that theory and research were intertwined in a more complex way than the simple reciprocal cycle described by Merton (1957) or the more elaborate cyclical process described by Klein (2005, p. 17). This means it is not possible to describe a sequence or cycle in the methods because there was a constant and complex fluidity in ways the conceptualizing, observing, generalizing, measuring, inducing, organizing, integrating, deducing, speculating, inferring, and revising occurred and influenced each other. We need to describe some aspects of the methods before others, but it is difficult, perhaps impossible, to identify which methods were used first, or last, or in what sequence, because they were intertwined in multifaceted ways.

Another aspect of the methods is that the methodology in constructing and improving theories is different in a number of ways from that used in doing empirical research. Research methods are more precise, prescriptive, technical, and detailed; and the processes that are used in creating and revising theories are more varied, subjective, intuitive, and creative. This means the methods in theorizing are more complex but less mature. They are less clear and systematic, and there are fewer rules and guidelines. For example, there is little consensus about the nature of evidence about theories, the criteria for evaluating theories, or the processes in creating and revising them.

The methods that are used in theory building also have changed substantially since the pioneering descriptions by Braithwaite (1953), Nagel (1961), Zetterberg (1965), Glaser and Strauss (1967), Stinchcombe (1968), Blalock (1969, 1971), Dubin (1969), Hage (1972), Gibbs (1972), and Burr (1973). For example, there is considerably more attention paid to the use of qualitative data, narrative analysis, and grounded theory (Chase, 2005; Denzin & Lincoln, 1994; Gilgun, 2001, 2005; Glaser, 1978; Strauss & Corbin, 1990), and there is greater appreciation for subjectivity in theory building (D. L. Thomas & Wilcox, 1987). The methodological discussions in the Boss et al. (1993) sourcebook expanded attention to contextual and ideological factors, and the methodological discussions in the Bengston et al. (2005) sourcebook expanded the diversity and inclusiveness. More recent discussions of methods have developed other ways of improving theory, such as authorizing (Knapp, 2002), examining consistency and paying attention to the evolution of theories (Tudge et al., 2009), and modeling (Jaccard & Jacoby, 2010).

METHODS IN THE GENERATION STAGE

One of our methods was to gather several different types of new data that we then used as the basis for generating ideas in the theory. Four different methods were used; some of them were fairly conventional and widely used whereas others were relatively unconventional, innovative, and almost never used. The four methods were (a) interviews and discussions, (b) observations, (c) historical analysis, and (d) analyzing literature. Each of these methods has advantages, limitations, shortcomings, and weaknesses, but the combination of them in one project is more valuable than any of them alone.

Interviews and Discussions

We have talked with hundreds of people about the ways aspects of the sacred play a role in their families. Some of these sessions were structured and semistructured interviews whereas others were more open-ended; and some of them were discussions rather than interviews. We talked with individuals, couples, families, and groups. We also talked with people in different parts of the world and with people who are affiliated with a variety of religious persuasions. The interviewees comprised men, women, and children of a wide range of ages, and the interviews were conducted over a span of many years.

Between 2001 and 2010, Loren Marks and David Dollahite conducted interviews with almost 500 individuals in 200 U.S. families. Detailed information about the methods and families is in other publications, such as Dollahite and Marks (2009). But to briefly summarize, the interviews yielded in-depth, qualitative data from highly religious families residing in all eight regions of the United States, including New England (Massachusetts, Connecticut), the Northwest (Oregon, Washington), the Pacific region (California), the Mountain West (Idaho), the Mid-Atlantic region (Delaware, Maryland, Pennsylvania), the Midwest (Ohio, Wisconsin), the Southern Crossroads region (Kansas, Oklahoma), and the South (Florida, Louisiana).

Locale was considered due to significant regional variation in U.S. religiosity, culture, and subculture (Roof & Silk, 2005). The families included members of conservative and mainline Protestant churches, the Catholic Church, New Christian Religions, and the Muslim, Mormon, and Jewish (Hasidic, Modern Orthodox, Conservative, and Reformed) faiths. Some of the interviews were with husbands and wives separately but most were as a couple. Seventy-seven adolescent children were also interviewed. An additional strength of these data are that 50% of the sample were from ethnic/racial minorities: 32 African Americans, 22 Asian Americans, 15 Native Americans, 15 Latinos, 11 Middle Easterners, 4 East Indians, and 1 Pacific Islander—with the balance of the families being Caucasian.

These interviews were conducted in the homes of the individuals, and most of them used semistructured interview schedules. Some new questions were added and others were deleted as new issues and questions were dealt with. The interviews varied in length from 1 to 4 hours, averaging about 2 hours, and audio recordings were made. The transcribed interviews resulted in 5000+ pages of qualitative data. The transcripts were examined and reexamined by several different groups in research methods and research internship classes, and these analyses led to the conceptual models in Dollahite and Marks (2005, 2009).

Another source of data was that Wes Burr and his wife lived in the northland in New Zealand during 2000 and 2001. This area of New Zealand is primarily rural, and a large percentage of the population have Maori heritage. Wes and Ruth talked extensively with a sizeable number of Maori people about their culture, history, and family life. The format for these discussions was more of a participant observation style than an interview style, and they occurred in homes, churches, and marais (sacred enclosures or temples).

These sessions were not recorded, but Wes kept a detailed journal. This format allowed for extensive discussions about and analysis of a wide variety of ideas, and Wes steered many of the conversations to beliefs and behavior about how sacred matters influenced family life. The Maori people tend to be relatively family oriented and religious, and they typically were eager to join in these discussions. Several hundred people participated in these discussions, with some being involved in many of them and others participating for just a short time. It was impossible to keep detailed statistics about who participated in which ways because the Maori have a very informal lifestyle, and people were joining and leaving the groups during the discussions. These discussions were helpful in clarifying and refining many of the ideas that are discussed in this book and in understanding their role in a non-Western culture and with a number of different religions.

Wes also discussed the ideas in this book in considerable depth with an additional 76 individuals in Utah between 2008 and 2010, and had less involved discussions with many more. These sessions were with relatives, friends, and neighbors. One of the objectives in these discussions was to learn more about the ways people felt the principles in sacred theory made a difference in their lives. Another goal was to learn more about aspects of life that are viewed as sacred by some and not sacred by others. We were also trying to learn more about how people thought living and not living the various principles made a difference in various aspects of their life. We had developed the opinion that there were differences in the family processes and outcomes that were influenced by different principles, but we had little evidence that this is actually true. We therefore wanted to learn more about what people thought about how different principles helped them with different aspects of their lives. We also had little information about whether sacred processes help as a unified cluster or whether certain aspects of the sacred make a difference in unique ways.

Observations

The dominant pattern in contemporary research methods is to give the most credence to quantitative and impersonal sources of data, but Strauss and Corbin (1990) argued that "personal experience represents still another source of theoretical sensitivity" (p. 43). Strauss and Corbin used the experiences of divorce and death of a loved one as examples, noting both differences and similarities between the experiences, and they suggested: "By drawing upon the *personal experience* of divorce, the analyst can have a basis for making comparisons that in turn stimulate the generation of potentially relevant concepts and their relationships that pertain to loss through death" (p. 43, italics added).

We have drawn considerably from our personal experiences as children, siblings, spouses, parents, and grandparents, and many of the narratives in this book are drawn from these observations. We also have observed for many years our immediate and extended families and the families of people we have come to know well in community, counseling, and educational settings; and we have found these observations very helpful. We believe this source of data may actually be the most useful and rich source in studying families. Social scientists are strangers in families, and when they try to get data from families with questionnaires, interviews, and observers they do not have full access to many of the complexities and subtleties in family processes. It is only the people who are living in families and who are observing firsthand the almost infinitely variable and intricate aspects of family life who have access to the many complex and nuanced and also subtle but powerful aspects of what goes on in families. Therefore we believe that our observations inside our own families have been very valuable; and we believe that the methods that are usually given more credence in the academic community are often more superficial, partial, fragmented, and limited in usefulness.

Therefore as we have worked at the generation of the ideas in sacred theory, we have relied heavily on our own observations of family processes and the observations of colleagues. We openly admit that many of our observations are subjective, unique, and unsystematic, but we find them very helpful in improving and expanding theoretical ideas because they provide some of the most valuable, in-depth, and contextualized insights into family processes. By contrast, many of the dominant approaches in the social sciences call for researchers to become "invisible" and to become "objective" tools. They are not allowed to experience per se—only to reason objectively, collect data, and make a logically consistent case, as if presenting evidence at a murder trial. We find this approach sterile and superficial and think it is wise to acknowledge and use personal experiences—especially as we try to discuss *family* in as valid and authentic a way as possible.

Fortunately, there is considerable precedent for scholars using their own personal observations in their theorizing. For example, Cooley (1902, 1909) used observations of his own children in his home as one of the important sources of his insights as he created his theory of the emergence of the self. Piaget also used his own family observations for many of the ideas he contributed about child development. More recently, Allen (2000) also argued for the value of personal experiences in scholarly inquiry. Her term for these observations was reflexive consciousness.

There are a number of other reasons we've found our personal observations helpful. Family life is an intensely private and personal experience. When people are behind the closed doors of their own homes, they are, as Goffman (1959) captured it, "off-stage," and family members live the familial part of their lives in a private and complex sphere that includes an enormous number of past experiences that influence what goes on in the present. Additionally, there is often the element of shared familial dreams and aspirations for the future. Those who are "insiders" in this experience know and understand a complex array of phenomena that are largely unavailable to social sciences researchers who come with questionnaires and interview schedules. Also, even though many ethnographers are not aware of it, many aspects of family life are also not accessible to scholars, even those who spend months living in communities to try to study them.

This means that many of the most valuable and in-depth insights about the nature of family processes come from *living in a family*. As we have lived in our families, we have interacted with grandparents, extended family, and our immediate family as children and then as adults; and these experiences have provided us with a rich source of ideas and information about family life. Our personal observations are, of course, subjective and biased, and this is why the generating stage of the theory development project is complemented by a larger set of processes that include later development, verification, and refinement. There are also, of course, important limitations to the subjective and unique observations and experiences that are provided in one's own family, and these also should be taken into account. Therefore after generating sacred theory and describing it in this volume, it is important to acquire evidence from other sources that will lead to testing and revising. By the same token, we believe that those who try to rely on only "objective" data collection as their primary research tool will miss many of the key and important aspects of family life.

Along with our personal observations, we also have relied on the observations and ideas of colleagues in family studies, philosophy, and the humanities. These colleagues have brought to bear their subjective observations and the observations they have from their professional experiences with students and clients. We also view this as a rich source of ideas, and have talked with and relied on a sizeable group of colleagues in our search for insights about family processes.

Historical Analysis

Wes Burr also brought a different source and kind of data to this project. He became interested in the history of his family heritage and began in 1988 to work at the process of gathering and publishing histories. This led to a number of discussions, some of them fairly extensive, with many of his close and distant relatives about their ancestors and genealogy.

Some of these discussions were with close relatives in Utah, and others were with more distant relatives in Connecticut, New York, England, and Sweden. These discussions created the opportunity for further discussions about the role of sacred matters with a diverse group of relatives and others, and this historical research led to a number of publications and over 3200 pages of histories (Burr, 2000a, 2000b, 2002; Burr & Burr, 2009; Burr, 2006; Burr & Burr, 1995).[1]

---

[1] A limited number of these books were published so they are not widely available; but if anyone is interested in these publications, there are copies available through the Harold B. Lee Library at Brigham Young University, Provo, Utah 84601.

At the time Wes began his foray into this type of history, he did not expect it to be one of the helpful methods in improving and expanding theoretical ideas about the role of sacred matters in families. He began doing it because of personal interest and a desire to have more of his heritage written down for his posterity. However, he gradually came to realize these experiences were deepening his insights into a number of aspects of sacred matters in families. They helped clarify and expand a number of ideas about the role of generational relationships described in Chapter 10, but also the role of other processes such as sacrifice, forgiveness, loving, faith, and sanctification. They helped him better understand the nature of family and some of the more essential and enduring aspects of being a family. They also helped deepen and refine his insights into what is important in families and what helps and harms in family life.

Some of the insights from these observations and involvement with the historical method led to new developments and major changes in the conceptualizing and theorizing in sacred theory. For example, in the early stages of developing the theory, we relied on the extensive literature about the importance of self-esteem and programs to enhance self-esteem (Burr et al. 1982, Chapter 4). However, we eventually came to believe that the emphasis on self-esteem is misguided, and we eliminated these ideas from the theory in favor of ideas about the dignity and importance of all people and a mutual orientation or communal orientation (Beck & Clark, 2010; Clark & Mills, 1979) rather than a self-orientation. A paper was then published that argued that the extensive attention to self-esteem is actually more harmful than beneficial in families (Burr & Christensen, 1992).

Analyzing Literatures

Another of our methods was to examine three different bodies of literature to gather ideas about how aspects of the sacred are involved in families. One of these was the research and theory in family studies. We began this process in the 1970s, and have tried to keep abreast of the literature since then. In the last stages of completing this book, we undertook searches on EBSCO (Academic Search Premier, Family & Social Studies Worldwide, and PSYCHinfo), Google Scholar, Web of Science, and CSA databases to try to find relevant literature in recent years. We searched key terms such as *peacemaking*, *contention*, *patience*, *cooperation*, *competition*, *negative emotions*, *negative affect*, *anger*, *unity*, *consensus*, *agreement*, and *conflict*, as well as synonyms such as *amicable*, *calm*, *conciliatory*, *gentle*, *placatory*, *quiet*, *tranquil*, *quarreling*, *aggression*, *hostility*, *helping*, *sharing*, *assistance*, *problem solving*, *common good*, and *social conflict*. Each of these terms was combined with *family*, *relationship*, or *couple*. In each database we set limiters to find articles published in peer-reviewed journals since 2000.

Another type of literature we found helpful was sacred literature such as the Bible and Qur'an, and summaries and analyses of the ideas and traditions in the other world religions such as Smith's volumes (1991, 1992). We found these bodies of literature to be rich with individualistic ideas and moral ideals, but they rarely focused explicitly on family processes. However, our observations of the dynamics in our own families and our interview data suggested that many of the individualistic ideas are so consistent with the widely shared goals in families that are described on pages 18–21 that it was a minor logical leap to generalize many of the individualistic ideas to family processes.

Initially, our search of these bodies of literature was a fairly informal process, but it became more systematic and thorough when a group of about a dozen colleagues began meeting twice a month during the 2008–2009 academic year to identify ways the sacred could have a more central role in family studies. These analyses of religious literatures led to a long list of ideas, and about 50 of them were relevant for sacred theory. This list was slowly pared down to a more manageable group, and we eventually settled on the 25 principles that are briefly described in Figure 1.1 on page 32 and discussed in Chapters 2–12.

The third type of literature we examined was artistic literature such as novels, poetry, and drama. Two of our colleagues, Kathleen Bahr and Mae Blanch, taught a class for many years that focused on ways artistic literature is helpful in understanding family processes, and Wes and Randy worked with Kathleen in writing a text titled *Family Science* (Burr, Day, & Bahr, 1993). They benefited from Kathleen's expertise in how literature can inform the study of the family and used some of the insights in generating ideas in the theorizing in this volume. This is not an area where we have expertise, but these experiences helped us clarify, refine, and illustrate the principles we were assembling. We hope that in the future others who have more expertise in this type of literature will examine it more thoroughly than we have. We think it is a promising type of scholarship because the artistic literature is considerably more sophisticated than the social science literature in identifying, describing, and illustrating ideas that are helpful and harmful in families. Classical works such as Homer's *Odyssey* and the Shakespearean plays illustrate profound ideas. Some of the more modern works we have found helpful are Tolstoy's *Anna Karenina* (1965), Tyler's *Searching for Caleb* (1975), and Browning's "How Do I Love Thee?"

METHODS IN IMPROVING AND EXPANDING IDEAS

At the same time we were gathering new data and examining these three bodies of literature, we also began the rather complicated process of trying to improve and expand the theory and research. This process turned out to be more challenging and complicated than we anticipated, and included a large number of strategies and methods. We started out with a relatively vague idea of what we wanted to do, but we didn't have a very good understanding of the many strategies and methods that would come into play. Therefore this process became a series of learning experiences about the many processes and methods that are involved.

This means this section of this chapter is fairly long and very complicated. To make our description of these methods as simple and understandable as possible, we have divided the discussion of the improving and expanding methods into five parts. First, we describe the methods we used as we tried to integrate sacred and secular ideas. Second, we describe a group of methods we used as we moved from data to theory. Third, we describe a pattern in our theory building we didn't expect or anticipate. Fourth, we describe the methods we used when we were working with concepts and propositions and the different aspects of the relationships in propositions. Fifth, we describe methods we found helpful in a stage of theory building we didn't previously realize was a separate stage in theory building. We now call this stage of theory building "the describing stage."

Methods in Integrating the Sacred and Secular

We think it will help us describe the methods we've used if we briefly review the history of the way sacred ideas have been included and excluded in scholarly inquiry. Ideas about sacred matters dominated intellectual thought in the Middle Eastern and European cultures during the Middle Ages, but this was changed by the Renaissance and the Protestant Reformation. These changes led to improvements in the scientific method; but although the scientific method was becoming more sophisticated and gaining in credibility, most scholars had an epistemology that assumed knowledge gained through scientific and sacred methods could be integrated. Many of even the most eminent scholars, such as Galileo and Newton, saw little or no conflict in integrating their scientific theories and empirical observations with their religiously derived beliefs.

Several events during the early 1500s brought dramatic changes in these views. Copernicus developed his theory about the earth rotating around the sun, but the dominant belief at the time was that the earth was the center of the universe. This idea was developed by Greek philosophers such as Aristotle; and it eventually became known as the Ptolemaic theory because it was formulated in its most sophisticated way in the second century by a Greco-Egyptian astronomer named Claudius Ptolemy.

Copernicus developed the idea that the sun is the center of the universe and the earth revolves around the sun. As this new theory became widely known throughout Europe, it became a problem because the Catholic Church had adopted the Ptolemaic theory as part of its dogma. This and similar scientific discoveries began a struggle between what was emerging as a new way to get knowledge and the religious ways of getting knowledge that had dominated Western thought for more than a millennium.

In the next century, the controversies between science and religion spread to other ideas and became more heated. For example, the Catholic Church at the time also believed the Aristotelian idea that the moon gave off its own light rather than reflected light. Galileo turned this idea into a major controversy. He was the first person to put two lenses together in a tube and look through it. We call his invention the telescope, and when he used it to study the moon he realized that the light of the moon is reflected light from the sun. When he published this and a number of other ideas, he was arrested, sent to Rome, and tried and convicted of heresy. He lived the rest of his life in house arrest and with more than a few restraints on what he could and could not do.

During the next century, the Catholic dogma was shown to be wrong with respect to other ideas as well, but church leaders resisted and fought against the new ideas. This led to many extensive debates about whether religious ideas were credible. Scholars such as Francis Bacon (1561–1626) argued that scientific ideas rather than religious ideas ought to be the master of things, whereas René Descartes (1596–1650) and Isaac Newton (1643–1727) argued for the validity of theistic and scientific ideas.

Gradually, the majority of the scientific community developed negative attitudes toward ideas that came from religious sources, and this was the dominant pattern when the social sciences began to appear in late nineteenth century. Therefore this pattern became the prevailing approach in all of the social sciences. There were a few isolated individuals, such as Hall (1891), James (1902), and Allport (1950; Allport & Ross, 1967), who advocated the inclusion of ideas about sacred phenomena, but these ideas were ignored by the majority of social scientists until the last part of the twentieth century (Richards & Bergin, 2005; Thomas & Henry, 1985).

Like Richards and Bergin (2005), we have wondered why sacred phenomena were excluded so long in the social sciences and mainstream mental health professions. They suggested: "There is not a simple answer to this. The relationships among religion, psychological thought, and psychotherapy are long and complex. Historical, philosophical and theoretical influences all seem to have contributed to this alienation from spirituality during the 20th century" (p. 31).

Part of the problem during modernism was that science and religion rely on very different ways of getting and verifying knowledge. Science relies on reason and observation in ways that can be interpersonally replicated to increase the confidence that can be placed in the ideas. Religious ideas, on the other hand, come from mystical sources such as revelation and inspiration, and they rely on authority, faith, and uniquely subjective experiences for confidence.

We are not interested in getting into denominational controversies or doctrinal debates. We also are not interested in whether ideas gleaned from and about the sacred are true or false noumenologically. Rather, we make the assumption that ideas from and about the sacred are phenomenologically real, pervasive, important to a large number of humans, and related to so many important parts of family life that they deserve attention.

We also have been persuaded by scholars such as Bergin (1980), Jones (1994), and Barbour (2000) that the sacred and scholarly can be integrated and that the integration will contribute to the progress of scholarly inquiry "by suggesting new modes of thought . . . and new theories" (Jones, 1994, p. 194). This integration, however, is neither simple nor easy, and calls for a number of unique methodological strategies. However, so few scholars have worked at this integration that the methodology for it is not well developed. Jones suggested in one place that it will help if a "dialogical" approach is used, and in another place he suggested it ought to be a "dialectical" approach (p. 195), but little has been written about what these strategies involve.

As we have tried to bring the sacred closer to center stage in the scholarly study of families, one strategy we have found helpful is to search for conceptualizations and ideas to include that have not been part of family studies. As Stephen Marks (1996) suggested, "A proper inclusion of spirituality within the social and behavioral sciences will mean an eagerness to find it wherever it might appear, and this will mean bridging the boundaries between the domestic and the nondomestic" (p. 570). He further urged that "when we do look for transcendence within those vessels we call families, we should be uncompromisingly inclusive in our readiness to hear a full range of voices" (p. 570).

Another strategy we have found helpful is to differentiate between several different aspects of ideas about the sacred. There is a difference between the epistemological sources of ideas and the ideas themselves. Many ideas about the sacred are derived from spiritual or mystical epistemological sources, and these sources are matters of faith that cannot be subjected to the rational and observational tools of scholarly scrutiny. We have not tried to incorporate into scholarly inquiry the study of these sources of beliefs and knowledge. However, many of the ideas that are derived from spiritual or mystical sources are not fundamentally different from ideas that have been derived from observation or reason, and some of these ideas can and should be included in scholarly inquiry.

However, even though the tools of scholarly inquiry can deal with many of the ideas that are about and from sacred sources, there are some sacred matters that the rational and empirical tools of academia cannot deal with. For example, the scientific method does not have the tools to address questions about noumenological reality or the nature of the supernatural and heavenly. Therefore questions and answers to issues such as there are not candidates for integration. However, ideas that are phenomenological beliefs and the consequences of these beliefs can be dealt with using the rational and empirical tools of academia. Therefore ideas such as these can be integrated. This means it is important when trying to integrate the sacred with the scholarly to try to integrate only the parts of sacred matters that can be studied with the intellectual, observational, and linguistic tools that are accepted and recognized parts of scholarly inquiry.

We also found it useful to distinguish between abstract ideas that can be a part of abstract or general conceptual frameworks and theories and ideas that can be subjected to empirical observation. Abstract ideas that cannot be observed directly can be included in scholarly theories, and they can be evaluated, compared, and contrasted with reasoning and logic. But they cannot be dealt with directly using empirical methods. However, it is possible to deduce less general ideas and hypotheses; and as these deductions become more specific and concrete, they gradually come into the realm where empirical methods can be used to assess and evaluate them. And these differences are the same for dealing with both sacred and secular matters.

When we have less general and observable ideas, it is possible to then determine with empirical methods whether conditions and relationships that are predicted by the more abstract ideas actually exist. When the empirically expected relationships do not emerge, this provides information that can be used to examine the logic in deductions and whether some of the phenomenological conceptions about sacred and secular phenomena ought to be reexamined and/or modified. This process is also the same for the ideas derived from sacred sources and those derived from other methods, because they are all human understandings of what we think are realities rather than the realities themselves. Therefore all of the ideas in sacred theory are subject to modification as new data and analyses emerge. We hope that when changes about sacred ideas are suggested by empirical findings, we will not be as troubled and resistant as church leaders were when Galileo and others brought new ideas to the scene a few hundred years ago.

A growing number of scholars seem to be agreeing with the idea that we ought to work at the task of integrating sacred and scholarly ideas. For example, Mahoney, Rye et al. (2005) concluded that "it would seem important for social scientists to integrate religiously based beliefs and behaviors into models of how people interpret and come to terms with interpersonal violations" (p. 57). We hope we and others accomplish this in connection with a number of ideas that are currently viewed only as religious ideas. And in addition to just integrating these ideas, another of our goals has been to give some of them a major role in sacred theory, even though there will, of course, continue to be some sacred phenomena that cannot be a part of scientific inquiry.

One of the interesting aspects of our journeys is that this book, with its attempt to integrate ideas originating in the sacred parts of life with scholarly ideas and methods, is an example of a type of scholarship that would have been scorned and rejected a half century ago. We are curious about whether what we have created and the methods we have used will be accepted and appreciated or scorned and rejected. As with so many aspects of what we are trying to do in this book, we will need to wait a few years to learn such things.

Making Inferences From Data to Theory

In our quest to understand methods that have been helpful in theory building, we reviewed the work of a number of scholars who have contributed theories that have been widely appreciated to try to learn more about methods and strategies that were helpful to them in building theory from data. We examined and in some cases reexamined the contributions of Plato (1979), Smith (1776), Newton (Gleick, 2003), Marx and Engels (1848), Darwin (1859), Pavlov (1927), Freud (1927, 1965), Mead (1934), Erikson (1950, 1959, 1968), Rogers (1951), Bateson et al. (1956), and Bertalanffy (1968).

We found it interesting that the writings of these scholars focused primarily on their ideas and the data that helped them. They gave little attention to describing their methods of theory building. However, inferring from the little they did say, it appears all of them were aware of previously existing research data and theories in which there were inadequacies, complexities, inconsistencies, contradictions, or unanswered questions that were puzzling to them. These various situations piqued their intellectual curiosity, and motivated them to try to do something about these problems.

For a period of time, they were not sure what could be done to improve their problematic situation, and apparently this condition lasted for quite a while for many of them. During this time of "stewing," they seem to have wrestled with their various puzzling and confusing situations. Many of them tried a variety of ideas that were not successful, and most of the innovations that turned out to be helpful came slowly and gradually—sometimes in a cumulative way and with occasional "aha" moments.

We see a number of similarities between what we have experienced and the experiences of these other scholars. For example, as Darwin observed the unusual diversity on the Galapagos Islands, he said that he kept asking himself, over and over again, questions such as "What is going on here?"; "What makes sense of all of this?"; "How can all of this be?"; "What will help in understanding what I'm seeing?"; "What will explain all of this variation?"; "There have to be clues here we haven't put together in the right way. What are they?" (Darwin, 1859).

Darwin was observing plants and animals and thinking about the theories that existed in his time. We have been observing families and thinking about the theories of our time; and we have been asking essentially the same questions. As we have searched the ideas in existing theories, just as Darwin examined and reexamined many times the theories in his day, we found them helpful in providing understanding about some parts of what we are studying, but we also felt and continue to feel that there are some additional important things going on—more than are captured in the previously existing theories.

Some other examples are that Marx, Freud, and Pavlov all seemed to go through similar processes. During the period when they were searching for explanations, they turned to any type of data that looked like it would be helpful, and much of the research and data gathering was not very systematic or interpersonally replicable. For example, Freud's observations of clients such as little Hans were not quantified and analyzed with standardized instruments that demonstrated validity and reliability and sophisticated statistical tests. They were fairly unsystematic clinical observations. They also were subjective, and he continually compared them to his own personal experiences. Even Newton was not very systematic as he watched pendulums swing in his chapel and observed how feathers and apples fell (Gleick, 2003).

The point of these examples is that the process of creating general or widely applicable theories involves intellectual movement from other theories and from data to new theories. Further, scholars are influenced by a variety of different kinds of data; and much of the data they find useful are not all that sophisticated methodologically. We found the same pattern in that other theories and several different kinds of data from different sources helped us when we were searching for the general ideas that ought to be in sacred theory.

The literature on methods of theory building might lead a novice to believe theoretical ideas are created primarily from quantitative data in research publications. For example, the discussion in Chapter 1 of the Bengston et al. (2005) sourcebook is almost entirely about the role of quantitative data. This idea suggests that theories are created from the findings in tables, the findings in journal articles, or the many ways of listing, classifying, and categorizing described by Strauss and Corbin (1990). Our analysis of the theory building by earlier scholars and our own experience indicate that the coding, classifying, and categorizing strategies described by Strauss and Corbin are helpful when dealing with data, developing conceptual insights, and generating modest, less general, less abstract, and limited theoretical insights, but they are of limited value in generating general, abstract, broad, and inclusive theoretical ideas.

These views of our methods should not be interpreted as depreciating or a bias against quantitative data. We believe quantitative and qualitative data are both valuable and have a place in theory construction and revision, but they contribute different kinds of ideas and have different roles. We find qualitative data and relatively unsystematic and intuitive analyses and creativity of more value in the generating and describing stages in theory construction, and quantitative data of more value in the testing and revising of theories. This is illustrated by the qualitative narratives in Chapters 2–12 wherein the ideas in sacred theory are generated and described, and the quantitative analyses in Chapter 14 wherein we move into the testing, corroborating, and revising stages of scholarly inquiry.

We found that the strategies described by Chase (2005) as "narrative inquiry" were very helpful in generating abstract ideas (p. 669). These strategies involve an almost indescribably complex set of intellectual processes that are simultaneously working at assembly, analysis, integration, extrapolation, and creativity with a variety of ideas and data, as well as what Chase called lenses, approaches, and voices (pp. 656–667). We also found strategies such as theoretical sampling and sensitivity and elaboration analysis helpful in generating general ideas. As we worked at the generating process, we found it useful to simultaneously entertain (a) insights from previous research, (b) previous theorizing, (c) patterns in a variety of pieces of new data, (d) the more general ideas in our theorizing (if we were deducing) and the less general ideas in the theory (if we were trying to induce more general ideas), (e) ideas in sacred literature, and (f) a wide variety of inductive, deductive, analytic, interpretive, listening, dissecting, and creating strategies that are described in the literature about the methodology of theory building.

Some readers may wish we would identify the table or finding or interview quote that provided the specific basis for the generation of various ideas. Sometimes this is possible, and we do this for a few theoretical ideas that have low generality and are close to data. We wish we could discuss the origins all of our theoretical ideas in a way that wouldn't take volumes for each idea, but that is just not the way the generation of abstract and general theoretical ideas worked for us. They were generated in a series of gradual improvements and insights and occasional "aha" moments that in many situations were almost imperceptible at first and gradually became more clear; and they emerged from such a complex cluster of trends and patterns in data, from such a variety of studies and observations, and from so many other ideas that the generation process cannot be described in detail or as a step-by-step process. As those who have been through this process can attest, and those who haven't can't fully understand or appreciate, the best we can do is what has been done dozens of times in this volume by saying things like "the patterns in our data suggest . . ." or "the trends in our data indicate . . ." or "we gleaned ________ from our data and other ideas."

An Unanticipated Pattern

As we look back on our journeys during the generating stage in our theory building, we now see a pattern we didn't anticipate or see when we were in the middle of the process. We don't know if this pattern is the same for others who build theories, or if it will eventually become a part of theory-building methods, but it is systematic and intriguing, and it may be helpful to describe it.

The 25 less general principles were the first ideas that were generated in our theory-building efforts. These ideas were generated in a rather complex interaction of generalizing individualistic ideas in the sacred literature to family processes, reviewing the literature in family studies, and induction from data gleaned in our fairly specific observations and interviews.

The idea that is at an intermediate level of generality about the importance of a *loving style* of relating became clear after we had a cluster of the less general ideas in our minds and as we realized it was a more general idea that included many of the less general ideas. The next step in our theory building was the generation of the three more general propositions that are labeled 2, 3, and 4 in the Figure 1.1 on page 32. These ideas were relatively vague, unclear, and blurry at first, and they became clearer in an uneven way. For example, we wrote down some of our ideas about Proposition 4 first and then Proposition 2 and then Proposition 3. Then, after these three ideas were described in a way that was a little clearer, we were able to describe them more clearly and concisely. Subsequently, we developed the ideas that are associated with them, such as the model of family we've used and the widely shared goals in families that are described on pages 18–21.

After these ideas were clear and were described in our manuscript, we felt that these ideas were improving and expanding the theorizing in helpful ways, but we also had a nagging feeling that something else was needed. We didn't know if it was a fourth principle at the same level of generality as the three general principles, or if we ought to try to find a more general idea, but we had a muddled sense that the cluster of ideas was not as adequate as it ought to be. It wasn't complete or finished. There was something still missing, but we didn't know what it was, and we spent several months in this uncomfortable, wondering, and searching stage.

About this time the idea that became Proposition 1 and is the most general idea began to gradually appear. The term *sacred matters* was suggested as one of the possibilities for a title for the book, and although we were attracted to it as a book title, we did not see it as a valuable theoretical idea. We didn't do any more with this term or idea for several months. It was just an idea that was in the back of our minds as we were considering different titles for the book. During these months we didn't realize the potential this idea had as a general idea in the theory. It wasn't until a colleague suggested the idea in Proposition 1 that we realized this idea is more general than just an idea about family processes and was an excellent culminating explanation of why all of the other ideas in the theory fit together, provide valuable insights, and strike us as valid.

The interesting pattern in this sequence is that the less general ideas came first and the more general ideas were generated by moving from the least general ideas to the ideas that are slightly more general. Then the slightly more general ideas appeared next, and the most general idea was generated last. At each stage, the ideas were relatively fuzzy and unclear at first, but they became clearer as we worked with them and tried to write them down, and this helped us describe the rationale and basis for them. Before we experienced this pattern, we were open to the possibility that the most general ideas might come first in theory building, but we now suspect the pattern we experienced is probably the way many theories are created.

Methods With Different Aspects of Theories

There are several different components of theories (i.e., concepts, propositions, relationships between propositions, etc.). The process of improving and expanding a theory requires that each of these components or aspects of theory be addressed and developed, but some of the methods for doing so are unique.

Concepts Sprey (1990) argued that "theorizing about marriage and the family in all its manifestations essentially remains a linguistic endeavor" (p. 9). Therefore the most basic building blocks of theories are words or terms. These are called *concepts*, and when concepts are interdefined they create a *conceptual framework*.

There are two different kinds of definitions of concepts. *Rational definitions* are the type found in dictionaries. *Operational definitions* are provided by the tools that are used in research. Having both of these definitions is helpful, but it takes considerable time to create operational definitions, and it isn't very practical to even try to create them until the describing stage of theorizing is reasonably advanced.

We have provided rational definitions for many of the concepts in sacred theory, but we have not devoted much time and energy to the creation and testing of operational definitions. The result is that now that the theory is described, there is a need to create more operational definitions of at least the less general concepts. This is a chicken-and-egg situation in that innovations in either definitions or descriptions lead to progress, and progress in either area helps the other. The primary contributions in this book are to generate a conceptual framework and theory that is more general, integrated, and expanded than it has been before, and to rely on rational definitions in this process. We have chosen this approach because, with a few exceptions, such as with the concept of forgiveness, there are no well-developed operational definitions.

Some may wish we had made a different choice and spent more time providing operational definitions. However, if we had taken the time to create operational definitions of the concepts, it would have detracted from the theoretical generation and description we have been able to create, and we think the best contribution we can make is to emphasize the generation and description. We also hope and assume that future scholarship will increase the quality and number of operationalized concepts in the theory.

Another of the methods we used with concepts is to analyze and improve some of them. It took several pages of analysis of terms such as religion, spiritual, and sacred to conclude that the term *sacred* is more helpful in theorizing because it is more general and less tied to cultural, historical, and denominational factors. By comparison, we also concluded that the term *religion* is more helpful in conducting empirical research because it is less general and more easily operationalized (Marks & Dollahite, in press).

Another method we used with regard to the conceptual framework was an effort to identify and describe different levels of generality. This involved identifying which concepts are more and less general and which of the more general concepts include which less general concepts.

Propositions The payoff parts of theories are the truth assertions that describe the ways the concepts are interrelated. There are a number of different kinds of truth assertions in social science theories. Some of them deal with ways concepts or patterns change and evolve over time, ways they are different in different populations, and ways they are distributed in populations. Others that are important in some theories are when scholars use the concepts to analyze patterns and processes with individuals or populations. The kind we find the most useful are those that describe present-to-future relationships that are useful in understanding, explaining, and intervening. Understanding and explaining are intermediate and instrumental goals, whereas intervening is a more ultimate end because it can directly help family life professionals and families themselves.

There is considerable consensus in the way propositions are different from hypotheses. The term *proposition* is usually used to refer to relatively general and abstract truths. Many of the propositions in theories are so general and abstract that they cannot be observed or measured in a direct sense. The term *hypothesis* is usually used to refer to deductions that are made from propositions that are sufficiently specific and concrete that they can be empirically tested by finding corroborating or refuting evidence. Some scholars, however, use the term hypothesis as synonymous with proposition. Therefore care should be taken to determine how these terms are used.

In our theory building, our goals have been to generate and describe propositions rather than test them, so we spent most of our time trying to find ways to state propositions clearly and to find ways propositions are related to each other, whereas we have little to say about hypotheses. There is, therefore, considerable analysis and evaluation in this book, and more inferring than deducing, because we've made inferences from observations in our families, from the lives of relatives, friends, and others we have known, and from interviews and questionnaire data.

The term *principle* is also used to refer to some propositions. But becausee the word *principle* is also used in several other ways, scholars need to determine how it is used in each context. One definition of *principle* is a law or truth that is sufficiently fundamental, primary, or general that other truth assertions can be derived from it. When the term is used this way, it is virtually synonymous with *proposition*.

Another way the term principle is widely used is as a guide for moral conduct. When used this way, it is referring to moral principles. These are abstract or general statements about ethics or morality that can be used as the basis for making decisions about specific behaviors. Moral principles can be applied in a wide range of situations to help people determine how they ought to act or not act in various situations, but this way of defining principle is different from the way it is used in most scholarly inquiry and different from the way we use it herein.

The most helpful principles are those that are *present-to-future* statements that have utility because they describe ways present behaviors or processes are related to the probability of future events. The present aspects of the principles are aspects wherein choices and decisions can be made about behavior or processes. Therefore the "present" parts of principles are the parts people can control with their agency. People have much less control over the "future" phenomena than the "present" phenomena. For example, one of the principles in sacred theory is the idea that the amount of kindness and unkindness in families influences the probability that families will find successes and failures. People have considerable control over whether they are kind or unkind to each other. Therefore this part of the principle can be manipulated, changed, or controlled by family members. And what family members do in the present makes a difference in whether they will find successes or failure in the future, which cannot be as easily or directly controlled.

Another way of thinking about these aspects of principles is that family members can have considerable control over the "if" part of principles (behavior), but they have little ability to control the "then" part of principles. Said another way, family members have considerable control over their *behavior*, but they have little control, and sometimes no control, over the *consequences of their behavior*.

Principle-based thinking is economical because a few principles can have implications for a large number of specific behaviors. Therefore principles are a valuable, efficient, and helpful type of idea to employ in theories.

The most helpful principles are also fairly independent of culture, time, or social situations. They operate in a wide variety of societies, cultures, and circumstances. For example, a principle that says being loving in families helps them be successful would be true for old and young, Europeans and Asians, and males and females.

Principles can be used, but they are not used in the same way we use a supply of pencils. Using them is not a process of using something physically, as when we use an electrical appliance or an automobile. Principles are ideas that identify the probable consequences of various actions or situations, and it is the knowledge that the principles provide that is used in helping us make decisions about how to act in specific situations.

The value of principles can be seen by examining some of the findings in the research by Gottman (1994a, 1994b) and his colleagues. They asked questions about the way *present-is-related-to-future* to try to better understand how marital processes are related both to future marital success and, conversely, to divorce. They found that they were able to predict the probability of divorce fairly well, and that when couples have a 5:1 ratio of positive to negative interactions their chances of success are high. By contrast, when the ratio is lower than this the probability of divorce increases substantially. They also found that the presence of several negative patterns, such as criticism, contempt, defensiveness, and stonewalling (which they called the "Four Horsemen of the Apocalypse" [Gottman, 1994b, p. 72]), were strongly related to success and divorce.

These findings are informative, but the greatest value of the Gottman research is that they then looked for more general and abstract ideas that could be inferred from these more specific findings. After a series of studies, they eventually theorized that the basic marital nutrients they saw in a variety of styles of marriage and situations were two general, abstract, and influential factors they called *love* and *respect* (Gottman, 1994b, pp. 61–62).

These two ideas are good examples of principles because they are abstract, inclusive, and general, and they deal with present-to-future relationships. They cannot be directly observed in empirical data, but when a wide variety of data are examined, they provide inferences and have a set of characteristics that are summarized by these more general concepts. These two principles are also excellent examples of valuable principles because they deal with aspects of family that can be changed, aspects wherein individuals can learn how to alter the ways they behave, with the awareness that the behaviors that are examples of these two theoretical concepts are powerfully related to marital success and, inversely, to divorce. It is no accident or coincidence that these two principles have a central role in sacred theory. One of the reasons they have a central role is because of the persuasive scholarship of Gottman and his colleagues.

Relationships There are several aspects that relationship variables have with each other that are important in theory building, and different methods are used with each of them. Six of these are (a) existence, (b) direction, (c) shape, which includes the idea of thresholds, (d) contingencies or contextual factors, (e) temporal differences, and (f) strength or amount of influence.

Existence refers to whether relationships exist or nor, and this is the most elementary of the aspects. This has been a major concern in this book because our first goals were to identify or create propositions and principles that identify the existence of relationships. We focused on present-to-future relationships, and gleaned ideas from interviews and discussions, observations, historical analyses, previous research and theory, and other literature.

The direction of relationships becomes important after scholars believe there is a basis for asserting existence. Relationships are positive when the variation in the variables is in the same direction, and negative when increases or decreases in one variable are accompanied by changes in the opposite direction in the other variable.

Most scholars pay considerable attention to the existence and direction of relationships, and we are no different. As we moved through the generation and description stages of building sacred theory, these two aspects of relationships were always important, and all of the principles in sacred theory describe the direction in the relationships.

Some relationships are linear, and others are curvilinear. When relationships are linear, changes in one variable are accompanied by the same amount of variation in the other variable throughout their range of possible variation. When relationships are curvilinear, changes in one variable are accompanied by differing amounts of variation in the other one in different parts of its range of variation.

Some relationships also have thresholds. A threshold is when there is a point in the variation in one variable where the variation in the other variable makes a radical change. We tried to find a basis for assertions about shape and thresholds, but found little basis for speculating about these aspects of the relationships. However, these aspects are important, and future scholarship that focuses on the ideas in sacred theory will undoubtedly pay increasing attention to them.

There is one idea in sacred theory about which we have a little bit of evidence of curvilinearity and thresholds, and it will be helpful when future scholarship learns more about it. It deals with the idea on pages 135–138 about being wise as family members try to cope with their negative emotions. The theorizing of Bowen (1976) about what he called differentiation led us to believe that as the intensity of negative emotions increases, there is a threshold in the relationship it has with other variables, such as the amount of unkindness. We don't think that as the intensity of negative emotion increases, there is a linear decrease in self-control or increase in other effects such as unkindness. What we think occurs is that people reach a certain point as the intensity increases where they "lose their cool," where their ability to control themselves decreases rather dramatically. At this threshold, control decreases substantially and other effects such as selfishness and unkindness tend to increase dramatically. As scholars devise ways to quantify the intensity of emotions and the amount of control and unkindness, they will be able to determine if this speculation is true. If it is true, it has important implications for helping families.

Another aspect of relationships that is important has to do with contingencies. These are situational factors or contextual factors that make a difference in various aspects of relationships. For example, some contextual factors make a difference in the existence of relationships, and others change the shape or direction. We have paid little attention to the role of contingencies, but future research will probably provide new insights about how they make a difference.

This aspect of relationships is illustrated with the relationship described on page 176 between caring about ancestors and posterity and family outcomes. Based on the theorizing by Erikson (1950, 1959) about the role of generativity, it is likely that this relationship doesn't even exist or is a minor issue until family members reach adulthood. Erikson suggested that it is when people move into their adult stage of life that generativity becomes important. We don't know of any research that undergirds this idea, but it is likely that Erikson was right, and future research will probably provide more information about this aspect of this relationship.

Some family processes have more influence than others, and some have more influence on the probability of some outcomes than others. Research can help us learn which factors have substantial influence and which have less. The operational way of learning about these differences is to find differences in the strength of relationships.

These differences are important in the therapeutic parts of the field because it may be that certain family processes have more influence in helping people cope with some problems than others. It is important in educational parts of the field because some family processes may help certain aspects of families, such as the ease of transitions, and other processes may be strongly related to the probability of children cultivating their social competence.

There is little evidence about differences in the amount of influence in the ideas in sacred theory, and therefore we have said little about this aspect of relationships. There is one area, however, that illustrates that this is an important aspect, that is, the study by Lee et al. (1997) that found that unkindness in families accounted for considerably more of the variance in family success than did kindness. If future research provides additional evidence that this is true, it is an important finding that has significant implications, and it deserves attention in future scholarship.

One of the important parts of theories is accumulating evidence for and against the assertions in the propositions. Some of the ideas in sacred theory have more evidence than others. For example, there is a growing and considerable amount of evidence that forgiveness and prayer are helpful, but little evidence about other ideas such as the value of mercy and compassion.

In our theorizing, we have turned to four sources for evidence. They are (a) interviews, (b) observations of families by us and colleagues, (c) the historical method, and (d) data from the Flourishing Families Project at BYU, and we used slightly different methods with these different sources. There is still relatively little evidence for most of the ideas in the theory, but we hope future research will provide additional evidence.

METHODS IN THE DESCRIBING STAGE

In the early months of 2009, we were still in what Nisbet (1976) called the *discovery* stage and we have called the generating stage. Gradually, however, the pace of finding ways to improve and expand the theorizing slowed, and we found ourselves being more concerned with finding ways to describe the theory. This wasn't, however, an abrupt shift, because our efforts at trying to describe the theory also led to some additional improvements.

We did not expect the describing part of theory building to be very complicated or involved. However, it turned out to be such a complex and demanding process that we now think of it as a separate part of theory building, one that has a number of methods that are different from the methods used in the other parts of theory building.

As we began the describing stage, we tried several approaches that did not turn out to be very effective. We tried writing the theory as a novel, but the technical parts of the ideas interfered with the story, and the story interfered with the ideas, so this strategy stalled. We also tried using dialogues, similar to the strategy used by Plato in *The Republic*, but that didn't work very well either. By the middle of 2009, we settled on the approach we've used in this book. Initially, we had the philosophical and methodological issues in the first part of the book because that is the usual pattern in research reports, but eventually we decided to describe the theory first and the assumptions and methods later.

As we worked at describing the theory, we reviewed again and again many of the transcripts and notes from interviews we had previously conducted for several research projects. They helped clarify and expand our thinking; they also helped us decide which concepts and ideas ought to be included in this first attempt to describe sacred theory, and they provided examples of many of the ideas.

There were many challenges as we tried to find ways of describing the theory that would be effective. For example, how many narratives and stories should be included? They are the parts of our qualitative data that provide the basis for the ideas, and the more that are included, the greater the evidence for the ideas, but too many would detract from the presentation.

Another issue was deciding how many of the "less general" principles to include. We eventually settled on the 25 that are in this book, but we could have included another 25 that also seem valuable. Clearly we have only scratched the surface in studying aspects of the sacred that seem relevant for families. As we evaluated this issue and talked with several colleagues about it, we suspect we still may have more than is wise because the 25 are almost an overwhelming array. Time will tell how quickly it will be helpful to add additional ideas to sacred theory.

Another challenge was that it was sometimes difficult to find concepts that would communicate the ideas we wanted to communicate without creating unanticipated problems. An example of this was the series of changes we made in assembling the list of widely shared goals in families. The model of family that is described at http://familycenter:byu.edu/Assumptions.dhtml provided a basis for identifying these goals, but we had difficulty finding a way to conceptualize what this list is. We tried to use the term *needs*, but it has so many complications that it led to the demise of need theory in psychology. We also tried just using the term *goals*, but this is so unspecific and relativistic that anyone's goals can be included. We also tried the term essential processes, but we eventually concluded this would lead to endless debates about what is actually essential. Eventually, we settled on "widely shared" goals that are based on the model of family described in the Internet publication, and we hope this turns out to be helpful rather than create additional unanticipated problems.

We had the same problem in finding a name for the theory. It is helpful to have short and descriptive names for general theories—such as systems theory, exchange theory, and so forth. We were uncomfortable with the name sacred theory because the word *sacred* initially sounded like an adjective, and the theory is not a theory that is sacred. It is a theory about sacred matters, but sacred matters theory would be an awkward name. We also had to decide whether the theory was a religious theory or a theory about the spiritual. We tried to use several acronyms such as SIF theory as a shorthand name for "the sacred in families." We eventually returned to the name sacred theory because the more we used it the more we realized that *sacred* in this context is a noun rather than an adjective. The point of these examples is to illustrate that the describing stage in theory construction is not a part that can be ignored or lightly passed over. It creates the identity of the theory, and is a naming and branding process. These processes are important, but they are sometimes challenging and complicated.

We think the ideas that are described in this volume will be helpful, but they are not the only important ideas about the sacred in families. There are several ideas that we think are very important that we have not been able to clarify and describe at this stage of building sacred theory. We suspect that some of these will be added later. St. Paul used the analogy of seeing through the glass darkly (I Corinthians 13:12), and this is not a bad description of where we are with several ideas.

Also, after the theorizing described in this volume was completed, scores of transcripts from the Marks interviews were examined again for comments that would provide additional insights and evidence about the ideas in sacred theory. This led to a few new examples that illustrate the ideas in the theory. We then reexamined the manuscript and the examples that are included to try to find a balance by not having so many examples that they detract but having enough to effectively illustrate at least some of the sources of the ideas.

BROADER THAN SCIENCE

The term *family science* was coined a few decades ago, and many view it as the best way to describe the study of family. However, our experiences with sacred theory have led us to believe "science" is not the best way to describe what the study of families is or ought to be. The scholarly study of families is much broader than just science. One reason we believe this is illustrated in Nisbet's (1976) analysis of the limited role of the scientific method in generating theoretical insights. He reflected that as he was considering the sources of modern sociology, he realized that "none of the great themes which have provided continuing challenge and also theoretical foundation for sociologists during the last century was ever reached through anything resembling what we are today fond of identifying as 'scientific method'" (p. 3). By scientific method, Nisbet meant "the kind of method, replete with appeals to statistical analysis, problem, design, hypothesis, verification, replication, and theory construction, that we find describe in our textbooks and course on methodology" (p. 3).

We appreciate the role of the science in generating some theoretical ideas that are inferred from empirical observations, and we agree with Merton (1957) that the theoretical and empirical parts of this process do, and should, reciprocally inform and help each other. Also, we don't think either the theoretical or empirical part is more superior, ultimate, or original than the other. Neither is adequate alone. Systematically speaking, they are like the heart and lungs in our bodies. Both are essential and useful, and they are dependent on each other.

The scientific method is also helpful in seeing how well some aspects of ideas correspond to empirically observable phenomena, but philosophical inquiry and other sources of information and forms of analysis are also helpful in generating ideas and in examining the truth, history, nature, and implications of ideas. This suggests that science is helpful, but it is just one part of an array of methods that are useful in the scholarly study of families.

The medical field is widely referred to as an "art and science," and the study of family is less purely or exclusively scientific than medicine. Therefore we suggest that the study of family also ought to be considerably more pluralistic than the term family science asserts. We prefer terms such as *family scholarship*, the *scholarly study of family*, or *family studies*. These changes will help the field benefit from having a broader array of methodologies of theory construction, testing, evaluation, modification, and application, rather than just relying on science as the ultimate, best, or only way to formulate beliefs and obtain knowledge.

Our experience suggests that the scientific method is the most useful in the testing and revising stages of scholarship, but of less value in the generating, describing, and applying stages. A number of other forms of seeking knowledge are relatively more valuable in these other stages, including philosophy, history, theology, intuition, and arts (such as classical literature and drama). In studying families, we also have found a number of these other methods useful in the generation stage of theory building. These include fairly unsystematic personal, family, educational, and clinical experiences and observations.

One of the implications of these changes is that the theories in family studies ought to be viewed as *scholarly theories* rather than *scientific theories*. This is because the ideas in them are, and ought to be, derived from and tested by a wider range of sources and methods than just scientific methods. Science can help us deal effectively with many things, but it is restricted to the parts of reality that can be accessed with scientific tools, and there is a great deal about family that cannot be observed with the strategies and tools that are available in the scientific method. Science is not an effective tool for dealing with the more meaningful, profound, significant, weighty, teleological, spiritual, valued, important, and ultimate aspects of life in general, or family life in particular. Many have turned to science as a tool to try to deal with these more abstract aspects of life, and in doing so, they have expected more from science than it is able to deliver because it is not a strategy for answering life's more meaningful, general, and abstract issues and questions.

Scientific observations also demand interpersonal replication. However, much of what occurs in family life is so unique, subtle, multifaceted, spontaneous, creative, and simultaneously involved with only partially conscious perceptions and memories of the past, and anticipations, hopes, dreams, and aspirations for the future that, for all practical purposes, scientific observation is quite limited in what it can capture and study.

Another idea that is helpful in understanding how we ought to think about the role science should have in the study of family is to imagine an illustrative but hypothetical situation. What if we had to choose between the ideas that can be created and refined with scientific methods and those that can be created with philosophy, theology, personal experiences, and the arts? In this situation, what would most of us choose? It probably would not be science.

The bottom line is that the systematically acquired empirical findings from the scientific method are comparatively meager, superficial, less defensible, and less relevant. Some of the reasons for this are that scientific methods such as questionnaires, interview schedules, and observation schedules tend to deal primarily with short-term, observable, and mostly public aspects of family processes. Most of the really important parts of family life tend to be long-term, difficult to observe, fairly subtle, private, nuanced, and extremely complex processes; and the tools we have for social "science" provide little access to these parts of life.

Knapp (2002, 2006) called for more authorizing and more critical and dialogical theorizing—a plea for increases in the attention given to several innovative ways of reasoning that have not been parts of scientific methodology. Another way of expanding the methods in studying families is to increase the role of several aspects of philosophy—such as expanding the use of logic and the discussion of assumptions and applications of theories; and we have strived to use these methods in our theory building.

Philosophy is many different things to different people, but whatever it is, scholars cannot study family without using it. Knowingly or unknowingly, wisely or unwisely, we employ the ideas and tools provided by and honed by philosophical inquiry. Those who venture into the study of family and choose to minimize or pay little attention to the ways philosophical inquiry informs what they do will study less effectively than those who choose to use philosophy to help in the process.

Philosophy isn't a body of knowledge as much as it is a method of analysis, criticism, synthesis, and integration. It is problem seeking and solving, question asking and investigating. It is more of an enterprise or activity than a subject matter, and these processes can be helpful in studying family. For example, if family scholars had been using these powers of reason more, it would not have been necessary in the first part of this chapter to chide family scholars for relying so exclusively on the scientific method as a strategy for seeking answers and insights that the scientific method is not designed to provide.

Logic is one of the branches of philosophy that is helpful in scholarly study. It helps us learn how to reason effectively and defensibly. It helps us understand the differences between induction and deduction and when and why to use these processes. One specific way greater attention to the study of logic would help the study of family is in the use of statistics. Inferential statistics are designed to help scholars better understand the probability of making errors in generalizing findings from a sample to a population. However, statistical analyses are not designed to provide a basis for making inferences from data about the validity of theoretical ideas. Whenever those who study family shift back and forth intellectually between their data and the abstract ideas in their theories, they are using logic and reasoning, induction and deduction—some of the most fundamental tools in philosophy—and there are many instances in the literature in which these differences in logical processes are confused and inappropriately used.

Philosophy is also valuable in helping scholars better understand the fundamental assumptions that underlie their work. Had family scholars in the twentieth century, the authors included, paid more attention to the philosophical issues in theory building, testing, and application, it is likely that their work would have been more effective.

A side note to this aspect of methods is that graduate study in the family field includes substantial study in the research methods used in empirical research and in statistical methods used in the analysis of data, and little emphasis on the methods used in philosophical inquiry and theorizing. We believe this imbalance is ill advised and inappropriate and hinders the growth of the field. If more attention were given to the methods of philosophical and theoretical inquiry, we wonder how much more effective the family field would have been in its first century of existence, and we hope there is a shift in emphasis in the next several decades.

SUMMARY

This chapter described the methods we have used in trying to improve and expand the theorizing about the sacred in families. We used interviews, questionnaires, observations, and the historical method to acquire new data. We also searched for ideas about the role of the sacred by examining the scholarly literature in family studies, religious literature, and artistic literature such as poetry, novels, and drama.

This chapter also described the methods that we used in trying to improve different aspects of the theory. This includes a discussion of the methods we used to include more ideas about and from the sacred in family studies—methods of defining, clarifying, and organizing concepts and generating and evaluating propositions—as well as of methods of improving insights about aspects of relationships such as existence, direction, shape, contingencies, amount of influence, and amount of evidence.

We relied on the scientific method in some aspects of our theory building, but we also used a number of other ways of gaining knowledge, including philosophical and historical analyses. We also used literature and believe it should be used much more in the field, and therefore that the scholarly study of the family should be much broader than just science. Terms such as family studies are more broad and inclusive and are better descriptors of what we have done and what we think ought to be done in the field.

The methods we used make sacred theory something of a *grounded theory* (Glaser & Strauss, 1967), but it is also much more than just grounded theory. Grounded theory is built from empirical observations, and sacred theory is also *gleaned theory* because many of the ideas have been gleaned from sacred literature. It is also *reasoned theory* because the ideas result from complex ways of analyzing the previous research and literature and thinking about how various ideas are similar to and different from each other, inclusive and included, and more and less abstract and general.

References

Abbott, D. A., Berry, M., & Meredith, W. H. (1990). Religious belief and practice: A potential asset in helping families. *Family Relations*, *39*, 443–448.

Aldous, J. (1996). *Family careers: Rethinking the developmental perspective*. Thousand Oaks, CA: Sage.

Allen, K. R. (2000). A conscious and inclusive family studies. *Journal of Marriage and Family*, *62*, 4–17.

Allport, G. W. (1950). *The individual and his religion: A psychological interpretation*. New York, NY: Macmillan.

Allport, G. W., & Ross, J. M. (1967). Personal religious orientation and prejudice. *Journal of Personality and Social Psychology*, *5*, 432–443.

Allred, G. H. (1981). *On the level: The self, family society*. Provo, UT: Brigham Young University Press.

Al-Mabuk, R. H., & Downs, W. R. (1996). Forgiveness therapy with parents of adolescent suicide victims. *Journal of Family Psychotherapy*, *7*, 21–39.

Al-Mabuk, R. H., Enright, R. D., & Cardis, P. A. (1995). Forgiveness education with parentally love-deprived late adolescents. *Journal of Moral Education*, *24*, 427–444.

Amato, P. R., Booth, A., Johnson, D. R., & Rogers, S. J. (2007). *Alone together: How marriage in America is changing*. Cambridge, MA: Harvard University Press.

Anderson, E. (1999). *Code of the street: Decency, violence, and the moral life of the inner city*. New York, NY: Norton.

Arcus, M. E., Schvaneveldt, J. D., & Moss, J. (1993). *Handbook of family life education*. Newbury Park, CA: Sage.

Arterburn, S., & Felton, J. (1991). *Toxic faith*. Colorado Springs, Co: WaterBrook Press.

Bach, G. R., & Wyden, P. (1968). *The intimate enemy*. New York, NY: Avon Books.

Back, K. W. (1972). *Beyond words: The story of sensitivity training and the encounter movement*. New York, NY: Russell Sage Foundation.

Baden, A.D., & Howe, G. W. (1992). Mother's attributions and expectancies regarding their conduct-disordered children. *Journal of Abnormal Child Psychology*, *20*, 467–485.

Baefsky, P. M., & Berger, S. E. (1974). Self-sacrifice, cooperation, and aggression in women of varying sex-role orientation. *Personality and Social Psychology Bulletin*, *1*, 296–298.

Bahr, H. M., & Bahr, K. S. (2001). Families and self-sacrifice: Alternative models and meanings for family theory. *Social Forces*, *79*, 1231–1258.

Bahr, H. M., & Bahr, K. S. (2009). *Toward more family-centered family sciences*. New York, NY: Lexington Books.

Bailey, E. (1998). Sacred. In W. Swatos Jr. (Ed.), *Encyclopedia of religion and society* (pp. 443–444). Walnut Creek, CA: AltaMira Press.

Baker, T. R., Burr, W. R., & Yorgason, B. G. (1980). *A marital strengthening program for Latter-day Saints*. Provo, UT: Brigham Young University Family Living Center.

Baker, E. H., Sanchez, L. A., Nock, S. L., & Wright, J. D. (2009). Covenant marriage and the sanctification of gendered marital roles. *Journal of Family Issues*, *30*, 147–178.

Barber, B. K., Stolz, H. E., & Olen, J. A. (2005). Parental support, psychological control, and beavioral control: Assessing relevance across time, method, and culture. *Monographs of the Society for Research in Child Development*, *70*(4), 19.

Barbour, I. G. (2000). *When science meets religion: Enemies, strangers, or partners?* New York, NY: HarperCollins.

Bargh, J. A., Gollwitzer, P. M., Lee-Chai, A., Barndollar, K., & Trotschel, R. (2001). The automated will: Nonconscious activation and pursuit of behavioral goals. *Journal of Personality and Social Psychology*, *81*, 1014–1027.

Barry, J. W., Worthington, E. L., Parrott, L., O'Connor, L. E., & Wade, N. G. (2001). Dispositional forgiveness: Development and construct validity of the Transgression Narrative Test of Forgiveness (TNTF). *Personality and Social Psychology Bulletin, 27*, 1277–1290.

Bass, E., & Davis, L. (1994). *The courage to heal: A guide for women survivors of child sexual abuse* (3rd ed.). New York, NY: Harper and Row.

Bateson, G., Jackson, D. D., Haley, J., & Weakland, J. (1956). Toward a theory of schizophrenia. *Behavioral Science, 1*, 251–264.

Battle, C. L., & Miller, I. W. (2005). Families and forgiveness. In E. L. Worthington (Ed.), *Handbook of forgiveness* (pp. 227–243). New York, NY: Routledge.

Baucom, D. H. (2001). Religion and science of relationships: Is a happy marriage possible? *Journal of Family Psychology, 15*, 652–656.

Bauman, Z. (1993). *Postmodern ethics*. Oxford, UK: Blackwell.

Baumeister, R. F., Finkenauer, C., & Vohs, K. D. (2001). Bad is stronger than good. *Review of General Psychology, 5*, 323–370.

Beach, S. R. H., Fincham, F. D., & Stanley, S. M. (2007). Contextualizing the study of marital transformation: Points of convergence. *Journal of Marriage & Family, 26*, 315–319.

Beach, S. R. H., Fincham, F. D., Hurt, T. R., McNair, L. M., & Stanley, S. M. (2008). Prayer and marital intervention: A conceptual framework. *Journal of Social & Clinical Psychology, 27*, 641–699.

Beck, A. T. (1975). Cognitive therapy and the emotional disorders. New York, NY: International Universities Press Inc.

Beck, L. A., & Clark, M. S. (2010). What constitutes a healthy communal marriage and why relationship stage matters. *Journal of Family Theory and Review, 2*, 299–315.

Bellah, R. N., Madsen, R., Sullivan, W. M., Swidler, A., & Tipton, S. M. (1985). *Habits of the heart: Individualism and commitment in American life*. Berkeley: University of California Press.

Bengtson, V. L., Acock, A. C., Allen, K. R., Dilworth-Anderson, P., & Klein, D. M. (Eds.). (2005). *Sourcebook of family theory & research*. Thousand Oaks, CA: Sage.

Bengtson, V. L., & Allen, K. R. (1993). The life course perspective applied to families over time. In P. G. Boss, W. J. Doherty, R. LaRossa, W. R. Schumm, & S. K. Steinmetz (Eds.), *Sourcebook of family theories and methods: A contextual approach* (pp. 469–99). New York, NY: Plenum Press.

Benson, H. (1996). *Timeless healing: The power and biology of belief*. New York, NY: Scribner.

Berger, P. L. (1967). *The sacred canopy: Elements of a sociological theory of religion*. Garden City, NY: Doubleday.

Bergin, A. E. (1980). Psychotherapy and religious values. *Journal of Consulting & Clinical Psychology, 48*, 75–105.

Berkowitz, L. (1973). The case for bottling up rage. *Psychology Today, 7*, 24–31.

Bernard, J. (1973). My four revolutions: An autobiographical history of the ASA. *The American Journal of Sociology, 78*, 773–791.

Berscheid, E. (1985). Interpersonal attraction. In G. Lindzey & E. Aronson (Eds.), *Handbook of social psychology* (Vol. 2, pp. 267–286). New York, NY: Taylor & Francis.

Berscheid, E., & Hatfield, E. (1978). *Interpersonal attraction*. Reading, MA: Addison-Wesley.

Bertalanffy, L. V. (1968). *General system theory: Foundation, Development, Application*. New York, NY: Braziller.

Blalock, H. M. (1969). *Theory construction: From verbal to mathematical formulations*. Englewood Cliffs, NJ: Prentice-Hall.

Blalock, H. M. (1971). *Causal models in the social sciences*. Chicago, IL: Aldine-Atherton.

Blau, P. M. (1964). *Exchange and power in social life*. New York, NY: Wiley.

BLS: Bureau of Labor Statistics, Bureau, U. S. C. (2003). Current population report.

Blumer, H. G. (1938). Social psychology. In E. P. Schmidt (Ed.), *Man and society* (pp. 144–198). New York, NY: Prentice-Hall.
Blumer, H. G. (1969). *Symbolic interactionism: Perspective and method*. Englewood Cliffs, NJ: Prentice Hall.
Boss, P. G. (1999). *Ambiguous loss: Learning to live with unresolved grief*. Cambridge, MA: Harvard University Press.
Boss, P. G. (2002). *Family stress management: A contextual approach*. Thousand Oaks, CA: Sage.
Boss, P. G. (2006). *Loss, trauma, and resilience: Therapeutic work with ambiguous loss*. New York: Norton.
Boss, P. G., Doherty, W. J., LaRossa, R., Schumm, W. R., & Steinmetz, S. K. (Eds.). (1993). *Sourcebook of family theories and methods: A contextual approach*. New York, NY: Plenum Press.
Bossard, J. H. S., & Boll, E. S. (1950). *Ritual in family living*. Philadelphia: University of Pennsylvania Press.
Böszörményi-Nagy, I. (1987). *Foundations of contextual therapy*. New York, NY: Brunner/Mazel.
Böszörményi-Nagy, I., & Krasner, B. R. (1986). *Between give and take: A clinical guide to contextual therapy*. New York, NY: Brunner/Mazel.
Böszörményi-Nagy, I., & Spark, G. M. (1973). *Invisible loyalties: Reciprocity in intergenerational family therapy*. Hagerstown, MD: Harper and Row.
Bott, E. (1957). *Family and social network*. London, UK: Tavistock.
Boulding, K. E. (1973). *The economy of love and fear*. Belmont, CA: Wadsworth.
Bowen, C., Madill, A., & Stratton, P. (2002). Parental accounts of blaming within the family: A dialectical model for understanding blame in systematic therapy. *Journal of Marital & Family Therapy*, *28*, 129–144.
Bowen, C., Stratton, P., & Madill, A. (2005). Psychological functioning in families that blame: from blaming events to theory integration. *Journal of Family Therapy*, *27*, 309–329.
Bowen, M. (1976). Theory in the practice of psychotherapy. In P. Guerin (Ed.), *Family therapy* (pp. 42–90). New York, NY: Gardner.
Bowen, M. (1978). *Family therapy in clinical practice*. New York, NY: Aronson.
Bowker, J. (2000). *The concise Oxford dictionary of world religions*. Oxford, UK: Oxford University Press.
Boyce, W. T., Jensen, E. W., James, S. A., & Peacock, J. L. (1983). The family routines inventory: Theoretical origins. *Social Science Medicine*, *17*, 193–200.
Bradbury, T. N., & Fincham, F. D. (1991). A contextual model for advancing the study. In G. J. O. Fletcher & F. D. Fincham (Eds.), *Cognition in close relationships* (pp. 127–147). Hillsdale, NJ: Erlbaum.
Braithwaite, R. B. (1953). *Scientific explanation: A study of the function of theory, probability and law in science*. London, UK: Cambridge University Press.
Breunlin, D. C. (1988). Oscillation theory and family development. In C. J. Falicov (Ed.), *Family transitions: Continuity and change over the life cycle* (pp. 133–154). New York, NY: Guilford Press.
Broderick, C. B. (Ed.). (1971). *A decade of family research and action, 1960–1969*. Minneapolis, MN: National Council on Family Relations.
Broderick, C. B. (1993). *Understanding family process: Basics of family systems theory*. Newbury Park, CA: Sage Publications.
Bronfenbrenner, U. (1979). *The ecology of human development: Experiments by nature and design*. Cambridge, MA: Harvard University Press.

Bronfenbrenner, U., & Morris, P. A. (2006). The bioecological model of human development. In W. Damon & R. M. Lerner (Eds.), *Handbook of child psychology: Theoretical models of human development* (6th ed., Vol. 1, pp. 793–828). New York, NY: Wiley.

Buckley, W. F. (1967). *Sociology and modern systems theory*. Englewood Cliffs, NJ: Prentice-Hall.

Burchard, G. A., Yarhouse, M. A., Kilian, M. K., Worthington, E. L., Berry, J. W., & Canter, D. E. (2003). A study of two marital enrichment programs and couples' quality of life. *Journal of Psychology and Theology*, *31*, 240–252.

Burns, D. D. (1989). *The feeling good handbook*. New York, NY: William Morrow & Co.

Burr, R. J. (2000a). *The life story of Steven Lynn Burr, 1961–1984*. Provo, UT: Wesley and Ruth Burr Family Organization.

Burr, R. J. (2000b). *Our Darton ancestors*. Lehi, UT: Wesley and Ruth Burr Family Organization.

Burr, R. J. (2002). *Family histories of the ancestors of Klin and Nila Darton*. Lehi, UT: Wesley and Ruth Burr Family Organization.

Burr, R. J., & Burr, W. R. (2009). *The journeys of Ruth and Wesley Burr*. Lehi, UT: Wesley and Ruth Burr Family Organization.

Burr, W. R. (1973). *Theory construction and the sociology of the family*. New York, NY: Wiley-Interscience.

Burr, W. R. (1976). *Successful marriage: A principles approach*. Homewood, IL: Dorsey Press.

Burr, W. R. (2006). *A history of the Bryans from Erda*. West Jordan, UT: Wesley and Ruth Burr Family Organization.

Burr, W. R., & Beutler, I. F. (1995). *Toward more pragmatic family science theories: Part III: Loving as an example*. Paper presented at the Theory and Methods Workshop, NCFR, Portland, OR.

Burr, W. R., & Burgess, M. (1974). Notes and comments: On the indepdendence of tensions and satisfactions in marriage. *Journal of Marriage and Family*, *36*, 236–237.

Burr, W. R., & Burr, R. J. (1995). *A history of the Burr pioneers*. Provo, UT: Charles and Sarah Burr Family Organization.

Burr, W. R., & Christensen, C. (1992). Undesirable side effects of enhancing self-esteem. *Family Relations*, *41*, 460–464.

Burr, W. R., Day, R. D., & Bahr, K. S. (1993). *Family science*. Pacific Grove, CA: Brooks/Cole.

Burr, W. R., Dollahite, D. C., & Draper, T. W. (1995). *Toward more pragmatic family science theories: Part I: Philosophical and methodological issues*. Paper presented at the Theory and Methods Workshop, NCFR, Portland, OR.

Burr, W. R., Hill, R., Nye, I. F., & Reiss, I. L. (1979). *Contemporary theories about the family* (Vols. 1 and 2). New York, NY: Free Press.

Burr, W. R., Swenson, G. E., & Cannon, K. L. (1976). Marital satisfaction and conjugal control. *Home Economics Research Journal*, *4*, 121–125.

Burr, W. R., Yorgason, B., G., & Baker, T. R. (1982). *Creating a celestial marriage*. Salt Lake City, UT: Bookcraft.

Busby, D. M., Holman, T. B., & Taniguchi, N. (2001). RELATE: Relationship evaluation of the individual, family, cultural, and couple contexts. *Family Relations*, *50*, 308–316.

Butler, M. H., Gardner, B. C., & Bird, M. H. (1998). Not just time-out: Change dynamics of prayer for religious couples in conflict situations. *Family Process*, *37*, 451–478.

Butler, M. H., & Harper, J. M. (1994). The divine triangle: God in the marital system of religious couples. *Family Process*, *33*, 277–286.

Butler, M. H., Stout, J. A., & Gardner, B. C. (2002). Prayer as a conflict resolution ritual: Clinical implications of religious couples' report of relationship softening, healing perspective, and change responsibility. *The American Journal of Family Therapy*, *30*, 19–37.

Caillois, R. (1961). *Man, play, and games*. New York, NY: Free Press.

Carlo, G., Padilla-Walker, L. M., & Day, R. D. (in press). A test of the economic strain model on adolescents' prosocial behaviors. *Journal of Research on Adolescence.*

Carlson, C. R., Bascaseta, P. E., & Simonton, D. A. (1988). A controlled evaluation of devotional meditation and progressive relaxation. *Journal of Psychology and Theology, 16*, 362–368.

Carroll, J. S., Nelson, D. A., Yorgason, J. B., Harper, J. M., Ashton, R. H., & Jensen, A. C. (2010). Relational aggression in marriage. *Aggressive Behavior, 36*, 315–329.

Carter, E. A., & McGoldrick, M. (Eds.). (1989). *The changing family life cycle: A framework for family therapy*. New York, NY: Allyn and Bacon.

Carver, C. S., & White, T. L. (1994). Behavioral inhibition, behavioral activation, and affective responses to impending reward and punishment. *Journal of Personality and Social Psychology, 67*, 319–333.

Cashwell, C. S., & Young, J. S. (2005). *Integrating spirituality and religion into counseling: A guide to competent practice*. Alexandria, VA: American Counseling Association.

Cervantes, L. F. (1965). *The dropout: Causes and cures*. Ann Arbor: University of Michigan Press.

Charters, W. W. J., & Newcomb, T. M. (1958). Some attitudinal effects of experimentally increased salience of a membership group. In E. E. Maccoby, T. M. Newcomb, & E. L. Hartley (Eds.), *Readings in social psychology* (pp. 276–280). New York, NY: Holt, Rinehart and Winston.

Chase, S. E. (2005). Narrative inquiry: Multiple lenses, approaches, voices. In N. K. Denzin & Y. S. Lincoln (Eds.), *The Sage handbook of qualitative research* (3rd ed., pp. 651–675). Thousand Oaks, CA: Sage.

Chen, J. (1990). *Confucius as a teacher: Philosophy of Confucius with special reference to its educational implications*. Beijing: Foreign Languages Press.

Cheong, R. K., & DiBlasio, F. A. (2007). Christ-like love and forgiveness: A biblical foundation for counseling practice. *Journal of Psychology & Christianity, 26*, 14–25.

Cherlin, A. J. (2004). The deinstitutionalization of American marriage. *Journal of Marriage & Family, 66*, 848–861.

Cherlin, A. J. (2009). *The marriage-go-round: The state of marriage and the family in America today.* New York: Knopf.

Chibucos, T. R., Leite, R. W., & Weis, D. L. (2005). *Readings in family theory*. Thousand Oaks, CA: Sage.

Christensen, H. T. (1964). *Handbook of marriage and the family*. Chicago, IL: Rand McNally.

Christensen, H. T. (1969). Theory derived from cross-cultural family research. *Journal of Marriage & Family, 31*, 209–222.

Clark, M. S., & Lemay, E. P. (2010). Close relationships. In S. T. Fiske, D. T. Gilbert, & G. Lindzey (Eds.), *Handbook of social psychology* (pp. 898–940). New York, NY: Wiley.

Clark, M. S., Lemay, E. P., Jr., Graham, S. M., Pataki, S. P., & Finkel, E. J. (2010). Ways of giving benefits in marriage: Norm use, relationship satisfaction, and attachment-related variability. *Psychological Science, 21*, 944–951.

Clark, M. S., & Mills, J. (1979). Interpersonal attraction in exchange and communal relationships. *Journal of Personality and Social Psychology, 37*, 12–24.

Cohen, J. R. (2002). The ethics of respect in negotiation. *Negotiation Journal, 18*, 115–120.

Coleman, P. W. (1998). The process of forgiveness in marriage and the family. In R. D. Enright & J. North (Eds.), *Exploring forgiveness* (pp. 75–94). Madison: University of Wisconsin Press.

Collins, P. (2005). Thirteen ways of looking at a "ritual." *Journal of Contemporary Religion, 20*, 323–342.

Cook, J. C., Schoppe-Sullivan, S. J., Buckley, C. K., & Davis, E. F. (2009). Are some children harder to coparent than others? Children's negative emotionality and coparenting relationship quality. *Journal of Family Psychology, 23*, 606–610.

Cook, W. L. (1993). Interdependence and the interpersonal sense of control: An analysis of family relationships. *Journal of Personality and Social Psychology*, *64*, 587–601.

Cooley, C. H. (1902). *Human nature and the social order*. New York, NY: Scribner's.

Cooley, C. H. (1909). *Social organization: A study of the larger mind*. New York, NY: Scribner's.

Covey, S. R. (2001). *The 7 habits of highly effective people: Restoring the character ethic*. New York, NY: Free Press.

Coyle, C. T., & Enright, R. D. (1997). Forgiveness intervention with postabortion men. *Journal of Consulting & Clinical Psychology*, *65*, 1042–1046.

Crain, W. C. (1985). *Theories of development: Concepts and applications*. Englewood, NJ: Prentice-Hall.

Cramer, D. (2002). Satisfaction with romantic relationships and a four-component model of conflict resolution. In S. P. Shohov (Ed.), *Advances in psychology research* (Vol. 16, pp. 129–137). Hauppauge, NY: Nova Science.

Crocker, S. (1984). Prayer as a model of communication. *Pastoral Psychology*, *33*, 83–92.

Cuber, J. F., & Harroff, P. B. (1965). *The significant Americans: A study of sexual behaviors among the affluent*. New York, NY: Appleton-Century.

Cui, M., & Donnellan, M. B. (2009). Trajectories of conflict over raising adolescent children and marital satisfaction. *Journal of Marriage & Family*, *71*, 478–494.

Curran, D. (1983). *Traits of a healthy family: Fifteen traits commonly found in healthy families by those who work with them*. Minneapolis, MN: Winston Press.

Darwin, C. (1859). *The origin of species*. New York, NY: Modern Library.

Das, B. (1947). *The essential unity of all religions*. Benares, India: Ananda.

Davis, K. (1984). *The study of marriage and the family as a scientific discipline*. Paper presented at the meeting of the American Sociological Association. August, San Antonio, TX. Also published in the *Newsletter of the Task Force for the Development of the Family Discipline* (1985), Vol. 2, pp. 3–4.

Day, R. D., & Padilla-Walker, L. M. (2009). Mother and father connectedness and involvement during early adolescence. *Journal of Family Psychology*, *23*, 900–904.

de Cremer, D. (2002). Respect and cooperation in social dilemmas: The importance of feeling included. *Personality Social Psychology Bulletin*, *28*, 1335–1341.

de Cremer, D., & Tyler, T. R. (2005). Am I respected or not?: Inclusion and reputation as issues in group memberships. *Social Justice Research*, *18*, 121–153.

Denham, S. A., Neal, K., Wilson, B. J., Pickering, S., & Boyatzis, C. J. (2005). Emotional development and forgiveness in children: Emerging evidence. In E. L. Worthington (Ed.), *Handbook of forgiveness* (pp. 127–142). New York, NY: Routledge.

Denzin, N. K., & Lincoln, Y. S. (Eds.). (1994). *Handbook of qualitative research* (2nd ed.). Thousand Oaks, CA: Sage.

Deutsch, M. (1973). *The resolution of conflict: Constructive and destructive processes*. New Haven, CT: Yale University Press.

Deutsch, M. (1985). *Distributive justice: A social-psychological perspective*. New Haven, CT: Yale University Press.

DiBlasio, F. A. (1998). The use of a decision-based forgiveness intervention within intergenerational family therapy. *Journal of Family Therapy*, *20*, 77–94.

DiBlasio, F. A. (2000). Decision-based forgiveness treatment in cases of marital infidelity. *Psychotherapy*, *37*, 149–158.

Diesing, P. (1962). *Reason in society: Five types of decisions and their social conditions*. Urbana: University of Illinois Press.

Doherty, W. J. (1995). *Soul searching: Why psychotherapy must promote moral responsibility*. New York, NY: Basic Books.

Doherty, W. J. (1999). *The intentional family: Simple rituals to strengthen family ties*. New York, NY: Avon Books.

Doherty, W. J. (2001). *Take back your marriage: Sticking together in a world that pulls us apart*. New York, NY: Guilford Press.
Doherty, W. J., & Carlson, B. (2004). *Putting family first.* New York, NY: Owl Books.
Dollahite, D. C. (2003). Fathering for eternity: Generative spirituality in Latter-day Saint fathers of children with special needs. *Review of Religious Research*, *44*, 237–251.
Dollahite, D. C. (2007). Latter-day Saint marriage and family life in modern America. In D. S. Browning & D. A. Clairmont (Eds.), *American religions and the family: How faith traditions cope with modernization & democracy* (pp. 124–150). New York, NY: Columbia University Press.
Dollahite, D. C., & Lambert, N. M. (2007). Forsaking all others: How religious involvement promotes marital fidelity in Christian, Jewish, and Muslim couples. *Review of Religious Research*, *48*, 290–307.
Dollahite, D. C., Layton, E., Bahr, H. M., Walker, A. B., & Thatcher, J. Y. (2009). Giving up something good for something better: Sacred sacrifices made up religious youth. *Journal of Adolescent Research*, *24*, 691–725.
Dollahite, D. C., & Marks, L. D. (2005). How highly religious families strive to fulfill sacred purposes. In V. L. Bengtson, A. C. Acock, K. R. Allen, P. Dilworth-Anderson, & D. M. Klein (Eds.), *Sourcebook of family theory & research* (pp. 533–542). Thousand Oaks, CA: Sage.
Dollahite, D. C., & Marks, L. D. (2006). Family and community nurturing spirituality in Latter-day Saint children and youth. In K. Yust, A. N. Johnson, S. E. Sasso, & E. C. Roehlkepartain (Eds.), *Nurturing childhood and adolescent spirituality: Perspectives from the world's religious traditions* (pp. 394–408). Lanham, MD: Rowman & Littlefield.
Dollahite, D. C., & Marks, L. D. (2009). A conceptual model of family and religious processes in highly religious families. *Review of Religious Research*, *50*, 373–391.
Dollahite, D. C., Marks, L. D., & Goodman, M. A. (2004). Families and religious beliefs, practices, and communities: Linkages in a diverse and dynamic cultural context. In M. Coleman & L. H. Ganong (Eds.), *Handbook of contemporary families: Considering the past, contemplating the future* (pp. 411–431). Thousand Oaks, CA: Sage.
Dollahite, D. C., Marks, L. D., & Olson, M. M. (1998). Faithful fathering in trying times: Religious beliefs and practices of Latter-day Saint fathers of children with special needs. *Journal of Men's Studies*, *7*, 71–93.
Dollahite, D. C., Marks, L. D., & Olson, M. M. (2002). Fathering, faith, and family therapy: Generative narrative therapy with religious fathers. *Journal of Family Psychotherapy*, *13*, 259–289.
Dollahite, D. C., Slife, B. D., & Hawkins, A. (1998). Family generativity and generative counseling: Helping families keep faith with the next generation. In D. P. McAdams & D. S. Aubin (Eds.), *Generativity and adult development: How and why we care for the next generation* (pp. 449–481). Washington, DC: American Psychological Association.
Dollahite, D. C., & Thatcher, J. Y. (2008). Talking about religion: How highly religious youth and parents discuss their faith. *Journal of Adolescent Research*, *23*, 611–641.
Dollahite, D. C., Ward, M. R., & Hawkins, A. J. (2009). Something more vs. something less: Exploring the meaning of marriage for religious couples.
Dossey, L. (1993). *Healing words: The power of prayer and the practice of medicine*. San Francisco, CA: HarperCollins.
Dubin, R. (1969). *Theory building*. New York, NY: Free Press.
Durkheim, E. (1915). *The elementary forms of the religious life* (J. W. Swain, Trans.). London: Allen and Unwin.
Duvall, E., & Hill, R. H. (1948). *Report of the committee on the dynamics of family interaction*. Paper presented at the National Conference on Family Life, Washington, DC.
Duvall, E. R. M. (1957). *Family development*. Chicago, IL: Lippincott.

Edmonds, V. H., Withers, G., & Dibatista, B. (1972). Adjustment, conservatism, and marital conventionalization. *Journal of Marriage & Family*, *34*, 96–103.

Edwards, H. (1973). *Sociology of sport*. Homewood, IL: Dorsey Press.

Elkins, D., Anchor, K. N., & Sandler, H. M. (1979). Relaxation training and prayer behavior as tension reduction techniques. *Behavioral Engineering*, *5*, 81–87.

Ellis, A. (1961). *A guide to rational living*. Englewood Cliffs, NJ: Prentice-Hall.

Ellis, A. (1975). *How to live with a neurotic: At home and at work*. Oxford, UK: Crown.

Ellis, A. (1980). Psychotherapy and atheistic values: A response to A. E. Bergin's "Psychotherapy and Religious Values." *Journal of Consulting & Clinical Psychology*, *48*, 635–639.

Ellison, C. G., Burdette, A. M., & Wilcox, W. B. (2010). The couple that prays together: Race and ethnicity, religion, and relationship quality among working-age adults. *Journal of Marriage & Family*, *72*, 963–975.

Emler, N., & Reicher, S. (1995). *Adolescence and delinquency: The collective management of reputation*. Oxford, UK: Blackwell.

Enright, R. D. (2001). *Forgiveness is a choice: A step-by-step process for resolving anger and restoring hope*. Washington, DC: APA Life Tools.

Enright, R. D., & Fitzgibbons, R. P. (2000). *Helping clients forgive: an empirical guide for resolving anger and restoring hope*. Washington, DC: American Psychological Association.

Enright, R. D., & North, J. (Eds.). (1998). *Exploring forgiveness*. Madison: University of Wisconsin Press.

Epstein, N. B., Baldwin, L. M., & Bishop, D. S. (1983). The McMaster family assessment device. *Journal of Marital & Family Therapy*, *9*, 171–180.

Erikson, E. H. (1950). *Childhood and society*. New York, NY: Norton.

Erikson, E. H. (1959). *Identity and the life cycle*. New York, NY: International Universities Press.

Erikson, E. H. (1968). *Identity: Youth and crisis*. New York, NY: Norton.

Erikson, E. H., & Erikson, J. M. (1997). *The life cycle completed*. New York, NY: Norton.

Falicov, C. J. (1988). *Family transitions: Continuity and change over the life cycle*. New York, NY: Guilford Press.

Feeney, J. A., Noller, P., & Ward, C. (1997). Marital satisfaction and spousal interaction. In R. J. Sternberg & M. Hojjat (Eds.). *Satisfaction in close relationships* (pp. 160–189). New York: Guilford.

Fenell, D. (1993). Characteristics of long-term first marriages. *Journal of Mental Health Counseling*, *15*, 446–460.

Fernando, A. (1985). *Buddhism made plain: An introduction for Christians and Jews*. Maryknoll, NY: Obis Books.

Festinger, L. (1954). A theory of social comparison processes. *Human Relations*, *7*, 117–140.

Fiese, B. H. (2006). *Family routines and rituals*. New Haven, CT: Yale University Press.

Fiese, B. H., Hooker, K. A., Kotary, L., & Schwagler, J. (1993). Family rituals in the early stages of parenthood. *Journal of Marriage & Family*, *55*, 633–642.

Fiese, B. H., & Tomcho, T. J. (2001). Finding meaning in religious practices: The relation between religious holiday rituals and marital satisfaction. *Journal of Family Psychology*, *15*, 597–609.

Fincham, F. D. (2000). The kiss of the porcupines: From attributing responsibility to forgiving. *Personal Relationships*, *7*, 1–23.

Fincham, F. D. (2003). Marital conflict: Correlates, structure, and context. *Current Directions in Psychological Science (Wiley-Blackwell)*, *12*, 23–27.

Fincham, F. D., & Beach, S. R. H. (1999). Conflict in marriage: Implications for working with couples. *Annual Review of Psychology*, *50*, 47–77.

Fincham, F. D., & Beach, S. R. H. (2002). Forgiveness in marriage: Implications for psychological aggression and constructive communication. *Personal Relationships*, *9*, 239–251.

Fincham, F. D., Beach, S. R. H., & Davila, J. (2004). Forgiveness and conflict resolution in marriage. *Journal of Family Psychology*, *18*, 72–81.

Fincham, F. D., Beach, S. R. H., Lambert, N. M., Stillman, T., & Braithwaite, S. (2008). Spiritual behaviors and relationship satisfaction: A critical analysis of the role of prayer. *Journal of Social & Clinical Psychology*, *27*, 362–388.

Fincham, F. D., & Bradbury, T. N. (1987). The assessment of marital quality: A reevaluation. *Journal of Marriage & Family*, *49*, 797–809.

Fincham, F. D., Davila, J., & Beach, S. R. H. (2007). Longitudinal relations between forgiveness and conflict resolution in marriage. *Journal of Family Psychology*, *21*, 542–545.

Fincham, F. D., Hall, J., & Beach, S. R. H. (2005). "Till lack of forgiveness doth us part": Forgiveness and marriage. In E. L. Worthington (Ed.), *Handbook of forgiveness* (pp. 207–225). New York, NY: Routledge.

Fincham, F. D., Hall, J., & Beach, S. R. H. (2006). Forgiveness in marriage: Current status and future directions. *Family Relations*, *55*, 415–427.

Fincham, F. D., Lambert, N. M., & Beach, S. R. H. (2010). Faith and unfaithfulness: Can praying for your partner reduce infidelity? *Journal of Personality and Social Psychology*, *99*, 649–659.

Fincham, F. D., & Linfield, K. J. (1997). A new look at marital quality: Can spouses feel positive and negative about their marriage? *Journal of Family Psychology*, *11*, 489–502.

Fincham, F. D., Stanley, S. M., & Beach, S. R. H. (2007). Transformative processes in marriage: An analysis of emerging trends. *Journal of Marriage & Family*, *69*, 275–292.

Finkel, E. J., Rusbult, C. E., Kumashiro, M., & Hannon, P. A. (2002). Dealing with betrayal in close relationships: Does commitment promote forgiveness? *Journal of Personality and Social Psychology*, *82*, 956–974.

Framo, J. L. (1970). Symptoms from a family transactional viewpoint. In N. W. Ackerman, J. Lieb, & J. K. Pearce (Eds.), *Family therapy in transition* (pp. 125–171). Boston, MA: Little, Brown.

Framo, J. L. (1976). Family of origin as therapeutic resource for adults in marital and family therapy. *Family Process*, *15*, 193–210.

Frankl, V. E. (1984). *Man's search for meaning*. New York, NY: Pocket Books.

Freedman, S. R., & Enright, R. D. (1996). Forgiveness as an intervention goal with incest survivors. *Journal of Consulting and Clinical Psychology*, *64*, 983–992.

Frei, J. R., & Shaver, P. R. (2002). Respect in close relationships: Prototype definitions, self-report asessment, and initial correlates. *Personal Relationships*, *9*, 121–139.

Freud, S. (1927). *The future of an illusion*. Garden City, NY: Doubleday.

Freud, S. (1965). *New introductory lectures on psychoanalysis* (J. Strachey, Trans.). New York, NY: Norton.

Friedlander, M. L., Heatherington, L., & Marrs, A. L. (2000). Responding to blame in family therapy: A constructionist/narrative perspective. *American Journal of Family Therapy*, *28*, 133–146.

Fritz, H. L., & Helgeson, V. S. (1998). Distinctions of unmitigated communion from communion: Self-neglect and overinvolvement with others. *Journal of Personality and Social Psychology*, *75*, 121–140.

Fromm, E. (1956). *The art of loving*. New York, NY: Perennial Library.

Fromm, E. (1965). *Escape from freedom*. New York, NY: Avon Books.

Furlong, M., & Young, J. (1996). Talking about blame. *Australian and New Zealand Journal of Psychiatry*, *17*, 191–200.

Gable, S. L., & Reis, H. T. (2001). Appetitive and aversive social interaction. In J. Harvey & A. Wenzel (Eds.), *Close romantic relationships: Maintenance and enhancement* (pp. 169–195). Mahwah, NJ: Erlbaum.

Gaines, S. O., Jr. (1994). Exchange of respect-denying behaviors among male-female friendships. *Journal of Social and Personal Relationships, 11*, 5–24.

Gaines, S. O., Jr. (1997). Classifying dating couples: Gender as reflected in traits, roles, and resulting behavior. *Basic and Applied Social Psychology, 16*, 75–94.

Gall, T. L., Basque, V., Damasceno-Scott, M., & Vardy, G. (2007). Spiriuality and the current adjustment of adult survivors of childhood sexual abuse. *Journal for the Scientific Study of Religion, 46*, 101–117.

Gallagher, S. K. (2003). *Evangelical identity and gendered family life*. New Brunswick, NJ: Rutgers University Press.

Gelles, R., & Straus, M. A. (1979). Determinants of violence in the family: Toward a theoretical integration. In W. R. Burr, R. Hill, I. F. Nye, & I. L. Reiss (Eds.), *Contemporary theories about the family: Research-based theories* (Vol. 1, pp. 549–581). New York, NY: Free Press.

Gibbs, J. P. (1972). *Sociological theory construction*. Hinsdale, IL: Dryden Press.

Giles, L. (1976). *The analects of Confucius: Translated from the Chinese, with an introduction and notes*. Norwalk, CT: Easton Press.

Gilgun, J. F. (2001). Grounded theory and other inductive research methods. In B. A. Thyer (Ed.), *The handbook of social work research methods* (pp. 345–364). Thousand Oaks, CA: Sage.

Gilgun, J. F. (2005). Deductive qualitative analysis and family theory building. In V. L. Bengtson, A. C. Acock, K. R. Allen, P. Dilworth-Anderson, & D. M. Klein (Eds.), *Sourcebook of family theory & research* (pp. 83–84). Thousand Oaks, CA: Sage.

Glaser, B. G. (1978). *Theoretical sensitivity: Advances in the methodology of grounded theory*. Mill Valley, CA: Sociology Press.

Glaser, B. G., & Strauss, A. L. (1967). *The discovery of grounded theory: Strategies for qualitative research*. Chicago, IL: Aldine.

Gleick, J. (2003). *Isaac Newton*. New York, NY: Pantheon Books.

Goffman, E. (1959). *The presentation of self in everyday life*. Garden City, NY: Doubleday.

Gollwitzer, P. M., & Moskowitz, G. B. (1996). Goal effects on action and cognition. In A. W. Kruglanski & E. T. Higgins (Eds.), *Social psychology: handbook of basic principles* (pp. 361–399). New York, NY: Guilford Press.

Goode, W. J. (1959). The theoretical importance of love. *American Sociological Review, 24*, 38–47.

Goode, W. J. (1963). *World revolution and family patterns*. New York, NY: Free Press of Glencoe.

Goode, W. J., Hopkins, E., & McClure, H. M. (1971). *Social systems and family patterns: A propositional inventory*. New York, NY: Bobbs-Merrill.

Goodman, M. A., & Dollahite, D. C. (2006). How religious couples perceive the influence of God in their marriage. *Review of Religious Research, 48*, 141–155.

Gordon, K. C., & Baucom, D. H. (1998). Understanding betrayals in marriage: A synthesized model of forgiveness. *Family Process, 37*, 425–449.

Gordon, K. C., & Baucom, D. H. (2003). Forgiveness and marriage: Preliminary support for a measure based on a model of recovery from a marital betrayal. *American Journal of Family Therapy, 31*, 179–199.

Gordon, K. C., Baucom, D. H., & Snyder, D. K. (2000). The use of forgiveness in marital therapy. In M. E. McCullough, K. I. Pargament, & C. E. Thoresen (Eds.), *Forgiveness: Theory, research, and practice* (pp. 203–227). New York, NY: Guilford Press.

Gordon, K. C., Baucom, D. H., & Snyder, D. K. (2005). Forgiveness in couples: Divorce, infidelity and couples therapy. In E. L. Worthington (Ed.), *Handbook of forgiveness* (pp. 407–422). New York, NY: Routledge.

Gordon, K. C., Hughes, F. M., Tomcik, N. D., Dixon, L. J., & Litzinger, S. C. (2009). Widening spheres of impact: The role of forgiveness in marital and family functioning. *Journal of Family Psychology*, *23*, 1–13.

Gottman, J., & Silver, N. (2004). *The seven principles for making marriage work*. New York: Three Rivers Press.

Gottman, J. M. (1979). *Marital interaction: Experimental investigations*. New York, NY: Academic Press.

Gottman, J. M. (1994a). *What predicts divorce? The relationship between marital processes and marital outcomes*. Hillsdale, NJ: Erlbaum.

Gottman, J. M. (1994b). *Why marriages succeed or fail: And how you can make yours last*. New York, NY: Simon & Schuster.

Gottman, J. M. (1999). *The marriage clinic: A scientifically-based marital therapy*. New York, NY: Norton.

Gottman, J. M., & Krokoff, L. J. (1989). Marital interaction and satisfaction: A longitudinal view. *Journal of Consulting & Clinical Psychology*, *57*, 47–52.

Gottman, J. M., Murray, J. D., Swanson, C. C., Tyson, R., & Swanson, K. R. (2002a). *The mathematics of marriage: Dynamic nonlinear models*. Cambridge: MIT Press.

Gottman, J. M., Swanson, C., & Swanson, K. (2002b). A general systems theory of marriage: Nonlinear difference equation modeling of marital interaction. *Personality & Social Psychology*, *6*, 326–340.

Gouldner, A. W. (1960). The norm of reciprocity: A preliminary statement. *American Sociological Review*, *25*, 161–178.

Granovetter, M. S. (1983). The strengths of weak ties. In R. Collins (Ed.), *Sociological theory* (pp. 201–233). San Francisco: Jossey-Bass.

Gray, J. A. (1987). *The psychology of fear and stress* (2nd ed.). New York, NY: Cambridge University Press.

Greeley, A. M. (1991). *Faithful attraction: Discovering intimacy, love, and fidelity in American marriage*. New York, NY: Tor Books.

Griffith, J. L. (2010). *Religion that heals, religion that harms: A guide for clinical practice*. New York, NY: Guilford Press.

Grimes, R. L. (1995). *Beginnings in ritual studies* (Revised ed.). Columbia, SC: University of South Caolina Press.

Gruner, L. (1985). The correlation of private, religious devotional practices and marital adjustment. *Journal of Comparative Family Studies*, *16*, 47–59.

Guerney, B. G. (1977). *Relationship enhancement*. San Francisco, CA: Jossey-Bass.

Hage, J. (1972). *Techniques and problems of theory construction in sociology*. New York, NY: Wiley.

Hajii, (2006). Four faces of respect. *Reclaiming children and youth*, *15*, 66–70.

Haley, A. (1976). *Roots*. Garden City, NY: Doubleday.

Haley, J. (1963). *Strategies of psychotherapy*. New York, NY: Grune & Stratton.

Hall, G. S. (1891). The moral and religious training of children and adolescents. *Pedagogical Seminary*, *1*, 196–210.

Hargrave, T. D., & Sells, J. N. (1997). The development of a forgiveness scale. *Journal of Marital & Family Therapy*, *23*, 41–62.

Harper, J. M., & Dome, L. J. (in press). Materialism and forgiveness in couples. *Family Relations*.

Harper, J. M., & Hoopes, M. H. (1990). *Uncovering shame: An approach integrating individuals and their family systems*. New York, NY: W. W. Norton & Co.

Harris, A. H. S., & Thoresen, C. E. (2005). Forgiveness, unforgiveness, health and disease. In E. L. Worthington (Ed.), *Handbook of forgiveness* (pp. 321–348). New York, NY: Routledge.

Harvey, J., Heath, G. C., Spencer, M., Temple, W., & Wood, H. G. (1917). *Competition: A study in human motive*. London, UK: Macmillan.

Harvey, J. H., Stein, S. K., Olsen, N., & Roberts, R. J. (1995). Narratives of loss and recovery from a natural disaster. *Journal of Social Behavior and Personality, 10*, 313–330.

Hastings, P. D., & Rubin, K. H. (1999). Predicting mothers' beliefs about preschool-aged children's social behavor: Evidence for maternal attitutdes moderating child effect. *Child Development, 70*, 722–741.

Hawkins, A. J., & Dollahite, D. C. (1997). *Generative fathering: Beyond deficit perspectives*. Thousand Oaks, CA: Sage.

Hawkins, A. J., Bradford, K. P., Palkovitz, R., Christiansen, S. L., Day, R. D., & Call, V. R. A. (2002). The inventory of father involvement: A pilot study of a new measure of father involvement. *Journal of Men's Studies*, 10, 183–196.

Helgeson, V. S., & Fritz, H. L. (1998). A theory of unmitigated communion. *Personality & Social Psychology Review, 2*, 173–183.

Hendrick, S. S. & Hendrick, C. (2006). Measuring respect in close relationships. *Journal of Social and Personal Relationships, 6*, 881–899.

Hendrick, S. S., Hendrick, C., & Logue, E. M. (2010). Respect and the family. *Journal of Family Theory and Review, 2*, 126–136.

Henslin, J. M. (1980). *Marriage and family in a changing society*. New York, NY: Free Press.

Hetherington, E. M., & Kelly, J. (2002). *For better or for worse: Divorce reconsidered*. New York, NY: Norton.

Hill, E. W. (2001). Understanding forgiveness as discovery: Implications for marital and family therapy. *Contemporary Family Therapy: An International Journal, 23*, 369–384.

Hill, R., & Hansen, D. A. (1960). The identification of conceptual frameworks utilized in family study. *Marriage and Family Living, 22*, 299–311.

Hill, R., & Rodgers, R. (1964). The developmental approach. In H. T. Christensen (Ed.), *Handbook of marriage and the family* (pp. 171–211). Chicago, IL: Rand McNally.

Hoffman, J. (Ed.). (2011). *Religious rituals*. New York: Routledge.

Holden, G. W. (2001). Psychology, religion, and the family: It's time for a revival. *Journal of Family Psychology, 15*, 657–662.

Holman, T. B., & Burr, W. R. (1980). Beyond the beyond: The growth of family theories in the 1970s. *Journal of Marriage & Family, 42*, 723–729.

Holmes, J. G. (1989). Trust and the appraisal process in close relationships. In W. H. Jones & D. Perlman (Eds.), *Advances in personal relationships* (Vol. 2, pp. 57–104). London, UK: Kingsley.

Holmes, J. G., & Boon, S. D. (1990). Developments in the field of close relationships: Creating foundations for intervention strategies. *Personality and Social Psychology Bulletin, 16*, 23–41.

Holmes, J. G., & Rempel, J. K. (1989). Trust in close relationships. In C. Hendrick (Ed.), *Review of personality and social psychology* (Vol. 10, pp. 187–220). London, UK: Sage.

Holyoake, G. J. (1896). *English secularism: A confession of belief*. Chicago, IL: Open Court.

Homans, G. C. (1950). *The human group*. New York, NY: Harcourt Brace.

Homans, G. C. (1961). *Social behavior: Its elementary forms*. New York, NY: Harcourt, Brace & World.

Honer, S. M., & Hunt, T. C. (1987). *Invitation to philosophy: Issues and options*. Belmont, CA: Wadsworth.

Horowitz, L. M., Rosenberg, S. E., & Bartholomew, K. (1993). Interpersonal problems, attachment styles, and outcome in brief dynamic psychotherapy. *Journal of Consulting & Clinical Psychology, 61*, 549–560.

Huizinga, J. (1955). *Homo ludens: A study of the play-element in culture*. Boston, MA: Beacon Press.

Hyman, H. H. (1942). The psychology of status. *Archives of Psychology, 269*.

Hymowitz, K. S. (2006). *Marriage and caste in America: Separate and unequal families in a post-marital age*. Chicago, IL: Ivan R. Dee.

Ibrahim, E., & Johnson-Davies, D. (1976). *Nawawi's forty hadith/Al-Arba'in al-Nawawiyya*. Beirut: Holy Koran.

Imber-Black, E., Roberts, J., & Whiting, R. A. (1988). *Rituals in families and family therapy*. New York, NY: Norton.

Impett, E. A., Gable, S. L., & Peplau, L. A. (2005). Giving up and giving in: The costs and benefits of daily sacrifice in intimate relationships. *Journal of Personality and Social Psychology, 89*, 327–344.

Ingoldsby, B. B., Smith, S. R., & Miller, J. E. (2004). *Exploring family theories*. Los Angeles, CA: Roxbury.

Jaccard, J., & Jacoby, J. (2010). *Theory construction and model-building skills: A practical guide for social scientists*. New York, NY: Guilford Press.

Jack, D. C. (1991). *Silencing the self: Women and depression*. Cambridge, MA: Harvard University Press.

Jack, D. C., & Dill, D. (1992). The silencing the self scale. *Psychology of Women Quarterly, 16*, 97–106.

Jackson, A. P., Fischer, L., & Dant, D. R. (Eds.). (2005). *Turning Freud upside down: Gospel perspectives on psychotherapy's fundamental problems*. Provo, UT: Brigham Young University Press.

Jacobson, N. S., & Margolin, G. (1979). *Marital therapy: Strategies based on social learning and behavior exchange principles*. New York, NY: Brunner/Mazel.

James, W. (1890). *Principles of psychology,* New York, NY: Holt.

James, W. (1892). *Psychology*. New York, NY: Holt.

James, W. (1902). *The varieties of religious experience: A study in human nature*. New York, NY: Longmans, Green.

James, W. (1947). *Essays on faith and morals*. New York, NY: Longmans, Green.

Johnson, R. T., Johnson, D. W., & Tauer, M. (1979). The effects of cooperative, competitive, and individualistic goal structures on students' attitudes and achievement. *Journal of Psychology, 102*, 191–199.

Johnston, C., & Freeman, W. (1997). Attributions for child behavior in parents of children without behavior disorders and children with attention-deficit-hyperactivity disorder. *Journal of Consulting and Clinical Psychology, 65*, 636–645.

Johnston, C., & Patanaude, R. L. (1994). Parent attributions for inattentive-overactive, and oppositional-defiant child behaviors. *Cognitive Theory and Research*, 18, 261–175.

Jones, S. L. (1994). A constructive relationship for religion with the science and profession of psychology: Perhaps the boldest model yet. *American Psychologist, 49*, 184–199.

Jordan, J. V. (1991). The relational self: A new perspective for understanding women's development. In J. Strauss & G. R. Goethals (Eds.), *The self: interdisciplinary approaches* (pp. 136–149). New York, NY: Springer-Verlag.

Jourard, S. M. (1971). *The transparent self*. New York, NY: Van Nostrand Reinhold.

Kamiar, M. (2009). *Brilliant Biruni: A life story of Abu Rayhan Mohammad Ibn Ahmad*. Lanham, MD: Scarecrow Press.

Kaminer, D., & Stein, D. J. (2000). Forgiveness: Toward an integration of theoretical models. *Psychiatry: Interpersonal & Biological Processes, 63*, 14.

Kelley, H. H., & Thibaut, J. W. (1978). *Interpersonal relations: A theory of interdependence*. New York, NY: Wiley.

Kelly, E. L. (1955). Consistency of the adult personality. *American Psychologist, 10*, 659–681.

Kennedy, L. W., & Forde, D. R. (1999). *When push comes to shove: A routine conflict approach to violence*. Albany: State University of New York Press.

Kerr, M. E. (1981). Family systems theory and therapy. In A. S. Gurman & D. P. Kniskern (Eds.), *Handbook of family therapy* (pp. 226–266). New York, NY: Brunner/Mazel.

Kim, E. Y., & Miklowitz, D. J. (2004). Expressed emotion as a predictor of outcome among bipolar patients undergoing family therapy. *Journal of Affective Disorders, 82*, 343–352.

Klein, D. M. (2005). The cyclical process of science. In V. L. Bengtson, A. C. Acock, K. R. Allen, P. Dilworth-Anderson, & D. M. Klein (Eds.), *Sourcebook of family theory & research* (pp. 17–21). Thousand Oaks, CA: Sage.

Klein, S. L., Horton, B., & Zhang, S. (2008). Communicating love: Comparisons between American and East Asian university students. *International Journal of Intercultural Relations, 32*, 200–214.

Kluwer, E. S., & Johnson, M. D. (2007). Conflict frequency and relationship quality across the transition to parenthood. *Journal of Marriage & Family, 69*, 1089–1106.

Knapp, S. J. (2002). Authorizing family science: An analysis of the objectifying practices of family science discourse. *Journal of Marriage & Family, 64*, 1038–1048.

Knapp, S. J. (2006). *Critical theorizing: Enhancing theoretical rigor in family research*. Paper presented at the TCRM workshop at the annual meeting of the National Council on Family Relations.

Knapp, S. J. (2009). Critical theorizing: Enhancing theoretical rigor in family research. *Journal of Family Theory and Review, 1*, 133–145.

Koenig, H. G., McCullough, M. E., & Larson, D. B. (2001). *Handbook of Religion and Health*. New York: Oxford University Press.

Kohn, A. (1986). *No contest: The case against competition*. Boston, MA: Houghton Mifflin.

Kroll, B., & Taylor, A. (2003). *Parental substance misuse and child welfare*. London, UK: Kingsley.

Krumrei, E. J., Mahoney, A., & Pargament, K. I. (2009). Divorce and the divine: The role of spirituality in adjustment to divorce. *Journal of Marriage & Family, 71*, 373–383.

Kunce, L. J., & Shaver, P. R. (1994). An attachment-theoretical approach to caregiving in romantic relationships. In K. Bartholomew & D. Perlman (Eds.), *Attachment processes in personal relationships* (Vol. 5, pp. 205–237). London, UK: Kingsley.

Lakritz, K. R., & Knoblauch, T. M. (1999). *Elders on love: Dialogues on the consciousness, cultivation, and expression of love*. New York, NY: Parabola Books.

Lambert, N. M., & Dollahite, D. C. (2006). How religiosity helps couples prevent, resolve, and overcome marital conflict. *Family Relations, 55*, 439–449.

Lambert, N. M., & Dollahite, D. C. (2008). The threefold cord. *Journal of Family Issues, 29*, 592–614.

Lambert, N. M., Fincham, F. D., Braithwaite, S. R., Graham, S. M., & Beach, S. R. H. (2009). Can prayer increase gratitude? *Psychology of Religion and Spirituality, 1*, 139–149.

Lambert, N. M., Fincham, F. D., Marks, L. D., & Stillman, T. F. (2010). Invocations and intoxication: Does prayer decrease alcohol consumption? *Psychology of Addictive Behaviors, 24*, 209–219.

Lambert, N. M., Fincham, F. D., Stillman, T. F., Graham, S. M., & Beach, S. R. M. (2010). Motivating change in relationships: Can prayer increase forgiveness? *Psychological Science, 21*, 126–132.

LaRossa, R. (1997). *The modernization of fatherhood: A social and political history*. Chicago, IL: University of Chicago Press.

Larson, D. B., & Larson, S. S. (2003). Spirituality's potential relevance to physical and emotional health: A brief review of quantitative research. *Journal of Psychology & Theology, 31*, 37–51.

Lasswell, M. E., & Lobsenz, N. M. (1980). *Styles of loving: Why you love the way you do*. New York, NY: Doubleday.

Lazarus, A. A. (1958). New methods in psychotherapy: A case study. *South African Medical Journal*, *32*, 660–664.

Lazarus, A. A. (1971). *Behavior therapy & beyond*. New York, NY: McGraw-Hill.

Lee, G. R. (1987). Comparative perspectives. In M. B. Sussman & S. K. Steinmetz (Eds.), *Handbook of marriage and the family* (pp. 59–80). New York, NY: Plenum Press.

Lee, T. R., Burr, W. R., Beutler, F. I., Yorgason, F., Harker, H. B., & Olsen, J. A. (1997). The family profile II: A self-scored, brief family assessment tool. *Psychological Reports*, *81*, 467–477.

Lee, T. R., & Goddard, H. W. (1989). Developing family relationship skills to prevent substance abuse among high-risk youth. *Family Relations*, *38*, 301–305.

Legaree, T.-A., Turner, J., & Lollis, S. (2007). Forgiveness and therapy: A critical review of conceptualizations, practices, and values found in the literature. *Journal of Marital & Family Therapy*, *33*, 192–213.

Lerner, H. G. (1985). *The dance of anger: A woman's guide to changing the patterns of intimate relationships*. New York, NY: Harper & Row.

Lerner, H. G. (1988). *Women in therapy: Devaluation, anger, aggression, depression, self-sacrifice, mothering, mother blaming, self-betrayal, sex-role stereotypes, dependency, work and success inhibitions*. Northvale, NJ: Aronson.

Levinger, G. (1976). A social psychological perspective on marital dissolution. *Journal of Social Issues*, *32*, 21–47.

Lévi-Strauss, C. (1967). *Structural anthropology*. Garden City, NY: Anchor Books.

Lewis, C. A., Shevlin, M., McGuckin, C., & Navratil, M. (2001). The Santa Clara strength of religious faith questionnaire: Confirmatory factor analysis. *Pastoral Psychology, 49*, 379–384.

Lidz, T. (1963). *The family and human adaptation*. New York, NY: International Universities Press.

Linder, J. R., Crick, N. R., & Collins, W. A. (2002). Relational aggression and victimization in young adults' romantic relationships: Associations with perceptions of parent, peer, and romantic relationship quality. *Social Development, 11*(1), 69–86.

Lindgren, K. N., & Coursey, R. D. (1995). Spirituality and serious mental illness: A two-part study. *Psychosocial Rehabilitation Journal*, *18*, 92–111.

Loser, R. W., Hill, E. J., Klein, S. R., & Dollahite, D. C. (2009). Perceived benefits of religious rituals in the Latter-day Saint home. *Review of Religious Research*, *50*, 345–362.

MacCrimmon, K. R., & Messick, D. M. (1976). A framework for social motives. *Behavioral Science*, *21*, 86–100.

Machiavelli, N. (1531). *The discourses* (L. J. Walker, Trans.). London: Penguin Books.

MacKinnon-Lewis, C., Lamb, M. E., Hattie, J., Baradaran, L. P. (2001). A longitudinal examination of the associations between mothers' and sons' attributions and their aggression. *Development and Psychopathology, 13*, 69–81.

Magoun, F. (1948). *Love and marriage*. New York, NY: Harper & Brothers.

Mahoney, A. (2010). Religion in families, 1999–2009: A relational spirituality framework. *Journal of Marriage & Family*, *72*, 805–827.

Mahoney, A., Carels, R. A., Pargament, K. I., Wachholtz, A., Edwards Leeper, L., Kaplar, M., & Frutchey, R. (2005). The sanctification of the body and behavioral health patterns of college students. *International Journal for the Psychology of Religion*, *15*, 221–238.

Mahoney, A., Pargament, K. I., Cole, B., Jewell, T., Magyar, G. M., Tarakeshwar, N., Murray-Swank, N. A., & Phillips, R. (2005). A higher purpose: The sanctification of strivings in a community sample. *International Journal for the Psychology of Religion*, *15*, 239–262.

Mahoney, A., Pargament, K. I., Jewell, T., Swank, A. B., Scott, E., Emery, E., & Rye, M. (1999). Marriage and the spiritual realm: The role of proximal and distal religious constructs in marital functioning. *Journal of Family Psychology, 13*, 321–338.

Mahoney, A., Pargament, K. I., Murray-Swank, A., & Murray-Swank, N. (2003). Religion and the sanctification of family relationships. *Review of Religious Research, 44*, 220–236.

Mahoney, A., Pargament, K. I., Tarakeshwar, N., & Swank, A. B. (2001). Religion in the home in the 1980s and 1990s: A meta-analytic review and conceptual analysis of links between religion, marriage, and parenting. *Journal of Family Psychology, 15*, 559–596.

Mahoney, A., Rye, M. S., & Pargament, K. I. (2005). When the sacred is violated: Desecration as a unique challenge to forgiveness. In E. L. Worthington (Ed.), *Handbook of forgiveness* (pp. 57–72). New York, NY: Routledge.

Maio, G. R., Thomas, G., Fincham, F. D., & Carnelley, K. B. (2008). Unraveling the role of forgiveness in family relationships. *Journal of Personality and Social Psychology, 94*, 307–319.

Mamalakis, P. M. (2001). Painting a bigger picture: Forgiveness therapy with pre-marital infidelity: A case study. *Journal of Family Psychotherapy, 12*, 39–54.

Marciano, T. D. (1987). Families and religions. In M. B. Sussman & S. K. Steinmetz (Eds.), *Handbook of marriage and the family* (pp. 285–316). New York, NY: Plenum Press.

Marks, L. D. (2002). *Illuminating the interface between families and faith.* (Unpublished doctoral dissertation), University of Delaware, Newark.

Marks, L. D. (2004). Sacred practices in highly religious families: Christian, Jewish, Mormon, and Muslim perspectives. *Family Process, 43*, 217–231.

Marks, L. D. (2005). Religion and bio-psycho-social health: A review and conceptual model. *Journal of Religion & Health, 44*, 173–186.

Marks, L. D. (2006). Religion and family relational health: An overview and conceptual model. *Journal of Religion & Health, 45*, 603–618.

Marks, L. D. (2008). Prayer and marital intervention: Asking for divine help . . . or professional trouble? *Journal of Social & Clinical Psychology, 27*, 678–685.

Marks, L. D., & Dollahite, D. C. (2001). Religion, relationships, and responsible fathering in Latter-day Saint families of children with special needs. *Journal of Social & Personal Relationships, 18*, 625–650.

Marks, L. D., & Dollahite, D. C. (2007). Fathering and religious contexts: Why religion makes a difference to fathers and their children. In S.E. Brotherson & J. M. White (Eds.), *Why fathers count* (pp. 335–351). Harriman, TN: Men's Studies Press.

Marks, L. D., & Dollahite, D. C. (in press). Mining the meanings from psychology of religion's correlation mountain. *Journal of Psychology of Religion and Spirituality*.

Marks, L. D., Dollahite, D. C., & Barker, K. (2011). "Don't forget home": The importance of sacred ritual in families. In J. Hoffman (ed.), *Religious rituals* (pp. 186–203). New York: Routledge.

Marks, L. D., Dollahite, D. C., & Dew, J. (2009). Enhancing cultural competence in financial counseling and planning: Understanding why families make religious contributions. *Journal of Financial Counseling and Planning, 20*, 14–26.

Marks, L. D., Nesteruk, O., Hopkins-Williams, K., Swanson, M., & Davis, T. (2006). Stressors in African American marriages and families: A qualitative exploration. *Stress, Trauma & Crisis: An International Journal, 9*, 203–225.

Marks, L. D., Nesteruk, O., Swanson, M., Garrison, B., & Davis, T. (2005). Religion and health among African Americans. *Research on Aging, 27*, 447–474.

Marks, L. D., & Palkovitz, R. (2004). American fatherhood types: The good, the bad, and the uninterested. *Fathering, 2*, 113–129

Marks, L. D., & Palkovitz, R. (2007). Fathers as spiritual guides. In S. E. Brotherson & J. M. White (Eds.), *Why fathers count: The importance of fathers and their involvement with children* (pp. 209–223). Harriman, TN: Men's Studies Press.

Marks, S. R. (1996). The problem and politics of wholeness in family studies. *Journal of Marriage & Family, 58*, 565–571.

Marshall, A. (1961). *Principles of economics* (9th ed.). New York, NY: Macmillan.

Marx, K., & Engels, F. (1848). *Manifesto of the Communist Party.*

Marx, K., & Engels, F. (1964). *On religion*. New York, NY: Schocken Books.

Maslow, A. H. (1943). A theory of human motivation. *Psychological Review, 50*, 370–396.

Maslow, A. H. (1954). *Motivation and personality*. New York, NY: Harper.

Maslow, A. H. (1962). *Toward a psychology of being*. New York, NY: Van Nostrand Reinhold.

Maslow, A. H. (1966). *The psychology of science: A reconnaissance*. Chicago, IL: Henry Regnery.

Maslow, A. H. (1971). *The farther reaches of human nature*. New York, NY: Viking Press.

Masters, W. H., & Johnson, V. E. (1966). *Human sexual response*. Boston, MA: Little, Brown.

Mawadudi, A. A. (1988). *Towards understanding Islam.* London, UK: The Islamic Foundation.

May, R. (1969). *Love and will*. New York, NY: Norton.

McCullough, M. E. (1995). Prayer and health: Conceptual issues, research review, and research agenda. *Journal of Psychology and Theology, 25*, 15–29.

McCullough, M. E., Sandage, S. J., Brown, S. W., Rachal, K. C., Worthington, E. L., & Hight, T. L. (1998). Interpersonal forgiving in close relationships: II. Theoretical elaboration and measurement. *Journal of Personality and Social Psychology, 75*, 1586–1603.

McCullough, M. E., & Worthington, E. L. (1994). Models of interpersonal forgiveness and their applications. *Counseling & Values, 39*, 2–14.

McCullough, M. E., Worthington, E. L., & Rachal, K. C. (1997). Interpersonal forgiving in close relationships. *Journal of Personality and Social Psychology, 73*, 321–336.

McIntosh, D. N., Silver, R. C., & Wortman, C. B. (1993). Religion's role in adjustment to a negative life event: Coping with the loss of a child. *Journal of Personality and Social Psychology, 65*, 812–821.

McNulty, J. K. (2008). Forgiveness in marriage: Putting the benefits into context. *Journal of Family Psychology, 22*, 171–175.

Mead, G. H. (1934). *Mind, self and society*. Chicago, IL: University of Chicago Press.

Meredith, W. H. (1985). The importance of family traditions. *Wellness Perspectives, 2*, 17–19.

Meredith, W. H., Abbott, D. A., Lamanna, M. A., & Sanders, G. (1989). Rituals and family strengths: A three-generation study. *Family Perspective, 23*, 75–84.

Merton, R. K. (1957). *Social theory and social structure*. Glencoe, Ill: The Free Press.

Miller, W. R., & Thoresen, C. E. (2003). Spirituality, religion, and health: An emerging research field. *American Psychologist, 58*, 24–35.

Minuchin, S. (1974). *Families and family therapy*. Cambridge, MA: Harvard University Press.

Mizruchi, S. L. (1998). *The science of sacrifice: American literature and modern social theory*. Princeton, NJ: Princeton University Press.

Montada, L. (1992). Attribution of responsibility for losses and perceived injustice. In L. Montada, S.-H. Filipp, & M. J. Lerner (Eds.), *Life crises and experiences of loss in adulthood*. Englewood Cliffs, NJ: Erlbaum.

Müller, F. M. (1901). *The sacred books of the East* (Vol. 12). New York, NY: Scribner's.

Murdock, G. P. (1934). *Our primitive contemporaries*. New York, NY: Macmillan.

Murphy, J. G. (2002). Forgiveness in counseling: A philosophical perspective. In S. Lamb & J. G. Murphy (Eds.), *Before forgiving: Cautionary views of forgiveness in psychotherapy* (pp. 41–53). London, UK: Oxford University Press.

Murray-Swank, N., Pargament, K. I., & Mahoney, A. (2005). At the crossroads of sexuality and spirituality: The sanctification of sex by college students. *International Journal for the Psychology of Religion*, *15*, 199–219.

Murstein, B. I., Cerreto, M., & MacDonald, M. G. (1977). A theory and investigation of the effect of exchange-orientation. *Journal of Marriage & Family*, *39*, 453–548.

Myerhoff, B. (1978). *Number our days*. New York, NY: Simon & Schuster.

Myers, M. (1983). *The morality of kinship*. Paper presented at the the Virginia Cutler lecture, Brigham Young University, Provo, UT.

Nagel, E. (1961). *The structure of science: Problems in the logic of scientific explanation*. New York, NY: Harcourt, Brace & World.

Neff, K. D., & Harter, S. (2002). The authenticity of conflict resolutions among adult couples: Does women's other-oriented behavior reflect their true selves? *Sex Roles*, *47*, 403–417.

Neff, P. (1982). *Tough love: How parents can deal with drug abuse*. Nashville, TN: Abingdon.

Nelson, D. A., & Carroll, J. S. (2006). *Couples relational aggression and victimization scale (CRAViS)*. Provo, UT: RELATE Institute.

Nisbet, R. A. (1976). *Sociology as an art form*. New York, NY: Oxford University Press.

Nix, R. L., Pinderhughes, E. E., Dodge, K. A., Bates, J. E., Pettit, G. S., & McFadyen-Ketchum, S. A. (1999). The relation between mothers' hostile attributon tendencies and children' externalizing behavior problems: The mediating role of mothers' harsh discipline pratices. *Child Development*, *70*, 896–909.

Noller, P. (2005). What is this thing called love? Defining the love that supports marriage and family. *Personal Relationships*, *3*, 97–115.

Norville, D. (2009). *The power of respect: Benefit from the most forgotten element of success*. Nashville, TN: Nelson.

Nottingham, E. K. (1971). *Religion: A sociological view*. New York, NY: Random House.

Novak, A., & Vallacher, R. R. (1998). *Dynamical social psychology*. New York: Guilford Press.

Nye, I. F., & Berardo, F. M. (1966). *Emerging conceptual frameworks in family analysis*. New York, NY: Macmillan.

Ohaeri, J. U., Shokunbi, W. A., Akinlade, K. S., & Dare, L. O. (1995). The psychosocial problems of sickle cell disease sufferers and their methods of coping. *Social Science and Medicine*, *40*, 955–960.

Onedera, J. D. (2008). *The role of religion in marriage and family counseling*. New York, NY: Routledge.

Orden, S. R., & Bradburn, N. M. (1968). Dimensions of marriage happiness. *The American Journal of Sociology*, *73*, 715–731.

Osmond, M. (1987). Radical-critical theories. In M. B. Sussman & S. K. Steinmetz (Eds.), *Handbook of marriage and the family* (pp. 103–124). New York, NY: Plenum Press.

Osmond, M. W., & Thorne, B. (1993). Feminist theories: The social construction of gender in families and society. In P. G. Boss, W. J. Doherty, R. LaRossa, W. R. Schumm, & S. K. Steinmetz (Eds.), *Sourcebook of family theories and methods: A contextual approach* (pp. 591–622). New York, NY: Plenum Press.

Page, J. R., Stevens, H. B., & Galving, S. L. (1996). Relationships between depression, self-esteem, and self-silencing behavior. *Journal of Social & Clinical Psychology*, *15*, 381–396.

Palazolli, M. S., Boscolo, L., Cecchin, G., & Prata, G. (1978). *Paradox and counter-paradox*. New York, NY: Aronson.

Palazolli, M. S., Cirillo, S., Selvini, M., & Sorrentino, A. M. (1989). *Family games: General models of psychotic processes in the family*. New York, NY: Norton

Paleari, F. G., Regalia, C., & Fincham, F. D. (2005). Marital quality, forgiveness, empathy, and rumination: A longitudinal analysis. *Personality and Social Psychology Bulletin, 31*, 368–378.

Palmer, S. J., & Keller, R. R. (1993). *Religions of the world*. Provo, UT: BYU Press.

Paloutzian, R. F., & Park, C. L. (Eds.). (2005). *Handbook of the psychology of religion and spirituality*. New York, NY: Guilford Press.

Pargament, K. I. (1997). *The psychology of religion and coping: Theory, research, practice*. New York, NY: Guilford Press.

Pargament, K. I. (2007). *Spiritually integrated psychotherapy: Understanding and addressing the sacred*. New York, NY: Guilford Press.

Pargament, K. I., & Koenig, H. G. (2000). The many methods of religious coping: Development and initial validation of the RCOPE. *Journal of Clinical Psychology, 56*, 519–543.

Pargament, K. I., Magyar, G. M., Benore, E., & Mahoney, A. (2005). Sacrilege: A study of sacred loss and desecration and their implications for health and well-being in a community sample. *Journal for the Scientific Study of Religion, 44*, 59–78.

Pargament, K. I., & Mahoney, A. (2002). Spirituality: Discovering and conserving the sacred. In C. R. Snyder & S. J. Lopez (Eds.), *Handbook of positive psychology* (pp. 646–659). New York, NY: Oxford University Press.

Pargament, K. I., & Mahoney, A. (2005). Sacred matters: Sanctification as a vital topic for the psychology of religion. *International Journal for the Psychology of Religion, 15*, 179–198.

Pargament, K. I., Zinnbauer, B. J., Scott, Allie B., Butter, E. M. Zerowin, J., & Stanik, P., (1998). Red flags and religious coping: Identifying some religious warning signs among people in crisis. *Journal of Clinical Psychology, 54*, 77–79.

Parkin, D. (1992). Ritual as spatial direction and bodily division. In D. DeCoppet (Ed.), *Understanding rituals* (pp. 11–25). London: Routledge.

Patton, J. (2000). Forgiveness in pastoral care and counseling. In M. E. McCullough, K. I. Pargament, & C. E. Thoresen (Eds.), *Forgiveness: Theory, research, and practice* (pp. 281–298). New York, NY: Guilford Press.

Pavlov, I. P. (1927). *Conditioned reflexes* (G. V. Anrep, Trans.). London, UK: Oxford University Press.

Peperzak, A. T. (1993). *To the other: An introduction to the philosophy of Emmanuel Levinas*. West Lafayette, IN: Purdue University Press.

Percesepe, G. J. (1991). *Philosophy: An introduction to the labor of reason*. New York, NY: Macmillan.

Peterson, C., & Seligman, M. E. P. (2004). *Character strengths and virtues: A handbook and classification*. Washington, DC: Oxford University Press.

Pew Research Center. (2010). *The decline of marriage and rise of new families.* New York, NY: Author.

Pickering, M. (1997). A new look at Auguste Comte. In C. Camic (Ed.), *Reclaiming the sociological classics: The state of the scholarship* (pp. 11–44). Malden, MA: Blackwell.

Plato. (1979). *The republic* (R. Larson, Trans.). Wheeling, IL: Harlan Davidson.

Pleck, J. (2010). Paternal involvement: Revised conceptualization and theoretical linkages with child outcomes. In M. E. Lamb (Ed.), *The role of the father in child development* (5th ed., pp. 58–93). Hoboken, NJ: John Wiley & Sons Inc.

Poloma, M. M., & Pendleton, B. F. (1991). The effects of prayer and prayer experiences on measures of general well-being. *Journal of Psychology and Theology, 19*, 71–83.

Powell, J. J. (1974). *Why am I afraid to love*? London, UK: Fontana/Collins.

Putnam, R. (2000). *Bowling alone*. New York, NY: Simon & Schuster.

Radloff, L. S. (1977). The CES-D scale: A self-report depression scale for research in the general population. *Applied Psychological Measurement, 1*, 385–401.

Random House dictionary of the English language: The unabridged edition. (1967). New York, NY: Random House.

Richards, P. S., & Bergin, A. E. (2005). *A spiritual strategy for counseling and psychotherapy* (2nd ed.). Washington, DC: American Psychological Association.

Ripley, J. S., & Worthington, E. E. (2002). Hope-focused and forgiveness-based group interventions to promote marital enrichment. *Journal of Counseling and Development, 80*, 452–463.

Roberts, J. (1988). Setting the frame: Definition, functions, and typology of rituals. In E. Imber-Black, J. Roberts, & R. A. Whiting (Eds.), *Rituals in families and family therapy* (pp. 3–48). New York, NY: Norton.

Robinson, L. C. (1994). Religious orientation in enduring marriage: An exploratory study. *Review of Religious Research, 35*, 207–218.

Rodgers, R. H. (1973). *Family interaction and transcation: The developmental approach*. Englewood Cliffs, NJ: Prentice-Hall.

Rogers, C. R. (1951). *Client-centered therapy: Its current practice, implications and theory*. Boston, MA: Houghton Mifflin.

Rogers, C. R. (1961). *On becoming a person: A therapists view of psychotherapy*. Boston, MA: Houghton Mifflin.

Roof, W. C., & Silk, M. (2005). *Religion and public life in the Pacific region*. Lanham, MD: Altamira.

Rose, A. M. (1962). *Human behavior and social processes: An interactionist approach*. Boston, MA: Houghton Mifflin.

Rousseau, J. J. (1762). *Emile* (B. Foxley, Trans.). London, UK: Dent & Sons

Rousseau, J. J. (1763). *The social contract* (G. Hopkins, Trans.). New York, NY: Oxford Univesity Press.

Rubin, Z. (1973). *Liking and loving: An invitation to social psychology*. New York, NY: Holt, Rinehart and Winston.

Ruddick, S. (1989). *Maternal thinking: Toward a politics of peace*. Boston, MA: Beacon Press.

Rusbult, C. E., Bissonnette, V. L., Arriaga, X. B., & Cox, C. L. (2008). Accommodation processes during the early years of marriage. In T. N. Bradbury (Ed.), *The developmental course of marital dysfunction* (pp. 74–113). New York, NY: Cambridge University Press.

Scanzoni, J., & Arnett, C. (1987). Enlarging the understanding of marital commitment via religious devoutness, gender role preferences, and locus of marital control. *Journal of Family Issues, 8*, 136–156.

Schvaneveldt, J. D., & Lee, T. R. (1983). The emergence of practice of ritual in the American family. *Family Perspective, 17*, 137–143.

Schüutz, A. (1999). It was your fault! Self-serving biases in autogiographical accounts of conflicts in married couples. *Journal of Social & Pesonal Relationships, 16*, 193–209.

Schwartz, S. (1975). The justice of need and the activation of humanitarian norms. *Journal of Social Issues, 31*, 111–136.

Seligman, M. E. P. (2011). *Flourish: A visionary new understanding of happiness and well-being*. New York: Free Press.

Shams, M., & Jackson, P. R. (1993). Religiosity as a predictor of well-being and moderator of the psychological impact of unemployment. *British Journal of Medical Psychology, 66*, 341–352.

Sherif, C. W., & Sherif, M. (1967). *Attitude, ego-involvement, and change*. New York, NY: Wiley.

Sherif, C. W., Sherif, M., & Nebergall, R. E. (1965). *Attitude and attitude change: The social judgment-invovlement approach*. Philadelphia, PA: Saunders.

Shorter, E. (1975). *The making of the modern family*. New York, NY: Basic Books.

Shostrom, E. L. (1967). *Man, the manipulator: The inner journey from manipulation to actualization*. New York, NY: Abingdon Press.

Siegel, A. E., & Siegel, S. (1957). Reference groups, membership groups, and attitude change. *Journal of Abnormal and Social Psychology*, *55*, 360–365.

Silva, J., Marks, L. D., & Cherry, K. (2009). The psychology behind helping and prosocial behaviors: An examination from intention to action in an adult population. In K. Cherry (Ed.), *Lifespan perspectives on natural disasters: Coping with Katrina, Rita and other storms* (pp. 219–240). New York, NY: Springer.

Skinner, B. F. (1948). *Walden two*. New York, NY: Macmillan.

Skinner, B. F. (1971). *Beyond freedom and dignity*. New York, NY: Bantam.

Slife, B. D., & Williams, R. N. (1995). *What's behind the research?: Discovering hidden assumptions in the behavioral sciences*. Thousand Oaks, CA: Sage.

Smedes, L. B. (1984). *Forgive and forget: Healing the hurts we don't deserve*. New York, NY: HarperCollins.

Smith, A. (1776). *An inquiry into the nature and causes of the wealth of nations*. Oxford, UK: Oxford Univeristy Press.

Smith, C. (2003). Theorizing religious effects among American adolescents. *Journal for the Scientific Study of Religion*, *42*, 17–30.

Smith, H. (1991). *The world's religions: Our great wisdom traditions*. San Francisco, CA: Harper.

Smith, H. (1992). *Forgotten truth: The common vision of the world's religions*. San Francisco, CA: Harper.

Smith, H. (2001). *Why religion matters*. San Francisco, CA: Harper.

Snarey, J. R., & Dollahite, D. C. (2001). Varieties of religion-family linkages. *Journal of Family Psychology*, *15*, 646–651.

Sorokin, P. A. (1967). *The ways and power of love*. Chicago, IL: Henry Regnery.

Sprey, J. (1990). *Fashioning family theory: New Approaches*. Newbury Park, CA: Sage.

Stanley, S. M. (1998). *The heart of commitment*. Nashville, TN: Nelson.

Stanley, S. M. (2005). *The power of commitment*. San Francisco, CA: Jossey-Bass.

Stanley, S. M., & Markman, H. J. (1992). Assessing commitment in personal relationships. *Journal of Marriage & Family*, *54*, 595–608.

Stanley, S. M., Whitton, S. W., Sadberry, S. L., Clements, M. L., & Markman, H. J. (2006). Sacrifice as a predictor of marital outcomes. *Family Process*, *45*, 289–303.

Stark, R., and Finke, R. (2000). *Acts of faith: Explaining the human side of religion*. Berkeley, CA: University of California Press.

Steinmetz, S. K., & Straus, M. A. (1974). *Violence in the family*. New York, NY: Dodd, Mead.

Sternberg, R. J. (1997). Construct validation of a triangular love scale. *European Journal of Social Psychology*, *27*, 313–335.

Sternberg, R. J., & Barnes, M. L. (Eds.). (1988). *The psychology of love*. New Haven, CT: Yale University Press.

Stinchcombe, A. L. (1968). *Constructing social theories*. New York, NY: Harcourt, Brace & World.

Stratton, P. (2003). Causal attributions during therapy II: Reconstituted families and parental blaming. *Journal of Family Therapy*, *25*, 161–180.

Straus, M. A. (1974). Leveling, civility, and violence in the family. *Journal of Marriage & Family*, *36*, 13–29.

Straus, M. A., Gelles, R. J., & Steinmetz, S. K. (1978). *Behind closed doors: Violence in the American family*. New York, NY: Doubleday/Anchor.

Strauss, A. L., & Corbin, J. M. (1990). *Basics of qualitative research: Grounded theory procedures and techniques*. Newbury Park, CA: Sage.

Subkoviak, M. J., Enright, R. D., Wu, C. R., Gasin, E. A., Freedman, S., Olson, L. M., et al. (1995). Measuring interpersonal forgiveness in late adolescence and middle adulthood. *Journal of Adolescence*, *18*, 641–655.

Sullivan, K. T. (2001). Understanding the relationship between religiosity and marriage: An investigation of the immediate and longitudinal effects of religiosity on newlywed couples. *Journal of Family Psychology*, *15*, 610–626.

Sussman, M. B., & Steinmetz, S. K. (1987). *Handbook of marriage and the family*. New York, NY: Plenum Press.

Swenson, D. (2009). *Society, spirituality, and the sacred: A social scientific introduction* (2nd ed.). New York, NY: University of Toronto Press.

Tangney, J. P. (1990). Assessing individual differences in proneness to shame and guilt: Development of the self-conscious affect and attribution inventory. *Journal of Personality and Social Psychology, 59*, 102–111.

Tangney, J. P. (1991). Moral affect: The good, the bad, and the ugly. *Journal of Personality and Social Psychology, 61*, 598–607.

Tangney, J. P. (1994). The mixed legacy of the superego: Adaptive and maladaptive aspects of shame and guilt. In J. M. Masling & R. F. Borenstein (Eds.), *Empirical perspectives on object relations theory* (pp. 1–28). Washington, DC: American Psychological Association.

Tangney, J. P., Wagner, P., & Gramzow, R. (1992). Proneness to shame, proneness to guilt, and psychopathology. *Journal of Abnormal Psychology, 101*, 1–10.

Taylor, A. C., & Bagdi, A. (2005). The use of explicit theory in family research. In V. L. Bengtson, A. C. Acock, K. R. Allen, P. Dilworth-Anderson, & D. M. Klein (Eds.), *Sourcebook of family theory* (pp. 22–25). Thousand Oaks, CA: Sage.

Taylor, C. (1991). *The ethics of authenticity*. Cambridge, MA: Harvard University Press.

Taylor, C. (2007). *A secular age*. Cambridge, MA: Belknap Press of Harvard University Press.

Thibaut, J. W., & Kelley, H. H. (1959). *The social psychology of groups*. New York, NY: Wiley.

Thomas, D. L., & Cornwall, M. (1990). Religion and family in the 1980s: Discovery and development. *Journal of Marriage & Family*, *52*, 983–992.

Thomas, D. L., & Henry, G. C. (1985). The religion and family connection: Increasing dialogue in the social sciences. *Journal of Marriage & Family*, *47*, 11.

Thomas, D. L., & Wilcox, J. E. (1987). The rise of family theory: A historical and critical analysis. In M. B. Sussman & S. K. Steinmetz (Eds.), *Handbook of marriage and the family*. New York, NY: Plenum Press.

Thomas, W. I. (1923). *The unadjusted girl: With cases and standpoint for behavior analysis*. Boston, MA: Little, Brown.

Thomas, W. I., & Znaniecki, F. (1918). *The Polish peasant in Europe and America*. Boston, MA: Badger.

Tolstoy, L. (1965). *Anna Karenina* (C. Garnett, Trans.). New York, NY: Random House Inc.

Toma, C., Yzerbyt, V., & Corneille, O. (2010). Anticipated cooperation vs. competition moderates interpersonal projection. *Journal of Experimental Social Psychology*, *46*, 375–381.

Toussaint, L. L., Williams, D. R., Musick, M. A., & Everson, S. A. (2001). Forgiveness and health: Age differences in a U.S. probability sample. *Journal of Adult Development*, *8*, 249–257.

Townsend, M., Kladder, V., & Mulligan, T. (2002). Systematic review of clinical trials examining the effects of religion on health. *Southern Medical Journal*, *95*, 1429–1434.

Tudge, J. R. H., Mokrova, I., Hatfield, B. E., & Karnik, R. B. (2009). Uses and misuses of Bronfenbrenner's bioecological theory of human development. *Journal of Family Theory and Review*, *1*, 198–210.

Turillo, C. J., Folger, R., Lavelle, J. J., Umphress, E. E., & Gee, J. O. (2002). Is virtue its own reward? Self-sacrificial decisions for the sake of fairness. *Organizational Behavior and Human Decision Processes*, *89*, 839–865.

Tutu, D. (1998). Without forgiveness there is no future. In R. D. Enright & J. North (Eds.), *Exploring forgiveness* (pp. xiii–xiv). Madison: University of Wisconsin Press.

Tyler, A. (1975). *Searching for Caleb*. New York: Alfred A. Knopf.

Tyler, T. R., & Blader, S. L. (2000). *Cooperation in groups: Procedural justice, social identity, and behavioral engagement*. Philadelphia, PA: Taylor & Francis.

Tyler, T. R., & Huo, Y. J. (2002). *Trust in the law: Encouraging public cooperation with the police and courts*. New York, NY: Russell Sage Foundation.

Umberson, D., Williams, K., Powers, D. A., Liu, H., & Needham, B. (2005). Stress in childhood and adulthood: Effects on marital quality over time. *Journal of Marriage & Family*, *67*, 1332–1347.

van Lange, P. A. M., Agnew, C. R., Harinck, R., & Steemers, G. E. (1997). From game theory to real life: How social value orientation affects willingness to sacrifice in ongoing close relationships. *Journal of Personality and Social Psychology*, *73*, 1330–1344.

van Lange, P. A. M., Rusbult, C. E., Drigotas, S. M., Arriaga, X. B., Witcher, B. S., & Cox, C. L. (1997). Willingness to sacrifice in close relationships. *Journal of Personality and Social Psychology*, *72*, 1373–1395.

Vaux, A. (1987). Appraisals of social support: Love, respect, and involvement. *Journal of Community Psychology*, *15*, 493–502.

Von Arnim, E. (2007). *The enchanted April*. Charleston, SC: Bibliobazaar.

Wade, S. H. (1989). The development of a scale to measure forgiveness. *Dissertation Abstracts International: Section B. Sciences and Engineering*, *50*, 5338.

Waldron, V. R., & Kelley, D. L. (2008). *Communicating forgiveness*. Thousand Oaks, CA: Sage.

Walls, G. B. (1980). Values and psychotherapy: A comment on "Psychotherapy and Religious Values." *Journal of Consulting & Clinical Psychology*, *48*, 640–641.

Walsh, F. (2003). Family resilience: Strengths forged through adversity. In F. Walsh (Ed.), *Normal family processes: Growing diversity and complexity* (3rd ed., pp. 399–423). New York, NY: Guilford Press.

Walsh, F. (2006). *Strengthening family resilience*. New York, NY: Guilford Press.

Walsh, F. (2009). *Spiritual resources in family therapy* (2nd ed.). New York, NY: Guilford Press.

Warner, C. (1995). *Bonds of anguish, bonds of love*. Salt Lake City, UT: Arbinger.

Weber, M. (1904). *The Protestant ethic and the spirit of capitalism* (1958, Trans.). New York, NY: Scribner's.

Weissman, M. M., Orvaschel, H., & Padian, N. (1980). Children's symptom and social functioning self-report scales: Comparison of mothers' and childrens' reports. *Journal of Nervous Mental Disorders*, *168*, 736–740.

White, J. M. (1991). *Dynamics of family development: A theoretical perspective*. New York, NY: Guilford Press.

White, J. M. (2005). *Advancing family theories*. Thousand Oaks, CA: Sage.

White, J. M., & Klein, D. M. (2008). *Family theories* (3rd ed.). Thousand Oaks, CA: Sage.

Whitton, S. W., Stanley, S. M., & Markman, H. J. (2002). Sacrifice in romantic relationships: An exploration of relevant research and theory. In A. L. Vangelisti, H. T. Reis, & M. A. Fitzpatrick (Eds.), *Stability and change in relationships* (pp. 156–181). Cambridge, UK: Cambridge University Press.

Whitton, S. W., Stanley, S. M., & Markman, H. J. (2007). If I help my partner, will it hurt me? Perceptions of sacrifice in romantic relationships. *Journal of Social & Clinical Psychology*, *26*, 64–91.

Wiener, N. (1948). Cybernetics. *Scientific American*, *179*, 14–18.

Wieselquist, J., Rusbult, C. E., Foster, C. A., & Agnew, C. R. (1999). Commitment, pro-relationship behavior, and trust in close relationships. *Journal of Personality and Social Psychology, 77*, 942–966.

Wilcox, W. B. (2004). *Soft patriarchs, new men: How Christianity shapes fathers and husbands*. Chicago, IL: University of Chicago Press.

Wilcox, W. B. (Ed.). (2010). *The state of our unions*. Charlottesville, VA: National Marriage Project at the University of Virginia.

Wile, D. B. (1993). *After the fight: A night in the life of a couple*. New York, NY: Guilford Press.

Williams, D. R., Larson, D. B., Buckler, R. E., Heckman, R. C., & Pyle, C. M. (1991). Religion and psychological distress in a community sample. *Social Science and Medicine, 11*, 1257–1262.

Wilson, C., Gardner, F., Burton, J., & Leung, S. (2006). Maternal attributions and young children's conduct problems: A longitudinal study. *Infant & Child Development, 15*, 109–121.

Winch, R. F. (1955). The theory of complementary needs in mate selection: Final results on the test of the general hypothesis. *American Sociological Review, 20*, 552–555.

Winch, R. F. (1958). *Mate-selection: A study of complementary needs*. New York, NY: Harper.

Winch, R. F., & Blumberg, R. L. (1968). Societal complexity and familial organization. In R. F. Winch & L. W. Goodman (Eds.), *Selected studies in marriage and the family* (pp. 70–92). New York, NY: Holt, Rinehart and Winston.

Winton, C. A. (1995). *Frameworks for studying families*. Guilford, CT: Dushkin.

Wise, G. W. (1986). Family routines, rituals, and traditions: Grist for the family mill and buffers against stress. In S. Van Zandt (Ed.), *Family strengths 7: Vital connections* (pp. 243–256). Lincoln, NE: Center for Family Strengths.

Wolin, S. J., & Bennett, L. A. (1984). Family rituals. *Family Process, 23*, 401–420.

Wolin, S. J., Bennett, L. A., Noonan, D. L., & Teitelbaum, M. A. (1980). Disrupted family rituals: A factor in the intergenerational transmission of alcoholism. *Journal of Studies on Alcohol and Drugs, 41*, 199–214.

Wolpert, M. (2000). Is anyone to blame? Whom families and their therapists blame for the presenting problem. *Clinical Child Psychology & Psychiatry, 5*, 115–132.

Worthington, E. L. (1998). An empathy-humility-commitment model of forgiveness applied within family dyads. *Journal of Family Therapy, 20*, 59–76.

Worthington, E. L. (2005). *Handbook of forgiveness*. New York, NY: Routledge.

Young, W. A. (1995). *The world's religions: Worldviews and contemporary issues*. Englewood Cliffs, NJ: Prentice-Hall.

Zetterberg, H. L. (1965). *On theory and verification in sociology*. Totowa, NJ: Bedminster Press.

Zhai, J. E., Ellison, C. G., Stokes, C. E., & Glenn, N. D. (2008). "Spiritual, but not religious": The impact of parental divorce on the religious and spiritual identities of young adults in the United States. *Review of Religious Research, 49*, 379–394.

Zimmerman, C. C., & Broderick, C. B. (1954). Nature and role of informal family groups. *Marriage and Family Living, 16*, 107–111.

Zimmerman, C. C., & Broderick, C. B. (1956). The family self-protective system. In C. C. Zimmerman & L. F. Cervantes (Eds.), *Marriage and the family* (pp. 101–117). Chicago, IL: Regnery.

Zimmerman, C. C., & Cervantes, L. F. (Eds.). (1956). *Marriage and the family*. Chicago, IL: Regnery.

Zimmerman, C. C., & Cervantes, L. F. (1960). *Successful American families*. New York, NY: Pageant Press.

Author Index

A

Abbott, D. A., 56, 57, 60, 65, 200, 202, 289
Ackrman, J., 297
Acock, A. C., 5, 290, 298, 302, 310
Adams, B., ix
Agnew, C. R., 73, 311, 312
Akinlade, K. S., 56
Aldous, J. 237, 289
Allen, K. R., 5, 238, 266, 289, 290, 298, 302, 310
Allport, G. W., 271
Allred, G. H., 132, 289
Al-Mabuk, R. H., 40, 51, 289
Amato, P.R.228, 289
Anchor, K. N., 56, 296
Anderson, E., 106, 289
Arcus, M. E., 71, 289
Aristotle, 158, 159, 221, 227
Arnett, C., 16, 308
Aronson , E., 290
Arriaga, X. B., 73, 308, 311
Arterburn, S., 163, 289
Ashton, M., 250, 293
Aubin, D. S., 295

B

Bach, G. R., 125, 289
Back, K. W., 125, 289
Bacon, F., 270
Baden, A. D., 153, 289
Baefsky, P. M., 72, 289
Bagdi, A., 234, 310
Bahr, H. M., ix, 14, 69, 71. 72, 75, 88, 91, 92, 202, 251, 289, 295
Bahr, K. S., ix, 14, 69, 71. 72, 75, 88, 91, 92, 289, 292, 251, 269, 292
Bailey, E., 7, 289
Baker, T. R., ix, 136, 237, 289, 292
Baldwin, L.M., 248, 296
Barber, B. K., 120
Barbour, I. G., 271, 289
Bargh, J. A., 62, 289
Barker, K., 211
Barndollar, K., 62, 289
Barnes, M. L., 88, 309
Barry, J. W., 40, 290
Bartholomew, K., 110, 300, 302
Bascaseta, P. E., 293,
Basque, V., 2
Bass, E., 38, 290
Bateson, G., 235, 273, 290
Battle, C. L., 42, 43, 290
Baucom, D. H., 3, 36, 37, 40, 41, 42, 290, 298, 299
Bauman, Z., 109, 290
Baumeister, R. F., 48, 49, 249, 290
Baxter, L. A., 208
Beach, S. R. M., 2, 37, 440, 41, 42, 58, 59, 61, 62, 63, 64, 67, 71, 72, 74, 91, 117, 149, 251, 290 , 296, 297, 302
Beck, A. T., 290
Beck, L. A., 111, 224, 236, 268, 290
Bellah, R. N., 70, 98, 99, 165, 188, 220, 290
Bengtson, V. L., 5, 165,185, 238, 263, 274, 290, 298, 302, 310
Bennett, L. A., 202, 203, 204, 205, 206, 312
Benore, E., 22
Benson, H., 56, 290
Berardo, F. M., 15
Berger, P. L., 7, 215, 290
Berger, S. E., 72, 289
Bergin, A. E., 7, 56, 65, 234, 271, 271, 290, 308
Berkowitz, L., 125, 290
Bernard, J., 290
Berry, J. W., 292
Berry, M., 56, 289
Berscheid, E., 72, 88, 290
Bertalanffy, L. V., 235, 237, 273, 290
Beutler, I. F., 292, 303
Bird, M. H., 2, 292
Biruni, 13
Bishop, D.S., 248, 296
Bissonnette, V. L., 73, 308
Blader, S.L., 106, 311
Blalock, H. M., 11, 263, 290
Blanch, M., ix, 269
Blau, P. M., 110, 290
Blumberg, R. L., 36, 149, 312
Blumer, H. G., 173, 237, 291
Boll, E. S., 202, 204, 291
Boon, S. D., 72, 300
Booth, A., 228, 289
Borenstein, R. F., 310
Boscolo, L., 178
Boss, P. G., ix, 42, 53, 165, 192, 243, 263, 290, 291
Bossard, J. H. S., 202, 204, 291
Boszormenyi-Nagy, I., 42, 75, 176, 177, 180, 184, 291
Bott, E., 147, 291
Boulding, K. E., 75, 80, 93, 112, 291
Bowen, C., 152, 153, 291
Bowen, M., 135, 280, 291
Bowker, J., 7. 291
Boyatzis, C. J., 35, 294
Boyce, W. T., 202, 291

Bradburn, N. M., 36, 91, 149
Bradbury, T. N., 42, 291, 297, 308
Bradford, K.P., 300
Braithwaite, R. B., 11, 291
Braithwaite, S. R., 58, 59, 263, 297, 302
Brelsford, G., x
Breunlin, D. C., 238, 291
Broderick, C. B., 15, 173, 196, 197, 18, 199, 235, 291, 312
Bronfenbrenner, U., 201, 243, 291
Brotherson, S. E., 304, 305
Brown, S. W., 305
Browning, D. S., 88, 269
Buckler, R. E., 56, 312
Buckley, C. K, 235, 293
Buckley, W. F., 235, 292
Burchard, G. A., 51, 292
Burdette, A. M., 296
Burgess, M., 37, 292
Burns, D. D., 248, 292
Burr, R. J., 265, 267, 292
Burr, W. R., 11, 15, 37, 71, 136, 159, 165, 202, 222, 235, 238, 263, 265, 267, 268 269, 289, 292, 298, 300, 303
Burton, J., 153, 312
Busby, D. M., 246, 248, 292
Bush, E. G., 208
Butler, M. H., ix, 2, 57, 58, 60, 61, 62, 64, 65, 66, 67, 236, 240, 292

C

Caillois, R., 132, 292
Call, V. R. A., 300
Calvin, J. 219
Cannon, K. L., 292
Canter, D. E., 292
Cardis, P. A., 40, 289
Carels, R. A., 12
Carlo, G., 244, 292
Carlson, B., 295
Carlson, C. R., 293
Carnelley, K. B., 43
Carroll, J. S., 244, 250, 293
Carter, E. A., 237, 293
Carver, C. S., 81, 293
Cashwell, C. S., 7, 293
Cecchin, G., 178
Cerreto, M., 110
Cervantes, L. F., 173, 196, 293, 312
Chan, L. Y., 293
Charters, W. W. Jr., 173, 293
Chase, S. E., 263, 274, 293
Chen, J., 293
Cheong, R. K., 45, 293
Cherlin, A. J., 21, 228, 293
Cherry, K., 75, 309
Chibucos, T. R., 15, 293
Choen, J. R., 106
Christensen, C., 222, 268, 292
Christensen, H. T., 15, 72, 165, 185,187, 192, 193, 293, 300
Christiansen, S.L., 300
Cirillo, S., 178
Clairmont, D. A., 295
Clark, C. L., 208, 224
Clark, M. S., 72, 111, 224, 268, 290, 293
Clements, M. L., 71, 309
Cohen, J. R., 293
Cole, B., 303
Coleman, M., 42
Coleman, P. W., 293
Collins, P., 202, 293
Collins, R., 299
Collins, W. A., 250
Confucious, 88
Cook, J. C., 293
Cook, W. L., 294
Cooley, C. H., 237, 266, 294
Corbin, J. M., 11, 263, 265, 266, 274, 309
Corneille, O., 310
Cornwall, M., 1, 2, 5, 11, 31, 310
Coursey, R. D., 56
Covey, S. R., 74, 158, 183, 294
Cox, C. L., 73, 308, 311
Coyle, C. T., 51, 294
Crain, W. C., 238, 294
Cramer, D., 80, 294
Crick, N. R., 250
Crocker, S., 65, 294
Cuber, J. F., 125, 126, 127, 294
Cui, M., 294
Curran, D., 202, 294

D

Damasceno-Scott, M., 2, 298
Damon W., 291
Dant, D. R., 227, 301
Dare, L. O., 56
Darwin, C., 14, 273, 274, 294
Das, B., 10, 294
Davila, J., 2, 37, 149, 297
Davis, E. F., 293
Davis, K., 19, 294
Davis, L., 38, 2900
Davis, T., 2, 56
Day, R. D., 292, 244, 269, 292, 294, 300
de Cremer, D., 106, 294
Denham, S. A., 35, 294
Denzin, N. K., 11, 263, 294
Descartes, R., 271
Deutsch, M., 43, 73, 105, 127, 129, 131, 132, 294
Dew, J., 304
Dibatista, B., 16, 296

DiBlasio, F. A., 38, 45, 51, 293, 294
Diesing, P., 131, 132, 294
Dill, D., 80, 301
Dilworth-Anderson, P., 5, 290, 298, 302, 310
Dixon, L. J., 37, 299
Doherty, W. J., x, 65, 74, 185, 202, 203, 208, 221, 294, 295
Dollahite, D. C., ix, x, 1, 2, 3, 4, 5, 13, 24, 55, 60, 61, 71, 79, 186, 201, 211, 264, 265, 290, 291, 292, 294, 295, 298, 300, 302, 309
Dome, L. J., 244, 299
Donnellan, M. B., 294
Dosscy, L., 56, 295
Downs, W. R., 51, 289
Draper, T. W., ix, 292
Drigotas, S. M., 311
Dubin, R., 11, 263, 295
Dumas, A., 154
Durkheim, E., 13, 207, 208, 295
Duvall, E., 237, 295

E

Edwards, H., 131, 296
Edmonds, V. H., 16, 296
Edwards Leeper, L., 303
Elkins, D., 56, 296
Ellis, A., 164, 214, 236, 237, 296
Ellison, C. G., 7, 59, 296, 312
Emery, E., 304
Emler, N., 106, 296
Engels, F., 214, 273
Enright, R. D., 36, 40, 41, 51, 289, 293, 294, 296, 297, 310, 311
Epstein, N.B., 248, 296
Erikson, E. H.176, 180, 184, 273, 281, 296
Erikson, J. M., 176, 296
Everson, S. A., 41, 310

F

Falicov, C. J., 237, 296
Feeney, J. A., 107, 296
Felton, J., 163, 289
Fenell, D., 41, 296
Fernando, A., 39, 296
Festinger, L., 173, 296
Fiese, B. H., 202, 204, 208, 296
Filipp, S. H., 305
Fincham, F. D., 2, 37, 40, 41, 42, 43, 51, 56, 58, 59, 61, 62, 63, 64, 65, 71, 72, 74, 91, 149, 251, 290, 291, 296, 297, 302
Finke, R., 186, 309
Finkel, E. J., 42, 293, 297
Finkenauer, C., 48, 290
Fischer, L., 227, 301
Fiske, S. T., 293
Fitzgibbons, R. P., 36, 41, 296
Fitzpatrick, M. A., 311
Fletcher, G. J. O., 291
Folger, R., 72, 311
Forde, D. R., 106, 302
Foster, C. A., 73, 312
Framo, J. L., 178, 297
Frankl, V. E., 74, 82, 83, 118, 183, 217, 297
Freedman, S., 297, 310
Freedman, S. R., 51, 297
Freeman, W., 153, 301
Frei, 107, 297
Freud, S., 214, 217, 273, 274, 297
Frielander, M. L., 152, 297
Fritz, H. L., 80, 110, 297, 300
Fromm, E., 88, 93, 112, 217, 297
Frutchey, R., 303
Furlong, M., 152, 297

G

Gable, S. L., 75, 81, 298, 301
Gaines, S. O. Jr., 106, 298
Gall, T. L., 2, 298
Gallagher, S. K., 22, 226, 298
Galving, S. L., 80
Ganong, L. H., 295
Gardner, B. C., 2, 240, 292
Gardner, F., 153, 312
Garrison, B., 2
Gasin, E. A., 310
Gee, J. O., 72, 311
Gelles, R., 125, 189, 298, 309
Gibbs, J. P., 11, 263, 298
Gilbert, D. T., 293
Giles, L., 88
Gilgun, J. F., 11, 263, 298
Glaser, B. G., 11, 263, 287, 298
Gleick, J., 273, 274, 298
Glenn, N. D., 7, 312
Goddard, H. W., 103, 303
Goethals. G. R., 301
Goethe, J. W., 158
Goffman, E., 20, 237, 266, 298
Gollwitzer, P. M., 62, 289, 298
Goode, W. J., 71, 92, 298
Goodman, L. W., 312
Goodman, M. A., 1, 4, 295, 298
Gordon, K. C., 36, 37, 40, 41, 42, 51, 149, 298, 299
Gottman, J. M., 61, 62, 73, 80, 92, 106, 125, 127, 134, 135, 178, 250, 279, 280, 299
Gouldner, A. W., 43, 73, 105, 127, 128, 299
Graham, S. M., 59, 293, 302
Gramzow, R., 255, 310
Granovetter, M. S., 198, 299
Gray, J. A., 37, 81, 149, 299
Greeley, A. M., 57, 60, 65, 299

Griffith, J. L., 16, 164, 173, 299
Grimes, R. L., 202, 299
Gruner, L., 56, 65, 66, 299
Guerney, B. G., 43, 93, 112, 299
Gurman, A. S., 302

H

Hage, J., 11, 263, 299
Hajii, 106, 299
Haley, A., 176, 178, 179, 180, 184, 299
Haley, J., 235, 290, 299
Hall, G. S., 40, 41, 271
Hall, J., 297, 299
Hancock, R., ix
Hannon, P. A., 42, 297
Hansen, D. A., 15, 300
Hardy, S., ix
Hargrave, T. D., 40, 299
Harinck, R., 311
Harker, H. B., 303
Harper, J. M., 57, 64, 65, 236, 240, 244, 246, 250, 292, 293, 299
Harris, A. H. S., 41, 300
Harroff, P. B., 125, 126, 127, 294
Harter, S., 81
Harvey, J. H., 56, 300
Harvey, J., 130, 298, 300
Hastings, P. D., 153, 300
Hatfield, B. E., 310
Hatfield, E., 88
Hawkins, A. J., ix, 55, 248, 295, 300
Heath, G. C., 132, 300
Heatherington, L., 152, 297
Heaton, T. B., 293, 303
Hecht, M., ix
Heckman, R. C., 56, 312
Helgeson, V. S., 80, 110, 297, 300
Hendrick, C., 106, 107, 300
Hendrick, S. S., 106, 107, 300
Henry, G. C., 271, 310
Henslin, J. M., 92, 300
Hetherington, E. M., 21, 300
Higgins, E. T., 298
Hight, T. L., 305
Hill, E. J., 2
Hill, E. W., 38
Hill, R., 11, 15, 109, 237, 238, 292, 295, 298, 300
Hoffman, J., 211, 300
Holden, G. W., 300
Holman, T. B., ix, 15, 235, 246, 292, 300
Holmes, J. G., 72, 300
Holyoake, G. J., 214, 216, 300
Homans, G. C., 110, 300
Homer, 88, 269
Honer, S. M., 116, 227, 300
Hooker, K. A., 228, 296
Hoopes, M., 246, 299
Hopkins, E., 71
Hopkins-Williams, K., 56
Horowitz, L. M., 100, 300
Horton, B., 302
Howe, G. W., 153, 289
Hughes, F. M., 37, 299
Hugo, V., 154, 157
Huizinga, J., 132, 301
Hunt, T. C., 116, 227, 300
Huo, Y. J., 106, 311
Hurt, T. R., 2, 290
Hyman, H. H., 173, 301
Hymowitz, K. S., 228, 301

I

Ibrahim, E., 88, 301
Imber-Black, E., 202, 204, 206, 207, 301, 308
Impett, E. A., 75, 80, 81, 301
Ingoldsby, B. B., 15, 240, 301

J

Jaccard, J., 11, 264, 301
Jack, D. C., 80, 301
Jackson, A. P., 227, 301
Jackson, D. D., 235, 290
Jackson, P. R., 56, 308
Jacobson, N. S., 73, 301
Jacoby, J., 11, 263, 301
James, S. A., 202, 291
James, W., 9, 13, 69, 116, 211, 237, 271, 301
Jensen, A. C, 293
Jensen, E. W., 202, 250, 291
Jewell, T., 303, 304
Johnson, D. R., 228, 289
Johnson, D. W., 132, 301
Johnson, M. D., 302
Johnson, R. T., 132, 301
Johnson, V. E., 136, 305
Johnson-Davies, D., 88, 301
Johnston, C., 301
Jones, S. L., 271, 301
Jones. W. H., 300
Jordan, J. V., 80, 301
Jourard, S. M., 43, 93, 112, 301

K

Kamiar, M., 13, 301
Kaminer, D., 37, 301
Kant, I., 9, 227
Kaplar, M., 303
Karnik, R. B., 11, 310
Keller, R. R., 106
Kelley, D. L., 38, 311
Kelley, H. H., 72, 110, 240, 301, 301, 310

Kelly, J., 21, 173, 300, 301
Kennedy, L. W., 106, 302, 302
Kerr, M. E., 135, 302
Kilian, M. K., 292
Kim, E. Y., 152, 302
Kladder, V., 56, 310
Klein, D. M., 5, 6, 15, 109, 165, 185, 240, 263, 290, 298, 302, 310, 311
Klein, S. L., 2, 302
Kline, C. A., 107, 208
Kluwer, E. S., 302
Knapp, S. J., ix, 11, 264, 285, 302
Kniskern, D. P., 302
Knoblauch, T. M., 89, 302
Koenig, H. G., 17, 56, 302
Kohn, A., 131, 132, 302
Koski, J., x
Kotary, L., 208, 296
Krasner, B. R., 42, 176, 177, 291
Krokoff, L. J., 80, 299
Kroll, B., 56, 302
Kruglanski, A. W., 298
Krumrei, E. J., 2, 3, 12, 17, 22, 97, 302
Kumashiro, M., 42, 297
Kunce, L. J., 110, 302

L

Lakritz, K. R., 89, 302
Lamanna, M. A., 202
Lambert, N. M., 2, 4, 56, 58, 59, 61, 65, 295, 297, 302
LaRossa, R., 226, 290, 291, 302
Larsen, J., 250
Larson, D. B., 56, 302, 312
Larson, S. S., 56, 302
Lasswell, M. E., 88, 303
Lavelle, J. J., 72, 311
Layton, E., 295
Lazarus, A. A., 236, 303
Lee, G. R., 21, 103, 104, 303
Lee, T. R.. 49, 205, 249, 281, 303, 308
Lee-Chai, A., 62, 289
Legaree, T. A., 37, 38, 303
Lehninger, A. L., 63
Leibniz, 227
Leite, R. W., 15, 293
Lemay Jr., E. P., 111, 293
Lerner, H. G., 80, 303
Lerner, M. J., 305
Lerner, R. M., 291
Leung, S., 153, 312
Levinger, G., 16, 303
Levi-Strauss, C., 43, 303
Lewis, C. A., 251, 242, 303
Lidz, T., 178, 303
Lieb, J., 297
Lincoln. Y. S., 11, 263, 294
Linder, J. R. 250, 303
Lindgren, K. N., 56, 303
Lindzey, G., 290, 293
Linfield, K. J., 297
Litzinger, S. C., 37, 299
Liu, H., 249, 311
Lobsenz, N. M., 88, 303
Logue, E. M., 106, 300
Lollis, S., 37
Loser, R. W., 2, 204, 208, 303
Lu, Y., x
Luther, M. 219

M

Maccoby, E., 293
MacCrimmon, K. R., 72, 303
MacDonald, M. G., 110
Machiavelli, N., 109, 303
MacKinnon-Lewis, C., 153, 303
Madill, A., 152, 153, 291
Madsen, R., 70, 290
Magoun, F., 92, 112, 303
Magyar, G. M., 22
Mahoney, A., ix, 1, 2, 3, 4, 5, 7, 10, 12, 16, 17, 22, 57, 97, 117, 161, 167 195, 196, 198, 200, 207, 229, 251, 259, 273, 302, 303
Maio, G. R., 43
Mamalakis, P. M., 38
Marciano, T. D., 1
Margolin, G., 73, 301
Markman, H. J., 71, 72, 74, 80, 251, 309, 311
Marks, L. D., 1, 2, 3, 4, 5, 24, 26, 56, 59, 60, 63, 64, 75, 79, 159, 168, 186, 201, 208, 209, 210, 211, 226, 264, 265, 283, 295, 302, 309
Marks, S. R., 271
Markson, S., 208
Marrs, A. L., 152, 297
Marshall, A., 234, 305
Marshall, D., 211
Marx, K., 21, 273, 274
Masling, J. M., 310
Maslow, A. H., 20, 74, 238,
Masters, W. H., 136
Mawadudi, A. A., 186
May, R., 88
McAdams, D. P., 295
McClure, H. M., 71, 298
McCullough, M. E., 41, 56, 298, 302
McGoldrick, M., 237, 293
McGuckin, C., 251
McIntosh, D. N., 56
McNair, L. M., 2, 290
McNulty, J. K., 44
Mead, G. H., 108, 109, 173, 237, 273
Melling, B., ix

Meredith, W. H., 56, 202, 204, 205, 207, 289
Merton, R. K., 6, 263
Messick, D. M., 72
Miklowitz, D. J., 152, 302
Miller, I. W., 42, 43, 290
Miller, J. E., 15, 301
Miller, W. R., 165
Mills, J., 72, 111, 224, 265, 293
Minuchin, S., 178
Mizruchi, S. L., 72
Mokrova, I., 11, 310
Montada, L., 152
Morris, P. A., 201, 243, 291
Moskowitz, G. B., 62, 298
Moss, J., 71, 289
Muhammad, 88
Muller, F. M., 112
Mulligan, T., 56, 310
Murdock, G. P., 13
Murphy, J. G., 43
Murray, J. D., 299
Murray-Swank, N. A., 12, 97
Murstein, B. I., 110, 111, 154
Musick, M. A., 41, 310
Myerhoff, B., 183
Myers, M., 72, 75, 223

N

Nagel, E., 11, 263
Navrtil, M., 251
Neal, K., 35, 294
Nebergall, R. E., 173, 308
Needham, B., 249, 311
Neff, K. D., 81, 149
Neff, P., 81, 149, 306
Neff, K. D., 306
Nelson, D.,, 250
Nesteruk, O., 2, 56
Newcomb, T. M., 173, 293
Newton, I., 271, 273
Nisbet, R. A., 282, 284
Nix, R. L., 153
Nock, S. L., 289
Noller, P., 88, 296
Noonan, D. L., 206, 312
North, J., 41, 293, 296, 311
Norton, R., 246
Norville, D., 106
Nottingham, E. K., 7
Novak, A., 62
Nye, I. F., 11, 15, 292, 298

O

O'Connor, L. E., 40, 29
Ohaeri, J. U., 56
Olen, J. A., 289
Olsen, J. A., 120, 303
Olsen, N., 56, 300
Olson, L. M., 310
Olson, M. M., 2, 295
Onedera, J. D., 7, 65
Orden, S. R., 35, 91, 4
Orvaschel, H., 247, 311
Osmond, M. W., 224
Ostenson, J., ix

P

Padian, N., 247, 311
Padilla-Walker, L. M., 244, 292, 294
Page, J. R., 80
Palazolli, M. S., 178
Paleari, F. G., 41
Palkovitz, R., 79, 226, 300
Palmer, S. J., 106
Paloutzian, R. F., 7
Parata, 178
Pargament, K. I., ix, 1, 2, 4, 7, 8, 10, 12, 14, 16, 17, 22, 75, 97, 164, 207, 208, 298, 302
Park, C. L., 7
Parkin, D., 202
Parrott, L., 40, 29
Pataki, S. P., 293
Patanaude, R. L. 153, 301
Patton, J., 38
Pavlov, I. P., 14
Peacock, J. L., 291
Pendleton, 56
Peperzak, A. T., 109
Peplau, L. A., 75, 301
Percesepe, G. J., 116
Perlman, D., 300, 302
Peterson, C., 248, 307
Phillips, R., 303
Pickering, B. J., 294
Pickering, M., 35, 92
Pickering, S., 294
Pierce, J. K., 297
Plato, 214, 227, 231, 273, 282
Pleck, J., 248, 307
Poloma, M.M., 56
Powell, J. J., 88, 93, 112
Powers, D. A., 311
Prata, G., 306
Putnam, R., 201, 307
Pyle, C. M., 56, 312

R

Rachal, K. C., 305
Radloff, L. S., 248, 307
Regalia, C., 41
Reicher, S., 106, 296
Reis, H. T., 81, 298, 311

Reiss, I. L., 11, 292, 298
Rempel, J. K., 73, 300
Reynolds, E., ix
Richards, P. S., 7, 56, 65, 234, 271, 308
Riegert, D., ix
Ripley, J. S., 51, 308
Roberts, J., 202, 203, 301, 308
Roberts, R. J., 56, 300
Robinson, L. C., 57, 60, 308
Rodgers, R., 237, 300
Rodgers, R. H., 308
Rogers, C. R., 14, 228, 238, 273, 308
Rogers, S. J., 289
Roof, W. C., 264, 308
Rose, A. M., 173, 237, 308
Rosenberg, S. E., 110, 300
Ross, J. M., 271
Rousseau, J. J., 238, 308
Rubin, K. H., 153, 300
Rubin, Z., 88, 308
Ruddick, S., 89, 308
Rusbult, C. E., 42, 72, 73, 74, 251, 297, 308, 311, 312
Rye, M. S., 97, 273

S

Sadberry, S. L., 71, 309
Sanchez, L. A., 289
Sandage, S. J.
Sanders, G., 202
Sandler, H. M., 56, 296
Saxe, J. G., 232
Scanzoni, J., 16, 308
Schmidt, E. P., 291
Schoppe-Sullivan, S., 292, 293
Schumm, W. R., 290, 291, 306
Schutz, A., 152
Schvaneveldt, J. D., 71, 207, 289, 308
Schwagler, J., 208, 296,
Schwartz, S., 72
Scott, E., 304
Seligman, M. E. P., 248, 255, 308
Sells, J. N., 40, 299
Selvini, M., 178
Shakespeare, W., 88, 269
Shams, M., 56, 308
Shaver, P. R., 107, 110, 297, 302
Sherif, C. W., 173, 308
Sherif, M., 173, 308
Shevlin, M., 251
Shokunbi, W. A., 56
Shorter, E., 89, 308
Shostrom, E. L., 125, 309
Siegel, A. E., 173, 309
Siegel, S., 173, 309
Silk, M., 264, 308
Silva, J., 75, 309
Silver, R. C., 56, 178, 299
Simonton, D. A., 293
Skinner, B. F., 116, 236, 237, 309
Slife, B. D., 31, 295, 309
Smedes, L. B., 35, 50, 309
Smith, A., 14, 273, 309
Smith, C., 2, 3, 5, 309
Smith, H., 10, 150, 186, 218, 268, 309
Smith, S. R., 15, 301
Snarey, J. R., 1, 4, 5, 309
Snyder, D. K., 47, 40, 298, 299
Sorokin, P. A., 88, 92, 93, 112, 309
Sorrentino, A. M., 178
Spark, G. M., 42, 75, 176, 291
Spencer, M., 132, 300
Spinoza, 227
Sprey, J., 277, 309
Stanley, S. M., 2, 41, 62, 63, 71, 72, 74, 75, 80, 83, 84, 91, 251, 290, 297, 309, 311
Stark, R., 185, 186, 309
Steemers, G. E., 311
Stein, D. J., 38, 301
Stein, S. K., 56, 300
Steinmetz, S. K., 72, 165, 185, 290, 291, 303, 309, 310
Sternberg, R. J., 88, 309
Stevens, H. B., 80
Stillman, T. F., 56, 58, 59, 297, 302302
Stinchcombe, A. L., 11, 263, 309
Stokes, C. E., 7, 312
Stoll, R., 250
Stolz, H. E., 120, 289
Stout, J. A., 2, 240, 292
Stratten, P., 152, 153, 291, 309
Straus, M. A., 125, 189, 298, 309
Strauss, A. L., 11, 263, 265, 266, 274, 287, 298, 309
Strauss, J., 301
Stubbs, J. x
Subkoviak, M. J., 40, 310
Sullivan, K. T., 3, 310
Sullivan, W. M., 70, 290
Sussman, M. B., 72, 165, 185, 303, 310
Swank, A. B., 2
Swanson, C. C., 3, 299
Swanson, K. R., 299
Swanson, M., 2, 56, 304
Swenson, D., 7, 310
Swenson, G. E., 292
Swidler, A., 70, 290

T

Tangney, J. P., 255, 310
Taniguchi, N., 246, 292
Tarakeshwar, N., 2
Tauer, M., 132, 301
Taylor, A. C., 197, 214, 234, 302, 310

Taylor, C., 310
Teitelbaum, M. A., 206, 312
Temple, W., 132, 300
Thatcher, J. Y., 71, 295
Thibaut, J. W., 72, 110, 240, 301, 310
Thomas, D. L., ix, 1, 2, 5, 11, 15, 31, 263, 271, 310
Thomas, G., 43
Thomas, W. I., 9, 310
Thoresen, C. E., 41, 165, 298, 300, 305, 307
Thorne, B., 225
Thyer, B. A., 298
Tipton, S. M., 70, 290
Tolstoy, L., 88, 269, 310
Toma, C., 310
Tomcho, T. J., 208, 296
Tomcik, N. D., 37, 299
Toussaint, L. L., 41, 310
Townsend, M., 56, 310
Trötschel, R., 62, 289
Tudge, J. R. H., 11, 243, 264, 310
Turillo, C. J., 72, 311
Turner, J., 37
Tutu, D., 50, 311
Tyler, 311
Tyler, T. R., 106, 269, 294, 311
Tyson, R., 299
Tzu Kung, 88

U

Umberson, D., 249, 311
Umphress, E. E., 72, 311

V

Valjean, J. 153, 157
Vallacher, R. R., 62
Vangelisti, H. T., 311
Van Lange, P. A. M., 70, 72, 73, 74, 251, 311
Van Zandt, S., 312
Vardy, G., 2, 298
Vaux, A., 107, 311
Vohs, K. D., 48
Von Armin, 154, 311

W

Wachholtz, A., 303
Wade, N. G., 40, 290
Wade, S. H., 40, 311
Wagner, P. E., 255, 310
Waldron, V. R., 38, 311
Walker, A. B., 244, 295
Walker, L. J., 303
Walker, L. M., 292, 294
Walls, G. B., 164, 311
Walsh, F., 7, 42, 65, 190, 311
Ward, C., 296
Ward, M. R., 295
Warner, C. T., 165, 187, 188, 192, 193, 311
Watson, 236
Weakland, J., 235, 290
Weber, M., 12, 311
Weis, D. L., 15, 293
Weissman, M. M., 247, 311
Wenzel, A., 298
White, J. M., 15, 109, 165, 185, 234, 237, 238, 240, 311
White, T. L., 81, 293
Whiting, R. A., 202, 301, 308
Williams, K., 56, 311
Williams, R. N., ix, 31, 309
Wilson, B. J., 35, 294
Wilson, C. 153, 312
Winch, R. F., 36, 139, 149, 312
Winton, C. A., 15, 232, 312
Wise, G. W., 312
Witcher, B. S., 311
Withers, G., 16, 296
Wolin, S. J., 202, 203, 204, 205, 206, 312
Wolpert, M., 152, 312
Wood, H. G., 132, 300
Worthington, E. E., 51, 308
Worthington, E. L., 2, 37, 40, 41, 42, 45, 51, 290, 292, 299, 300, 305, 312
Wortman, C. B., 56
Wright, J. D., 289
Wu, C. R., 310
Wyden, P., 125, 289

Y

Yarhouse, M. A., 292
Yorgason, B., G., ix, 136, 289, 292
Yorgason, F., 303
Yorgason, J. B., 250, 293
Young, J. S., 7, 293
Young, J., 152, 297
Young, W. A., 7, 312
Yzerbyt, V., 310

Z

Zekus, A. ix
Zetterberg, H. L., 11, 263, 312
Zhai, J. E.. 7, 312
Zhang, S., 302
Zimmerman, C. C., 173, 196, 197, 312
Znaniecki, F., 9, 310

Subject Index

A

Abrahamic faiths, 4, 71, 105–106, 161–162, 192
Absolute, 9, 185–186, 192,
Abuse, 27, 40, 49, 134, 163, 205, 220, 230
Accountability, 44, 57, 58, 65, 118, 190
Acquisition, viii, 109, 114, 214, 222–224
Adolescence, 206
Adoption, 207, 245
Adversity, 190–191
Affective involvement, 248
Affective responsiveness, 248
Aggression, 37, 41, 48, 268,
Agreeableness, 43–44
Ahimsa, 106
American youth, 5
Analyzing literature, 264, 268–269
Ancestors, 177–181, 209, 267, 281,
Anger, 37, 40, 44, 66, 108–109, 124, 133, 135, 145, 164, 187, 268
Anthropology, 13, 43, 76, 202
Art of loving, 93
Asking and seeking, 53–68
Attraction, 113
Attributions, 8, 9, 12, 113, 153,
Authorizing, 264, 285
Autonomy, 176, 216–219, 221, 229

B

Bad and good, 48–50, 104, 186
Balancing stability and change, 20–21
Behavior–belief congruence, 26
Behaviorism, viii, 166, 234, 236–238
Belonging, 20, 200, 207, 211
Bickering, 126
Blind men analogy, 232–233
Bonding, 20, 76, 178, 191, 215, 231
Bonds, 37, 54, 77, 96, 104, 177, 182, 184, 188, 198, 207, 212, 217
Bounding, 173, 197, 199, 211
Bridging, 20, 173, 197, 199, 211, 271
Bronfenbrenner's theory, 201, 243
Buddhism, 39, 112, 150, 186
Burning in bosom, 53
Burning sensations, 53

C

Capitalism, 12
Caring, 19–21, 90, 96, 101, 124, 163, 169, 178, 218, 222, 224–225, 281
Catholic Church, 216, 219, 264, 270,
Caucasian, 245, 264
Causal laws, 116
Caution, 113
Ceteris paribus 234
Change, 3, 19–21, 46–47, 48–49, 55, 58, 66, 74, 89
Christensen's research 187
Christianity, 4, 39, 54, 71
Chronic stress, 249
Church of Jesus Christ of Latter–day Saints, viii, 209
Close relationships, 72, 92, 107, 111
Coercion, 225
Cognitive, 35–37, 166, 192, 233–234, 236–237, 239–240
Cognitive–behavioral theory 236–237
Cohesion, 43–44, 77, 96, 105, 207, 212
Combativeness, 43, 124, 127
Commitment, ix, 14, 19, 41, 44, 58–59, 65 72–75, 84, 168, 208
Communal, 110–111, 219, 224, 268
Communication, 37–38, 41, 44, 53–54, 65, 108–109, 204, 208, 212, 235
Compassion, 32, 37–39, 61, 66, 101–102, 129–130, 147, 150–151, 155, 157–160, 190, 223, 225, 282
Competing ideas, ix, 98, 212–231
Competition, 102, 130–132, 144–145, 268
Complementary needs, 139
Compromise, 84, 108–109, 112, 127–128, 138–139
Concepts, 7–11, 30–31, 277
Conceptual frameworks, vii, 1, 6–11, 15, 30–31, 109, 175, 213, 231–239, 272, 277
Conceptual improvements, 7–11, 30–31, 35–38, 53–54, 61, 67, 69–71, 83, 88–93, 106–107, 108–111, 113–115, 118, 124–125, 151–153, 185–186, 202–204
Conceptualization, 5, 6, 7–11
Conciliatory, 41, 44, 268
Condemning, 43, 45, 150, 152, 155, 1167, 172, 191
Conditioning, 14
Confidence, 96, 103, 105, 108, 113, 127, 188, 244, 271
Conflict habituated, 125–126
Conflict resolution, 2, 58, 60, 62
Conflict theory, 240
Conflict, 22, 37, 40–44, 58, 60–62, 64–66, 81, 103, 123, 125, 207, 246–248, 253, 258, 268
Conflict–avoiding, 2, 126, 134
Confucius, 88, 175
Congenial options, 73

Consecration, 82
Consensus, 102, 123, 138–141
Consequences, 25, 27, 29, 48–49, 73, 80–81, 99, 149, 163, 171, 177, 185, 187–191, 213, 215, 221, 231, 241, 272, 279,
Conservative, 264
Consistency, 95, 112, 126, 264
Contagious, 43, 153
Contemporary Theories About the Family, ix, 165
Contention, 96, 101–105, 124–128, 144, 147, 204, 208, 212, 268
Contexts, 4, 35, 197, 201
Contextual factors, see contingencies
Contingencies, 3–5, 42–48, 76, 80–85, 93, 127, 162–164, 172–173, 187, 188–192, 204–210, 260, 263, 280–281, 287
Continuum, 110–111
Control processes, 62
Control, viii, 22, 55, 64, 66, 84, 101, 120, 219–220, 222, 279, 281
Controlling emotions, 135–136
Cooperation, 32, 102, 104, 124–127, 130–132
Copernican theory, 270
Coping strategies, 22, 66
Coping theory, 17
Coping with disagreements, 32, 102, 123–146
Coping with divorce, 22
Coping with undesirable behavior, 32, 52, 102, 147–160, 200
Coping with undesirables, 19, 21
Coping, 20, 52, 54, 56, 64–65, 84, 97, 164, 180, 206, 230, 236
Cornerstone, 15, 91
Correlation, 1–2, 4–5, 16, 23, 44, 58, 67, 153
Correlations in new research, 252–254
Crime, 27, 30, 103, 105, 181, 229
Critical theory, 240,
Critical, 26, 87, 136, 150, 152, 159, 218, 224, 285
Cultural differences, 14, 15
Cultural survival of the fittest, 23–24
Curvilinear, 93, 136, 168, 280
Cycles, 56, 61, 66, 74–75, 154, 170, 235–236
Cyclic, 76–77
Cyclical, 6, 65, 73–74, 263

D

Data set, 244–249, 251, 257
Debt, 36, 38
Defensiveness, 43, 48, 92, 96, 103, 105, 108–109, 127–128, 134–135, 139, 151, 153, 279
Definitions, 18, 35–38, 40, 48, 63, 69–71, 88–91, 150, 158, 166–167, 202,204, 223
Definitions, operational, 277
Definitions, rational, 277
Democracy, 217
Dependence, 62, 66, 74, 75
Depression, 22, 27, 37,49, 56, 80–81, 228, 245–248, 253–256, 258–259
Descendants, 178, 182
Describing stage, 270, 275, 277, 282–283
Descriptive strategy, 89
Desecration, 22, 189, 190, 193, 215
Determinism, 116–118, 237
Developmental, 21, 22, 26, 70, 89, 118, 177, 183–184, 205, 237–238, 243, 255
Dialogical, 217, 285
Dichotomous thinking, 2
Dimensions two, 36–37, 91, 149
Dimensions, 2, 5, 11, 70, 124, 133, 193
Disagreeableness, 48
Disagreements, 32, 64, 66, 77, 96, 102, 103, 105, 121, 123–146
Discontinuous transformation, 63
Disillusionment, 169
Dispositional forgiveness, 43
Disrespect, 101, 105–109, 119, 131, 145
Distal, 2, 229, 251–252, 257, 259
Distance, 132, 150–151
Distinctiveness, 205, 206
Diversity, 8, 89, 123, 139, 237, 245, 263, 273
Divorce, 12, 21–22, 27, 74, 97, 187, 197, 205–207, 230, 254, 266, 279–280
Doubt, 187
Duplicity, 112
Duration, 189, 190, 193

E

East Indian, 264
Eclectic, 234–238, 242
Elephant analogy, 232–233
Elites, 12, 214, 216, 218–219, 229, 230
Emotional
  abuse, 21, 190
  flooding, 62, 66, 92
  needs, 19–21, 44, 167
  reactivity, 58, 66, 135
  softening, 60, 66
  stability, 43–44
  validation, 58, 65
Emotionality, 135–138
Emotionally charged, 62
Empathize, 126
Empathy, 37, 41, 44, 58, 65–66, 111, 143, 150–151, 170, 209
Empirical observations, 9, 23, 197
Empirical, 1, 4, 6, 8, 11–13, 30–31, 41, 45, 51, 56, 64, 67, 76, 80, 85, 91–93, 95, 112, 125, 157, 192, 228, 243, 244, 263, 272, 277, 279, 284–286, 287
Empiricism, 227

Enlightenment, 53
Enlightenment, The, 216–220
Entropy, 63
Epistemological, ix, 18, 32, 214, 227–228, 27,
Epistemology, 270
Erikson's theory, 176, 180, 184
Escalation, 230
Ethics, 8, 42, 164, 177, 185–186, 223, 278
European, 270, 279
Evolution of theories, 264
Excesses, 22, 96, 99, 173, 218–219, 221, 226, 230
Excessive individualism, 98, 99, 221–222
Excessiveness, 80–81, 85, 216–219
Exchange orientation, 98, 110–112, 154, 222–226
Exchange theory, 110, 224, 283
Expand theories, vii, 2, 5–6, 11, 30–31, 102, 205, 231, 237, 240, 244, 266, 268–269, 276–277, 282
Expand, 89, 118, 127–130, 159, 191, 260, 269, 285, 286
Expanded, 12, 16, 76, 89, 176, 233, 235, 263
Explanation, 4, 11–14, 16, 24, 48, 63, 89, 133, 228–230, 232, 239, 274 276
Expressiveness, 43–44

F

Faith community, 201, 210–211
Family development theory, 237–238
Family home evening, 209
Family Profile, 103
Family studies, vii, 284
Family therapy, vii
Fasting, 53, 63
Fatalism, 64
Feminist, 880, 185, 225–226, 240
Fidelity, 2, 40–41, 49, 59, 65
Fighting, 104
Flourishing Families Project, 243–249
Folklore, 139
Force, 13, 42, 56, 71, 81, 87, 92, 119, 123, 138, 145, 163, 171, 175, 189, 220–221, 225, 238
Forgetting, 50–51
Forgiving, 35–52
Four general ideas, vii, viii, 11–18, 21, 32, 97, 260
Four horsemen, 92, 134, 279
Fragmented theories, 6, 30
Fragmented, 3, 266
Freedom, 10, 22, 27, 70, 99, 115–121, 216–221, 226, 229, 236, 238
Functionalism, 240
Fusion, 135
Future research, 42–43, 47, 51, 76, 83, 104, 108, 115, 129, 135–136, 149, 151, 161, 172, 177, 201, 206, 236, 244, 257, 259–260, 281–282

G

Gain ethic, 98, 223, 227
Genealogical research, 179
Genealogy, 180, 267
General ideas, vii, viii, 11–18, 31–32, 275–276
General theory, 1, 4, 31
Generation stage in theory building, 264–269, 284
Generational alliances, 176, 177–178, 184
Generations, 1–3, 11, 23, 30, 32, 76, 103, 175–184, 201, 203, 206, 209, 230, 260–261
Generativity, 176, 180, 182, 281
Genetic, 117
Gentle, 25, 87, 94, 101–102, 104, 118, 120, 124, 148–151, 158, 250, 268
Gleaned theory, 287
Goals in defining love, 88–90
Goals in families, 18–22, 23, 25, 30, 32, 55, 61, 66, 163, 170, 213, 215, 218, 224, 231, 246, 250, 269
Goals in this book, 6, 11, 69, 195, 205, 218, 273
Goals of individuals, 219
Goals, 70, 84, 99, 109, 111, 116, 117, 119, 152, 167, 169, 211, 219, 246,
Golden mean, 80, 131, 158, 159, 197, 204, 218, 221, 226
Good and bad, 48–50, 104, 167, 186, 199,
Grants, 76
Gratitude, x, 59, 65, 73, 77, 209, 255
Greed, 112, 169, 223–224, 229
Greek, 130, 238, 270
Grounded theory, 263, 287

H

Harmful, 1–5, 16–19, 21–24, 32, 35, 43–44, 46, 49, 52, 64, 76, 80–85, 96–97, 103, 111, 115, 124–127, 130–134, 147, 150, 152–154, 157, 162–164, 173, 189–193, 195, 200, 204–211, 213–231, 268–269
Harmony, 24, 47, 55, 76–77, 95, 141, 163, 172, 188, 231, 238
Hasidic, 264
Health, 2, 4, 11, 12, 27, 41, 56, 81, 93, 249
Health-related stressors, 249
Heart, 10, 47, 53–54, 99, 131, 164–167, 173
Hedonism, viii, 84, 98, 120, 169, 214, 226–227, 229

Helpful, viii–ix, 1, 4–5, 8, 10, 12, 14, 16–24, 29, 31–32, 35, 41–43, 46, 51, 53–55, 58–66, 72–79, 84, 91, 95–96, 204–210
Helping patterns, 19, 102
Hermeneutics, 240
Hesitancy, 113
Hierarchal regressions, 252–259
High–risk conditions, 169, 174
Hindu, 88
Historical analysis, 264, 267–268
Historical conditions, 6, 11, 14, 15, 19, 106, 201,
Home, 19, 20, 24, 26, 59, 77, 96, 121, 136, 141, 164, 203, 205, 209, 244, 255, 256, 264, 265, 266
Hostility, 41, 44, 58, 108–109, 124, 133, 268
How questions, 1, 4–5, 21
Humanistic theories, 238–239
Humanists, 239
Humility,55, 158, 170
Hyperindividualism, 221
Hypocrisy, 26, 101, 112–113, 121, 158
Hypotheses, 31–32, 243, 244, 245, 272, 278

I

Iceberg analogy, vii–viii
Identification, 96, 105
Identity, 76, 144, 162, 176, 180, 183, 207, 222, 283
Ideological factors, 263
Ideologies, ix, 23, 24, 213–214, 225
Ideology, 109, 111, 165, 215, 216, 219–220, 223, 225
Implemental intentions, 62, 66
Improve conceptualization, 6, 7–11, 88–91, 277
Improve courses, vii
Improve relationships, 60, 179
Improve research, 2–4, 6, 31 69, 76, 205, 269
Improve, ix, 1, 24, 51, 74, 191, 222, 239, 261, 273
Improvements in forgiveness, 51
Improvements, 30, 84, 202, 217, 231, 270, 275, 282
Improving theory, 264,269
Inclusive, 6–8, 11, 32, 46, 214, 245, 260, 263, 272, 274, 279, 287
Independence, 8, 37, 103, 162, 165, 216–221, 229, 244
Indeterminism, 116–118
Individualism, 70, 84, 98–99, 109–110, 115, 219–222, 227, 229, 238
Indostan fable, 232–233
Inferences from data, 273–275, 286
Influence processes, 4, 62, 66
Integrated, vii–viii, 3, 6, 11–12, 26, 30, 52, 61, 67, 85, 158, 160, 180, 184, 187, 231, 233–234, 237, 238, 242, 270–273, 277
Integrating sacred and secular, 270–273
Integrating theories, 231–239
Integration, 3, 11, 24, 26, 63, 207, 208, 212, 228, 233, 271–272, 275, 286
Integrity, 32, 101–102, 112–113, 121, 246–248, 253, 255–257
Intensity of emotions, 136,141–142, 281
Interaction effects, 3, 59
Interest in others, 102, 140
Interest in self, 221
Interview data, 25–27, 184, 264–265, 268
Intimacy, 20, 21, 41–42, 44, 81, 120, 126, 131, 142, 176, 180, 198, 206, 231, 245, 246–248, 252–255, 258
Intimidate, 119, 123
Intrinsic, 125
Intrusive control, 120
Invisible hand, 14
Invisible loyalties, 76, 177
Irrational thinking, 214
Islam, 4, 54, 71, 88, 117, 186, 207

J

Judaism, 4, 54, 71, 117, 168, 207
Judeo–Christian, 39, 87, 130, 175
Judgmental, 11, 32, 147, 151–153, 155, 157–160, 167, 172, 191

K

Kindness, 30, 32, 39, 43, 49, 90, 96, 101–105, 107, 127–130, 135, 147–151, 204, 208, 212, 223, 245–261

L

Latino, 60, 264
Liberating values, 214, 216–222, 224, 229
Liberty, 10, 22, 217–221, 226
Life course, 19, 238
Likert scale, 246–251
Linear, 93, 136, 168, 235, 260–261, 280–281
Literature, 23, 35, 37, 40, 154, 160, 163, 268–269, 284–287
  previous, 1–6
sacred, 40, 61, 55, 67, 71, 112–114, 115, 118, 130, 140, 157, 170, 183, 268, 275–276, 287
Longevity, 2, 41
Long–term perspectives, 66
Love, 87-160
  as a noun, viii, 90–91
  as a verb, viii, 90–91

defining it, 88–91
God, 161–175
Loving, 20, 31–32, 84, 87–100, 101–122, 127

M

Maori, 265
Marai, 265
Marital
happiness, 57
intimacy, 245–246, 252–255
quality, 41, 107, 167, 245–247, 252–255, 258
satisfaction, 1–2, 12, 41, 43, 208
stability, 92, 167, 255
Market, 19, 199, 215, 222–226, 229, 231
Marriage rates 228–231
Materialism, 223–224, 227, 229
Meaning, 14, 20–22, 23–24, 108–109, 120, 169, 177, 180–182, 184, 203–204, 208, 212, 217, 230, 252
Meaninglessness, 169
Measurement, 3, 52, 67, 72, 107, 153
Mechanism, 3, 4, 171, 206
Mercy, 32, 43, 101–102, 146–151, 158–160, 167, 190, 225, 282
Metaphysical, ix, 18, 32, 227
Methodological, 32, 196, 263, 271, 274, 282
Methodology of theory building, 11, 243, 263–264, 270, 273–275, 280, 282–287
describing stage, 270, 275, 277, 282–283
generating stage 267, 269–282
Methods, vii, ix, 1,57, 107, 263–288
in new research, 244–252
inferring from data, 270–273
integrating sacred and secular, 270–273
multiple, vii
with concepts, 277
Middle Eastern, 130, 163, 264, 270
Mini theories, 6
Mistrust, 105, 113
Moderation, 80, 131, 172, 197, 205–206, 212, 216–221, 229, 231
Modern Orthodox, 264
Modernism, 271
Moral beliefs, 169 185–189, 191, 193
Moral order, 5
Morality, 32, 76–77, 109, 175, 185–194
Mormon Church, viii
Morphogenesis, 47, 157, 203–204, 212
Morphostasis, 157, 203–204, 212
Multifaceted, 24, 35, 52, 87, 89, 95, 99, 101–102, 142, 203, 263, 285
Multivariate models, 2
Mutual interest, 32, 108–112

N

Nagy's theory, 42, 76, 176–177, 180, 184
Narrative analysis, 263
Narrative inquiry, 275
Native American, 22, 264
Negative
attributions, 113, 153
coping, 141–144
emotion definitions, 133
emotion research, 134–135
emotion, 36–37, 45, 81, 102, 108, 124, 133–138, 141–144, 145, 147, 268, 280
Negativity, 61, 96, 104, 134–135
Negotiation, 106
Neighbors, 21, 140, 167, 172, 173–174, 198, 265
New York City, 10
New Zealand, 265
Nihilism, 21, 169
Noncyclic, 236
Nonexchange orientation, 110
Nontheistic, 10–11, 15, 84
Nontraditional families, 3, 260
Norm of reciprocity, 43, 105, 154
Normative theory, 187
Noumenological, 9, 15, 15, 239, 271–272
Noun, viii, 90–93, 98, 99, 221, 283

O

Obedience, 164, 186
Observation, 9, 11, 22, 208, 227–228, 232, 265, 271, 272, 285
advantages, 27
data, 27–30, 243
Observational, 243, 272
Observations, 8–9, 22, 25, 29, 39, 55, 71, 92, 126, 164, 199, 227, 244, 265–268, 270, 274, 275, 278, 280, 284–285, 287
Observations and interviews, 11, 17–18, 24, 27–31, 43, 45, 48, 81, 87–88, 92–95, 97, 101–105, 107–108, 111–113, 115, 120, 121, 123–124, 127–129, 133, 136, 138–140, 147, 150–151, 154–156, 160–161, 171–172, 175, 180, 189, 192, 264, 276, 282, 286
Omission, 192
Ontological, ix, 18, 32, 177, 186, 188
Openness, 55, 108–109, 120, 132, 135, 140–141, 168, 170
Operational definitions, 166, 277
Opium of the people, 214
Opposites attract, 123, 139
Oppression, 216–220
Optimism, 27, 140–141, 153, 170
Other, 109
interest, 108–112, 135
orientation, 65
Overarching underpinnings, 15
Overview of sacred theory, 1–34

P

Pacific Islander, 264
Parental alliances, 44, 178
Parental anxiety, 248
Parental involvement, 248
Parenting, 3–4, 22, 43, 55, 96, 172, 195, 197, 204, 208, 212
Patience, 11, 32, 101–102, 127–130, 135, 144, 147–151, 167, 170, 190, 209, 225, 268
Peacemaking, 32, 102, 124–130, 135, 144, 147, 167, 268
Perceptions, 4, 8–10, 12, 14, 32, 43, 45, 65, 76, 80, 141, 236, 285
Personal responsibility, 58, 60
Pessimism, 153, 238
Phenomenological, 9–10, 15, 215, 239, 271–272
Philosophy, vii, 23, 98, 101, 108–109, 111, 168–169, 174, 213–228
Positive affect, 37, 52, 109, 127–128, 132, 140
Positive cognitions, 44
Positivity, 96, 134
Posterity, 175–184, 268, 281
Postmodern, 45, 188, 238
Power, 13–18
Prayer, vii, 2,6,11, 32, 53–68
Predecessors, 175, 179–180, 182, 183
Present–to–future questions, 278–280
Principles advantages of, 279
Principles defined, 278–280
Principles, vii–viii, 31, 49, 63, 95, 97–98, 103, 141, 147, 150, 157–160, 166, 174, 185, 209, 234, 238, 244, 259, 265, 269, 275–279
Proposition 1, 12–16, 31–32, 276
Proposition 2, 16, 47, 82, 189, 276
Proposition 3, 16–17, 276
Proposition 4, 18–19, 276
Propositions, 11, 11–18, 24, 32, 89, 95, 98, 116, 162, 243, 270, 277, 278–281, 288
  general, 11–18, 21, 24, 32, 97, 181, 260, 276
  less general, vii–viii, 12, 32, 260
Protestant ethic, 12
Protestant reformation, 216, 219, 270
Proximal, 2–3, 5, 201, 229, 251–252, 257, 259
Psychoanalytic theory, 185, 234, 236, 240
Psychological, 41–42, 44
Psychological control, 120
Psychosocial aspects of sacred, 4, 195–212
Psychosocial functions, 4, 195
Ptolemaic, 270
Public realms, 20, 131–132, 141
Purpose of theories, 5, 90
Purpose, 14–15, 21, 24, 169, 177, 180–182, 184, 186, 208, 212, 224, 244

Q

Qualitative, vii, 1, 4, 40, 57–58, 60, 63, 84, 91, 99, 113, 136, 156, 172, 210, 243, 251, 255, 260–265, 274–275, 282
Quality of communication, 44, 65
Quantitative, vii, ix, 1, 70, 156, 172, 243–244, 255, 257, 259–261, 265, 274–275
Questions
  how questions, 1, 4–5, 21
  present–to–future questions, 278–280
  what questions, 2, 5, 8, 11, 15–16, 17, 18, 21, 26
  when questions, 1, 4–5
  why questions, 1, 4–5, 13, 21

R

Rapport, 141, 143–144
Rational definitions, 277
Rationale, 169, 174, 217, 276
Rationalism, 218, 227–2289
Reasoned theory, 287
Reciprocity avoiding, 153–155
Reciprocity, 32, 43, 62, 72–73, 80, 102, 105, 106, 108, 127–129, 157–159, 160, 170
Reconciliation, 27, 58, 61, 65, 66, 207, 236
Refinement of concepts, 7–11
Refinement, 42, 76, 243, 260, 267
Reformed, 264
RELATE, 246, 248
Relating
  communal, 110–111, 201, 219, 224
  exchange orientation, 98, 110, 111, 154, 224
  market, 223–224, 229
  non–exchange orientation, 110–111, 224
ways of, 95, 99, 102, 113–115, 119, 121, 124, 140, 150, 156, 160, 163, 170, 191, 214, 218, 222, 224–226, 230, 236, 276
Relational aggression, 250, 252, 255, 261
Relational spirituality framework, 4
Relationship persistence, 72, 75, 77, 255
Relationships with competing ideas, ix, 98, 213–231
Relationships with institutions, 241
Relationships with other theories, 231–241
Religion, defined, 7–11
Religiosity, 2–3, 6, 12, 17, 23–26, 49–50, 57, 59, 61, 196, 214, 264
Religious affiliation, 1, 251, 256
Religious attendance, 228–229, 244–245, 249, 252, 254–256, 257, 259
Religious networks, 200–201
Renaissance, 216, 270
Repenting, 10, 31, 51, 102, 147, 152, 156–157, 159–160, 190, 207
Research
  new, vii, 5, 76–79, 93, 243–262

previous, 1–4
ways to improve, 3–4
Resilience, 177, 182, 189–193
Resistance, 43, 81, 120, 127–128, 139, 153
Respect, 7, 10, 14, 32, 43, 92, 96, 101–102, 104, 105–108
Responsibility, 36, 58, 60, 66, 115–120, 152, 215, 217–219
Restoration effect, 159
Retaliation, 96, 104–105, 154, 250
Retaliatory, 41,44–45
Reticence, 132
Richly interconnected, 196–199, 211
Rights of individuals, 216–222
Ripple effect, 159
Rituals, 2, 6, 8, 11–12, 32, 51, 163, 196, 201–212, 237
Romantic love, 92
Roots, 28, 38, 46, 83, 106, 175, 178–180, 216, 238,
Routines, 202–204, 211
Rules, 8, 131,–132, 145, 190, 205, 250, 263

S

Sacred, ignored, 15
Sacred theory general ideas, 11–18
Sacred theory summary, 32
Sacrifice, 69–86
Safe haven, 96
Salience, 12–18, 47–48
Samples, vii, 4, 41, 47–48, 57–59, 187, 200, 245–251, 264, 286
Sanctification, vii, 6, 11–13, 22, 32, 51, 57, 59, 82–83, 85, 97, 216, 268
School performance, 103, 105
Scientific method, 46, 55, 270, 272, 284–287
Seattle, 245
Secular perspectives, 52, 69, 215–218
Secularism, 214–216, 218, 229
Security, 114, 140–141, 164
Self actualization, 74
Self interest, 70, 102, 110, 219, 221–222, 227, 238
Self–esteem, 98, 222, 229, 268,
Self–interest, 102, 108–112
Selfishness, 90, 108–110, 222, 229, 281
Self–orientation, 268
Self–transcendence, 74
Seriousness, 40, 189–190, 193
Service orientation, 101, 114–115, 121
Service, 32, 102, 113–115, 121, 147, 169, 210, 225, 251
Sexual abuse 2, 21, 49, 190,
Sexual, 2, 21, 136, 169, 187, 189–190, 192, 214, 226, 230, 246–247, 252, 255
Shame, 50, 150, 183, 246–247, 252–253, 255–256
Shared history, 208
Sheilaism, 188
Six blind men, 232–233
Sixth sense, 53
Skepticism, 15, 96, 103, 105
Social and organizational ties, 5
Social networks, 32, 196–201, 210–211
Social work, vii, 199
Socialism, 219
Socialization, 19, 167
Sociology, vii, 43, 202, 284
Soft voice, 53
Softening, 58, 60, 66
Solidarity, 76–77, 96, 105, 198, 207, 212
Sourcebook, ix, 165, 263, 274
Specific factors, 2, 3, 5, 6, 26, 32, 49, 127, 152, 164, 196, 229
Spiritual senses, 54
Spiritual, 3, 4, 6, 7–11, 22, 31, 41, 53–54, 56, 63, 65, 71, 75, 161, 163, 165–168, 177, 191, 199, 204, 208, 210, 212, 215, 219, 221, 224, 239, 272, 277, 283, 285
Spirituality, 2, 6, 7–11, 19, 31, 66, 190, 271
Spying, 132
Stability, 1, 19, 20–21, 29, 43–44, 75, 77, 92, 157, 167, 203–206, 208, 228, 246–247, 252–255, 258
Stagnation, 176, 182
Still voice, 53
Stress, 75, 81, 197, 247, 249, 253, 255, 258
Striving for consensus, 124, 135, 138–141, 145
Striving, 19, 43, 90, 96, 120, 127, 132, 170, 239
Substance abuse, 30, 103, 105
Substance, 21, 36, 181, 230
Substantive aspects of sacred, 4–5, 17, 35, 195–196
Surplus value, 73
Surrender selfishness, 108–109
Survival of fittest, 14, 23
Suspicion, 48, 113, 132, 142
Symbolic interaction, viii, 95, 109, 173, 234, 237, 240
Systems theories, viii, 42, 235–236

T

Tabula rasa, 236
Temporal differences, 280
Testable, vii, 11, 89
The Enlightenment, 216–220
The Republic, 214, 231, 282
Theistic, 10, 15, 84, 169, 271
Theories, ways to improve them 5–6, 282
Theorizing strategy, 90
Theory building methodology, 11, 243, 263, 270, 273–275, 280, 282–287
Therapeutic individualism, 70
Thread analogy, 13–14

Thresholds, 3, 6, 136, 168, 260, 280
Tough love, 149–150, 158
Traditional families, 3, 41, 226, 260
Transition theory, viii, 237–238, 140
Triangles, 57
Trust, 37, 41–42, 44, 49–50,59, 65, 73–75, 77, 96, 103, 105, 108, 113, 132, 176, 248, 251
Truth assertions, 11, 14–15, 16, 278
Two dimensions, 36–37, 91, 149
Typological strategies, 88–90
Tyranny, 216–219

U

Unanticipated pattern, 75, 275–276
Unconditional positive regard, 14
Undesirable behavior, 147–160, 207
Undesirables, 19, 21
Unity, 32, 59, 65, 96, 101, 123, 130, 135, 138–141,168, 204, 212, 268
Unkindness, 43, 49, 102–105, 149, 247, 249–258, 278–281
Unmoderated liberating values, 214, 216–219
Utilitarian, 125

V

Validating, 65, 120, 126
Validation, 58, 65, 134, 243
Values, 164–166
Valuing the sacred, 167–168
Verb, viii, 90–91, 97, 98, 99
Verification, 243, 267, 284
Violence, 21, 27, 56, 138, 189, 197, 226, 229
Visual summary, 31–32, 43, 64, 75–76, 127, 129, 132, 140, 151
Volatile, 126

W

Warner's theory, 165, 187–188, 192
Waves in study, 245
Wellbeing, 2, 67, 70, 81, 244, 246, 248, 255, 257
What questions, 2, 5, 8, 11, 15–16, 17, 18, 21, 26
When questions, 1, 4–5
Whole person, 19, 152, 166
Why questions, 1, 4–5, 13, 21
Why, vii, 1, 3–4, 8, 13, 14–16, 18, 21, 24, 45, 48, 52, 60–64, 83, 133, 135, 170, 177, 180–181, 186, 189, 197–198 211, 230, 240, 267, 271, 276, 286
Widely shared goals, 18–21, 25, 30, 32, 55,170, 213, 215, 231, 269, 276, 283,
Winning, 61, 126, 131, 144
Wrangling 124